The Space
of Love and
Garbage

A Companion Volume to *The Space of Love and Garbage:*

All We Need Is a Paradigm: Essays on Science, Economics, and Logic from The Harvard Review of Philosophy,
edited by S. Phineas Upham

The Space of Love and Garbage

And Other Essays from
The Harvard Review of Philosophy

EDITED BY
S. PHINEAS UPHAM

OPEN COURT
Chicago and La Salle, Illinois

To order books from Open Court, call toll-free 1-800-815-2280, or visit our website at www.opencourtbooks.com.

Open Court Publishing Company is a division of Carus Publishing Company.

Copyright © 2008 by *The Harvard Review of Philosophy. The Harvard Review of Philosophy* (ISSN 1062-6239) is an official student organization of Harvard University.

First printing 2008

Library of Congress Cataloging-in-Publication Data

The space of love and garbage : and other essays from the Harvard review of philosophy / edited by S. Phineas Upham.
     p.   cm.
   Summary: "A collection of essays from the Harvard review of philosophy focusing on personal, emotional, and political issues"— Provided by publisher.
   Includes bibliographical references and index.
   ISBN-13: 978-0-8126-9620-2 (trade paper : alk. paper)
   ISBN-10: 0-8126-9620-4 (trade paper : alk. paper)
   1. Philosophy, Modern. I. Upham, S. Phineas. II. Harvard review of philosophy.
   B791.S73 2007
   190—dc22
                                          2007029579

Contents

Foreword

I know of no more rational and attractive place to begin and to continue to survey the reaches of philosophical possibility than that provided in the pages of *The Harvard Review of Philosophy*. This is amply verified by the quality and range of the essays in *The Space of Love and Garbage* and its companion volume, *All We Need Is a Paradigm*, by the high quality of the contributors to these volumes, and by their quite unmatched (in any comparable journal I am aware of) range of subjects and modes of thinking.

Professional journals are the life's blood of every field of instruction and investigation throughout the modern university. National and international reputations of scholars can be begun and established by publication in them; collections of journal articles are assigned in virtually every university lecture hall and seminar room; graduate students and assistant professors characteristically make the cases for their initial positions and their advancement for tenured positions on the basis of their texts' selection for publication in journals whose articles are subject to blind review. In the field of philosophy, although this has undergone some change in recent years, the publication of books rather than articles by prominent figures in the field remains distinctly rarer than in the other humanities disciplines and in humanistically inclined registers of social inquiry, and a book by a philosopher is itself characteristically a collection of articles separately published over a period of years by its author, sometimes revised for their conjunction and perhaps for their reading beyond the profession.

The particularity of the value of the fact of students at the origin of *The Harvard Review of Philosophy*'s existence must be a function of its value simultaneously for students and for the profession of philosophy. For those directly involved in its publication and the imagination of that fact by their fellows, at Harvard and beyond, the heightened attention to issues and words destined to be made public and at stages before a final version is arrived at makes real and immediate for them the world of a community of scholarship as little else can. For *The Harvard Review of Philosophy*, the fact that potential recruits to the profession are involved in the work of the profession before they have become credentialed professionals is an irreplaceable reminder that institutions, indeed the institutionalization of the profession of philosophy itself, the field of study and instruction dedicated to self-reflection, will tend to become complacent and to resist change when change may be called for.

I think here especially of resistance to pedagogical change, of what is regarded as essential to philosophical learning and training. This is in at least three obvious ways a more fateful matter in the study of philosophy than in any other field.

First, at least in the United States, the study of philosophy, unlike the other humanities and the sciences, is only exceptionally offered in high schools, so it is mostly first encountered systematically in university courses, where time for intellectual experimentation rapidly diminishes.

Second, there is no general agreement among philosophers on the best way to begin study of the subject. Like every other feature of the field, any particular beginning is open to criticism. A case may well be made that history or epistemology or logic or ethics should come first, or that one should postpone things until a schedule can accommodate more than one of these regions in the same semester.

Third, whichever path is entered upon is apt to shape the future course of your philosophical expectations. Professional philosophers inevitably take pains to define what they expect of philosophy—to declare and exhibit what mode or modes of thinking count for them as philosophically pertinent and fruitful—and these expectations are inevitably somewhat at variance with a student's own expectations, so often formed, to the extent they have reached articulate form, by rumor, by one-sided enthusiasms or disappointments expressed by more experienced students, perhaps by a puzzling yet fascinating book (from a strange culture or an ancient time) that may or may not pass as current philosophy.

We might summarize these registers of perplexity by saying that there is no substitute for acquiring philosophical experience in charting and evaluating your own course of philosophical education. Here is an initial paradox in studying philosophy: You already have to possess philosophical experience in order to acquire it. An initial relief from the paradox is the discovery that we all have more such experience than, we have, left to ourselves, recognized.

The service *The Harvard Review of Philosophy* has provided over the years simultaneously to the continuity of the profession of philosophy and to those in search of introductions to its riches is something for which its community of teachers and its students owe permanent debts of gratitude. I am honored to congratulate those who have devoted themselves to so superbly valuable a project.

STANLEY CAVELL

Preface

This book collects for the first time nineteen of the most outstanding works from the *Harvard Review of Philosophy*. Focusing on personal, emotional, and political issues, these chapters illuminate just those areas of philosophy and life that are most important to living 'the good life' to its fullest as an individual and as a citizen.

What are our responsibilities to each other, to the ones we love, to our community, to our country? In this book we bring philosophy back to its roots – asking questions that are both important and instructive to the general public, lovers, philosophers, and scholars alike.

We at the *Harvard Review of Philosophy* believe philosophy to be a vibrant and exciting way to address some of the most pressing and deepest concerns in life. The essays included here flow from analytic, continental, and ancient philosophical roots, and they address a variety of topics ranging from immigration to moral intuition. Each essay focuses on questions central to the practical aspects of human experience—especially those involving life, love, and politics.

In "The Space of Love and Garbage," Stephen Erickson emphasizes being *in* the present—being open and receptive to understandings that transcend the logical. He draws from Kant and Heidegger to explore the "openness to openness." Clearing the cluttering "garbage" of everyday life is a worthy goal, though the pursuit of being in the present may itself be an obstacle. In the spirit of Wittgenstein, Erickson furthers the place philosophy has in clearing away garbage and re-discovering philosophical clarity.

In "Rousseau and the Modern Cult of Sincerity," Arthur Melzer discusses how sincerity and "being oneself" has become a core virtue in our modern "culture of narcissism." How did it come about that sincerity became the only required virtue and hypocrisy the only unforgivable sin? How did acknowledgment of vices become the new virtue? Melzer says, "What piety is for Saint Augustine, what contemplation is for Plato, sincerity is for Rousseau."

Delving into the historic origins of the ideal of sincerity, Meltzer analyzes how sincerity became the goal of some alienated intellectuals. He finds that we are all alienated intellectuals now, and that hypocrisy, Rousseau's "bourgeois hypocrisy," has come to be for everyone the vice of modern commercial bourgeoisie. Meltzer describes the progression, "today everyone denounces conformity and longs for sincerity" and therefore "everything that once seemed so resolutely anti-bourgeois has now come to light as only late-bourgeois."

In another essay Hubert and Stephen Dreyfus think through the philosophical implications of the movie *The Matrix* examining the film's question of elemental skepticism—do we exist in reality as we seem to ourselves?—and extend that skepticism to question the value of reality. Is it "better to live in the real world no matter how miserable rather than living in an illusory world that makes us feel good?" Hubert and Stephen Dreyfus,, father and son, give their provocative answers.

Gisela Striker asks the question: "Why Study the History of Philosophy?"—after all, she points out, students of chemistry, biology, and astronomy can do well without anything more than a current snapshot of the history of their respective fields while ignoring outdated research and theories. But, she argues, though advances have been made and mistakes corrected, overall "progress in philosophy does not seem to be of the cumulative sort" and studying past philosophy not only contains valuable insights but helps us avoid costly mistakes—in discussion and in life—and find valuable arguments including some that have been overlooked or forgotten. Further, the value, beauty and usefulness of philosophy rests in the power and subtleties of its best arguments and in its ability to further rigorous and meaningful thought.

Love, reality, or hubris—these essays enlist the reader into the philosophic tackling of modernity's central questions.

S. Phineas Upham

1

Rousseau and the Modern Cult of Sincerity

ARTHUR M. MELZER

Arthur M. Melzer is a professor of political science at Michigan State University and Co-director of the Symposium on Science, Reason, and Modern Democracy. He is the author of The Natural Goodness of Man: On the System of Rousseau's Thought *and co-editor of* Technology and the Western Tradition. *He is currently working on Aristotle's moral philosophy.*

Any true effort at collective self-knowledge, any attempt to understand ourselves as a society and a culture, must give particular attention to the question of sincerity. For the canonization of sincerity or authenticity, its elevation to the highest or most fundamental human virtue, would seem to be one of the defining characteristics of our age. This has been the observation of a long line of critics.

One might immediately object, of course, that the goal with which we are truly obsessed is rather wealth or material success. But one of the strangest things about our society is that while everyone chases money, few wholeheartedly believe in it. Virtually every American will tell you that Americans are too materialistic and sell-out too easily. Somehow, we have all internalized the old critique of bourgeois culture; we are all critics of our own lives. And on this second, critical level, when we ask ourselves what it means not to sell out, a little voice within us always gives the same reply: "Be true to your inner self." This is our obsession with sincerity.

Thus, by the ideal of sincerity, I mean something very general—more general, perhaps, than is sanctioned by common usage. In the largest sense, I mean the phenomenon that Allan Bloom describes in saying that in our thinking about human happiness and human excellence, we have replaced the traditional vocabulary of virtue and vice with such new pairs of opposites as inner directed/other directed, real self/alienated self, sincere/hypocritical.[1]

For example, if one asks what character trait has been the single greatest subject of condemnation and loathing by the intellectuals and artists of the past two centuries, one would have to answer: hypocrisy. Even today, as Judith Shklar remarks:

> Hypocrisy remains the only unforgivable sin, perhaps especially among those who can overlook and explain away almost every other vice, even cruelty. However much suffering it may cause, and however many social and religious rules it may violate, evil can be understood after due analysis. But not hypocrisy, which alone now is inexcusable.[2]

Conversely, if one seeks to name the positive characteristic that our culture uses to define the happy and healthy soul, one would have to say: "Being Oneself." If the modern age had a theme song, it would be "I Gotta Be Me."

But also included in the ideal of sincerity is the assumption that the self that I gotta be is the private self, even the secret self. Thus the turn to sincerity also entails the "Fall of Public Man," to use the title of a recent work of sociology, that is, the demotion of the public, political realm of life and the concomitant elevation of the world of the personal, the private, and the intimate.[3]

Thus, for example, Lionel Trilling suggests that it was the new ideal of sincerity that was responsible for the sudden florescence—during the seventeenth century—of such sincere art-forms as autobiography, memoir writing, and portrait painting.[4] And certainly this phenomenon continues today in our self-obsessed society, with its hunger for every form of personal disclosure and disburdening self-display from psychoanalysis to tell-all memoirs to est to Oprah Winfrey. And so when Christopher Lasch speaks of our "Culture of Narcissism," this too seems yet one more feature of our new world of sincerity.[5]

But sincerity is not to be confused with frankness or plainspokeness, an opposite virtue and very much on the wane in our age of euphemism. A person is supposed to show himself to others, not others to themselves. The frankness of one would only inhibit the sincerity of another. Nor is sincerity the same as honesty. The latter involves a self-disciplined adherence to the truth or to one's word, the former an adherence to the self.

So, in sum, if it is true that we are obsessed with sincerity — that above everything else, we loathe hypocrisy, cherish self-disclosure, and long to be ourselves — the question is: Why? How did this ideal emerge?

Sincerity as an Outgrowth of Democratic Egalitarianism

Let me make a first stab at an explanation—a first stab that will prove inadequate and thus prepare the way for a somewhat different approach. In seeking to understand any major feature of American life usually the best place to begin is Tocqueville's *Democracy in America*. One consults him, first, to see if he explicitly discusses the particular issue in question, and if he does not—as is more or less the case with sincerity—then one can at least attempt to apply his general method of explanation. This method, which, as I understand it, is a variation on a long tradition dating back to Plato and Aristotle, endeavors to understand every characteristic of a given society as an outgrowth of the fundamental political principles structuring that society—in the case of America, the principles of equality and freedom. In Tocqueville's view, for example, even our penchant for materialism ultimately derives from these more basic principles.[6]

So can we understand the ideal of sincerity as a direct outgrowth or expression of the democratic principles of equality and freedom? Ultimately, I think the answer is: No. But, it is likely that our love of sincerity springs from more than one source, and certainly one of these sources is our hunger for equality. So, let us very briefly consider this Tocquevillian explanation before moving beyond it.

To begin with the points that Tocqueville himself makes, the equality, freedom, and mobility of democratic society destroy the rigid hierarchy and ceremonious formality of aristocratic life, liberating men for a greater spontaneity, sincerity and naturalness. "Democracy loosens social ties, but it tightens natural ones" (p. 589). In the realm of social etiquette, to take the most obvious example, "democratic manners are neither so well thought out nor so regular [as aristocratic ones], but they often are more sincere [sincère]. They form, as it were, a thin, transparent veil through which the real feelings and personal thoughts of each man can be easily seen" (p. 607). Similarly, the democratic family, being more egalitarian, dispenses with cold, aristocratic formality, and appeals instead to natural affection, openness, and intimacy (pp. 587–89). Above all, aristocratic societies "liked to entertain a sublime conception of the duties of man"; and these lofty morals, straining human nature, inevitably were honored more in speech than in deed. Strenuous ideals generate hypocrisy. Democratic equality, by contrast, encourages a more realistic and open acknowledgement of human selfishness and thus engenders a moral doctrine—"self-interest properly understood"—that is "wonderfully agreeable to human weaknesses." As such, it is followed more easily and so also more sincerely (pp. 525–27).

All of these points show how a decrease in aristocratic hypocrisy and corresponding increase in sincerity are unintended by-products, as it were, of democracy and equality. They do not, however, address the precise phenomenon we are examining, which presumably was not yet present in Tocqueville's America: the rise of sincerity as a conscious goal, indeed as the highest ideal and virtue.[7]

Thus, still in the spirit of Tocqueville, but beyond the letter, we might add the following points relating equality to the virtue of sincerity. Sincerity calls upon us to admit and reveal our true inner feelings, and this means especially the feelings we would otherwise want to hide, that is, the base and shameful feelings. There is no virtue, after all, in revealing our most noble impulses. Thus the ideal of sincerity serves equality, because it encourages self-unmasking, self-debunking, and the public renunciation of the pretence to superiority. Sincerity would have all of us declare: "Beneath my public mask, I too am weak."

Taken to an extreme, sincerity is even more leveling. On television talk shows, for example, we see a daily parade of reformed drug addicts, child molesters, and other moral unfortunates who, speaking loquaciously of their crimes, end up receiving the admiration of the audience for their courageous openness and sincerity. The more horrible their secrets, the nobler they are for revealing them. Thus, on a certain level, the worse they are, the better they are: heroes of sincerity are to be found only among the most unfortunate or depraved. In short, the ideal of sincerity, when taken to an extreme, has that transvaluing power—made famous by Nietzsche—by which established hierarchies and inequalities are not only subverted but reversed.

Sincerity as a Countercultural Ideal

Notwithstanding all of this service that sincerity renders to equality, however, it still does not seem that one can rest with a Tocquevillian explanation. One cannot adequately explain the rise of sincerity as an ideal as a direct outgrowth of the principle of equality that stands at the core of our regime. A new kind of analysis is needed.

My primary reason for saying this is that the ideal of sincerity did not first arise from within our liberal, democratic regime, but rather as a reaction against it. As is well known, sincerity was first embraced by intellectuals and artists who, standing outside and against the dominant bourgeois culture, denounced it for its rampant hypocrisy and conformism. In other words, what is crucial for understanding the virtue of sincerity and our obsession with it is to see that it is a new kind of virtue—a "countercultural virtue" if you like. It is distinguished from other virtues in at least three ways.

First, as we have just seen, it is not a direct virtue embodying the ideals of the society, but a reactive or countercultural one, embraced out of revulsion for our direct traits and primary impulses. Sincerity was canonized not because it expressed the regime and its principles, but precisely because it seemed so clearly missing from the regime.

Secondly, sincerity is, at least in its origins, not a collective virtue, stemming from the principles or conscience of the nation as whole, but rather a specialized virtue, being the discovery and unique property of the intellectual class which stands in an adversarial relation to the culture at large.

And thirdly, because sincerity is defined against the prevailing culture, it is not a "natural" virtue like courage which grows out of permanent features of the human condition, but rather a historical virtue, which arises in reaction to particular, historically contingent conditions. Courage, for example, is recognized pretty much everywhere as a virtue and as at least a contender for the highest virtue, whereas sincerity is much less often singled out for praise and, before our time, has perhaps never been viewed as the highest virtue.

Now if it is true, in particular, that sincerity is not a natural but a historical virtue, then to understand it fully, we ought to study it historically. And if we search back to find the first emergence of the ideal of sincerity in the full modern sense, we come eventually to Rousseau. The proof of this assertion will require the whole remainder of my essay, but, for initial evidence, let me offer three observations.

One, Rousseau was the first philosopher to adopt the posture of the modern alienated intellectual—the first who stood outside society not in order to escape or transcend it, but in order to look back at it in criticism and blame.

Second, if we look at the content of this criticism and blame, we find that the fundamental vice for which Rousseau condemns the men of his time is precisely: insincerity and hypocrisy.[8] Indeed, he is the inventor of the critical concept of "bourgeois hypocrisy."

Third, if we turn to the positive goal Rousseau promotes, we find at its core a new ideal of sincerity, understood for the first time as an end in itself. This ideal, moreover, is illustrated and exemplified in the life of Rousseau himself, who was, for example, the only philosopher whose longest writing is his own autobiography. This writing, moreover, focuses not primarily on the events of his life or on his ideas but on his inner feelings and sentiments. And it is a document committed to intimate self-disclosure, recounting in excruciating detail, for example, his youthful desire to expose himself and his protracted love affair with a woman he liked to call "Mama."

So if we are seeking the historical origins of our peculiar ideal of sincerity, Rousseau, I believe, is our man. Let us then ask him our question: why are you so obsessed with sincerity?

I think he would give a two-part answer to this question—the first, concerning the unique prevalence of hypocrisy or insincerity in modern or bourgeois society; the second part, concerning the unique goodness of sincerity as such. Let us consider each in turn.

But one initial word of caution. We will be examining one particular strand of Rousseau's thought—an especially important one, but still not the whole garment. Rousseau's attack on hypocrisy is something he never mutes or qualifies. His positive ideal of sincerity, on the other hand, is something that is meant to apply, undiluted, only to those compelled or enabled to live isolated, withdrawn, private lives. It does not apply to that alternative ideal of Rousseau's works: the denatured, public-spirited citizen living in the legitimate state. There is no talk of sincerity in the *Social Contract*. To be sure, the citizen is no hypocrite, like the people Rousseau sees about him in Paris. He is sincere in the important sense that he is self-consistent and acts as he speaks. But since he places loyalty to the fatherland and the general will above loyalty to his unique inner self, indeed since he is a self-combatter, continually at war with his most natural impulses, he is not sincere in the deepest sense. Similarly, Rousseau believes that, even in private life, it is never good for a young woman to be altogether sincere. He considers female sexual modesty to be necessary precisely because it is untrue.[9] Again, Rousseau makes it quite clear that strict honesty or sincerity is not wholly compatible with the role of the great Legislator who founds a nation, or with that of the tutor who raises Émile.[10] Thus, the ideal of sincerity, while in a sense the deepest stratum of Rousseau's thought, nevertheless had an elaborately hedged and qualified status in his writings which it has mostly lost in our own time and which, at any rate, must be abstracted from in the analysis to follow.

The New Prevalence of Hypocrisy

Rousseau would say that if he seems to be obsessed with insincerity, constantly railing and fulminating against hypocrisy, that is only because hypocrisy is the most fundamental and characteristic feature of the men of his time. Many others, in fact, had pronounced the same judgment, including Montesquieu, who wrote a brief essay entitled "A Praise of Sincerity." In this work, which is roughly contemporaneous with Rousseau's writings and thus a useful term of comparison, Montesquieu calls flattery and false politeness "the virtue of the century; it is the whole study of today."[11] He attributes this regrettable phenomenon partly to the natural preference men always have for pleasant flattery over troublesome frankness and partly to the particular influence of the French monarchy of his time, which produced and propagated the courtier spirit (pp. 102, 104–05).

Rousseau's description of, as well as his explanation for, the same phenomenon is far more radical. He describes how:

> Everything being reduced to appearances, everything becomes factitious and deceptive: honor, friendship, virtue, and often even vices themselves about which men finally discover the secret of boasting; how, in a word, always asking others what we are and never daring to question ourselves on this subject, in the midst of so much philosophy, humanity, politeness, and sublime maxims, we have only a deceitful and frivolous exterior.[12]

This condition of hypocrisy is certainly not natural or historically universal, according to Rousseau, who maintains, on the contrary, that men are naturally good. Therefore, this vice must result from certain corrupting social conditions. It is not a natural vice but a historical one. Furthermore, according to Rousseau, the historical cause of our hypocrisy is not anything isolated or relative to a particular form of government. The French courtliness criticized by Montesquieu is only one manifestation, if a particularly egregious one, of a much broader phenomenon. The true source of our hypocrisy is to be found in the fundamental structure of modern society as such.

To understand this, let us begin somewhat further back. Rousseau adopts but radicalizes the theoretical individualism of the thinkers he is attacking, the early modern thinkers like Hobbes and Locke whom Rousseau blames for the new prevalence of hypocrisy. Human beings, in his view, are not by nature social, but rather solitary and selfish. They can, however, be artificially transformed and made into social beings by properly devised political institutions—those which are able to engender sympathetic fellow feeling and a patriotic love of the common good. To the extent that a society succeeds in thus denaturing human beings and transforming them into patriotic citizens, these human beings will live happily, healthily, and free of hypocrisy.

But, according to Rousseau, the defining characteristic of modern societies is precisely their conscious renunciation of this difficult effort to transform men into citizens. Encouraged by the theoretical individualism of such thinkers as Hobbes and Locke, modern or bourgeois societies attempt the experiment of leaving men as they are, as naturally selfish individuals, and uniting them by showing them that cooperation with others is in their own selfish interest.[13]

The crucial modern claim, then, is that selfishness of the proper kind actually fosters sociability. The more that people are selfish, after all, the more they feel the need for things, and the more they need things, the more they depend on other men to supply them, and the more they depend on others, the more they must be willing to serve others so that these others will serve them in return. In this way, sociability can be generated from selfishness.

But in Rousseau's view this grand modern experiment is an unmitigated disaster. He agrees that materialism, individualism, and selfishness can indeed be used to hold people together in society through bonds of mutual self-interest, but such a society will have the precise and unavoidable effect of forcing each of its members to become a phony, an actor, and a hypocrite.

The reason for this is beguilingly simple. The whole idea of generating sociability from selfishness relies—obviously—on a contradiction within human selfishness: the more I am selfish, the less I love others, but the more I need them. Thus the more I care only about myself, the more I am driven to seek the services of others. And this elemental contradiction of human selfishness is what creates the modern character: the other-directed egoist, who is prevented by his need to use others from ever being himself.

Think it through. The egoistic individual is forced by his very selfishness to appear just and benevolent towards others—so that they will help him—but, because he is selfish, he never sincerely desires to be this way for its own sake. The same thing that makes him need to appear moral—his selfishness—makes him dislike being moral. In short, among selfish but mutually dependent human beings, it is necessarily bad to be what it is necessarily good to seem. In such a society, there is an unavoidable gulf between seeming and being; and this is why it becomes psychologically necessary that all men become phonies, actors, role-players, and hypocrites.

From now on we must take care never to let ourselves be seen such as we are: because for every two men whose interests coincide, perhaps a hundred thousand oppose them, and the only way to succeed is either to deceive or to ruin all those people. That is the fatal source of the violence, the betrayals, the deceits and all the horrors necessarily required by a state of affairs in which everyone pretends to be working for the others' profit or reputation, while only seeking to raise his own above them and at their expense.[14]

In sum, the modern commercial republic, generating sociability from selfishness, necessarily creates a society of smiling enemies, where each individual pretends to care about others precisely because he cares only about himself.

So this is the first half of Rousseau's answer to our question: Why is he, and why are we in his footsteps, so obsessed with sincerity? His answer is that, for the reasons just given, hypocrisy is everywhere: it is the universal and essential characteristic of the man of our time, the modern bourgeois. And indeed since Rousseau, the concept of "bourgeois hypocrisy" and the irritable tendency to find it everywhere has been a staple of Western literature and philosophy.[15]

The Character of Bourgeois Hypocrisy

Before going on to the second half of Rousseau's response to our question, it is necessary at least briefly to evaluate this first argument, which, despite its considerable influence, would seem to be too extreme. Why must we all be secret enemies, one wants to ask, given the relative harmony that exists among our selfish interests? Rousseau anticipates the objection:

> If I am answered that society is so constituted that each man gains by serving the others, I shall reply that this would be very well, if he did not gain still more by harming them. There is no profit, however legitimate, that is not surpassed by one that can be made illegitimately, and wrong done to one's neighbor is always more lucrative than services. (*Second Discourse*, pp. 194–95)

But does this statement remain true if one looks, not only at immediate profit, but at one's long term self-interest? Should one not rather conclude with Adam Smith that, for people in the middle classes, who have no significant power other than their reputation, success "almost always depends upon the favor and good opinion of their neighbors and equals; and without a tolerable regular conduct, these can very seldom be obtained. The good old proverb, therefore, that honesty is the best policy, holds, in such situations, almost always perfectly true."[16]

Indeed, honesty would seem to be precisely the characteristic bourgeois virtue. If Rousseau failed to see this, it is because (his terminology notwithstanding) the world he observed was late aristocratic, not bourgeois. And honesty does not flourish in corrupt aristocracies, as Montesquieu pointed out and Smith goes on to argue:

> In the superior stations of life the case is unhappily not always the same. In the courts of princes, in the drawing-rooms of the great, where success and preferment depend, not upon the esteem of intelligent and well-informed equals, but upon the fanciful and foolish favour of ignorant, presumptuous, and proud superiors; flattery and falsehood too often prevail over merit and abilities. (p. 129)

More generally, in traditional and aristocratic societies, where people are bound to one another with a hundred duties not of their own choosing, doubtless one of them is honesty; but should a person find it necessary on

occasion to lie—like the "wily Odysseus"—his standing as a man of honor
and virtue need not be fundamentally compromised. But in a bourgeois society, where this web of duties has been swept away and where people face each
other as free, atomized, but needy individuals, almost all serious human relationships are voluntarily contracted on the basis of free promise or consent.
Here, agreement and trust are everything. Precisely here, then, a man is only
as good as his word. Thus, as W.E.H. Lecky remarks in his *History of European Morals*:

> Veracity is usually the special virtue of an industrial nation, for although indus-
> trial enterprise affords great temptations to deception, mutual confidence, and
> therefore strict truthfulness, are in these occupations so transcendently impor-
> tant that they acquire in the minds of men a value they had never before pos-
> sessed. Veracity becomes the first virtue in the moral type, and no character is
> regarded with any kind of approbation in which it is wanting. . . . This constitutes
> probably the chief moral superiority of nations pervaded by a strong industrial
> spirit.[17]

Even if all of this is granted, however, Rousseau would not be without
reply. Under the right social and economic conditions, he might argue, people's long-term self-interest may indeed incline them to behave honestly, especially if this calculation is buttressed by additional moral or religious impulses
(as in fact Locke, Smith, Tocqueville, and Weber, among others, all assume).
But the question is: What is the character of this bourgeois honesty and
respectability? No matter how deeply ingrained, Rousseau suspects, at bottom it is false. It still grows out of the fundamental contradiction of selfish
sociability or egoistic other-directedness. It is not a virtue embraced for its
own sake as something intrinsically good, but only for the useful impression
it makes upon others. It is only a necessary evil. Each man earnestly praises
it in public—to encourage others to be honest and to convince them that he
is so—but in private he knows that it contradicts his heart's desire. Thus, the
bourgeois may indeed be honest, but he is not sincere; his whole moral posture is a mask worn for others, an act, a role, a lie.[18]

This is the account of bourgeois hypocrisy in its toned-down form, the
form that flourished in most of the nineteenth century. In the last fifty years,
however, the old, straitlaced honest bourgeois seems gradually to have given
way to a new type, closer in many respects to Rousseau's original model.
Such writers as C. Wright Mills, Eric Fromm, and above all David Riesman have argued that the increasing bureaucratization of the corporation
and the state have revived something like the old courtier spirit. The "inner-
directed" man of early capitalism—whose hypocrisy always remained a
somewhat controversial hypothesis—is being replaced by the "other-directed"

man—whose eager posturing, conformity, and hollowness are far more widely acknowledged.[19]

At any rate, without trying to settle here the precise degree of prevalence of bourgeois hypocrisy, it should be possible, in light of the preceding discussion, at least to characterize more exactly this new kind of hypocrisy identified by Rousseau and how it differs from earlier forms. Wherever there is a lofty and strenuous moral ideal, as in aristocratic societies or piously Christian ones, there will inevitably be moral hypocrites. But in most cases such persons might more accurately be called "boasters" because their claims ultimately stem from a genuine (if wavering) admiration for the prevailing moral ideal, and they err only in exaggerating the degree to which they attain it.

The new, bourgeois hypocrisy is fundamentally different. The skeptical unmasking of Christian and aristocratic moral hypocrisy is the very precondition for the emergence of the new hypocrisy of interest. Liberated from the pretense to aristocratic self-sufficiency and to divine protection, the bourgeois faces, unprotected, his mortal exposedness, his selfish neediness and therefore his utter dependence on others. Thus, when he raises his exaggerated claims to honesty, he does so not from a genuine faith in or admiration of honesty (as a Christian or aristocratic hypocrite might), but from a calculated desire for the material benefits of being thought honest. Unlike the moral hypocrite, that is, he has no genuine desire to be what he endeavors to seem; on the contrary, a contradiction exists between his claims and his motive for asserting them. His other-directedness is egoistic. He pretends to care for others precisely because he cares only for himself.

That is why the bourgeois hypocrite seems so particularly loathsome. The claims he makes for himself are surely less grandiose and probably even less false (as judged by behavior) than the aristocratic or Christian hypocrite, but they are more profoundly insincere. He is no longer merely boasting; he is dissimulating, acting, role-playing. His public claims constitute a direct denial of his true self. For this reason, his hypocrisy is actually worse the more it is successful, for it involves a falsification of the inner life, a fundamental self-betrayal. That is why, in confronting this new hypocrisy, Rousseau and those who follow him invent a new vocabulary of criticism, unknown to earlier moralists, involving such terms as inner nothingness, emptiness, hollowness, phoniness, inauthenticity, and so forth.

Related to this are two other distinctive features of the modern preoccupation with hypocrisy, which also point to its Rousseauian provenance. The condemnation of hypocrisy is obviously not a new phenomenon. The most prominent earlier example is perhaps the "Sermon on the Mount." But in all earlier condemnations, this vice is regarded as a moral problem of the individual, a natural human foible like cowardice or immoderation. By contrast, in Rousseau and in the view prevailing after him, hypocrisy is regarded as a social and historical problem: it is seen as a widespread deformity of character systematically produced by the evils of modern society. It is "bourgeois" hypocrisy. Consequently, hypocrisy in the modern understanding is necessarily a countercultural concept—indicting the existing social order—and the attack on it has more the character of social criticism than of moral exhortation.

Moreover, because this vice is blamed on society, the specifically modern concept of hypocrisy tends to go along with the view that only the bohemian intellectual, who is defined by his stance outside and against society, can free himself from and so recognize this deformity. And this in turn leads to the view that the intellectual has the unique ability and therefore the unique duty to act as the conscience of society and to denounce its hypocrisy wherever and whenever he sees it.[20]

In sum, Rousseau and those who followed him were obsessed with hypocrisy because of the new prevalence of this vice, resulting from the rise of the bourgeois state, and because of their perceived duty as intellectuals to denounce it. And since Rousseau's time, this duty has been well fulfilled, producing a torrent of anti-bourgeois attacks on hypocrisy.

Sincerity as the Highest Good

There is a second part, however, to Rousseau's explanation for his obsession with sincerity. If the first points to the prevalence of hypocrisy in his time, the second gives new arguments for the positive good of sincerity. This second part is indeed a necessary addition to the first because attacking hypocrisy does not automatically lead to praising sincerity. The mere fact that hypocrisy is bad and prevalent by no means proves that sincerity is the highest good. The "Sermon on the Mount," for example, contains a famous attack on hypocrisy, but this does not lead to a praise of sincerity as such but rather to the praise of piety, sincere piety. There is no suggestion here that the nonbeliever could justify himself before God by emphasizing his sincerity.

Similarly, in Shakespeare and Molière we find much emphasis on the falseness of men's claims to virtue and nobility, but the opposite of hypocritical nobility is still taken to be genuine nobility—not sincerity as such. Thus, Rousseau (and we after him) is doing something fundamentally new when he makes the seemingly obvious move from blaming hypocrisy to praising sincerity—that is, not praising sincere piety, or sincere righteousness, but sincerity itself and by itself. In other words, Rousseau is the first to define the good as being oneself regardless of what one may be. And that is a radically new position—a position which is at the core of his and our unique obsession with sincerity.

To defend this new view is the point of the second part of Rousseau's answer, which consists of a defense of the goodness of sincerity as such. But this argument actually brings us into the most fundamental level of Rousseau's thought, for his defense of sincerity is really a consequence of his whole new understanding of human nature, his comprehensive redefinition of the human self.

According to Rousseau, the fundamental principle of human nature is self-love: the innate inclination to delight in, preserve, and actualize ourselves.[21] But this claim is certainly not new; many earlier thinkers had taken such a view. The crucial issue is: what is the self that we love in this way? What is the human self that we incline to delight in, preserve, and actualize? Here is where Rousseau will give a new answer.

Aristotle, for example, makes the famous statement: man is a political animal. And by this he means that the true human self is a public or communal self, that a human being cannot be himself by himself, that he can truly realize himself and come into his own only by performing his function within the larger political whole. Plato maintains that our truest self is our reason or mind, and that we actualize ourselves most fully through the act of philosophic contemplation. St. Augustine holds that our highest good and truest self is God; and that self-love, fully conscious of itself, is the same as the love of God.

Rousseau rejects all of these earlier accounts of the human self. The starting point for his new reflections on the self is the same as that, seen above, for his analysis of the modern state and the origins of hypocrisy: it is the theoretical individualism of early modern thought—only deepened and radicalized.

Rousseau maintains that the true foundation of the human self is not God or reason or the community but the elemental self-consciousness of the individual. Although he does not present a systematic derivation of his views, Rousseau's argument would seem to run as follows. In every act of awareness or perception, I am always simultaneously aware of the fact that I perceive. And furthermore, in thus perceiving that I perceive, I necessarily perceive myself. Therefore, there is a self-awareness which necessarily accompanies every act of awareness as such. This is the famous "sentiment of existence": the sheer awareness that I am, that I exist. And it is in this elemental self-consciousness that Rousseau locates the true human self and the foundation of our being. Somehow, a human being exists not through his relation to God or to the essence of man, but through a relation to himself. Our being is our presence to ourself, our sentiment of existence.[22]

The precise meaning and ground of these claims is, to be sure, not altogether clear. But what can be seen fairly clearly are their consequences, which emerge if we plug them back into the theory of self-love with which we began. The fundamental human inclination, we have seen, is self-love, which impels us to preserve and actualize ourselves. We want, as fully as possible, to become what we are, to realize ourselves, to become as alive and actualized as possible, to really live. But how, concretely, we ought to go about this depends on the true nature of the human self.

In this context, Rousseau's new definition of the self has the following meaning: the true way to actualize oneself is not through the love of God or philosophic contemplation of the cosmos, or participation in the political order, but through withdrawal from everything else and communion with one's inner self. In a word, through sincerity.

Here, in short, is Rousseau's argument for the positive good of sincerity. As we can see now, it is not merely an ethical argument praising the morally virtuous character of sincerity. Nor is it a political argument about the social usefulness of sincerity. Rather it is an argument issuing from the deepest claims regarding the nature of human existence. Rousseau argues that sincerity is the highest good in life because it is the essential path to genuine selfhood and self-realization. What piety is for St. Augustine, what contemplation is for Plato, sincerity is for Rousseau. It is the unique means through which we draw closer to Being and make ourselves most real.[23]

Let me try to elaborate this point, and render it more precise, by distinguishing six fundamental characteristics of the new Rousseauian self and by showing how each of these, in its own way, leads to the canonization of sincerity as the royal road to self-realization. In doing this, I may be forced, in places, to extend Rousseau's ideas beyond his own formulations of them—yet not beyond the general tendency of his thought, or so I believe.

First, because the sentiment of existence is a completely internal phenomenon, the true self is emphatically private. The real me is not my social self or communal self: it is not what I am in other people's eyes nor is it my role in the community, my public activity and political participation. The real me is the one that is there when I am alone.

Rousseau is aware that the public world of honor, power, and status seems to us more real and important. But he endeavors with all his force to convince us that this is a deadly illusion: that the public world is an alienation from the true self, that the private world of feelings and intimacies is actually the more real one. Rousseau consciously strives to subvert the public world and to make people more withdrawn, inward, intimate, self-absorbed, and introspective.

Rousseau also knows, indeed emphasizes, that for civilized, socialized and, especially, urbanized human beings it is no easy matter to get free of the social self, which does not simply disappear behind closed doors. But he believes that those who live in relative isolation, or those who are willing to retreat there, if they will commune with themselves in the company of nature and a few close friends or family members, can succeed over time in recovering contact with a good part of their natural sentiments and selves. In other words, Rousseau has a faith, if a very qualified one, in the power of introspection—a crucial presupposition of the ideal of sincerity. Self-knowledge does not require a rigorous dialectical examination of our opinions and beliefs, nor an externally applied psychoanalytic examination of the subconscious mind. The Rousseauian self is more immediately accessible. Ultimately, we can find and know and be ourselves through introspection and sincerity.[24]

Second, for Rousseau, the true self is not the rational self. We are not our intellect, our mind, but our feelings. The ground of our being is the sentiment of existence, which is a sentiment, a feeling: "to exist, for us, is to feel [sentir]."[25]

As for reason, in Rousseau's view, it is a recently acquired and rather unnatural faculty. It may indeed be the most impressive or powerful of our faculties, but it is not a very deep part of us: it does not control our behavior and, more importantly, it is not the ground of our being or existence. Therefore, we do not actualize ourselves by reasoning or contemplating reality, but by communing with our sentiments and feelings. From the standpoint of Rousseauian selfhood, it is less important to be true to reality than to be true to oneself. So, the ideal of wisdom must be replaced with that of sincerity.

Third, the true self is not the moral self. Rousseau knows that human beings, though by nature solitary and free, have the capacity to invent laws, contract obligations, create ethical and religious duties, and then force themselves to comply with these. Civilized human beings are self-overcoming animals who will conquer and repress their spontaneous inclinations and natural selves in the name of certain ethical ideals. We human beings can transform ourselves into moral beings, into persons of character and principle.

Rousseau sees this as socially salutary, indeed necessary, and spends much time admiring it; but ultimately he sees it as unnatural. The true self is the spontaneous self, not this invented and forcibly imposed moral character. The real me is the one that remains when I let go and stop trying, when I just let it be. I truly find myself when, rejecting all the strenuous talk about my higher self, and liberated from shame and guilt, I just freely observe and sincerely acknowledge all that goes on within my soul. I must "be myself" regardless of what I may be. So again, the true me is accessed through sincerity.[26]

Fourth, my true self is not primarily what I have in common with others—my share of universal human nature—but rather what is particular and unique to me. For, in nature, only the individual or particular is real; everything universal is a human creation, indeed a falsification, a distorting imposition on reality. Thus everything in myself that I have in common with others probably derives from the alien influence of society; it does not really come from me. But on the other hand, everything in me that is particular, unique and idiosyncratic is likely to derive from my true inner self.[27]

One consequence of this is as follows. If my truest being were something universal—like participation in the universal nature or essence of man—then I could come to recognize and understand myself best through a kind of rational knowledge. Then the Delphic imperative to "know thyself" would mean "know human nature." But if the deepest thing in me is unique, then I can only know myself personally, and the whole enterprise of rational self-knowledge must be replaced by each individual's introspection and sincerity.

Fifth, just as the Rousseauian self is not universal but rather particular, so also it does not have the character of a form or a formal cause. The elemental self-consciousness that is the ground of our being does not have any form or idea or essence: it is a pure sentiment of existence. It is a pure awareness that we are—without any specification of what we are. Thus, the human self has the character, not of a form but, as it were, of a source or a well-spring. And so self-realization does not mean arranging one's soul in the proper order, or being in conformity with the formal essence or objective nature of man. Rather, self-realization means being in touch with our source, "connecting" with our well-spring, being "on line." For Rousseau, being oneself does not mean corresponding to oneself but rather coming from oneself—and thus it means sincerity. For the sincere person is precisely he who always makes his true self his source and origin.

The sixth and last characteristic involves a twist. The true self is "expansive." After one has finally retreated from all the social sources of falsehood and hypocrisy and turned back to the plenitude of the natural self, one finds that an important part of that self is a quasi-erotic inclination to "expand" the self outward in pursuit of a still greater aliveness.[28] The presence of other human beings alienates me from myself as long as I hold up my social self to greet and confront theirs. But when, withdrawing within, I discover my true, private self, it also becomes possible to discover and "identify with" theirs, to connect inside to inside, to be witness to the intense, trembling reality that another's life has for himself, and in this way to excite and heighten the experience of my own life, to make my existence more real to me. To the extent, then, that the Rousseauian self seeks to connect up to some larger reality, it is to the inner flow of human life and suffering. Rousseau, one might say, replaces classical contemplation with a caring voyeurism. And once again, sincerity, both one's own and others', is the essential condition of this experience.[29]

Conclusion

In sum, Rousseau radically reinterprets the character of human existence, arguing that the true human self, rooted in the sentiment of existence, is private rather than public, sentimental rather than rational, spontaneous rather than moral, unique rather than universal, originary rather than formal, and compassionately expansive rather than closed. And each one of these changes, in a different way, makes sincerity the key to self-actualization. This fact, together with the new prevalence of hypocrisy in the emerging bourgeois order, explains why Rousseau was so obsessed with sincerity. And I believe that an experience of hypocrisy and a conception of the self similar to Rousseau's also lies behind much of our own preoccupation with sincerity.

By way of conclusion, I would like briefly to speculate how the character of Rousseau's argument may also help us to understand one further feature of our love of sincerity. As we have seen, the hatred of hypocrisy and longing for sincerity first emerged, not as an expression of the dominant culture, but as a reaction against it, as a counter-cultural ideal employed by bohemian intellectuals in their critique of bourgeois society. But in recent decades, the ideal of sincerity has clearly become general, permeating the whole of society. Today, everyone denounces conformity and longs for sincerity. In other words, as suggested above, one of the strangest characteristics of our society is that, in some measure, everyone has internalized the intellectual critique of bourgeois life. Everyone contains some mix of culture and counter-culture. And everything that once seemed so resolutely anti-bourgeois has now come to light as only late-bourgeois.

If this observation is correct, it might be useful to look once again to Rousseau for an explanation. We have seen that the theoretical principles underlying both parts of Rousseau's analysis are largely borrowed from the very thinkers he is attacking. Specifically, Rousseau's central premise, his extreme individualism, is only an extension and radicalization of the bourgeois individualism of Hobbes and Locke. But this means that Rousseau's critique of modern culture is essentially a dialectical critique: he shows that the very principles of that culture, when thought through in all their inner tensions, lead one to a counter-cultural stance. Rousseau's main argument is indeed that modern society builds on a massive contradiction: it is based on individualism and, for this very reason, it destroys all sincere individuality. Both sides of this contradiction combine, in Rousseau, to produce an intense and redoubled longing for individuality—an obsession with sincerity.

Nothing prevents others from eventually re-enacting this same dialectical process. Indeed, if one can generalize from the argument and the example of Rousseau, it would seem that bourgeois culture contains the seeds of its own critique, and that the anti-bourgeois intellectual is the inevitable out-growth of the thing he criticizes. But if he is that, then he is also an outgrowth that will tend to spread. To generalize still further, it looks as if a society based upon Lockean individualism will tend sooner or later to generate a kind of Rousseauian anti-Lockeanism which will slowly become general while remaining in permanent and unresolved tension with the original, Lockean substratum. Some such process, at any rate, would seem to be at work in our ever-spreading and ever-frustrated longing for sincerity.

2

Existential Phenomenology and the Brave New World of *The Matrix*

HUBERT L. DREYFUS and
STEPHEN D. DREYFUS

Hubert Dreyfus is Professor of Philosophy in the graduate school at the University of California, Berkeley. His research interests bridge the analytic and Continental traditions in twentieth century philosophy, and include phenomenology, existentialism, philosophy of psychology, philosophy of literature, and philosophical implications of artificial intelligence; his most recent work is On the Internet *and he is working on a second edition of his commentary on Heidegger's* Being and Time.

The Matrix raises familiar philosophical problems in such fascinating new ways that, in a surprising reversal, students all over the country are assigning it to their philosophy professors. Having done our homework, we'd like to explore two questions raised in Christopher Grau's book of essays on the film.[1] Grau points out that *The Matrix* dramatizes René Descartes's worry that, since all we ever experience are our own inner mental states, we might, for all we know, be living in an illusion created by a malicious demon. In that case most of our beliefs about reality would be false. That leads Grau to question the rationality of Cypher's choice to live in an illusory world of pleasant experiences, rather than facing painful reality.

We think that *The Matrix*'s account of our situation is even more disturbing than these options suggest. *The Matrix* is a vivid illustration of Descartes's additional mind-blowing claim that, even if our *minds* were directly in touch with the world, our *brains* could *never* be in direct touch with reality. For all we could know, we are, in fact, all brains in vats. So in choosing to return from the "desert of the real" to the Matrix world, Cypher is merely choosing between two sets of systematic appearances. To counter these disturbing ideas we have to rethink what we mean by contact with the real world, illusion, freedom, and control. Only then will we be in a position to take up Grau's question as to why we feel it is better to live in the real world, no matter how miserable, rather than living in an illusory world that makes us feel good.

I. The Myth of the Inner

Thanks to Descartes, we moderns have to face the question: How can we ever get outside of our *private inner experiences* so as to come to know the things and people in the *public external world*? While this seems an important question to us now, it has not always been taken seriously. For the Homeric Greeks human beings had no inner life to speak of. All their strong feelings were expressed outwardly. Homer considered it one of Odysseus's cleverest tricks that he could cry inwardly while his eyes remained dry.[2]

A thousand years later, people still had no sense of the importance of their inner lives. St. Augustine had to work hard to convince them otherwise. For example, he called attention to the fact that one did not have to read out loud. In his *Confessions*, he points out that St. Ambrose was remarkable in that he read to himself. "When he read, his eyes scanned the page and his heart explored the meaning, but his voice was silent and his tongue was still."[3]

But the idea that each of us has an inner life made up of our private thoughts and feelings didn't really take hold until early in the seventeenth century when Descartes introduced the modern distinction between the contents of the mind and the rest of reality. In one of his letters, he declared himself "convinced that I cannot have any knowledge of what is outside me except through the mediation of the ideas that I have in me."[4]

Thus, according to Descartes, all each of us can directly experience is the content of our own mind. Our access to the world is always *indirect*. Descartes then used reports of people with phantom limbs to call into question even our seemingly direct experience of our own bodies. He writes:

> I have been assured by men whose arm or leg has been amputated that it still seemed to them that they occasionally felt pain in the limb they had lost—thus giving me grounds to think that I could not be quite certain that a pain I endured was indeed due to the limb in which I seemed to feel it.[5]

For all we could ever know, Descartes concluded, the objective external world, including our body, may not exist; all we can be certain of is our subjective inner life.

This Cartesian conclusion was taken for granted by thinkers in the West for the next three centuries. A generation after Descartes, Gottfried Leibniz postulated that each of us is a windowless monad.[6] A monad is a self-contained world of experience, which gets no input from objects or other embodied people because there aren't any. Rather, the temporally evolving content of each monad is synchronized with the evolving content of all the other monads by God, creating the illusion of a shared real world. A generation after that, Immanuel Kant argued that human beings could never know reality as it is in itself but only their own mental representations, but, since these representations had a common source, each person's experiences were co-ordinated with the mental representations of all the others to produce what he called the phenomenal world.[7] In the early twentieth century, the founder of phenomenology, Edmund Husserl, was more solipsistic. He held, like Descartes, that one could bracket the world and other minds altogether since all that was given to us directly, whether the world and other minds existed or not, was the contents of our own "transcendental consciousness."[8] Only recently have philosophers begun to take issue with this powerful Cartesian picture.

Starting in the 1920s existential phenomenologists such as Martin Heidegger[9] and Maurice Merleau-Ponty,[10] in opposition to Husserl, contested the Cartesian view that our contact with the world and even our own bodies is mediated by internal mental content. They claimed that, if one paid careful attention to one's experience, one would see that, at a level of involvement more basic than thought, we deal directly with the things and people that make up our world.

As Charles Taylor, the leading contemporary exponent of this view, puts it:

> My ability to get around this city, this house comes out only in getting around this city and house. We can draw a neat line between my picture of an object and that object, but not between my dealing with the object and that object. It may make sense to ask us to focus on what we believe about something, say a football, even in the absence of that thing; but when it comes to playing football, the corresponding suggestion would be absurd. The actions involved in the game can't be done without the object; they include the object.[11]

In general, unlike mental content, which can exist independently of its referent, my coping abilities cannot be actualized or, in some cases, even entertained (consider imagining how you tie your shoelaces) in the absence of what I am coping with.

This is not to say that we can't be mistaken. It's hard to see how I could succeed in getting around in a city or playing football without the existence of the city or the ball, but I could be mistaken for a while, as when I mistake a façade for a house. Then, in the face of my failure to cope successfully, I may have to retroactively cross off what I seemingly encountered and adopt a new set to act or readiness (itself corrigible) to encounter a façade rather than the house I was set to deal with.

II. Brains in Vats

So it looks as if the inner-outer distinction introduced by Descartes holds only for thoughts. At the basic level of involved skillful coping, one is, Merleau-Ponty claims, simply an empty head turned towards the world.[12] But this doesn't show that *The Matrix* is old fashioned or mistaken. On the contrary, it shows that *The Matrix* has gone further than philosophers who hold we can't get outside our *mind*. It suggests a more convincing conclusion—one that Descartes pioneered but didn't develop—that we can't get outside our *brain*.

It was no accident that Descartes proclaimed the priority of the inner in the seventeenth century. At that time, instruments like the telescope and microscope were extending human beings' perceptual powers. At the same time, the sense organs themselves were being understood as transducers bringing information from the objective external world to the brain. Descartes pioneered this research with an account of how the eye responds to light energy from the external world and passes the information on to the brain by means of "the small fibers of the optic nerve."[13] Likewise, Descartes used the phantom limb phenomenon to argue that other nerves brought information about the body to the brain and from there the information passed to the mind.

It seemed to follow that, since we are each a brain in a cranial vat,[14] we can *never* be in direct contact with the world or even with our own bodies. So, even if phenomenologists like Heidegger, Merleau-Ponty, and Taylor are right that we are not confined to our inner *experiences*, it still seems plausible to suppose that, as long as the impulses to and from our nervous system copy the complex feedback loop between the brain's out-going behavior-producing impulses and the incoming perceptual ones, we would have the experience of directly coming to grips with things in the world. Yet, in the brain in the vat case, there would be no house and no city, indeed, no real external objective world, to interact with, and so we might seem to be confined to our inner experiences after all. As Morpheus[15] says to Neo in the construct:

> How do you define "real"? If you're talking about what you can feel, what you can smell, what you can taste and see, then "real" is simply electrical signals interpreted by your brain.

But this Cartesian conclusion is mistaken. The inner electrical impulses are the *causal basis* of what one can taste and feel, but we don't see and taste *them*. Even if I have only a phantom arm, my pain is not in my brain but in my phantom hand. What the phenomenologist can and should claim is that, in a Matrix world which has its causal basis in bodies in vats outside that world, the Matrix people whose brains are getting computer generated inputs and responding with action outputs, are directly coping with *perceived* reality, and *that* reality isn't *inner*.[16] Even in the Matrix world, people directly cope with chairs by sitting on them, and need baseballs to bring out their batting skills. Thus coping, even in the Matrix, is more direct than conceived of by any of the inner-outer views of the mind's relation to the "external world" that have been held from Descartes to Husserl.

Yet, wouldn't each brain in the Matrix construct have a lot of false beliefs, for example that its Matrix body is its real body whereas its real body is in a vat? No. If the Matrix dweller has a pain in his damaged foot it's in his Matrix foot, not in his brain, nor in the foot of a body in a vat—a foot that is not damaged and about which he knows nothing at all.[17] It's a mistake to think that each of us is experiencing a set of neural firings in a brain in a cranial vat. True, each of us has a brain in his or her skull and the brain provides the causal basis of our experience, but we aren't our brain. Likewise, the people in the Matrix world are not brains in vats any more than we are. They are people who grew up in the Matrix world and their experience of their Matrix body and how to use it makes that body their body, even if another body they can't even imagine has in its skull the brain that is the causal basis of their experience.

After all, the people who live in the Matrix have no other source of experience than what happens in the Matrix. Thus, a person in the Matrix has no beliefs at all about the vat-enclosed body and brain that is his causal basis, and couldn't have any. That brain is merely the unknowable cause of that person's experiences. Since the only body a Matrix dweller sees and moves is the one he has in the Matrix world, the AI programmers could have given him a Matrix body radically unlike the body in the vat. After all, the brain in the vat started life as a baby brain and could have been given any experience the AI programmers chose. They could have taken the brain of a white baby who was going to grow up short and fat, and given it the Matrix body of a tall, athletic African-American.[18]

But there is still at least one problem. The Matricians' beliefs about the properties and uses of their perceived bodies, as well as about chairs, cities, and the world may be shared and reliable, and in that sense true, but what about the *causal* beliefs of the people in the Matrix? They believe, as we do, that germs cause disease, that the sun causes things to get warm, gravity causes things to fall, and so forth. Aren't all these beliefs false? That depends on one's understanding of causality. People don't normally have explicit *beliefs* about the nature of causality. Rather, they simply *take for granted* a shared sense that they are coping with a shared world whose contents are causing their experience. Unless they are philosophizing, they do not believe that the world is real or that it is an illusion, they just count on it behaving in a consistent way so that they can cope with things successfully. If, however, as philosophers, they *believe* that there is a physical universe with causal powers that makes things happen in their world, they are mistaken. And, if the causal theory of perception requires this strong sense of causality for perceptions to be veridical, they are not perceiving anything. But if they claim that belief in causality is simply a response to the constant conjunctions of experiences as David Hume did, or that causality is the necessary succession of experiences according to a rule, as Kant held, then their causal beliefs would be true of the causal relations in the Matrix world, and most of their perceptual experiences would be veridical.[19]

Kant claims that we organize the impact of things in themselves on our mind into the experience of a public, objective world, and science relates these appearances by causal laws, but we can't know the ground of the phenomena we perceive. Specifically, according to Kant, we experience the world *as* in space and time but *things in themselves* aren't in space and time. So Kant says we can know the *phenomenal* world of objects and their law-like relations but we can't know the things in themselves that are the ground of these *appearances*.

The Matricians are in the same epistemological position that we are all in according to Kant. So, if there are Kantians in the Matrix world, most of their beliefs would be true. They would understand that they are experiencing a co-ordinated system of appearances, and understand too that they couldn't know the things in themselves that are the ground of these appearances, that is, that they couldn't know the basis of their shared experience of the world and the universe. But Kantians don't hold that our shared and tested beliefs about the world, and scientists' confirmed beliefs about the universe, are false just because they are about phenomena and do not and cannot correspond to things in themselves. And, as long as Kantians, and everyone in the Matrix, didn't claim to know about things in themselves, most of their beliefs would be true.

Nonetheless, the implicit philosophy of *The Matrix* obviously does not subscribe to the Kantian view that we can *never* know things in themselves. In *The Matrix* one can come to know reality. Once Neo's body is flushed out of the vat and is on the hovercraft, he has a broader view of reality and sees that his previous understanding was limited. But that doesn't mean he had a lot of *false beliefs* about his body and the world. When he was in the Matrix, he didn't think about these philosophical questions at all.[20] But once he is out, he has a lot of new *true beliefs* about his former vat-enclosed body—

beliefs he didn't have and couldn't have had while in the Matrix. We have seen that existential phenomenologists acknowledge that we are sometimes mistaken about particular things and have to retroactively take back our readiness to cope with them. But, as Merleau-Ponty and Taylor add, we only do so in terms of a *prima facie* new and better contact with reality. Likewise, in *The Matrix* version of the brain in the vat situation, those who have been hauled from the vat into what they experience as the real world can see that much of what they took for granted was mistaken. They can, for example, understand that what they took to be a world that had been around for millions of years was a recently constructed computer program.

Of course, things are not so simple. Most of Neo's current beliefs might still be false. His experience might, after all, be sustained by a brain in a skull in a vat, and the AI programmers might now be feeding that brain the experience of Neo's being outside the Matrix and in the hovercraft. Given the conceivability of the brain-in-the-vat fantasy, the most we can be sure of is that our coping experience reveals that we are directly up against some boundary conditions independent of our coping—boundary conditions with which we must get in sync in order to cope successfully. In this way, our coping experience is sensitive to the causal powers of these boundary conditions. Whether these independent causal conditions have the structure of an independent physical universe discovered by science, or whether the boundary conditions as well as the causal structures discovered by science are both the effect of an unknowable thing in itself that is the ground of appearances as postulated by Kant, or even whether the cause of all appearances is a computer, is something we could never know from inside our world. But Neo, once he seems to be on the hovercraft, does know that, as in waking from a dream, his current understanding of reality supersedes his former one.

III. An Ethical Interlude

The distinction between a Matrix person and the body that is the causal basis of that person has serious ethical implications. In the movie innocent people doing their job, like the police officers in the opening scene, are killed with casual unconcern, if not with relish by Morpheus and his band. Morpheus justifies these killings by explaining that the Matricians have been told that the intruders are dangerous terrorists and so the police and other defenders of law and order will kill Morpheus and his friends if they don't strike first. But when we remember that each time a Matrician is killed an associated human body somewhere in a vat dies, it seems that the killing of a virtual person in the Matrix must be morally wrong because it causes the death of a real human being.

But this can't be the right way to think about the moral issue. The bodies in the vats are not people; they are the causal basis of the people in the Matrix. They happen to be human bodies made of protoplasm but they could just as well be computers made of silicon as long as they process the inputs and outputs the way the human brain does. It is important to bear in mind that a body in a vat doesn't have a human personality apart from the active, vulnerable, feeling person in the Matrix of whom it is the causal basis.

Thus, when Neo is in the Matrix world, there are two Neo-related bodies. One is an active embodied Neo coping in the Matrix world, and the other is a non-coping, Neo-causing body in a vat (or chair) outside the Matrix world, but there is only one Neo and he stays the same in the Matrix world and later in the hovercraft because he has the same concerns, memories, and so forth—whatever accounts for personal identity—and there never was a Neo in the vat, any more than there is a person in your skull because to be the causal basis of a person is not to be a person.

It follows that when Morpheus and his followers kill the people in the Matrix world, it is murder, not because the killers cause a human organism in a vat to die, but because they kill Matricians who have personalities, act freely, love, suffer, and so forth. True, the way the Matrix world is set up, if one were to kill a body in a vat, the associated person in the Matrix would die. But the point to note is that the moral priorities are the reverse of one's first intuitions. The killing of a person in the Matrix world is intrinsically wrong because killing a person is wrong, and incidentally it results in the death of a human body in a vat; while killing the human body in the vat is wrong only as long as that body is at least potentially the causal basis of a person in the Matrix world. In our world, the tight causal connection between our biological body and our personhood keeps us from noticing these moral distinctions.

IV. A New *Brave New World*

We are now in a position to try to answer the question raised by Cypher's choice: Why live in the miserable world the war has produced rather than in a satisfying world of appearances? Some answers just won't do. It doesn't seem to be a question of whether one should face the truth rather than live in an illusion. Indeed, most of the beliefs of the average Matrician are true; they can cope by acting in some ways and not others. When they sit on a chair it usually supports them, when they enter a house they see the inside, when they walk around it they see the back. People have bodies that can be injured, they can kill and be killed. Even their background sense that in their actions they are coping with something independent of them and that others are coping with it too, is justified. As we have seen, Kant argued that, even if this were a phenomenal world, a world of appearances, most of our beliefs would still be true.

Likewise, living in the Matrix world does not seem to be less moral than living in our everyday world. The Matricians are dealing with real people, and they are free to choose what they will do; they can be selfish and betray their friends like Cypher, or they can be loyal to their friends and ready to risk their lives for their friends, like Trinity and Neo do for Morpheus. So, what, if anything, is wrong with the Matrix world?.[21]

To understand what's wrong with living in the Matrix we have to understand the source of the power of the Matrix world. Part of the power comes from the way the inputs and outputs from the computer are plugged directly into the brain's sensory motor-system. These correlations produce a powerful perceptual effect that is impervious to what they believe, like the wraparound IMAX illusion that forces one to sway to keep one's balance on a skateboard even though one knows one is sitting in a stationary seat watching a movie, or like when the moon looks bigger on the horizon even though one believes it is always the same size.

The inputs to the perceptual system of the brain in the vat produce an experience of a perceptual world whether we believe it is real or not, but once one realizes that the causality in the Matrix world is only virtual, since causality is not built into our perceptual system, one can violate the Matrix's causal laws. By the end of the movie, Neo can fly; if he wanted to, he could bend spoons.[22] About the causal principles governing the Matrix world, Morpheus tells Neo, "It is all in your mind."

If one doesn't believe in the causal laws governing appearances, one is free from the causal consequences. One's disbelief in the Matrix world somehow forces the computer to give one the experience one wills to have. To take a simple example, if one doesn't believe in the existence of a spoon, when one decides to see the spoon bending, the computer is forced to give one the visual input of the bending spoon. This is a literal example of what Morpheus calls "bending the rules." Likewise, if one believes that one can stop bullets, one will look for them where one stopped them and the computer will obediently display them there. So, after he learns that his experience of the Matrix world is not caused in the normal way, Neo doesn't *see* things differently— the impulses to his brain still control what he sees[23]—but he is able to choose to *do* things that he couldn't do before (like choose to stop bullets) and that allows him to see different things (the bullets stop). Unfortunately, how this suspension of belief in causality is able to affect the output of the brain's perceptual system is not explained in the film.

What, then, is the source of the sinister power of the Matrix world that keeps people conforming to the supposed constraints of a causal universe, even though there are no such constraints? If it isn't just that they are locked into the sensory motor correlations of their perceptual world, what sort of control is it? It has to be some sort of control of the Matricians' intellectual powers—powers which we learn early on in the movie are free from the control of direct sensory-motor computer correlations.[24] It must be some sort of mind control.

It seems that the Matrix simply takes advantage of a sort of mind control already operating in the everyday world. We are told that what keeps people from taking control of the Matrix world is their taking for granted the common-sense view of how things behave, such as, if you fall you will get hurt. More generally, what keeps people in line is their tendency to believe what the average person believes, and consequently keep doing (and not doing) what one does and doesn't do. (As in one eats peas with a fork, one doesn't throw food at the dinner table, and one goes out the door rather than the window.) Heidegger describes the resulting conformism as letting oneself be taken over by "the one" (*Das Man*).[25] Aldous Huxley similarly lamented the conformity of the brainwashed masses in *Brave New World*.

Thus, *The Matrix* can be seen as an attack on what Nietzsche calls herd mentality. Nietzsche points out that human beings are normally socialized into obeying shared social norms, and that it is hard to think differently. As he puts it, "as long as there have been humans, there have also been herds of men (clans, communities, tribes, peoples, states, churches) and always a great many people who obey, . . . considering, then, that nothing has been exercised and cultivated better and longer among men than obedience, one may fairly assume that the need for it is now innate in the average man."[26]

Waking in the movie, then, amounts to freeing oneself from the taken for granted norms that one has been brought up to accept. But how is this possible? Heidegger claims that human beings dimly sense that there is more to life than conforming. How fitting then that a barely expressible unease like a splinter in his mind seems to pervade Neo's and prompts him to begin the process of asserting his non-conformity by becoming a hacker and breaking all the rules.

V. A Really Brave New World

One might reasonably object that all the talk of dreaming in the film, even if it should not be taken literally, is too strong a religious metaphor to refer merely to what Heidegger calls living a tranquillized existence in the one. And waking seems to be more than becoming a non-conformist. After all, there are all those mentions of Jesus in connection with Neo collected by

Colin McGinn.[27] There can be no doubt that Neo is meant to be a kind of Savior, but what kind?

It's tempting to think that *The Matrix* is a Gnostic, Buddhist, or Platonic-Christian parable, in which what we take to be reality turns out to be a dream, and we are led to wake from the world of appearances to some kind of higher spiritual reality. On this reading, Neo would lead people out of the illusions of Plato's cave, the veil of Maya, or the darkness of the world into a higher disembodied life. But this association would be all wrong! In the film, salvation means the opposite of the traditional religious vision. True, the ones who see through the Matrix can get over some of the limitations of having a body as exemplified by their flying.[28] But such flying takes place *in* the Matrix world. In the real world to which Neo "awakes," and which we suppose will be reclaimed by human beings, there will be no more flying. People will have earthbound, vulnerable bodies and suffer cold, bad food, and death.

Neo has not escaped death. It may look, at the end of the film, as if Neo evades death, but his "resurrection" in the hovercraft is not into a world where death has been overcome by a miraculous divine love, rather, he has been saved by an earthly intervention—a sort of tender CPR—quite within the bounds of physics and chemistry. So he still has his vulnerable body and will have to die a real death one day. What he presumably has gotten over is not death but the herd's fear of death, thereby overcoming what, according to Heidegger, leads people to flee into tranquilized conformity in the first place.

But if bending the rules that are accepted by the average person just amounts to being able to bend spoons, fly, and stop bullets, it doesn't seem to be any kind of salvation. Breaking free of conformity must mean more than just being disruptive.[29] We are lead to expect that, in return for accepting everyday vulnerability and suffering, the people liberated by Neo will be reborn to a new and better life.

But what is wrong with life in the Matrix? It seems clear that if the AI intelligences do their job and make a complete simulation of our world, the people in the Matrix world should be able to do everything and experience everything that we can. Like them, we all have a causal basis in a brain in a vat. True, the causal link between their brains and the physical universe is different from ours, but why should that be a problem? How can the Matrix arrangement be, as Morpheus claims it is, "a prison for the mind," any more than our dependence on our brains and their inputs imprison us?

Morpheus has no idea of what such a prison would be and talks instead about enslavement and control. Early in the film, he says: "What is the Matrix? Control. The Matrix is a computer-generated dream world, built to keep us under control." James Pryor, at the end of his essay, "What's so Bad about Living in the Matrix?", tries heroically to make sense of this claim by speculating on what the AI programmers might do to control the Matrix dwellers, such as resetting their world back to 1980 if they so chose. If the machines had done any such thing, Pryor would have the right to say as he does:

> In the movie, humans are all slaves. They're not in charge of their own lives. They may be contented slaves, unaware of their chains, but they're slaves nonetheless. They have only a very limited ability to shape their own futures. . . . The worst thing about living in the Matrix would not be something metaphysical or episte-mological. The worst thing would be something political. It would be the fact that *you're a slave.*

In so far as the Matrix makers interfere in the lives of the Matricians, they *are* controlling them, but the moments of interference in the film (the taking away of Neo's mouth, inserting a bugging device, and then making him think it was a dream, and the changing of a door into a brick wall to trap Morpheus and his crew) do not show that the Matricians, in so far as they are being used as batteries, are not in charge of their own lives. In principle, the police and the UN ought to be able to keep the Matrix dwellers in order. As the police officer says at the beginning of the film, they can take care of lawbreakers and presumably hackers too. The Agents have been introduced to take care of people who hack into the Matrix from outside and those, like Neo, whom these intruders are trying to recruit. They do not and need not limit the lives of ordinary, Matricians but only the lives of those who are resisting the Matrix.[30] What is important is that those who live tranquilly in the Matrix have just as much ability to shape their everyday lives as we do, so having your causal basis used as batteries does not amount to being controlled and enslaved.

We therefore have to conclude that Morpheus and Pryor are simply mistaken. If you're a slave, there must be a master who controls what you *can* do or, in *Brave New World*, who even controls what you *want* to do, and, of course, if you were in such a world you would want your freedom. Having their causal basis used as a battery, however, doesn't interact with the Matricians' psychic lives and so doesn't limit what they can decide, what they can desire, or what they can do. What Morpheus doesn't understand (and Pryor doesn't bring out) is that having your causal basis used for some extraneous purpose is not *per se* enslaving. That is, although the Matricians' causal basis is being used to generate electricity; the Matricians themselves are not being used. Their "enslavement" in the Matrix is like our relation to our selfish genes. We don't feel that we are being controlled when our DNA is using our bodies to propagate itself. Likewise, the simple fact that the bodies the Matricians are linked to are serving some purpose outside their lives can't be what's wrong with living in the Matrix.

The movie never tells us what, in principle, is wrong with the Matrix world, so we will have to figure it out for ourselves. Our only clues are that Morpheus tells Neo there is some sort of limit on what people in the Matrix can think and experience, and Neo says at the end of the film that the AI intelligences don't like change. But what kind of internal change is so dangerous they can't leave it to the police to keep it under control? And why don't they like it?

The answer turns out to be barely hinted at in the film and figuring it out requires our going over some familiar philosophical ground as well drawing on Heidegger to help free us from certain Cartesian prejudices. Part of the answer is that, to make a Matrix world just like our world, the AI programmers have to copy the way that the electric impulses to and from our brains in our vat-like skulls are coordinated. For us, as Descartes already understood, physical inputs of energy from the universe impinging on our sense organs produce electric outputs that are sent to the brain and there give rise to our perceptual experience of other people and of things. This experience in turn, along with our dispositions, our beliefs, and our desires causes us to act, which produces electric outputs that move our physical body. How we act, alters, in turn, what we see, and so on, in a continual loop. The correlations between the perceptual inputs and the action outputs are mediated by the way the things and people in the world respond to being acted upon.

If each brain in a vat were cut off from the people and things in the world, in order to simulate our sensory-motor loops the AI intelligences would have to model how people and things respond to all types of actions. In the Matrix case, however, the AI programmers don't have to predict people's reactions, since the brains in the vats that are the causal basis of the people in the Matrix world respond as people do in our world, their responses can simply be fed back to the other envatted brains. But, since there is no world of things impinging on the sense organs of the brains in the vats, the AI intelligences have to program a computer simulation of our world.

They can't model the world on the physical level since modeling how the atoms are moving and interacting is beyond any theory and any computations that anyone can conceive. We can't even predict how a pencil balanced on its point will fall, or where the planets will be in their orbits a thousand years from now. It might take more atoms than there are in the universe to make a physical model of our world. So the AI intelligences have wisely decided to model how everyday things behave. That is, although they are unable to model how a swarm of electrons in the *universe* behaves like a desk; they could make a model of how desks in the everyday *world* behave. As the Oracle says in *Reloaded*:

See those birds? At some point a program was written to govern them. A program was written to watch over the trees, and the wind, the sunrise, and sunset. There are programs running all over the place.

Such a model, like the program for a shuttle simulator, would enable computers to produce the same correlations of electrical inputs and outputs, and therefore the same experiences of perception and action, in the world of the Matricians that the physical universe produces in our experience.

This would leave the higher brain functions unaffected, and, indeed, we are told that the Matricians are free to form their own desires, beliefs, goals, and so forth. But then it is hard to see how this set-up could be "a prison for the mind," any more than our dependence on the physical inputs from the universe to our brains imprisons us. Nor does there seem to be any problem with change. The Matrix world-model and the phenomenal world it simulates should be capable of being changed by people's actions in just the ways ours is and nonetheless remaining stable just the way our does.

So we are back at the question: What's wrong with the Matrix? How could a successful simulation of the electrical impulses to and from the brain, be "a limit on what we can think and experience." If there is an answer, no one in the film seems to know it. It must be subtle and hard to grasp. Indeed, it must be something that those who are in the Matrix can't grasp, and those outside find it almost impossible to articulate. To suggest a possible answer will require a detour through Heideggarian philosophy, since Heidegger claims there is something in our experience that, like the Matrix itself for the people in it, is nearest to us and farthest away. That is, something so pervasive that it has no contrast class to distingish it from, so that, like water to the fish, it is almost impossible to see or describe. Maybe this is what the AI intelligences have failed to simulate, and rightly fear.

Heidegger calls it "being." Being, in Heidegger, is "that on the basis of which beings are already understood."[31] One might say that the understanding of being is the style of life in a given period manifest in the way everyday practices are co-ordinated. These shared practices into which we are socialized provide a background understanding of what counts as things, what counts as human beings, and what it makes sense to do, on the basis of which we can direct our actions towards particular things and people. Thus the understanding of being opens up a disclosive space that Heidegger calls a clearing. Heidegger calls the unnoticed way that the clearing both limits and opens up what can show up and what can be done, its "unobtrusive governance."

For example, sociologists point out[32] that mothers in different cultures handle their babies in different ways that inculcate the babies into different ways of coping with themselves, people, and things. American mothers tend to put babies in their cribs on their stomachs, which encourage the babies to move around more effectively. Japanese mothers put their babies on their backs so they will lie still, lulled by whatever they see. American mothers encourage passionate gesturing and vocalizing, while Japanese mothers are much more soothing and mollifying.

In general American mothers situate the child's body and respond to the child's actions in such a way as to promote an active and aggressive style of behavior. Japanese mothers, in contrast, nurture a greater passivity and sensitivity to harmony in the actions of their babies. What constitutes the American baby as an *American* baby is its style, and what constitutes the Japanese baby as a *Japanese* baby is its quite different style.

The style of the culture governs how people and things show up for the people in it. The way things look reflects what people feel they can do with them. So, for example, no bare rattle is ever encountered. For an American baby a rattle-thing is encountered as an object to make lots of expressive noise with and to throw on the floor in a willful way in order to get a parent to pick it up. A Japanese baby may treat a rattle-thing this way more or less by accident, but generally we suspect a rattle-thing is encountered as serving a soothing, pacifying function like a Native American rain stick. So the rattle has a different meaning in different cultures depending on the style of the culture, and no one in AI has any idea how to program a style.[33]

But that's no problem. The different understandings of what it is to be a rattle and what it is to be in general don't have to be explicitly programmed since they are in the dispositions and beliefs of the people and, as we just saw, are passed on through socialization. If what happens when we perceive is that physical energy coming into the sense organs is taken up by the perceptual system and perceived as bare physical objects, and this is then interpreted by the mind, the AI programmers could capture cross cultural input-output perceptual experiences in their programs and leave the meaning and style of things to the interpretive powers of higher symbolic mental activity.

This is in fact the way philosophers from Descartes to Husserl thought about it. Husserl claimed in *Cartesian Mediations* that mere physical things are encountered first and then afterwards are given meaning as cultural objects.[34] But Heidegger contends that we don't normally experience bare physical objects and then interpret them in terms of what we can do with them. That is, we, don't first experience bare objects on the basis of the physical input to our perceptual system, and then assign each bare object a function predicate as Descartes thought and symbolic AI researches still believe. As Nietzsche already said, there is no immaculate perception. Or, to take Wittgenstein's convincing example, the same physical input to the visual system from the same lines on a page can be *seen*, not just interpreted, as a duck or a rabbit.

But, if a change in our understanding of things changes how they are *perceived*, there is, indeed, a problem for the AI intelligences programming the Matrix. For example, if you are making a world-model and want to include programs for simulating the experience of rattles, you will have to take account of what they will solicit one to do with them, and that means they will have to look like missiles or pacifiers. One can't just model the way the world is organized by the perceptual system by programs for bare objects, and leave the rest up to the mind. But, then, if the understanding of being in a culture changed so that objects looked different, that would pose a serious problem for the Matrix programmers. The case would be parallel to the one described to Morpheus by Agent Smith, when the AI intelligences had to scrap their program simulating a perfect world because humans didn't feel at home in it, and program one like ours with conflict, risk, or suffering. In other to do this reprogramming, the Matrix had to be shut down and in the process "whole crops were lost."

Unfortunately, where style is concerned, this sort of problem seems bound to recur. As Heidegger observes, the understanding of being that governs perception and action in our culture is not static, but has gone through a series of radical changes. In each stage, objects presented different possibilities for action and so looked different, and there were even different objects. For the early Greeks being meant welling up, and what welled up for the Greeks were gods, and heroes suddenly doing marvelous things. In the same way, the medieval understanding of being as being created by God made possible the appearance of miracles, saints, and sinners, and things looked as if they offered rewards and temptations. With Descartes and Kant, people in the Modern World became inner, autonomous, self-controlling subjects and things showed up as objects to be controlled. While now, in the Postmodern World, things show up as resources. Thus, many people, like Cypher, try to get the most out of their possibilities by maximizing the quality of their experiences.[35] And it is quite likely that some new change is just over the horizon. For example, if, as seems quite possible, we all come to believe in the Gaia principle and feel called to save the earth, nature will again look different to us.

One might think that this is still no problem for the Matrix programmers and their world model. If individual Homeric Greeks saw gods, and Christians saw miracles, it could be just something inner—a private dream or hallucination, and the Matrix apparently has no trouble dealing which such malfunctions in which the brain generates electric impulses that don't connect up with the world model. The AI intelligences could presumably even deal with collective hallucinations of gods or miracles. And what else could all these changed things be, since the physical universe presumably remains unchanged and has no place in it for gods and miracles. So it might seem, then, that all these Heideggerian different worlds and how things looked in them could be treated as private deviations from the one shared Matrix world produced by the programs for everyday objects and events. The perceptual world would then remain stable across changes of cultures and understandings of being.

The Heideggerian objection would be that a change of style is neither a private nor a collective hallucination, nor is it a change in the physical universe; it is precisely a change of the public shared world. Heidegger holds that such changes in the understanding of being like more local style changes, begin as local anomalies. These marginal practices then get focused by entrepreneurs like Ford, thinkers like Descartes, or Saviors like Jesus so that they produce a world wide change of style.[36] If Heidegger is right, the best the AI intelligences could do to avoid having to reprogram the Matrix and so lose whole crops of baby batteries, would be to try to stamp out the local anomalies and marginal practices before they add up to a major change of style. Thus, they are quite rightly afraid of change, and so introduce the agents into the Matrix. The agent's job, unlike that of the police who enforce the law, seems to be to suppress all anomalies, legal or not, that could bring about ontological revolutions.

But a hard question still remains. Now that we know what is *missing* from the Matrix—what Matricians can't think and experience—the possibility of radical change; we still have to ask why they need to think and experience it. But to account for *what's wrong* with life in the Matrix, and so why it is admirable to confront risky reality rather than remain in the safe and tranquilized Matrix world whatever the quality of experience in each, we need an account of human nature, so that we can understand why human beings need what the Matrix world fails to provide.

In our pluralistic world, there are many different cultures, each with its own understanding of human nature. As we have just noted, even our own culture has experienced many different worlds, created by new interpretations of human nature and the natural world, that changed what sorts of human beings and things could be perceived. But doesn't this just show, as Sartre famously observed, that there is no human nature? Here Heidegger makes an important meta-move. As the history of the West suggests, our nature seems to be able to open up new worlds and so to transform what is currently taken to be our nature. Perhaps *that* is our nature; human beings may be essentially world disclosers.

If being world disclosers is our nature, that would explain why we feel a special joy when we are being creative. Once we experience even a hint of world disclosing, we understand why it's better to be in the real world than in the Matrix, even if, in the world of the Matrix, one can enjoy steak and good wine. What's ultimately important to us is not whether most of our beliefs are true, or whether we are brave enough to face a risky reality, but whether we are locked into a world of routine, standard activities or are free to transform the world and ourselves. Nietzsche says we should "become those we are—human beings who are new, unique, incomparable, who give themselves laws, who create themselves."[37]

Creating new types of human beings and new worlds need not be as dramatic as Jesus creating a new world by defining us in terms of our desires rather than our actions, or Descartes inventing the inner and so helping usher in the Modern World. On a less dramatic scale, entrepreneurs like Ford, and poets like Dante change the world. Even an actress like Marilyn Monroe changed the style of the world of women and how they were related to men.[38] It is just such a freedom to open up new worlds that the Matrix world lacks. Perhaps, this lack of possibilities for radical change is what Neo experiences as the splinter in his mind. He does say to the AI intelligences at the end of the film, "I know you are afraid . . . of change."

There is, then, a subtle way that the AI computers have limited what the Matrix dwellers can think and experience, but it is not by limiting the possibilities available to them *in* their world. The limitation in question has nothing to do with not knowing whether we are brains in vats, nor whether the world is virtual or real. Nor, as long as the inputs to the brains are modeled on the way things normally behave in the world, and the outputs depend on the Matrix dwellers' own decisions, is there a problem of who is in control. The problem isn't epistemological, nor metaphysical, nor (pace Morpheus and Pryor) political. The problem is what Heidegger would call *ontological*. It has to do with the Matricians' freedom to choose all right, not with a limitation on choice *in* the current world, but a limitation on their freedom to change worlds—to change their understanding of being.

Heidegger holds that our freedom to disclose new worlds is our special human essence, and that this freedom implies that there is no pre-existent set of possible worlds. Each world exists only once it is disclosed. So it makes no sense to think that a computer could be programmed with a world-model that would anticipate the creation of all possible worlds in advance of their being opened by human beings. Artificial Intelligences couldn't program for such a radically openness if they wanted to. In fact, programmed creativity is an oxymoron.[39] By having no way to introduce radical freedom into their world-models and so, fearing all unconventional behavior, the AI intelligences have found it necessary to prevent any expression of the Martricians' ontological freedom. In this way, and only this way, could the Matrix world-model be said to limit what the Matricians can experience and think. And in only this way could the Matrix world be understood as a prison for the mind.

So Neo has to show the people in the Matrix world that their world can be creatively changed. As he says, "I'm going to show these people . . . a world where everything is possible." But, of course, that is not a possibility in the Matrix world. Challenged to integrate radical change into its world-model, the Matrix breaks down. We see on the computer screen: "System failure."[40]

3

On (and Beyond) Love Gone Wrong

STEPHEN A. ERICKSON

Stephen A. Erickson is the E. Wilson Lyon Professor of Humanities and Professor of Philosophy at Pomona College in Claremont, California. His latest book is The (Coming) Age of Thresholding. *He lectures extensively throughout the United States, England and Continental Europe on what he sees as the underlying sense of emptiness in contemporary life. His research involves the renewed exploration of what it means to be* in *but not altogether* of *this world.*

Christopher Lasch and others have suggested that the narcissistic personality is paradigmatic of our time—not that it is the only or all-determining paradigm of the late-twentieth-century human, but, certainly, that it is a contributing one, and one which greatly influences our self-understanding and the actions (and those more broadly conceived practices) which issue from this understanding.

Some go significantly further. Heinz Kohut, in fact, the recently deceased founder and leader of the "self-psychology" movement, has construed narcissistic personality disorder to be the most pervasive and explanatory malady of our historical age. Love, it seems, has somehow gone terribly wrong, and, as Dr. Krokowski, high up in the sanitarium in Thomas Mann's *Magic Mountain*, pointed out long ago, only emptiness, illness, and devastation are likely to follow. We are presented with a bleak picture of the human heart indeed.

At the same time ours has also been described as an age of considerable and even accelerating violence, disorganized as well as organized, domestic as well as tribal, national and regional. Do these two (alleged) circumstances of contemporary life—flawed love and intensifying violence—connect, and if so, how? This raises a more fundamental and troubling question. Is there a space left free for the pursuit of such questions, an opening in the midst of the overlapping territories (supposedly) conquered and most definitely claimed by the various academic disciplines, those relentlessly optimistic "sciences" of "man"? Does a space open itself in which a broadly philosophical reflection on these matters can not only take root, but find room in which to grow? Though I believe so, what follows can in the nature of things—in terms, that is, of the density of the thicket to be untangled, pruned, and explored—only trace and partially separate a few strands of the interwoven texture of destructive human entanglement.

Among other things, narcissism is said to be love gone wrong, love turned in upon itself as the result of the loss of its original, external and primary object. Depending upon how this loss is understood, its causes and its dynamic assessed, narcissism has also been claimed to be love wronged. This wronging of love is further said to result in the deepest of injuries being inflicted (however unwittingly) upon an individual, these through damage done to that most fundamental of modes of human relating (and thus being): attachment itself. How might one begin to understand these claims? Such assertions become particularly pressing when conjoined with still other, often conflicting beliefs which have infused (but perhaps more confused than informed) our age. Some of these beliefs include the following: that through further "enlightenment" and more effective education, we are becoming more tolerant, because liberated, and more liberated, because tolerant, further and more continuing exposure to others only enhancing the constructive dimensions of human interaction. Also included is the belief that love is the ultimate liberator, though acceptance and approval—perhaps first and (unfortunately) only tolerance—may often have to do. Two other beliefs are that love, even its far less effective precursors, enables its recipients to become and be themselves, this state of affairs coming about and maintaining itself in a manner quite free of coercive measures—measures deemed the antipodes of positive feeling; and that, whatever the intricacies of the human heart, the foundations upon which all human conflict must ultimately rest (and, equally, everything else human) are economic, thereby making improvement of those conditions not only (and whatever else) a benevolent act, but one productive of benevolence as well—this last claim being a translation of Brecht's famous aphorism that "*erst kommt das Fressen und dann die Moral*" (first comes material sustenance and then high-minded feelings).

Surely, taken together, these various and conflicting assertions can only bewilder. They run the gamut, all the way from warm and edifying commitments to positive human feeling, the "power of love" to the application, however constructively intended, of cold economic determinism. They range in societal orientation from "live and let live" to beliefs which provide a mandate, however covert, for social engineering. Underlying them all is a concern better to understand and, thereby, to overcome violence, both in essence and manifestation. What mapping, or at least glimpses of direction, might be secured in this tangled territory? Might this complex scheme of love, particularly its narcissistically inclined dimensions, provide, however partially, a compass giving direction? Let us consider.

I

In a recent and quite philosophical novel[1] a significant dichotomy is forwarded: love or liberalism. Though not altogether original in its reflections, one of its passages, a relatively brief one, will enable us to focus on a number of related issues.

> The choice [between love and liberalism[2]] has often been missed in an optimistic equation of the two terms, one considered the epitome of the other. But if they have been linked, it is always in an implausible marriage, for it seems impossible to talk of love and letting live, and if we are left to live, we are not usually loved. We may well ask why the cruelty witnessed between lovers would not be tolerated (or even considered conceivable) beyond conditions of open enmity. Then, to build bridges between . . . [individuals] and nations, we may ask related questions: Why do the countries that have no language of community or citizenship leave their members isolated but unmolested? And why do the countries that talk most of community, love, and brotherhood routinely end up slaughtering great swaths of their populations? (pp. 76–77)

These last are difficult questions, not made easier by the (seeming) fact that they issue from the tangled region of human affection and might, therefore, be construed as the legacy of love—however much love has been heralded by some as in its very nature supportive and liberating.

One of our earliest and most influential accounts of love—at least of what it has been pervasively understood to be—is found in Plato, though "love" is not the most perspicuous of terms for what Plato discusses.[3] The Greek word is ἐρος, which might best be translated as "desire." Desire is grounded in and motivated by an underlying lack or deficiency in the one who comes to have and, thus, experiences desire. There is, in short, something incomplete in (and about) the desirer, and it is this which produces desire itself. Further, one can only truly desire that which one lacks, and, whether or not fully (or even partially) comprehended, any given desire has as its ultimate and unalterable goal the overcoming of the specific lack which created and now defines it [4]—this through some sort of "oneness," some fusion, with the "object" deemed the appropriate "sufficiency" to overcome the underlying and motivating "deficiency," the lack, which generated the desire in the first place. Lack, of course, often construed as resulting from denial of access, can be painful, certainly frustrating, and hostility toward that which would impede the overcoming of the lack, toward that which is perceived as denying access to the remedy, the "sufficiency," is easily understandable. From anger and hostility to violence is clearly neither a long nor an illogical step, however deplorable that step may be.

Plato aside, such an account is replete with ambiguities and difficulties which have haunted discussions both of love and of "letting live (or be)" through the succeeding centuries. How, for example, could one possibly leave alone—simply let live and let be—that which is experienced as the "object" of one's love, now construed as that which would overcome one's deficiency, remedy one's lack, fulfill (and thereby alleviate the pain of) one's desire? A cluster of these and similar problems resides in the (seemingly) simple notion of "oneness with," alternatively termed "fusion." I overcome my slight hunger, for example, by eating an apple, by consuming, specifically, the apple which I experience myself as at this moment wanting—yes, *that* one over there. But to do so I must first have the apple in my *possession*. I must control what happens to it in a way which insures that it comes into my hands and becomes "mine" not just eventually, but at that time which is coincident with my desire for it. Hunger, of course, requires first the possession and then the consumption of the (putatively) desired object, the one which I believe would assuage my hunger, satisfy my desire. (All along, let us postulate, I have assumed that it was this apple which I desired and have assumed, also, that its consumption would overcome the deficiency in me, the hunger. Unless we assume that human beings are quite transparent to themselves, however, both of these assumptions are open to question.)

And what if it is not hunger but companionship I desire, this particular person as companion?[5] To satisfy this desire, I must at least have this person in my presence. The desired companion must be *with* me and at those times which are coincident with my desire for this person. Problematically, however, and altogether unlike the apple, the desired companion has a mind of his or her own. Others may compete with me for the apple, but the apple in and of itself will do nothing. It will resist none of us, nor, for that matter, will it seek any one of us out either. The desired companion, however, may simply resist me or may seek out another (or others) in a manner which excludes me. I must contend quite directly with the (sought after) companion in a way which would make no sense at all in relation to the apple. Consider one extreme form this contention might take: I "capture" the desired companion and lock that person away from everyone else, in a residence to which only I have access.

Legal considerations aside, one problem with this maneuver is obvious. Access to the physical presence of the desired companion, together with over-tures proposing companionship, is quite insufficient. There must be co-oper-ation, reciprocation, if the result I seek is to be achieved. Companionship requires mutuality, some significant measure of reciprocity. The apple need "do" nothing to be an apple. To be a companion, a person must do many things which cannot all be specified in advance. Further, a measure of spontaneity is required. Companionship involves not only an underlying script but sig-nificant (and unprogrammed) departures from it.

What, then, if I threaten harm, perhaps even death, if my overtures are not reciprocated?[6] And what if I demand that the reciprocation, the proffered companionship, be spontaneous and sincere? Though this surely sounds odd, it is not as odd as it may first seem. Coercion in interpersonal matters, after all, is seldom at the level of the overtly threatening or the clumsily (and cat-aclysmically) dramatic—though evidence of both forms of direct imposi-tion—of both strategies of forceful intrusion—is well documented, and not just in cases of domestic violence. This aside, however, and in any case, are the intricacies and subtleties of metaphorical threat, of implied psychologi-cal and emotional harm, not pervasive interpersonal strategies undertaken by countless individuals? And don't those who engage in these tactics often feel justified in doing so? And are the results of such interventions not often expe-rienced by these same perpetrators as both rewarding and vindicating?

The nexus of responses to this last set of questions is also less obvious than it might first appear. Taken to the extreme, of course, capture, incarcer-ation, and threat are bound to be counterproductive. Part of the meaning of companionship, of association in general, is that it be something in which parties freely engage, and overt coercion, the blatant use of force, negates this condition. To the extent that I insist on your doing something, it becomes dif-ficult for you to do it freely, even if it was your original intention to do so. The circumstances described in the previous paragraph, to be sure, are alto-gether overdrawn and exaggerated, and thus outrageous. Moreover, and in part because of this, they miss the subtly textured fabric of human interrela-tions within the complexity of everyday life. Much which occurs between people is largely covert to most of the parties involved, sometimes even to all the parties, including the perpetrating ones—though the accruing results can at the same time be extraordinarily significant and lasting. Three aspects of this circumstance (of often insufficiently comprehended human interpersonal subtlety) deserve special attention.

From a slightly different perspective, freely adopted patterns of behavior may be construed less grandly as forms of activity to which one has become habituated through some combination of repetition and (most probably, at least mild) enjoyment. In accordance with this model, free choice now looks more like the activation of pre-existing behavior patterns—more perspicuously, perhaps, like a failure to disengage from, alter, or impede them. Curiously then, liberty can almost be made to look like the victory of the *status quo* over the spirit of adventure, of stasis over change. Coercion, or some form of outside intervention at least, might initially be required to promote the latter in each pair (adventure and change) and, more significantly perhaps, to bring about development and improvement. This seemingly peripheral consideration bears repeating: "Negative" liberty, Isaiah Berlin's label for the fundamental commitment to leave people to their own affairs, need not always have positive outcomes, the freeing of dynamic (and typically entrepreneurial) individuals for risk-laden undertakings. It may not always stimulate adventure, either private or public. As Oakeshott, for example, saw, it can also simply reinforce routinized and largely stagnant behaviors, particularly of those people living in the largely ossified world of "communal ties." And this is a world in which we all find ourselves at one time or another, most especially in our childhood, but also during periods of stress or regression.

There are two other considerations to bear in mind. Preferences are often acquired, altered, and developed as the result of a learning process. Some sort of training or education is frequently required for a "sufficient appreciation" to have developed on the basis of which "informed and intelligent choices" can be made. If preferences are in this sense inculcated, however, they look to be very much conditioned, and thus determined. In any case, they give no appearance of being the result of some altogether unconstrained "act of will." Any bottle of wine, for instance, can be chosen from the list, if one is altogether "unencumbered" by knowledge of wines. Far fewer alternatives are appropriate, however, one's choices thereby becoming far more limited, if one is both conversant with wines and concerned to make an intelligent selection. In this situation who, then, makes the "freer" choice? Freedom sired by ignorance is placed in opposition to constraint born of knowledge. And how does the full range of relevant alternatives (and an algorithm of intelligent preference) come to any given individual's attention—not just in the first place, but in a sustainably effective manner?

Finally—and now we near the crux of the matter—it is often thought of others, and particularly of children, that they may initially resist the acquisition of certain habits, reject certain educational maneuvers on our part, either through shortsightedness, ignorance, or a more general (and, as it is typically construed, temporary) inability to understand and appreciate what is at stake. When this happens it is usually believed to be in the best interest of such benighted or otherwise deficient people that an attempt be made to inculcate the requisite habits in them anyway, that an effort be undertaken to educate these people in a manner which will, in fact, serve their (unfortunately unacknowledged, resisted, and often misconstrued) "best interests." Sometimes, of course, as is the case with vaccinations or medications for small children, force is applied. Understanding may not yet be possible and can, in any case, come later, if it is deemed necessary or appropriate at all. In other circumstances coercive training or forced education may be undertaken with an eye toward making the "student" in question self-sustaining with respect to a certain form and manner of activity. One wants not so much to do something *to* the learner (the inoculation case), as one wants to bring it about that the learner will do the something in question on his or her own, for example the detecting and avoiding of environmental hazards. The goal, then, is that repeatedly in the future and without the need for further instruction or prompting, the "proper" actions will be undertaken by the (perhaps reluctant, even resistant) student, and various "improper" actions will be avoided.

We have been largely in the realm of the preventive and, in this sense, the negative. What if the issue is no longer basic safety or maintenance, however, but the achievement of excellence and the excellent? What if the issue is the flourishing of those individuals who have demonstrated a capacity for such attainment—or, issues of excellence aside, at least the "betterment" of the life circumstances of specific individuals? It is said, for example, that one only wants "the best" for one's children—not just that the bad be avoided, but that the good, in fact the best, be acquired as well, this along with the skills necessary to secure and retain it. And surely one wants the same for one's friends—and for that particular someone one might know most intimately, the one one might be said most especially to "love."

A significant portion of one of love's tangles (together with its potential for promoting violence) is now before us, one which extends from children to companions to lovers. It is bound up with issues of excellence, recalcitrance, betterment, and "education." More often than not, it is also much clouded by the dynamics of desire and informed by strong, if unarticulated, opinions regarding value. Let desire stand as, minimally, the concern to secure, and thereby be able to enjoy, the presence of the one desired; not just the physical presence, of course, but an active and engaged reciprocation and cooperation with respect to the initiator's intentions. One should construe the efforts necessary to bring this circumstance about as coercive only quite covertly, if at all. No kidnap, confinement, or threat need be involved in the least. One simply positions oneself and is somewhat persistent, however guileful the positioning and persistence may need to be. Perhaps one first encounters indifference, reluctance, impatience or even irritation. Seemingly, the other party does not "understand," does not sufficiently appreciate what is being offered. The situation is inadequately comprehended by this person. But, then, why would the initiator continue? Though often not just unstated, but uncomprehended, the (continuingly successful and largely satisfying) desire for the presence of oneself—the initiator's own self-enjoyment, that is, together with its attendant implications—frequently comes into play. The underlying belief exists on the initiator's part that not only would the presence of the sought after (and proverbial) "other" prove to be enjoyable and enhancing for the initiator, but that the initiator's own presence (to his or herself especially, but also to others and very much to this particular other) is (or would prove to be) enjoyable and enhancing to those parties as well.[7] Benefit, it is deeply believed, is bound to be mutual.

We reach a level of considerable complexity. Desire for the other, coupled with the initiator's sense that his or her own presence to and for that other is at least a "good," both come into play. At the volatile extremes of intensity, of course, the reinforcing beliefs grow that the other is best for one and that one is oneself best *for* that other. This latter conviction, it is thought, is at least in a minimal sense certified in and through one's possession of a particular piece of knowledge: one claims to know what is best for the other, and, therefore, that one is in a position to provide it for and to that other. "Knowing" this, most unfortunately, can lead to puzzlement, annoyance, and outrage on the initiator's part. This tends to happen if the other fails to co-operate, an occurrence, it is then thought, which could only be a function of the other's ignorance (of one's own virtues or of the other's own true needs). If not ignorance, the alternative interpretation can only suggest some perversity on the other's part. How could what is implied, pointed out, perhaps even explained as *best* then be less than wholeheartedly embraced, possibly rejected? One stands at the verge of corrective instruction, discipline, even punishment, possibly violently administered, and these (almost) all in the other's interest, for the other's good. Force, even excesses motivated by hostility, perhaps overt violence, enters, not altogether inexplicably. These, in turn, are the unintended outgrowths of thwarted (and therefore pained) desire. It was desire more than anything else, after all, which first initiated those overtures meant to engender and secure the relationship.

There is more, access to which is made available through reference to Freud. Though subject to serious criticism, both methodological and substantive, there is much in Freud that repays careful study. He sometimes understood love as a combination of "object choice" (desire) and identification.

Desire we have already described. Identification, however, is a subtler notion. It involves a further choosing, now of someone who is drawn to one in the same manner as one is drawn to oneself, who appreciates one as and in the way in which one appreciates oneself. To appreciate anything, including oneself, implies, of course, a value judgment and, concurrently, a set of values. At the extreme, if one prefers oneself to anyone else, one has become for oneself the highest value, a circumstance, to be sure, which hardly anyone would condone: some would see it as moral error, others as pathological (and clearly as a deeply narcissistic pathology).

Love, for Freud, is most intense when desire and identification converged. The object of one's desire then appreciates one in the exact manner in which one appreciates oneself, thereby ratifying and reinforcing one's (largely unarticulated) sense (and scale) of value. Given that the one so appreciated, the initiator desires in any case the (possession, thus "guaranteeing" the) presence—equally, the (presence, thus enabling the) possession—of that other, the "object" of desire, the situation just described is bound to prove irresistible. What one wants enjoys one as one enjoys oneself, securing (doubly) one's satisfaction and at the same time confirming and reassuring one with regard to one's values.

But what if a circumstance arises in which rejection does not directly follow an initial overture, but comes sometime after the initiator's overtures have been accepted, together with all this implies? Given the value implications of identification—that a commitment to specific values is involved—something close to betrayal or perversity has entered the picture, a betrayal or perversity which is potentially contaminating. How could an extraordinary value, oneself in fact, a value experienced and accepted, even "adored," subsequently be spurned? How could this possibly happen? Further, just as the "other" as appreciator had adopted the desirer's values, following after them, so to speak, so will the seeming transformation of the appreciator's values now bring about a similar value change in the initiating and now potentially vulnerable desirer. Will the desirer, in experiencing rejection, run the danger of "following after" and become self-rejecting? In short, if I identify with a reinforcement of my underlying self-opinion, will I run the risk of continuing to identify with that reinforcement even as it becomes its opposite? At the extreme, complete abandonment by the "other" would have as its analogue utter self-abandonment, something psychologically analogous (and literally equivalent) to suicide. How to avoid the immense pain involved in a move even partially in this direction? One obvious answer is the recapturing of the original conditions that enabled identification to occur, in particular, the "reconversion" of the lapsed other as appreciator. For this purpose, much activity and considerable persistence may be necessary, and, given that the removal of a reinforcement of self-appreciation is invariably destabilizing, potentially disintegrating, and thus painful, the persistent recuperative activities undertaken may well be pursued (however irrationally) in a manner not untinged with elements of punishment and vengeance. Underlying what is a potentially frenzied and destructive attempt at reunion is a now precariously maintained assumption, *viz.*, that it is in the best interest of the incomprehensibly lapsed appreciator not to fail to lose contact with, not to fail sufficiently to appreciate, the truly valuable. Then, and only then, it is felt, can one oneself once again secure true peace of mind, having received reconfirmation and reassurance regarding what is truly valuable.

It is a short step from this tangled, though usually deep set of convictions, to the emotionally supercharged belief that these are life and death matters, that ultimates are at stake: order versus chaos, loyalty versus betrayal, honor versus shame, fulfillment versus emptiness, happiness versus despair, and continuance versus termination. These are just a few of the polarities experienced as at the heart of the matter, as present in a way which can quickly transform a major problem into a cataclysmic crisis. What surprise, then, that it quickly comes to be believed that drastic measures need to be taken, martial law imposed, all potentially contaminating (or further complicating) influences removed? One is reminded that the tribal gods, and the Israelites' God in particular, were jealous, wrathful, and vengeful.

I mention "martial law" as a means of moving, however provisionally, from the restrictedly interpersonal to the overarchingly societal and dangerously "national." The dynamics of identification provide the underlying and connecting link. Humans are not, nor do they see themselves as, billiard-ball individuals, existing in isolation from surrounding and sometimes relatively intangible realities. A significant part of their sense of themselves, and thus of their own perceived reality and identity, is in terms of their participation in and identification with values, sometimes embodied, sometimes abstract, which they experience as beyond themselves, yet in which they share. Though I am not my group, and my group is not me, insofar as I participate in and identify with it, I am part of it and, more importantly, it is part of me. Threats to it are therefore threats to me. Outsiders who attack my group, though through this they attack me, can partially, perhaps, be excused. They may be viewed as simply ignorant of what is truly valuable, unlearned, untrained, and uneducated with regard to it. Mere continuing exposure to the valuable could supposedly (and single-handedly) move them in the right direction, remove some of their resistance.

The certified insider, however, the actual group member, is another matter altogether. Lack of exposure, educational deficiencies of various sorts, cannot be adduced to explain this person's apostasy. Something less rational, and therefore less tractable, must be involved. And given the positioning of the insider as, by definition, inside, a further danger is involved: infection of other insiders. Something must clearly be done, decisively and quickly— incarceration perhaps, coupled with rehabilitative re-education or, as may become necessary, even more drastic actions. Not to know, not to have had exposure to the good is one thing. To commune with the good and then to reject it is something else, something evil and most likely a source of further contamination.

II

There is another way to tell the love story. Some might in fact call it a different love story altogether because it arises, seemingly, from a separate— some would say, singular—dimension of human experience. Consider the distinction between longing and belonging. On a certain level one feels the need to possess that for which one longs. One seeks its possession, something the dynamics of which, Heidegger and others have claimed, have brought about environmental devastation, the conversion of "high" culture into popular entertainment, and a curiously enervating secularism.[8] All of these developments—best perhaps termed "deteriorations"—derive, it is thought, from a pervasive commodification and subsequent mass-marketing of every alleged "reality" which purports to stand in any relation of otherness to the voracious consumer. This is particularly true in those cases of "realities" construed as requiring devotion or service from one, "realities" making demands, so to speak, and thereby limiting the "freedom" of the consumer to act in an immediate and unconstrained manner. "Easy" and "convenient appropriation" have been the watchwords of this soon passing century, with all forms of resistance construed merely as obstacles to be quickly and efficiently overcome.

Contrasted with this historical devolution is the quest for a quite different occurrence and outcome: the longing to belong—not to possess, but oneself to be possessed, yet remain oneself—within the life and ambiance of something larger and far more important than one's own individual existence. One of the many things which Nietzsche set out to discredit through his proclamation of God's death was this very possibility. And "narcissism," the (alleged) "love of self," might be said to result by way of exclusion, by way of an elimination of alternatives, brought about precisely through the loss of the "God" option construed in this broad manner. If there is nothing of significance beyond the autonomously and creatively shaped individual existence, then to what else could one possibly be devoted?

"Absorption" is a helpful word to juxtapose to "possession." One *establishes* and *takes* possession, which are actions, but one *undergoes* absorption, which, classically, is the essence of passion.[9] In the former (active) case, one's identity is of fundamental importance, for it is in its name that one takes "title" and claims one's various possessions and rights. Most particularly, one claims in one's name what is "rightfully" one's own, one's property,[10] which is thereby subordinated to one, now receiving its otherwise separate identity through one. Possession, in fact, is an inevitable function and outcome of agency, for agency seeks invariably to reflect its skills in the mirror of acquisition, which is seen as the "objective" validation of its efforts.[11]

These are somewhat complex matters which themselves come to reflect, among other things, the accelerating loss of objectivity in an eventual "will to power," once, that is, we reach the twentieth century. "It is John Smith's," for example, comes to mean that its existence is now partially constituted through a "belonging to" John Smith, and what John Smith will do or make of "it" will become its potentially altered (and, in relation to John Smith, derivative) identity and fate, the very meaning of its existence. Another way of putting this would be to say that John Smith comes to stand as the rightful agent of "its" fate, in relation to which "it" is, appropriately, the object of John Smith's agency. (And "it" becomes an "operator" capable of ranging over (nearly) everything, just as "John Smith" becomes the designator for a driven, if progressively horizonless "everyman.")

Absorption is a quite different matter. Again, one undergoes it. In some instances one might even be said to "suffer" it. For an essentially "activist" age such as ours, however, this has not been easy either to accommodate or to understand. In our era of pragmatic "doings," in fact, in an age of technological conquest, absorption cannot but appear impractical, inefficient, and even indulgent, if not altogether primitive and mysterious. Its reality is captured partially and most popularly in the notion of falling in love, something which one does not do, but which happens to one. Similarly and more generally, though usually less intensely and of shorter duration, *moods*, also, are experienced as coming over one, as happening and, thus and then, having to be undergone and, often, dealt with: encouraged, nurtured, or overcome. Though people are frequently urged to fight "negative" moods, for example, urged not to give in to them, these moods nonetheless occur, forming the substratum and substance of many of one's subsequent dealings—in extreme instances becoming the "objects" of various forms of treatment. Such moods do come upon people, sometimes taking over the individuals who have (or fall into) them. These moods thereby assume the status of passions to be undergone. And often much suffering is involved.

Classically, the entire panoply of moods, positive and negative, was discussed under the category of "the passions." All were instances of what I am now calling "absorption." Today, however, the very category of passion is subject to severe truncation and misunderstanding, thus presenting a problem. A "subjective," heavily psychologized age such as ours has understood passion largely in sexual and romantic terms. Given the pervasiveness of hostility in the world, mirrored theoretically in Freud's reflections on the death instinct, hate and antagonism have been given prominent play as well. But both of these passion clusters, ἐρος and θανατος, have been understood almost exclusively intrapsychically, understood as issuing forth from within the "psyche" and as finding the total dynamics of their explanation within this "subjectively" construed region. That there was something genuinely *beyond* the individual which might be not only the focus of passion, of absorption, but also the source and even cause of that passion was hardly considered.[12] Usually working at cross purposes, Nietzsche and the ambitions of "empirical" science came together in this instance to close the door on any serious consideration of such a possibility. Without it, however, the dynamics of experiential religion or creative inspiration could hardly be approached, much less comprehended.

A most controversial claim made by Heidegger was that moods were "disclosive," revealing our situation-as-a-whole. A brief excursus into the history of philosophy helps uncover some of the issues involved. At the threshold of the soon blossoming tradition of German idealism, Kant had made a seemingly sharp distinction between two dimensions of human cognition, spontaneity and receptivity. The latter, termed "sensibility," was a means of receiving data, the former, termed "understanding," was a means of acting upon this data, conceptualizing it. It was not long, however, before Kant's "categories," the active, conceptual dimension of knowing, was said to go "all the way down," meaning that the understanding, as Kant called it, had become everything as far as cognition was concerned. Though an essentially idealistic view, it has lived on in the twentieth century in the doctrine that all awareness is mediated through language: the limits of one's language become the limits of one's world, and language is understood as an essentially public (as opposed to private) phenomenon with diverse functions, all of which are derived from the broad and flexible pragmatics of everyday existence. In the midst of these epistemological commitments, however, together with their accompanying strategies, the underlying receptive dimension of human cognition seemed to get overlooked or lost. It was, otherwise, the largely unarticulated underpinning of sense datum theory. But once this latter theory was discredited by the diverse (and pervasively supported) attacks of common sense and conceptual realism, the notion of a fundamental stratum of receptivity was altogether disregarded. It was construed as somehow both beyond and beneath philosophical concern. Some combination of language games, social practices, and historical exegesis and commentary become the pre-occupying "business of philosophy."

It was in the midst of these developments that Heidegger's insistence on the disclosive feature of moods arose. His attempt was to recuperate human receptivity—more broadly, to return attention to openness as both the generator and, potentially, the expander and transformer of human experience and awareness. A new "beginning" was called for, and since philosophy itself was said to begin in wonder, a rekindling and renewal of wonder was clearly in order. If one were to categorize and conceptualize, to arrange and to put to use, then one first had to understand. But to understand one had to experience, and to experience one had first and above all to open oneself (or be opened) to that which would instigate that chain of "knowing" which was to end in conceptualization and control. In short, primordial and primal contacts with "reality," now something no longer taken for granted, had to be reinstigated.

One of Heidegger's own distinctions caught this very well. It was the distinction between calculative (*vorstellenes*) thinking and the thinking which recalls (*andenkenes Denken*). The former manipulated in various ways what was before (*vor*) one. But how did that something come to be before one in the first place, and was its current "presence" the result of numerous and, even if not numerous, nonetheless major transformative and (perhaps) distorting or even violating activities? To aid in answering these and other related questions, Heidegger called for a thinking which recalled that which first prompted whatever series of assimilative and appropriative processes subsequently occurred. He called for a remembering, and if we hyphenate this, we get re-membering, the re-newal of oneself as now separated, a re-newal taking the form of a fresh and no longer mediated contact with that from which one is now alleged, if only epistemologically, to have fallen away, *viz.*, the larger "reality" of which one is but a small part. Contact, perhaps even temporarily a fusion, is desired with that host in relation to which one is, paradoxically, both dependent parasite and alienated ex-member. (Thus the goal can partly be described as a re-membering.)

One can speak of falling in love, or of being consumed with (or by) hatred. And the experience of various moods coming over one is quite common. But to make moods fundamental cognitive indicators, to assign them a central position in the functioning of human receptivity, is a bold step and another matter altogether. If one adds to this the essentially Pauline-Augustinian claim that the (spiritual) love humans undergo, the passion which they suffer, is the major pathway to God (and that this human love simply reflects, however inadequately, divine love, which is God's fundamental and enduring pathway to human beings), then one has in dramatic, almost alarming, form a quite different sort of epistemology (if one can even call it by this essentially cognitivist name). Renewed connection, even fusion, appear to be the goals, and moods, intensified into the deeply positive dimensions of an as of yet not comprehended love, are their means. One does not so much *do* something to bring this ("prelapsarian" and now recuperated) state of affairs about. Rather, one puts oneself in the position to *undergo* something: the journey of return and reunion, re-union first through a re-turn (*Kehre*), and a journey in many ways characterized by suffering (again, an allowing to happen and subsequent nurturing, in this sense a suffering, of that ongoing and thus, continuing—and continual—happening of re-membering and remembering). More succinctly stated, and also as a means of historical indexing, it is helpful to remember that Kierkegaard called *suffering* the essential expression of religion, meaning, again, that religion was essentially the allowing, encouraging, and undergoing of a return to God from one's "fallen" state. If one now construes the highest of knowledge as that of reality, and further construes God and reality as equivalent conceptions, then knowing and the most fundamental of undergoings become one.[13]

We ourselves now stand at a significant threshold. What if love does get understood as an allowing and encouraging of an absorption—specifically, of oneself in that which is "beyond" one, yet of and in which one is, nonetheless, however uncognizantly, a member? What if openness and receptivity to this journeying are construed as the initiating "cognitive" acts, and the journeying itself is experienced as an undergoing which at the same time is a knowing, classically a passion, a suffering which not only deepens, but first secures the bond of knowledge? And, finally, what if moods get construed not just as internal occurrences, but as gateways to one's inner (and deeper) being and, through access and oneness with this being, to that which lies beyond, but to which, again, one nonetheless comes to experience that one belongs? At the very least "love" has now assumed a dynamic quite in contrast with that involved in ἔρος, in desire.

There are, nonetheless, connections between these two loves—so, at least, one cannot but assume (and every lover simply knows). The pursuit of these connections, however, would be premature, for it must first face up to the mysterious role played in these matters by the misleadingly named and too easily caricatured activity of *meditation*. It is this latter undertaking which almost certainly constitutes—forms and re-forms—the reintegrative bridge which relates and realigns possession and absorption, desire and (metaphysical) passion, erotic action and spiritual undergoing. In this, of course, the history of (not just Eastern) religions and the "metaphysics" of the ancients found no surprise. Contemporary thought, however, has yet fully to recognize this bridge, much less to begin its crossing. It is perhaps our sad, though exhilarating, fate that our new century either will cross it or will suffer personal and interpersonal emptiness and violence of a magnitude beyond, even, that of the last century. Let us all hope that the presence of a transformed philosophizing will be of guidance on our rapidly impending and perilous journey.[14]

4

The Space of Love and Garbage

STEPHEN A. ERICKSON

Stephen A. Erickson is the E. Wilson Lyon Professor of Humanities and Professor of Philosophy at Pomona College in Claremont, California. His latest book is The (Coming) Age of Thresholding. *He lectures extensively throughout the United States, England and Continental Europe on what he sees as the underlying sense of emptiness in contemporary life. His research involves the renewed exploration of what it means to be* in *but not altogether* of *this world.*

> Perhaps, it occurred to me, I was in some new space. I'd entered the place where oblivion was born. Or despair. And also understanding. Or perhaps even love— not as a mirage but as a space for the soul to move in.[1]

These meditations are in part occasioned by Ivan Klíma's provocative title to his recent novel *Love and Garbage*. Not just occasioned by the title, of course, but by the novel's content as well. This content, however, I wish to open to further investigation, and a somewhat controversial one. My inquiry will be guided by some (partially historical) reflections on the problematic, if not largely dismissed and abandoned notion of 'the spiritual present'. Each of the nine sections which follow involves an attempt to dis-close and, thus, open to questioning an aspect of this 'present'. 'Present' should be understood in time's broadest sense, the one which guides Hegel when he says that philosophy is *its* time comprehended in thought. Each section, also, is a beginning in the direction of making more—or has it (now) become "once more"?—credible experiences of the spirit. Any such undertaking is controversial, and to take cognizance of this a deliberate ambiguity is to be found in the preceding sentence, one grounded in syntactical form. The ambiguity engenders two readings, allowing, thereby, two quite different sorts of readers (or aspects of the 'same' reader): at one extreme the (problematically) devoted and at the other the (problematically) disdainful. In the more moderate undertaking in which I engage, it becomes all the more appropriate that each section, itself in varying ways questionable, also raises questions.

1

Receptivity might be called openness. In this respect Heidegger's concern with *Dasein*, which is said to *be* its disclosedness (*Erschlossenheit*) can be seen, also, as an attempt to radicalize, to bring into question (the limitations of) Kant's transcendental aesthetic, to question Kant's "sense-bound" epistemology, to probe his account of sensibility. Can we be open, receptive in a manner which makes possible (and explicable) access to something which is not analyzable (and thus explicable) in sensuous-cum-transcendentally-rationalist terms? Is an openness possible which in its very nature opens on to (and, thereby, provides direct access to) a non-sensuous? Kant and Heidegger scholarship might or might not engender an openness to these questions, an openness to openness.

2

Openness on ones own part, of course, is not sufficient for the emergence (manifestation, arrival) or even the existence of the (alleged) something toward which one opens. It would be hallucinatory or magical thinking to believe otherwise. Not only this. Ones own openness typically falls short of providing the setting (the circumstances, environment) in which an occurrence appropriate to that openness can happen. Might this tempt one to say that an openness which does not secure, perhaps merely by locating, but perhaps, also, by actively helping to produce, the appropriate setting is not 'really' an openness? Not a genuine one? Just for the moment let us say that genuine openness requires that that openness have secured an appropriate setting. It remains the case that (a now genuine) openness is no guarantee of the manifestation or, even again, the existence of its (sought after) "object." In this respect Nietzsche, Heidegger, and Derrida are, though in significant ways differing, very much *realist*. There are no guarantees, though a few hundred years ago and less, Fichte, Schelling, Hegel, and even Marx *gave* them. Might one construe our present era as one, precisely, of the loss of guarantee? If "it" was ever "there"—which means "here"—perhaps that which was guaranteed, the referent of the "it," "departed" prior to the demise of its guarantee. Perhaps the latter, however paradoxically, remained. If (possibly) so, then a first step toward (a possible) recovery of the "guaranteed" might be a working free of the guarantee itself, construed now as both misleading and obstructive.

Let us provisionally label the "constitutive elements" of the (failed) guarantee "garbage." On this basis it is possible to think in terms of clearing them away, a result of which will be the establishment of a clearing. Will such a clearing itself provide (or be) a guarantee? By the thinking upon which we are embarked, the "clearing" will only "guarantee" the *absence* of guarantee. This absence, in turn, will help provide (or itself perhaps be) access to what had been obfuscated, what had been hidden by the guarantee's presence: the absence of that (presence) which the guarantee's presence altogether erroneously guaranteed.

Consider, now, the "dynamics" of the situation: the presence of a guarantee purported to give access to (what may have been) a presence "beyond" (μετα) it. The latter (and, again, purported) presence (allegedly) became absent. This absence was hidden by the guarantee's presence. The removal of the guarantee, the bringing about of its absence, then, is for the purpose of making present the (purported) absence which the presence (of the guarantee) occluded. By turning a presence (the guarantee) into an absence, an absence underlying it, it is hoped, will be made present. In short, making a presence absent is meant to make an absence present. In this we find the beginnings of a logic of garbage re-moval. And why re-moval? Well, first, presumably, the guarantee was "moved in." Now it is to be moved "out." A second moving is a re-moval.

Ivan Klima speaks of garbage (re-moval) as an honorable calling, even a high, dangerous and most important one, for

> The Apocalyse can take different forms. The least dramatic, at first sight, is the one in which man perishes under an avalanche of useless objects, empty words, and excessive activity. Man becomes a volcano which imperceptibly sucks up the heat from below the ground until, in an instant, it trembles and buries itself. . . . we find it difficult to distinguish between what are still objects of our life and what are objects of our death. (p. 145)

Staying for a moment with the imagery, let us openly question. Whence the (metaphorical) fire providing (the volcano's, our) energy and what its "nature"? And how might we explain that fire getting used up? Much like Nietzsche, Klima speaks of the heat of explosion and a subsequent dwelling in the coldness of the void. Klima's void, however, is filled, littered; Nietzsche's empty. For Klima, thus, escaping the void will first require (garbage) re-moval, an emptying. For Nietzsche the issue is quite different, one of (creative) filling, a production. Both, however, exact from those who would hear them a recognition and acknowledgment of the void. How it is construed then determines, at least suggests, methods for its . . . avoidance, its a-voidance, the negating of its very negativity as void. But isn't the negation of negation a positive act? Isn't the re-moval of a (failed) guarantee a positive move, an affirmative gesture? We know that Heidegger, for example, was adamantly opposed to labelings of his thought as negative or nihilist. And even Derrida, as recently as 1991 can say:

> . . . one has to go through the experience of a deconstruction. This deconstruction (we should once again remind those who do not want to read) is neither negative nor nihilistic; it is not even a pious nihilism, as I have heard said."[2]

What makes voids voids? And what forms can they take? Can they range from vacuums, altogether "empty" spaces, to guarantees, to garbage? Again, Nietzsche and Klima, perhaps more so Heidegger and Derrida, can be studied. And such study might (or might not) engender openness to voids. Such study might (or might not) also prove a means of avoiding them. But why "openness to voids" at all? Our underlying direction suggests, but does not *guarantee* that voids mask, especially so if voids are not recognized as such. Perhaps genuine openness requires unmasking, however little such unmasking itself guarantees; but even, one wonders, if no thing, not even a face, thus nothing lies "behind" the mask? How otherwise to come to know? Openness to openness requires openness. Wouldn't all "masking" diminish such (and all and every) openness?

2

Garbage is an odd notion to introduce into (what might only controversially be called) . . . philosophy. Consider. What gets used up (and sometimes not even that) gets put into *your* garbage, but another might find it useful and claim it not to be garbage at all. So garbage is "relative"? To wants? But someone can want something and then be told, and become convinced, that it is "really garbage." Meaning? But perhaps a different approach is better, that garbage is relative to potential *use*. If no use is found, then what we have is . . . garbage.

Neither will this latest do, for, not just in literature but in life, garbage is often put to use, and sometimes, frequently even, just because it is . . . garbage, really garbage. It becomes, thereby, useful *to* certain people and useful to them *for* certain purposes. And they want it and will not be easily dissuaded, if at all.

Remember Wittgenstein saying that what to call a cow is for the public to decide. Doesn't this sound all the more applicable to "garbage"? And isn't it compounding empty manoeuvering, gamesmanship, if 'garbage' is then used to make large philosophical . . . (should we call them) statements: the masking void is . . . garbage? Or, garbage . . . masks the void? Or, the first task of philosophy is the re-moval of . . . garbage?

Lest it be thought that this notion is mere . . . rubbish—and what might *that* mean?—but also to make outrageous an already questionable undertaking, let us turn to some very ordinary language. We know that with somewhat differing motivations Heidegger and Wittgenstein agree that it is very important, methodologically valuable, to look closely at ordinary language. The language I now consult is quite pervasive, and I offer but a few examples in two separate groupings.

(1) Get rid of all that shit.
(2) Don't listen to this shit.
(3) It doesn't mean shit.
(4) No-one wants to be shit on by anyone.

And

(1) You're wasting her time.
(2) They are just wasting away.
(3) The waste around here is incredible.
(4) It's become a vast wasteland.

One might think such examples simply congregate street talk, ecological concern, and issues of efficiency into a locker room of everyday, colloquial discourse, shaded into the vulgar. But I don't think this is the whole story. Something else is suggested as well. The central and guiding trope is consumerist, and in varying ways 'garbage' and its recently exemplified cousins relate to what has been or ought to be disposed of (eliminated), or what should not be acquired (ingested) in the first place. Implied also is the notion of "using up." Suggested, further, at times and in places, is the notion of abuse.

4

Imagine a world in which everything simply gets viewed in terms of its usefulness, the uses to which each something can be put. What is useless is ignored, but if that same useless something is in some way obstructive, it is either moved out of the way or eliminated. Now a most obvious question regards the *sorts* of uses to which items are put.

Various pragmatisms recommend that we view the world not as something altogether separate from our interests, having an incomprehensible reality apart from us. The world as it is, rather, in any sense of "is" that can be said to matter, is supposedly revealed to us in and through our interests. More particularly, it is revealed in and through the uses to which we put the various things we encounter.

How should "interests" be construed? Seemingly there are broadly public interests which, through Dewey, Habermas and others, have largely been troped in democratic and egalitarian terms. But there are also seemingly private, or at least individual interests, which through Nietzsche, Heidegger and others, get understood in most aristocratic terms.

5

I have been trying to engender a frame in which a certain sort of discussion can take place, certain experiences occur and some possible responses to these experiences can then be suggested, even recommended. 'Frame', unfortunately, has a slightly subjective sound to it—not in terms of a private or idiosyncratic individuality, but in its suggestion of something linguistic or conceptual, as in "framework," something possessed by a "subject" and applied to "objects." Alternatives to 'frame,' however, are not easily found. The one I have chosen to employ is "space"—thus the *space* of . . . love and garbage.

"Space" is not without its own difficulties. For some it may sound too objective, suggesting a particular location traceable by means of mathematical coordinates geographically interpreted. When one then explores the space of . . . love, the suspicion is that the loosest of metaphors, perhaps even the vaguest, is in play.

But consider Kant's insight over against Leibniz, *viz.*, that things happen *in* space, but that the containment suggested by the "in" is not sufficiently analyzed by logical notions, most typically the notions of class inclusion and class membership. On the contrary, something "more" is involved than the logical, something which provides, in fact, the "playground" within and on which the relevant (spatial) items find their "place," move or get moved. This something "more" constitutes the ground for play, the ground on which it occurs. And when something "comes into play," it is there, on this ground, that it will be found.

Consider further, this time Heidegger's insight over against Kant, *viz.*, that the containment suggested by the "in" when one is said to be *in* love (or *in* art history), for example, is not sufficiently analyzed, if at all, by Euclidean-Newtonian notions such as Kant brought to bear in his quarrel with Leibniz. On the contrary, again something "more" is involved, something which also provides a "playground." Within and on this latter playground those items relevant to it find *their* place, and move and/or get moved. Such a playground *also* constitutes a ground for play, a ground on which it occurs. And when something—let us call it spiritual, as opposed to Newtonian (Kant) or logical (Leibniz)—"comes *into* play," it is "here," on this ground, that it will be found. It is necessary, in other words, that such ground be present, if "spiritual" play is to occur. Were one next to say that play is of the essence of spirit, then such ground would simply be necessary for spirit's existence, for the existence of the . . . spiritual.

There is always danger in a word like 'spirit' or 'spiritual', especially in the twentieth century. It is therefore helpful to remember that, provisionally, "spirit" is primarily exclusionary, referring to that which neither logic nor Newton (nor their combination) can exhaust, to that which such analyses miss, and thus exclude. More positive characterization has only been adumbrated, and then only marginally, through reference to such "fields" as love and art history.

Such (spiritual) space as (hopefully) I have now brought into better focus might be said to make possible (a kind of) play. From this it does not follow, however, that this space itself makes play, that it produces it. Nor could it be said to guarantee it either. Remember Kant in this regard: one can conceive space without objects, but never objects without space.

Let us follow Kant further. More particularly let us take note of his understanding that space is "transcendentally ideal," that is, not "out there," but (somehow) "in" the subject, but, again, "transcendentally" so. This brings us to a number of questions, but one in particular: Is that space which makes—let us now say—love and garbage possible itself a space to which we might relate, to some degree even control? If the Kantian analogy holds, we in fact find ourselves, in part at least, *in* it, which suggests that whatever we may (or may not) be able to do with it, it is most likely to have considerable effects on us. Ivan Klima captures a significant dimension of this with poignancy and, later, in a manner which provokes something close to dread. Commenting on a woman who became a collector of refuse, Klima writes:

> Like Sisyphus, that woman would never have completed her work, not only because the supply of new garbage will never stop, but also because an inner emptiness cannot be filled even with all the objects in the world. (*Love and Garbage*, p. 137)

But more tragically he writes:

> The Khmer Rouge did not fill the void in their souls with objects or with the money they so despised. They understood that the void in the soul cannot be filled even by all the objects in the world, and that was why they tried to fill that void by human sacrifices. But the emptiness of the soul cannot be filled by anything, not even if the whole of mankind were driven to the sacrificial block: the emptiness would continue, terrfying and insatiable." (p. 145)

6

I turn to a troping of "the void," by which I shall mean a "spiritual" space bereft of appropriate "objects," "objects" that might fill it or at least cancel out that space's emptiness. If we keep to Klima's vision, there will be some sorts of "objects" and events which will be unable to reach this space at all, which this space cannot embrace. It might even be thought of as analogous to a "category mistake" to relate such items (objects or events) to what we have now come to call "spiritual" space, as if one were trying to mix triangularity into one's orange juice. And this is by no means implausible. Consider. Can mathematical truths (as opposed to expressions *of* them) be found in Newtonian space? Could zebras take up residence in logical space? We dismiss these questions as misplaced, if not absurd. By analogy, thus, it is at least *prima facie* plausible to conclude that only certain "types" of items can find their way into spiritual space, that it only makes sense to speak of certain "sorts" of items as being (potentially, at least) *in* that space.

Nietzsche's proclamation of the "death of God" is the claim that spiritual space has become devoid of content, that it is now empty. Similarly such are Heidegger's assertions that ours is the age of the "not yet" and that to know how to question is to know how to wait, even a whole lifetime. I confess a similar experience, though with a quite different interpretation of its ultimate outcome. Using our language of this section both Heidegger and Nietzsche might be said, then, to be expressing the void.

Consider now possible modes of avoidance, construing avoidance (more perspicuously, a-voidance) as the attempt to escape the void—a-void now being construed as a privitive, negating form as occurs, say, in a-theism. One mode of (attempted) escape might be to deny that any void existed: traditional theism, for example. Another might be to deny that any such "space" existed as might then be (or become) empty, that is, void of habitation: materialisms. Still another would be to attempt to fill the empty space with "objects," either through locating or producing them. Either activity might (or might not) involve prior (or subsequent) recognition of that emptiness which the activity is an attempt to remedy. Now it is just such activities, recognized as such or not, which Klima is concerned to identify and to eject.. Their products he labels "garbage," and his own task, or the one he at least praises, is that of garbage removal.

How, then, to understand garbage? A number of options are available, and to some degree they complement one another.

(1) Garbage may occlude recognition of an underlying space which is devoid of content;

(2) garbage may (misleadingly) seem to "fill" such space, thereby making far less likely that "contents" in fact appropriate to that space arrive (or are found) in it;

(3) garbage may simply be any and all products of misguided attempts to fill spiritual space;

(4) the misguided attempts to fill spiritual space might themselves be construed as garbage.

What I wish to suggest is that philosophy deal with garbage, that it get openly into the business of garbage identification and removal.

7

Returning to themes with which this meditation began, I wonder whether openness might require considerable efforts at garbage identification and removal. But this in itself would not be enough. Required, also, would be something not "negative" but positive, the cultivation of openness in such a way as to make more likely—no guarantees—a space no longer empty. Nietzsche, of course, hoped for such results through the creativity of a dynamic, *uebermenschlich* will (-to-power). Heidegger deemed the cultivation of openness as itself necessary, but from a Nietzschen standpoint non-productive. Being would have to arrive (again) and in "its" own time. Zen, we know, counsels an emptying out.

8

Reflections on love. If reflection seeks the space of love *and* garbage, what about love? Yet it is not clear that love can be comprehended apart from the space it occupies and, perhaps in part, is. Giving something space can be construed in a number of ways. Most typically it is understood as not "crowding" that something, allowing it to be (itself) without interference. Giving space in this sense is the virtually "privative" act of leaving something alone. An underlying assumption is that the item to be left alone has (or needs) its own space and that movement into that space, its restriction or annulment, constitutes interference. Not only this. It is typical of such views to ascribe autonomy and, in large measure, self-sufficiency to that which is to be "given space." This last phrase, in fact, is perhaps better construed as granting something its *own* space, intrusions into which then are viewed precisely *as* intrusions, likely violations of that whose space the space is.

A slightly different view suggests that the space given is one's own space, that the item to be given space is thereby given place in what might be termed ones "world"—that world of ones concern, care, interest, even nurturing, which dies with one, though not thereby endangering those items occurring within it, finding place within it, during ones lifetime. Giving space in this sense is more akin to giving "place," but the suggestion is that place is within and part of one's schema of placement.

Whichever of these first two ways we consider, the suggestion remains that space is a *need*, that it can be diminished or enlarged, and that a full account of at least some items requires reference to be made to those items' space(s), with respect to size, condition and quality. Let us keep in mind in this regard the notion of "breathing space," a space which may need only to be allowed, but may in a stronger sense need to be provided. This is particularly helpful, for in terms of experience and etymology, for the Greeks at least, breath, life and spirit are initially fused and in that sense belong together. Only later do they get sorted out, and it is a deep issue as to whether the sorting out that occurred or any that might have, should be construed as an advance. The fusion may have been best. After the fusion may only have come con-fusion—a confusion born paradoxically from the womb of analytical reflection.

Note the opportunities engendered prior to analysis. And here, as often elsewhere, one looks for something analogous to the richness of metaphor, which is (perhaps erroneously) opposed to the clarity of distinction(s). Space is needed in which spirit may then breathe and, thereby, live. Spirit has a rhythm to it involving what is experienced as approach (exhalation) and withdrawal (inhalation). Note that such a way of experiencing spirit is from "outside" the particular spirit being experienced. From inside, that is, "autobiographically," the ascriptions are virtually reversed: inhalation is approach, exhalation withdrawal.

There is more. Inhalation, like ingestion, is restorative. Exhalation, like elimination, is discharge of the remainders, the used or unusable elements involved in restoration. In a very metaphorical sense, subject to considerable misunderstanding, the remainders are "garbage." But they can be understood in this manner only with very significant qualifications. The major one can be brought to light through reference to plants in their interrelations with animals. The exhalation from plants (oxygen) is the nourishing, restoring element, the appropriately inhaled material for human beings, and the humanly exhaled element (carbon dioxide) is the nourishing, restoring substance, the (again) appropriately inhaled element for plants.

Breathing is a using and a discarding, the rhythmic reality of which requires a space in which it can occur. But not just a space—co-respondent "realities" within that space as well. The space might be said to make the co-respondence—subsequently corrupted or merely degenerated into correspondence—possible. On the other hand the space might be said to be comprised in large part of the "transactional" elements of the co-respondence, the "spiritual" oxygen and carbon dioxide so to speak. 'Comprised' here means not so much that these elements are (simply) *within* the space, but that, beyond this, the elements can be said in large measure to *be* the space.

These, however, remain only suggestions at this point, for if we are to believe people like Klima or, for that matter, Nietzsche, a more fundamental problem than the filling of (spiritual) space is its emptying. Extraneous material must be emptied from it, so that it can itself be experienced as it in fact is, *viz.*, empty, void of appropriate content. In this resides somewhat of a problem, or at least an ambiguity, however. If nothing but content appropriate to spiritual space could in fact be in it, foreign or inappropriate material must, rather, be some place else, in some other space, diverting our attention or focus from spiritual space, rather than actually occupying it. Alternatively, such inappropriate or foreign material might stand in the way of us and the spiritual space we nonetheless occupy, occluding our vision of it or diminishing our experience and sense of it (and of ourselves within it).

Nietzsche makes a significant remark in this connection. He says that the wasteland grows, and then adds that one must beware, if one is among the group of those who hide wastelands within. Nietzsche's own specific meaning in this regard is less important than what such a text offers in the way of thoughtful opportunity for probings at the margins. Let us construe a wasteland, first somewhat materialistically, as a region of used up (and discarded) things, then alternatively, as an uncultivated region which, at least in its present state, offers nothing for what I will provisionally (and problematically) call "spiritual consumption." To say that such a region is growing, then, is to say two things: first, that the realm of the used up, the materially consumed, is advancing or expanding in terms of the number of items it contains and the boundaries which circumscribe its extension; and second, that the number and type of items appropriate (and available) for spiritual consumption are diminishing or contracting and that the region(s) in which they can be found are lessening in number and extent.

Can a more specific content be provided for such doctrines, thereby enhancing their plausibility? I believe so, and in fact Klima, however inadvertently suggests much in this regard.

. . . it occurred to me, even while he was reading to me about how man strayed off his path by deifying himself, that man can behave arrogantly not only by deifying his own ego, but equally when he proudly believes that he has correctly comprehended the incomprehensible or uttered the unutterable, or when he thinks up infallible dogmas and with his intellect, which wants to believe, reaches out into regions before which he should lower his eyes and stand in silence. We might debate for a long time about when that fatal shift occurred (if it occurred) which gave rise to the arrogant spirit of our age, and also about how far we must go back to put matters right, but what point would there be in such an argument when there is no return anyway, either in the individual's life or in that of humanity?" (pp. 111–12)

For our purposes a simple distinction needs first be made between the possessive and the absorptive. Possession and control tend to go together, as do absorption and surrender. The (hi)story to which Klima alludes is (the) Western (hi)story of progressive enhancement of the possessive at the expense of the absorptive. Possession puts the possessed at ones disposal. Disposing *over* it typically means first using, then disposing *of* it. Possession, thus, exists within the dynamic of self-enrichment. The possessor, not the possessed, is the center. Possessed items belong to the possessor, the center, as, so to speak, satellites. On this particular model it is the intellect's role to be a tool, even a weapon, in the service of possession/control/consumption/disposal. It is these latter, particularly the first two, which structure and circumscribe the parameters within which "knowing" moves. Note that what gets eliminated at the end of what might be called "the possessive process" is what gets in paradoxical sense "produced" through this process, *viz.*, waste—in other words, garbage. The purpose of the process, a pervasively consumptive one, is not, of course, to produce anything at all, and certainly not to produce garbage. The latter is only a by-product. This by-product, however, is what results (and remains) at the end of possessive activity. It therefore, and again, paradoxically, ironically, might be called the "final product," the populant of possessive drive's "kingdom of ends." The remains are what remain. They are the result, the "product."

Surely this is strange, leading to even stranger turns of phrase. "That the wasteland grows" now, at least, can be given more determinate content. As an age of consumption (seemingly) gains in strength, scope and duration—perhaps even intensity—its outcome is more and more garbage. Garbage is that in which it issues. In multiple senses garbage *is* its issue.

The contrast with absorption, possession's "other," is most helpful. To be absorbed in X, as opposed to the attempt to possess that X, involves a different dynamic. That in which one is absorbed becomes central. One then stands within its service, revolving, so to speak, around it.

Extreme states of absorption are revealing. In them one often (and usually self-forgetfully) seeks to *fuse* with that in or with which one is absorbed. One often experiences oneself "passively" as being "drawn toward," "guided by," "motivated in terms of" that something. It affects one, elicits a response in one. But the response is far less that of an agent seeking possession and the transportation of the relevant item into one's own space. It is better troped as the desire to be transported into the item's "space," not to draw it close, but to draw close to it. Let us consider the possibility that in the case of at least some items, a space exists which is experienced as *their* space and not one's own. We have an intuitive grasp of what this might mean through our dealings with other people. Sometimes even the growl of the dog suggests to us a potential violation of its space, the trespass on its territory. These examples are somewhat problematic, however, for they could be understood in altogether physical terms. For this reason it might be better to reflect on a very specific situation, which I shall label "the whore's kiss." It is said that the whore does not give her kiss to customers. Let us proximisally assume that this is because she does not wish to give them access to her space. The rejoinder is obvious. What space has the high-paying and polymorphously perverse customer not occupied? Surely no physical space, but what about personal space? Can a distinction be made on the basis of which it is possible to believe that a physical body (in physical space) has been *used*, but that in and through that use, however pervasive, no access was gained to the personal space of the person (*nor* to the person) whose body it is?

This last question is not idle, for there are those who would claim that personal space—itself dwindling through the spread of Orwellian and other agendas—is the last vestige of what might be called "sacred space," a space, supposedly, which is qualitatively different than other spaces, but which must "bestow" itself in the sense that there is no forced entry. One must be *granted* access, even proximity to it. However these larger issues are ultimately settled, we are nonetheless in a position, now, to understand better our second sense of wasteland-growth. It will mean the diminution, perhaps even the loss, of sacred and/or personal spaces—this in terms of their availability. And loss of availability may be for a number of reasons: the items (whose?) spaces the spaces are may no longer exist, may have gone elsewhere, or simply have withdrawn their "presence."

9

All that has preceded moves toward confrontation with one central question: do space, love, and garbage have any claim on philosophy? In this deliberately incomplete—what shall it be called, meditation?—I have begun to raise this question. I think it underlies much of contemporary concern. But to whom? Is it in any legitimate way the "business of philosophy?" I suppose what I am asking is whether the lovers of wisdom and the removers of litter could ever take up common cause? However temporarily and provisionally, could they be one? And whose questions are these?

5

The Contest of Extremes: An Exploration of the Foundations and the Peak of Nietzsche's Political Philosophy

PETER BERKOWITZ

Peter Berkowitz is an associate professor at George Mason University School of Law and a Research Fellow at the Hoover Institute at Stanford University. He is the author of Virtue and the Making of Modern Liberation. *He is Contributing Editor for* New Republic *and has written for a wide variety of other publications including* Atlantic Monthly, Times Literary Supplement, Weekly Standard, Wilson Quarterly, *and the* Yale Law Journal. *This chapter is the introduction to* Nietzsche: The Ethics of an Immoralist, *which won the Harvard University Press's Thomas J. Wilson Prize for the best book by a new author. Recently Berkowitz served as editor for* The Future of American Intelligence, Terrorism, the Laws of War, and the Constitution: Debating the Enemy Combatant Cases, *and* Never a Matter of Indifference: Sustaining Virtue in a Free Republic.

> She told me herself that she had no morality—and I thought she had, like myself, a more severe morality than anybody.
>
> —FRIEDRICH NIETZSCHE

The dazzling beauty of Nietzsche's writings may blind the reader to the extreme and explosive character of his opinions.[1] Nietzsche expounded a radical and aristocratic egoism; poured scorn on Platonism, Christianity, modernity, enlightenment, democracy, socialism, and the emancipation of women; denounced the belief in human equality as a calamitous conceit;

and ardently championed a rank order of desires, types of human beings, and forms of life.

Nietzsche's standpoint, which he describes as above politics (BT, Preface; A, Preface[2]), has implications for politics. But what he deplores in politics and would like to see abolished is more in evidence than what he approves of in politics and wishes to see accomplished. In fact, Nietzsche has little that is constructive to say about many of the leading themes in the history of political philosophy: the types of regimes and the characteristic citizen corresponding to each; the best regime; the laws or the rule of law; the fair distribution of property and the right arrangement of economic and social institutions. It is tempting, therefore, to conclude that Nietzsche does not practice or contribute to political philosophy, for a primary theme of political philosophy is the city or citizenship and the human being, that is, the relation between the common good and the good of the individual.

Yet Nietzsche's evident opinion that how human beings govern themselves is an illegitimate or marginal topic of philosophy is based upon a certain understanding of the desires and longings of the human soul and the kind of life or specific virtues most conducive to satisfying those desires. By starting from an analysis of what human beings desire and what is desirable for a human being, Nietzsche moves within the domain of moral and political philosophy. He poses a radical challenge to political philosophy by accepting the starting point of political philosophy—the inescapableness or fundamental importance of questions about what is good—while denying that the good is intrinsically connected to any political regime, system of economic and social institutions, or personal attachments. The radical devaluation of political life, and the comprehensive reflection in which that devaluation is ensconced, is a proper and indispensable subject of political philosophy.

A striking feature of Nietzsche's philosophical explorations, concealed by his reputation as the last of the modern philosophers and the first of the postmoderns, is the coexistence of, and indeed contest within his thought between, characteristically ancient and characteristically modern concerns. As in ancient political philosophy, the question of human perfection lies at the heart of Nietzsche's inquiries. At the same time, modern ideas about knowledge, freedom, and mastery pervade and continuously shape his investigations. In his most ambitious works Nietzsche elevates to new heights the characteristically modern aspirations to conquer fortune, to master nature, and to actualize freedom. Yet the dizzying perspective afforded by these new heights is by Nietzsche's own admission decisively determined by ancient notions of metaphysics and human excellence (UD, p. 1, GS, p. 344, BGE, p. 204). In effect, Nietzsche radicalizes modern principles but on the basis of, and constrained by, traditional moral and intellectual virtues. As he expounds a new ethics composed of ancient and modern elements, his thought becomes a battleground for extreme and rival opinions about history, art, morality, religion, virtue, nature, politics, and philosophy. Indeed, this contest of extremes forms his thought.

The death of God is the great speculation that drives Nietzsche's contest of extremes. Contrary to the reductivist approach exemplified by Alexander Nehamas's influential book *Nietzsche: Life as Literature*, in which the death of God functions as a premise in an argument that "allows Nietzsche to deny that the world is subject to a single overarching interpretation, corresponding to God's role or intention,"[3] the death of God describes the feeble worship of a God who is no longer vital or believable and, more important, represents the discovery that morality lacks a foundation in nature, divinity, or reason. This, at least, is the view of Nietzsche's madman who proclaims God's death and characterizes his murder as the greatest deed yet in history (GS, p. 125). For Nietzsche's madman, the death of God does not in the first place generate questions about knowledge and interpretation, but rather more urgently symbolizes a crushing loss of moral standards and gives rise to the intoxicating possibility and unnerving necessity of those few human beings who are fit to "become gods" (GS, p. 125).

Nehamas's favored doctrine, perspectivism, the view that every view, including the view called perspectivism, is only one among many interpretations (p. 1) is not even an implication or consequence of the death of God as Nietzsche understands it. For Nietzsche, the death of God—that is, the denial that nature, reason, or revelation provides moral standards for the governance of life, or for the belief that, as Nietzsche puts it a few sections earlier in *The Gay Science*, "The total character of the world . . . is in all eternity chaos" (GS, p. 109)—is the one true account of the circumstances in which human beings really dwell.[4] Paradoxically, the human condition so understood, at least in Nietzsche's view, generates specific and severe moral or practical imperatives.[5] And he views the clarification of these practical imperatives as his central task. The common tendency today to view questions about language, and interpretation as the central issues in Nietzsche's thought drastically shifts the actual center of gravity of his books. Nietzsche's fundamental concern with ethical and political questions is obscured when scholars make him over into a theorist primarily concerned with questions of how we know rather than of how we should live.[6] Actually, Nietzsche tended to avoid complicated theoretical analysis, giving pride of place instead to questions about the best life. When he does turn to epistemology and metaphysics it is usually with moral intent. For Nietzsche, as I shall argue, the chief question is not how we know but rather what we ought to do in response to the shattering knowledge within our grasp. And Nietzsche knows much—or at least his madman and his Zarathustra know much; from the true but deadly doctrine that morality lacks support in nature, reason, or God, they derive the moral imperative to invent festivals of atonement and sacred games which enable the very best human beings to make themselves gods by commanding the greatest things.[7] But what are the greatest things? What would a life in which the greatest things are commanded look like? And what makes self-deification necessary or desirable?

My book, *Nietzsche: The Ethics of an Immoralist*, clarifies the foundations and spells out the practical implications of Nietzsche's account of the best life. At the foundations of Nietzsche's thought there is a pervasive tension between his fundamental assumption that morality is an artifact of the human will and his unyielding conviction that there is a binding rank order among desires, types of human beings, and forms of life. On the basis of this contest of extreme and conflicting views Nietzsche expounds an ethics of creativity that culminates in a radical exaltation of the human power to both understand and control the world. Speaking very generally, human excellence for Nietzsche consists in facing squarely, comprehending accurately, and overcoming the ugly necessity that governs the human condition, by bringing that necessity under the will's dominion.

Human excellence so understood requires a coherent account of the disharmony between human desire and the cosmos in which human beings dwell, an account that explains why human beings are obliged to make themselves gods. But Nietzsche's robust conviction that there is an order of rank among souls and health proper to the soul contravenes his assumption or conviction that the world lacks a moral order. His view of human excellence and his conception of the fundamental character of the world are like two intimately related antagonists in a play who can never meet on stage because they are portrayed by the same actor. Nietzsche rejects the very idea of natural or rationally intelligible ends, yet he also affirms them and cannot do without them; this pervasive tension both binds his thought together and tears it apart.[8] His remarkable attempt to do justice to and overcome the contest of extremes that forms his thought culminates in *Thus Spoke Zarathustra* and *Beyond Good and Evil*, both of which envisage virtue without a natural end and promise redemption without God. Unable in good conscience to reject either cluster of opinions, Nietzsche thinks their conflict through to the breaking point and thereby powerfully suggests that the distinctions between just and unjust, noble and shameful, and good and bad are the hallmarks of our humanity and cannot be sustained if their foundation in nature, reason, or revelation is altogether abolished.

The Quarrel Between Ancient and Modern

Contemporary scholarship, both inspired by and devoted to Nietzsche, has obscured his bold examination of the character and the requirements of the best life. One particular prejudice that is cultivated by the new orthodoxy must be confronted at once. In Nietzsche: *The Ethics of an Immoralist*, I often use time-honored and old-fashioned words such as truth [*Wahrheit*], wisdom [*Weisheit*], soul [*Seele*], will [*Wille*], right [*Recht*], justice [*Gerechtigkeit*], nature [*Natur*], rank order [*Rangordnung*], nobility [*Vornehmheit*], and philosophy [*Philosophie*]. The reason is simple: Nietzsche uses these old-fashioned and time-honored words, and not just here and there, but pervasively, vigorously, and unabashedly both in criticism of others and in the service of his most characteristic convictions and doctrines.[9] Nonetheless, this language will jar and perhaps dismay those who approach Nietzsche on the basis of recent scholarship, and may at first glance appear as a tendentious attempt to bring foreign concepts and partisan moral categories to bear on Nietzsche's thought, a crude effort to impose terms and notions on Nietzsche that he himself sought to overthrow. Such reactions would be an unfortunate but understandable outgrowth of the new view that credits Nietzsche with overcoming morality, breaking free of traditional modes of thought, and founding new forms of life. This pious acceptance of Nietzsche's boldest claims at once selectively takes him at his word and surreptitiously puts words in his mouth. The new orthodoxy confuses Nietzsche's intention to overcome morality with its actual overcoming, mistakes the desire to discover or invent new modes and orders of thought for their discovery or invention, and mixes up the ambition to found new forms of life with their successful establishment. Propelled by a combination of credulity and enthusiasm, the new orthodoxy equates Nietzsche's wishes and promises with their fulfillment. If, however, one probes beyond the dominant opinion, one sees that Nietzsche's radical intentions are critically shaped and continuously nurtured by traditional ideas and hopes. Although it extends to the foundations, one does not have to probe deeply to discover manifestations of the traditional dimension of Nietzsche's thought: one need merely turn from popular opinions about Nietzsche to the textured surface of his writings.

This is not to say that Nietzsche's persistent use of traditional moral and philosophical language is without paradox. Although he tenaciously questions the value of truth and insists on "*perspective*, the basic condition of all life" (BGE, Preface), he denounces those who turn truth upside down and repeatedly equates serving or pursuing the truth with the supreme human type.[10] Although he delights in exposing pretensions to knowledge as desire for power, Nietzsche and his Zarathustra affirm that wisdom—human nature and of the fundamental character of existence—is the ground and goal of human excellence.[11] Although he condemns the soul as a pernicious invention of Christian priests and theologians, Nietzsche and his Zarathustra frequently use the term soul without irony or embarrassment to designate what is finest, deepest, and highest in human beings.[12] Although he criticizes the doctrine of the will as one of the four great errors and mocks the idea of both the free and the unfree will (TI, "The Four Great Errors," p. 7; BGE, p. 21), Nietzsche and his Zarathustra champion a self-determining will that wills itself and becomes its own law and Nietzsche considered himself a free spirit and regarded freedom and independence, rightly understood, as prerogatives of higher human beings.[13] Although he seeks to undermine the metaphysical basis for belief in the notion of right or rights, Nietzsche does not refrain from couching his vision of human excellence in terms of right and rights.[14] Although his Zarathustra mocks virtue as the opiate of the multitude, Nietzsche speaks of "our virtues," that is, the virtues of free-spirited philosophers like himself, and he identifies with the specific qualities of character on which human excellence depends. Although he argues that morality is an outgrowth or projection of desire and will, he also invokes justice as the rarest of virtues, that which governs the service of truth, giving and receiving, and valid legislation.[15] Although he affirms in unequivocal terms that nature is non-moral, chaotic, and senseless, he appeals to nature as a moral or ethical standard.[16] Although he asserts that good and evil are created by human beings, he routinely proclaims that there is an order of rank among desires, human types, and forms of life, and that the noble soul belongs to the upper echelons of the rank order.[17] And although he unleashes a devastating attack on the prejudices that have ruined philosophy in the past and bedevil it in the present, Nietzsche proudly proclaims himself a knower and philosopher and enthusiastically looks forward to a philosophy of the future.[18] Neither one side nor the other in these pairs of extremes is correctly designated by itself as "Nietzschean," or the core of Nietzsche's thought. This is not to say that in the contest of extremes that forms Nietzsche's thought one side does not gain the upper hand. It is, however, to insist upon the centrality of the contest that holds these rival and extreme opinions together and the fundamental assumptions about human beings and the cosmos that generate it.[19]

Some will argue that Nietzsche's reliance upon traditional language stems from a misplaced nostalgia from which he never quite broke free. Others will contend that he invokes traditional language ironically, subverting or transfiguring traditional terms and categories in the very process of using them. Still others will insist that although Nietzsche rejects traditional language in favor of something brand new, he is constrained to use it because traditional language has dominated the scene for ages and remains the only game in town. One must of course be alive to Nietzsche's famous irony and explore what Nietzsche aims to reveal and conceal through its use. Like Socrates, Nietzsche uses irony to call into question traditional understandings, but precisely in using irony, the very notion of which presupposes a gap between what one says and what one believes, and hence an intelligible and principled difference between appearance and reality, Nietzsche reveals his dependence on a traditional philosophical distinction.

To excuse or to rationalize away the traditional dimension of Nietzsche's thought risks transfiguring him into a miracle worker, exempting him from ordinary rules and standards and attributing to him extravagant feats, the philosophical equivalent of spinning straw into gold. I must emphasize that it is out of respect for his achievement as a writer and thinker that I do not approach Nietzsche as if he were able to walk on water or magically transform intractable tensions into redeeming visions. For now I want only to insist that his use of traditional language is a pervasive feature of his thought the significance of which must be determined if his philosophical explorations are to be understood. Nietzsche sometimes expresses his revolutionary aim as the revaluation of all values. Just as "revaluation" [*Umwertung*] embraces "value" [*Wert*], so too Nietzsche's attempts to conceive a new human type by revaluing all values, both by intention and of necessity preserves crucial elements of the tradition he sets out to overcome.

Heidegger's Challenge

Martin Heidegger provides almost unrivaled insight into Nietzsche's fundamental conceptions—the death of God, the will to power, the eternal return, and nihilism. In his pioneering confrontation with Nietzsche's thought Heidegger argues that Nietzsche's philosophy culminates in a vain desire, rooted in the very spiritual corruption that Nietzsche sought to overcome, for a supreme form of mastery. Heidegger, who regarded Nietzsche as primarily a "metaphysical thinker,"[20] indeed "the *last metaphysician* of the West,"[21] shows that the supreme questions raised by Nietzsche's philosophy revolve around fundamental metaphysical problems. Yet Heidegger, I think, mischaracterizes the significance of the moral intentions that motivate Nietzsche's philosophical explorations and misinterprets the results of his treacherous investigations.

On Heidegger's view, "Nietzsche's philosophy is inverted Platonism" (Volume 1, p. 188). Heidegger understands this inversion as the outcome of the countermovement to Western metaphysics that Nietzsche launches—where metaphysics is understood as the domain of "philosophy proper," that is, investigation of the basic structure and first principles or basic structure of the cosmos (Volume 2, pp. 184–197). Nietzsche's countermovement, Heidegger argues, necessarily remains, as a countermovement, entangled in metaphysics or "held fast in the essence of that over against which it moves."[22] But whereas Heidegger draws the conclusion that Nietzsche's attempt to overthrow the Platonism that constitutes the Western tradition in philosophy is a task that still awaits completion, I shall suggest that Nietzsche's failure to move beyond metaphysics attests to its inescapableness. Whereas Heidegger dreams of breaking free of "that over against which" Nietzsche's philosophy moves— that is the philosophical tradition inaugurated by Plato and supposedly completed by Nietzsche—I shall suggest that Nietzsche's inability to realize the highest ambitions of his philosophy requires reconsideration of the validity of "that over against which" his philosophy moves.[23]

Heidegger's encounter with Nietzsche represents a high point in Nietzsche interpretation because Heidegger discerned that the high point of Nietzsche's speculations, the peak where his fundamental conceptions collide, is in the effort to reconcile activities and concepts that, according to Heidegger's interpretation of the tradition, have traditionally been held apart: truth and art, knowing and making, necessity and freedom, Being and Becoming. According to Heidegger, Nietzsche attempts to achieve these reconciliations by making human power over the world absolute—but he fails. Nietzsche's failure, Heidegger insists, is tremendously important: it marks a turning point in the history of philosophy in the sense that it brings metaphysics to a close by thinking through its last possibility and revealing that its opposites could not be effectively reconciled. Following Heidegger, I see Nietzsche as a turning point. Yet, contrary to Heidegger's opinion that Nietzsche's thought represents the consummation and exhaustion of Western metaphysics, I suggest that Nietzsche's failure to overcome the tradition justifies a renewed encounter— one that is skeptical and curious rather than destructive or deconstructive— with the whole history of philosophy from which Nietzsche sought to break free.

One reason, I think, that Heidegger goes astray is that he pays too little attention to the movement of Nietzsche's thought. Although he was a great reader, Heidegger was also a great misreader.[24] By insisting that Nietzsche's fundamental question is the metaphysical question "what is being?" and that Nietzsche's philosophy is grounded in the doctrine of the eternal return, Heidegger projected a restrictive framework of his own making onto Nietzsche's thought, which although it revealed much also obscured plenty. With staggering irony, Heidegger's manipulation, exploitation, and selective use of Nietzsche's writings exemplifies the technological frame of mind that Heidegger himself deplored, purported to wish to overcome, and claimed to find in its most advanced form in Nietzsche's thought.[25]

If one places Nietzsche's unpublished notes, out of which Heidegger made so much, in perspective, and respects the context in which Nietzsche expounds his thoughts by turning to a consideration of his books, one will see the opportunity that Heidegger lost sight of and that his writings on Nietzsche buried. The opportunity consists in a nontraditional and skeptical encounter with the tradition. For the traditional notions and virtues that enliven Nietzsche's thought not only make possible the exhibition of the defects of his fundamental doctrines and highest aspirations; the crucial role of these traditional notions and virtues in his philosophical explorations also gives rise to the demand that they be given another hearing. This startling if tentative vindication of the tradition by one who set out to overcome it is perhaps a fitting tribute to a thinker who prefers to the courage of conviction the courage for an attack on one's convictions.

The Importance of Nietzsche's Books

Heidegger has contributed decisively to making legitimate an odd and indefensible practice that dominates efforts to reconstruct and expound Nietzsche's thought.[26] The common practice, cutting across a wealth of opinions about Nietzsche, is to lift Nietzsche's ideas, arguments, and philosophical explorations out of the context from which they derive the sense and significance Nietzsche gave them. In particular, Nietzsche's well-known statements about perspectivism, creativity, will, and reason have suffered at the hands of scholars and advocates a fate similar to that of a lion wrested from his natural habitat, hauled thousands of miles, and displayed for show in a cramped zoo cage where forced confinement silences its roar, dims its eyes, and breaks its spirit. While there may be good reasons for wrenching some of Nietzsche's ideas from their context and forcing them into new homes, what could justify passing off as the original these caged and broken speculations?

The standard practice involves making arguments about what Nietzsche intended or thought based on picking and choosing, mixing and matching, and cutting and pasting words, phrases, and ideas drawn from wherever they can be found in Nietzsche's *Collected Works*.[27] Wildly diverse materials, often with little or no mention of the argumentative or dramatic context from which they are taken, are marshalled to construct or reconstruct doctrines that are then attributed to Nietzsche. One sees the height of this perverse practice in the crude treatment to which *Thus Spoke Zarathustra* is routinely subjected. Even some of those who emphasize the literary character of Nietzsche's works do not hesitate to ascribe to Nietzsche isolated remarks or deeds of his literary creation, Zarathustra.[28]

What accounts for the strange manner in which many scholars rummage through Nietzsche's writings for useful material is, I think, a peculiar idea about how to read books in general and Nietzsche's books in particular. The common method is based on the assumption that Nietzsche's books are not unified works, that they do not present sustained philosophical views, that their parts do not derive their fundamental significance from their place in the whole. Judging by general practice, the consensus is that Nietzsche's books are potpourris of stimulating insights mixed in with clunkers, embarrassments, unfortunate fulminations, and irrelevant notions. The dominant view holds that the decisive unit of meaning in Nietzsche's writings is at one extreme a posthumously published, multivolume entity called *The Collected Works* and at the other extreme the brilliant, self-contained aphorism. In practice, these two extreme opinions amount to the same thing: they equally license scholars to become advocates, picking and choosing from Nietzsche's writings as they please, using what they find congenial, stimulating, or expedient, passing by in silence what they find mistaken or disadvantageous, and passing off the result as if it were faithful to Nietzsche's thought.

In fairness it must be said that Nietzsche himself advances extreme opinions that seem to sanction the crude interpretive approach to which his writings have been subject. After all, Nietzsche is the teacher of the will to power. Will to power implies that will is more fundamental than reason. Knowledge is not discovered by the mind but imposed or projected by the will on the world. As there is no enduring, stable order, interpretation is always only an expression of power. As there is no original, only text, there is no knowledge, only interpretation. We construct the text to suit our desire because we cannot do otherwise. As for books, there is no point in searching for the author's intention since interpretation always bears the indelible imprint of the interpreter's hierarchy of values. Since all reading is rewriting, and since all interpretation is ineradicably value-laden, the reader is fully justified in treating a text as grist for his or her mill. Thus, it seems that Nietzsche's own writing justifies the subjugation of his books to his readers' wills. Or does it? For to the extent that we establish that Nietzsche thought that all reading is writing we prove that some opinions, for example, Nietzsche's opinion that all reading is writing, may be read rather than rewritten.[29]

Although sophisticated authors may pay lip service to the idea that their interpretation is one among many, in practice those who champion the perspectival, willful, and aesthetic side of Nietzsche nonetheless purport to accomplish in the interpretation of Nietzsche what their interpretation of Nietzsche implies can never be accomplished, namely to grasp the basic or defining characteristics of Nietzsche's thought.[30] I am in sympathy with the quest to comprehend the fundamental features of Nietzsche's thought, in part because this comprehension is what Nietzsche explicitly wished for from his readers. My point is that scholars who attribute to Nietzsche, and themselves endorse, perspectival, constructivist, or aesthetic notions of understanding often claim, in quite traditional fashion, to understand what is basic or fundamental in Nietzsche's thought and give every appearance of wishing for their own writings to be read rather than rewritten. Thus their practice betrays their principle, undercutting the key presupposition—the idea that all interpretation is willful remaking of the world—that justifies disregarding the integrity of Nietzsche's books.

And something similar can be said about Nietzsche: his extreme theoretical speculations about the willfulness of interpretation notwithstanding, Nietzsche explicitly wrote, as the Prefaces to his books abundantly attest, in the hopes that some few readers would understand his meaning. To be sure, the speculation and the hope conflict. But which must yield? Is Nietzsche's hope that his writings would be understood undercut by his extreme speculations about language, interpretation, and knowledge? Or rather, must we understand Nietzsche's extreme speculations in light of his firm conviction that his writings as well as those of others were intelligible?

My view is that the extraordinary unity of conviction, purpose, and execution that marks Nietzsche's thought[31] comes to light only if we recognize the integrity of Nietzsche's books.[32] There is considerable *prima facie* evidence that this is how Nietzsche wished to be understood. First, the fact that he chose to write and publish books at all, and then books with titles, chapter headings, distinctive emphases, styles, and subjects gives rise to the presumption that the form of his presentation—the book—is meaningful.[33] Second, almost all of Nietzsche's books contain prefaces or prologues in which he discusses the specific intention informing the work at hand. Third, in *Ecce Homo*, Nietzsche surveys his life's work, and in so doing treats his books as distinct and ordered wholes. And more provisionally, attention to the structure, argument, and intention in Nietzsche's books yields rich rewards.[34] In the end, of course, the proof of the opinion that the key to Nietzsche's thought lies in his book is in the reading.[35]

A Path in Nietzsche's Thought

There are many paths in Nietzsche's thought. The path I trace proceeds by way of detailed explorations of a range of Nietzsche's major books, it goes to the foundations and the peak of his reflections on the best life, and it reveals the ethics of an immoralist.

Part I of my book, "Nietzsche's Histories," deals with Nietzsche's three major attempts, spanning his career, to clarify the significance of art, morality, and religion through the exploration of ancient history. The key to understanding how Nietzsche himself practices history is found in *On the Uses and Disadvantages of History for Life*, where he sets forth prescriptions for the right use of history. His prescriptions for the right use of history openly rest upon a bold claim to metaphysical knowledge and a definite view, at once descriptive and normative, of human nature. And these govern the manner in which he himself writes history. In harmony with the task that he assigns the "genuine historian" in *Uses and Disadvantages*, Nietzsche, in his own histories, subordinates the acquisition of exact historical knowledge to the poetic or mythic presentation of historical figures and events so as to display the enduring truth about human excellence and human degradation. In *The Birth of Tragedy* he analyzes the origins of ancient Greek tragedy to vindicate an ethics of art; in *On the Genealogy of Morals* he examines the origins of moral prejudices to elaborate an ethics of morality; and that in *The Antichrist* he exposes the origins of organized Christianity and praises the moral intentions governing Buddhism, Jesus, and the law of Manu to distinguish good and bad religions and to throw light on the ethics of religion. A major part of Nietzsche's enduring legacy is embodied in his histories where, in accordance with the task of the "genuine historian," he transforms history into poetry to defend wisdom, to distinguish nobility from baseness, and to establish the love of truth as a resplendent vice and noble faith.

Nietzsche's histories resolutely point to but do not fully articulate the character of human excellence, "the highest type [die höchste Art] of all beings" (EH III, on Z, p. 6). In his books there are two major attempts to articulate the character of his highest type. *Thus Spoke Zarathustra* presents the superman as the highest type. *Beyond Good and Evil* puts forward the "philosopher of the future" as the peak of human excellence. The obvious question, ignored right and left, is whether the superman and the philosopher of the future are distinct and rival types or whether they amount to one and the same type. Are the superman and the philosopher of the future, when all is said and done, two or one?

Part II, "The Highest Type," examines the character of the superman and the philosopher of the future. I argue that the philosopher of the future shares the superman's goal. In both *Thus Spoke Zarathustra* and *Beyond Good and Evil* Nietzsche teaches that human excellence requires absolute freedom, based on absolute knowledge and realized in absolute mastery. And just as in *Thus Spoke Zarathustra*, where Zarathustra eventually abandons the highest aims of the superman, Nietzsche retreats in the final parts of *Beyond Good and Evil* from the grandest aspirations of the philosopher of the future. Nevertheless, the perspectives of the two works differ. For example, whereas *Thus Spoke Zarathustra* throws light on the reasons why the superman must be rejected as the supreme type, *Beyond Good and Evil* leaves the reasons for tempering the ambitions of the philosopher of the future shrouded in shadows and silence. And whereas Zarathustra promises a new sobriety only at the very end, *Beyond Good and Evil* richly exemplifies throughout the free-spirited skepticism that is the identifying mark of this new sobriety. Nietzsche's two accounts of the supreme type provide complementary perspectives on the best life. Along with his histories, they constitute essential parts of his enduring legacy.[36]

A Point of Departure

Nietzsche's reputation as the philosopher of creativity, will, and power is not undeserved, yet it has worked to obscure the fundamental structure of his thought. For Nietzsche empathetically distinguishes good from bad exercises of creativity, willing, and power, and envisages a supreme type who practices both art and philosophy. Good art or right making in Nietzsche's thought depends upon good philosophy or right knowing.[37] Indeed, the account of the highest human activity that Nietzsche offers in *Zarathustra* and *Beyond Good and Evil* can be understood in terms of a formula: right making based upon right knowledge.[38]

Generally speaking, Nietzsche is, as postmodern interpretations suggest, a teacher of self-making or self-creation. Yet postmodern interpreters and "neo-Nietzschean" theorists overlook the foundations of Nietzsche's imperative to self-making and underestimate the severity of his ethics of the creative self. For Nietzsche, there is a rank order of creative activities according to which the ultimate form of making is self-making and the ultimate form of self-making is making oneself a god. What postmodern interpreters disregard is that Nietzsche is compelled to figure out the form of life suitable to a self-made god, one who engages in right making based on right knowing, but what he calls the "intellectual conscience." In other words, it is what he has been driven to discover about the human condition by his love of truth, or what is sometimes called his gay science, that impels Nietzsche to reach the fantastic conclusion that the good for human beings consists in the act of self-deification.

A brief glance at Nietzsche's *Gay Science*[39] can provide a useful introduction to the elements of the ethics of self-deification. In section 2, "*The Intellectual Conscience*," Nietzsche laments that "the great majority of people"—including "the most gifted men and the noblest women"—do not seek to rest their faith and judgments on reason (GS 2). Virtues, Nietzsche implies, are worthless if they are not supported by knowledge. "[H]igher human beings" are distinguished by the intensity of their desire for certainty. Hatred of reason is better than unquestioning faith inasmuch as it reflects skepticism or reasoned doubt about the competence of human reason; that is, hatred of reason is vindicated as an exercise in achievement of reason. Reminiscent of Socrates' assertion that philosophy begins in wonder (Theatetus 155d),[40] questioning, on Nietzsche's account, the key manifestation of the intellectual conscience, is grounded in the perception or experience of the "marvelous uncertainty and rich ambiguity of existence." Nietzsche finds those who lack the inclination to question contemptible. He admits that there is folly in this opinion, but explains that the folly lies not in his exalted estimation of the intellectual conscience but rather in the conviction that all human beings feel its sting. For a lively intellectual conscience is rare and the identifying mark of a higher human being.[41]

What would a higher human being amply endowed with an intellectual conscience know? How would such a person live? Section 125 of *The Gay Science*, "The Madman," presents Nietzsche's famous parable of the death of God. The madman, a seeker after God, is distinguished not only by what he seeks but also by what he knows. As a result of his searches, the madman knows that God is dead, that human beings have killed him, that God's murder is a catastrophe for the human spirit, and that the destruction of what was holiest and mightiest calls forth severe new obligations and fantastic opportunities. In language rich with Christian and theological overtones, Nietzsche's madman speculates that human beings who know that God is dead require comfort for their crime, need water to cleanse their blood-spattered spirits, and must invent "festivals of atonement" and "sacred games" to redeem their lives. For Nietzsche's madman, the proper and only worthy response to the death of God involves neither the negation of religious yearning nor the extirpation of the impulse to transcendence. On the contrary. Relieved of older obligations to worship or to imitate God, Nietzsche's madman discovers a new obligation for human beings: to appear worthy of having murdered God, the madman thinks, human beings must themselves "become gods."[42] By ascribing to human beings the power to kill God and the capacity to become a god, the madman effects a profound break with traditional Christianity. At the same time, the new obligation the madman assigns to human beings preserves an important element of the Christian tradition, because of the madman's heavy dependence upon Christian language and categories to articulate humanity's new goal, and indeed because of the very need for what is sacred and holy that underlies the quest to become a god were for Nietzsche's madman the supreme act of piety. Yet even if his madmen, yearning for "all that was holiest and mightiest," knowing that God was dead, and drawing the ethical consequences of this "tremendous event," were the supreme embodiment of piety, the question would remain as to Nietzsche's own evaluation of piety.

What could piety mean for Nietzsche's own evaluation of piety. What could piety mean for Nietzsche in view of his ruthless questioning of cherished pieties?

As it happens, Nietzsche tells us. Speaking in the first-person plural in Section 344, entitled "How we, too, are still Pious," Nietzsche proclaims the faith and the moral intention that govern his philosophical investigations, his gay science: "it is still a metaphysical faith upon which our faith in science rests—that even we knowers [*Wir Erkennenden*] today, we godless anti-meta-physicians still take our fire, too, from the flame lit by a faith that is thousands of years old, that Christian faith which was also the faith of Plato, that God is the truth, that truth is divine" (GS, p. 344). Nietzsche rejects the favorite words and special doctrines of Christianity and Plato. Although Nietzsche does proceed to raise the possibility of losing what he shares with Christianity and Plato—this faith in the divinity of truth—this loss remains, at least in *The Gay Science*, no more than a possibility. And a possibility, moreover, that Nietzsche is compelled to entertain by the internal standards imposed by faith in, or service to, the truth.[43]

Nietzsche's gay science is rooted in an ethics of knowing and a faith in the sanctity of truth. What then of willing, making, and creating? In Section 335, entitled "Long live physics!" Nietzsche presents the intellectual conscience as the judge of the moral conscience or the form of conscience that is recognized by conventional morality. In its restlessness and severity the intellectual conscience reveals that conventional morality rests upon hypocrisy and self-deception. Prizing knowledge above authority or tradition, the intellectual conscience undercuts the authority of conventional moral judgments by revealing that conventional morality, far from possessing a transcendent ground in nature, reason, or divine revelation, originates in the accidents of instincts, appetites, and circumstances. What follows the painful self-discovery that conventional morality lacks authoritative or lofty foundations, according to Nietzsche, is the task of understanding the imperative or necessity to undertake self-creation. The opinion that conventional morality is groundless is one of the grounds of Nietzsche's ethics of creativity.

To truly engage in self-creation requires knowledge so as to avoid mistaking the effect of some cause, a conditioned or reflexive response, for a freely chosen deed. Indeed, for Nietzsche, "*the creation of our won new tables of what is good*" rests upon the most ruthless forms of self-knowledge and knowledge of the world. Equating self-creation with making new laws for oneself, Nietzsche views this new lawgiving as dependent upon knowledge of the old laws that still bind human beings, especially the laws of physics, for conventional morality is not the only form of necessity that deprives human beings of freedom. Thus, to become self-creators, we must become the best learners and discoverers of everything that is lawful and necessary in the world: we must become physicists in order to be able to be creators in this sense—while hitherto all valuations and ideals have been based on ignorance of physics or were constructed so as to contradict it. Therefore: long live physics! And even more so that which compels us to turn to physics—our honesty! (*Gay Science*, p. 335)

Since creativity depends upon what is "lawful and necessary in the world," making depends upon knowing and right making depend upon right knowing. What exactly would those who, like Nietzsche, are governed by honesty see when they turn to physics to discover what is "lawful and necessary in the world"? One possibility is introduced by Nietzsche in the penultimate section of the first edition of *The Gay Science*, Section 341, "The Greatest Weight," which Nietzsche himself regarded as containing the basic idea of *Zarathustra*" (EH III, on Z, p. 1). Nietzsche asks the reader to imagine a demon who reveals that every life is condemned to infinite and exact repetition of all of its moments. Nor is this merely a thought about human life: "The eternal hourglass of existence is turned upside down again and again, and you with it, speck of dust!" This account of existence, which on first hearing, Nietzsche states, appears to be a crushing curse, is on closer inspection, he suggests, a divine thought. For the thought of eternal necessity somehow gives rise to a kind of test:

If this thought gained possession of you, it would change you as you are or perhaps crush you are or perhaps crush you. The question of each and every thing, "Do you desire this once more and innumerable times more?" would lie upon your actions as the greatest weight. Or how well disposed would you have to become to yourself and to life to crave nothing more fervently than this ultimate eternal confirmation and seal? (*Gay Science*, p. 341)

Nietzsche's question leaves mysterious how the fervent craving for eternal necessity confers eternal significance upon self, life, or existence.

Indeed, it would seem that satisfaction of the desire for eternal, unchanging necessity would have the opposite effect. Unless, somehow, the thought of eternal necessity were itself a freely chosen work of the will projected and stamped upon existence, a work of the will that renders existence desirable or beautiful (GS 276). This then—the form of making that beautifies the world by eternalizing necessity—might even be the highest example of right making based on right knowing. But what human being could hope to exercise to godlike a power? What would the exercise of such a power look like in practice? Question and considerations like these give a clue as to why the ultimate section of the first edition of *The Gay Science*, which contains almost verbatim the opening of *Thus Spoke Zarathustra*, is entitled "*Incipit tragoe-dia*," the tragedy begins.[44]

At this point the welcome objection may be raised that I have betrayed my own strictures by forming an interpretation of Nietzsche's thought from a few passages culled from one of his books supported by an opportunistic appeal to his notebooks. Indeed! To be sure, I have not shown that right mak-ing based on right knowing is the highest aspiration of *The Gay Science*, much less that it is the dominant ambition of Nietzsche's highest type. At best I have assembled some suggestive evidence that favors such an opinion and justi-fies further examination. The task of vindicating that opinion belongs to the detailed discussion of Nietzsche's works in my book.

Let me then end this chapter by anticipating my conclusion: a contest between a peculiar combination of convictions impels Nietzsche to identify self-deification as a human being's supreme perfection. A close study of a range of Nietzsche's books, however, indicates that for human beings such perfection is not attainable.

The imperative to make oneself a god is rooted in Nietzsche's teaching that in fact, and by right, will is the ruling element in the soul. Yet if the will rules over reason there are neither facts nor rights, only protections and cre-ations of the strongest or most efficacious wills. As I shall argue, this conun-drum ultimately proves fatal to Nietzsche's highest ambition; consequently, he does not succeed in establishing the will's sovereignty. Yet what is a defeat in one sense is a triumph in another. For Nietzsche's failed effort reveals that the attempt to transcend the human by making one's will a supreme law requires the principled denial of the distinction between political liberty and legal slavery, the ruthless denigration of political life, and in the end the mer-ciless reduction of history, nature, and human beings to artifacts of strong wills. Nietzsche's writings display how and to what a terrifying extent the coronation of the will withers the humane sensibilities, instills an indiscrim-inate contempt for authority, limitation, and form, and generates impossibly high and inevitably destructive standards for ethics and politics. The pathos of Nietzsche's exaltation of the will is that it subverts the rank order among desires, souls, and forms of life that he cherishes, and causes him to betray the intellectual conscience to which he professes allegiance and which in the first place dictated the will's exaltation. Yet in displaying the truth about this betrayal, above all in Zarathustra's self-betrayal, Nietzsche vindicates the intellectual conscience.

The explosive consequences of Nietzsche's thought will compel humane thinkers to question his assumptions, doubt his claims, and challenge his con-clusions. A different kind of thinker, impelled by the very skepticism that Nietzsche often incomparably exemplified, a free-spirited skepticism that treats nothing (not even Nietzsche's opinions) as too sacred to be questioned, doubted, or challenged, will strive to test and contest Nietzsche's thought. Finally, it is not the morality of the humane thinker but the reason of the skeptic that is decisive in requiring a reconsideration of Nietzsche's achievement. For reason is the not-so-secret power behind the throne on which Nietzsche sets the will. Nietzsche's efforts to exalt the will in the end bolster the claims of reason, because for him it is reason, not will, that crowns the will; reason, not will, that clarifies the "superroyal tasks" of the highest type; and reason, not will, that displays the confusion, the poverty, and the degradation stemming from the will's reign.

I do not take this conclusion to be at odds with the spirit of Nietzsche's thought. For I have been persuaded by Nietzsche's cautionary words directed to "philosophers and friends of knowledge," of whom he considers himself one, "that no philosopher so far has been proved right, and that there might be a more laudable truthfulness in every little question mark that you place after your special words and favorite doctrines (and occasionally after yourselves) than in all the solemn gestures and trumps before accusers and law courts" (BGE, p. 25). Would it not be a fitting tribute to thought such as Nietzsche's to place a question mark or two after his special words and favorite doctrines? Of course, such a tribute requires that one first accurately identify Nietzsche's special words and favorite doctrines.

Many roads converge in Nietzsche's thought; divergent paths lead out. Whatever the origin, whatever the stops along the way, whatever the destination, one will have squandered a golden opportunity if one passes by Nietzsche's thought without observing the love of truth, the courage, and the yearning for the good that animate his magisterial effort to live an examined life by giving an account of the best life.

6

A Psychological View of Moral Intuition

JONATHAN BARON

Jonathan Baron is a Professor of Psychology at the University of Pennsylvania. He is interested in decision-making, moral judgment, and their relation to public issues. He received a B.A. in psychology from Harvard in 1966 and a Ph.D. in psychology from the University of Michigan in 1970. His recent publications include "The Political Psychology of Redistribution," UCLA Law Review, *and "Cognitive Biases, Cognitive Limits, and Risk Communication,"* Journal of Public Policy and Marketing.

At least since the publication of John Rawls's *A Theory of Justice* in 1971, it has been standard practice in moral philosophy to develop theories by trying to explain and systematize our moral intuitions. Rawls made an analogy with linguistics. A few years before Rawls wrote, Noam Chomsky had advanced the field of linguistics through a similar move. Chomsky developed a mathematical theory of the structure of sentences by trying to account simply for his own intuitions about what was a sentence and what was not.

Rawls's view of theory construction through "reflective equilibrium" was subtle and elaborate. Much has been written about it. But a glance at current philosophy journals suggests that a simpler method has become common practice. Typically, the author presents a few carefully constructed cases and then tries to account for her own moral judgments about these cases.

This is especially true in the study of the set of issues concerned with causing harm through action *versus* omission, or causing harm *versus* letting it happen. For example, H.M. Malm describes a case in which two children, John and Mary, are in a crushing machine.[1] If you push a button, John will be killed but Mary will be unharmed. If you do not push, the reverse will happen. Malm thinks that you are wrong to push the button because it would be difficult to come up with a reason for doing so, while you do not need to give a reason for not pushing. Malm uses this example to derive substantive moral conclusions.

The question of where these intuitions come from and how they can be explained is indeed an interesting one. It may tell us something about human psychology. But, to someone who has been reading the literature on the psychology of heuristics and biases, it is unlikely to tell one much about the correct moral solution to these cases or others.[2]

It is easiest to see the problem if we get away from the moral domain and look at human intuitions about other cases where there is more agreement about the right answer. Psychologists have discovered—under different names—a variety of cases in which intuitions seem to be systematically incorrect.

One set of cases goes by the name of "naive theories." These are most easily found in science. In one study, students graduating from Harvard were asked why it was hot in the summer and cold in the winter. Many students said that the earth was closer to the sun in the summer.[3] This is reasonable: if you move closer to a fire, you get warmer. If this were the explanation, though, it would be warmer in July than in January in the Southern Hemisphere too. People's intuitions about science are often based on everyday experience, but this experience can mislead.

Many kinds of naive theories have been discovered. Some people think that a thermostat is like the accelerator in a car, so, when they walk into a cool house, they turn it from sixty to eighty degrees so that the house warms up (to seventy) more quickly. Again, not an unreasonable theory, just false. Of course, in science, we can show that the theory is false, though this may be more difficult in ethics. My point is that the same mechanisms that lead to incorrect intuitive theories in science may operate in ethics too.

A related phenomenon—probably the same phenomenon under a different name—is the use of heuristics in judgment and decision making. If you flip a coin six times, which is more likely, HHHTTT or HTHHTT? Many people say the latter, because it looks more similar to other random sequences. (The two sequences each have probability 1/64.) People tend to judge probability in terms of similarity, or "representativeness." Again, use of similarity to judge probability usually works, but it fails here.

Psychologists have cataloged dozens of such effects in decision making. In the "sunk cost effect," people consider the resources put into an option in deciding whether to abandon it, holding future consequences constant. For example, Ernie bought one TV dinner on sale for $4, decided to invite Bert over for dinner, then bought another for $8 (the sale being over). When both dinners were in the oven, Bert called to say he couldn't come. Which dinner should Ernie eat if he can eat only one, or does it matter? About forty percent of adults (and more children) say that he should eat the $8 one, because he wastes less money that way. The rule against waste is a good one, but it does not apply here. The money is already spent.

The "status-quo effect" increases the value of whatever is perceived as being the status quo. In one study, half of the (Cornell) students in a room were told that they had a Cornell mug, and they were asked how much money they would accept for it. The other half were asked how much money they would need so that they would prefer getting that amount of money to getting a Cornell mug. The former group gave answers about twice as high as the latter. Note that both groups were choosing between the same two outcomes. The only difference was in what they were told about the status quo. In general, sticking to the status quo is a reasonable heuristic; change is costly and risky. But in this case, these differences were not there. The heuristic was used anyway.

For another example of the status-quo effect, consider the following two cases:

A. The government plans to put a hazardous waste site 50 miles away and reduce your taxes, unless you (and others) are willing to give up the reduction, in which case the waste site will be 500 miles away;

B. The government plans to put the site 500 miles away unless you (and others) are willing to accept a tax reduction, in which case it will be 50 miles away.

In each case, what tax reduction would make you indifferent between the two locations? Many people would want more in B than in A. The move from 500 to 50 is a more serious loss than the move from 50 to 500 is a gain, despite the fact that the site is not built yet.[4]

Notice the analogy between these examples and Malm's example of John and Mary. Malm's intuition is easily explained as an extension of the same heuristic that yields the status-quo effect. Again, the point is not that Malm is necessarily wrong, but rather that this intuition can be understood without thinking that intuition is the royal road to moral truth.

A similar distinction occurs in cases of action *versus* omission. In questionnaire studies and in real life, most drivers given the choice of reducing auto insurance costs by limiting their right to sue will not take this option if they must act to do so. But if they must act to prevent the change, most people will accept it. The latter was the case in Pennsylvania, the former in New Jersey. About twice as many drivers chose the reduction in New Jersey as in Pennsylvania.

In general, the harm caused by action is more regrettable than the harm caused by omission, for a variety of reasons: acts are more often intentional; omissions are usually more easily corrected; and so on. So people develop a general rule against causing harm through omissions. When an action has both costs and benefits, people shy away from it, even when the usual factors that distinguish acts and omissions are absent. This intuition may lie behind some of the opposition to trade agreements, even among those who admit that the benefits outweigh the harms.

Suppose that a flu epidemic is going to kill ten out of 10,000 children. A vaccine will completely prevent the flu, but the vaccine may kill some number of children. You can tell nothing about which children will die from the flu or from the vaccine. All children have an equal chance in both cases. How much vaccine risk would you tolerate before you would decide not to vaccinate your child? (Or, if you were a policy maker, how much risk would you tolerate before you would no longer recommend the vaccine?) Many people will not tolerate very much risk. Some will tolerate none at all.

Notice that, if this intuition is put into effect, more children would die than if more children were vaccinated. This may have happened. In England and Japan, news stories about rare, isolated cases of brain damage or death possibly resulting from pertussis vaccine led many parents not to vaccinate their children. As a result, hundreds of children died or suffered brain damage from whooping cough, which the vaccine would have prevented. In the U.S. some parents still resist vaccination even though they admit that the risk of vaccination is lower than that of nonvaccination. The Sabin polio vaccine is another case.

If you were a rational child, you would probably want your risk to be minimized, and you would not care whether minimal risk was associated with someone's action or inaction. If we accept this account of what a child would rationally want and then fail to vaccinate the child, we are going against the child's interests, and not because someone else's interests are served instead, but rather because of our own moral beliefs. Why should we advocate moral principles—such as the relevance of the act-omission distinction—that go against some interests and serve no interests? (We could, of course, describe the situation *ex-post* as a conflict between those children who would die from the vaccine and those who would die from the disease. But the *ex-post* and *ex-ante* descriptions are the same case described differently. If we make a different decision, we must explain why the description is morally relevant.)

I have argued that moral intuitions can be understood as naive theories, or heuristics, so that they cannot be relied upon as the basis of normative moral theory.[5] Given that these heuristics exist and that at least some of them are clearly erroneous, how can we be sure that our moral intuitions are not in the same category? All of these heuristics can be understood as approximations that work most of the time (at best). If that is what they are, then they are not reliable guides to moral truth.

This view is consistent with the fact that people differ considerably in the heuristics they use and in the strength of their commitment to those heuristics. This is true in most of the examples I have given. In another study Mark Spranca and I gave subjects a story about a tennis player named John who wanted to beat Ivan Lendl (then ranked first in the world) by inducing Lendl to eat cayenne pepper. John knew that the house salad dressing at the club dining room where they were eating contained cayenne. He planned to recommend it to Ivan. In one version, John was about to do so, and Ivan ordered it himself, so John said nothing. In the other version, John recommended it. Some subjects felt quite strongly that John's behavior was morally different in the two cases (although they acknowledged the equivalence of intention). Others felt equally strongly that the behavior was equivalent. One subject wrote angrily, in large letters, that this distinction was at the root of Nazism: those who did nothing to stop it were fully responsible for their omissions. Possibly, philosophers also differ in the strengths of their intuitions, and this accounts in part for their disagreements.

Cultures, too, differ in their intuitions. U.S. college students, for example, have strong intuitions about the importance of autonomy and noninterference, but these intuitions were almost totally absent in a sample of students in India. Reliance on intuition can result in a culture-bound morality.[6]

I shall deal briefly here with three objections to my argument. One is that some moral intuitions are held very strongly by everyone, so they must be correct. It isn't clear to me why this follows. However, it is also true that some decision-making biases are held very strongly even though they are demonstrably illogical.

Second, it may be that the best moral system is to follow our strong intuitions, even if we cannot understand how these intuitions arise. I must grant this as a possibility. This is especially likely to be true when we can understand our intuitions as good approximations to ideal rules, and when any attempts to apply the ideal rules directly are more likely than not to lead to error. But this seems to me to be a practical matter, which I have called prescriptive rather than normative. If we want to understand morality, our intuitions are not enough, although as a guide to behavior they may be very good.

Third, if we disallow intuitions as primary data in moral philosophy, is anything left? The analogy with linguistics suggests a negative answer. I cannot answer this question here, although I and others have tried to answer it elsewhere. In brief, I think that alternative bases of moral philosophy can be found by asking ourselves about the ultimate aim of the enterprise.[7]

7

The Metaphysics of Ordinary Experience

STANLEY H. ROSEN

Stanley H. Rosen is Borden Parker Bowne Professor of Philosophy as well as a University Professor at Boston University and Evan Pugh Professor Emeritus at Penn State University. His books include Plato's Symposium, Plato's Sophist, Nihilism, The Question of Being, *and* The Mask of Enlightenment: Nietzsche's Zarathustra, *as well as, more recently,* The Metaphysics of Ordinary Experience.

I

Everyday experience provides us with the only reliable basis from which to begin our philosophical reflections. Radical deviations from ordinary experience are indistinguishable from arbitrary constructions or even fantasies if they are not mediated by a careful exposition of their nature as responses to problems in everyday understanding. A construction having nothing to do with the everyday would, of course, be initially meaningless. Those who wish to begin their philosophical activity by an instantaneous departure from ordinary experience, as though they were shot from a pistol, as Hegel says of certain proponents of the absolute, must after all explain to us why and how they are justified in undergoing the immediate detachment in question. To take a prosaic example, the recommendation to employ a new technical language in order to clarify ordinary English is accomplished via a meta-linguistic exposition that is largely ordinary. To go to the other extreme, even Heidegger prepares his readers for the new type of thinking with a few introductory pages on the origination of genuine problems from the everyday experience of things and the manner in which we speak about them.

I want once more to emphasize that by calling attention to ordinary experience as the basis of philosophy, I do not mean to imply that extraordinary experience and discourse are to be excluded. To the contrary, the ordinary demands that we speak in extraordinary ways. Everyday life is never self-sufficient, but it is impossible to depart from it entirely, and furthermore: Would we understand what such a departure could mean? This may be illustrated indirectly by an example from literature. James Joyce's *Ulysses* presents a long excerpt from the stream of consciousness of a single person, Leopold Bloom, which looks initially like a radical departure from normal syntax and the relative semantical stability of everyday speech. Underneath the hyperbolic representation, however, is the point of the imitation itself; we take our bearings by the very fact that we know ourselves to be listening to the flow of Bloom's consciousness, a flow that is not homogeneous but that occurs at different levels and in different registers. Joyce, in other words, is making a point about human nature in its normal or everyday condition, which is itself the manifestation of the extraordinary. As an artist, Joyce explains indirectly by the act of representation, which is mimetic only in the sense that it presents the human soul by means of an artifact. The artifact distorts, exaggerates, adorns, and in countless ways transforms the ordinary original, but it does not deviate entirely from it or replace it with something uniquely other or entirely unintelligible.

Stated as simply as possible, an artistic construction is designed for two reasons: to enrich and to illuminate our ordinary experience and understanding. The work of art assists us in experiencing more than we would be capable of experiencing by ourselves. But it also sheds light on experience and thereby helps us to understand what we already know about ourselves. Whereas philosophical disquisitions may be inner elements in a work of art (as for example in Thomas Mann's *Magic Mountain*), the artwork itself is not a philosophical disquisition. Marianne Moore says that a poem must not mean but be. In my opinion, this is not quite correct, but it points us in the right direction. Of course, poems or novels have meanings, but they are presented indirectly as the silent penumbra of significance emanating from the illusion of direct experience, whether in word or deed. The long and brilliant reflection on art by the character Marcel in the last volume of Proust's *Remembrance of Things Past* can be read apart from its function within the novel, as though it were an essay in a philosophical periodical. But to do this would be to do violence to Proust's central intention, since the reflection emerges from the detailed experiences of his entire life, as transmuted by recollection within the soul of a person who is literally reconstructing himself by a long act of what one could call hermeneutical memory. The conclusions of this act are invalid apart from our own re-appropriation of the experiences from which they emerge, a re-appropriation that allows us to translate them into the terms of our own lives precisely because, at bottom, these terms are the same for every human being. They are the terms of ordinary experience. And they are not fully accessible except to the extraordinary speaker. But the extraordinary speech would be empty of genuine significance if it were not rooted in ordinary experience.

I have been trying to suggest a fundamental difference between art and philosophy. Art does not express discursively or conceptually its own function but instead fulfills it. To the extent that the artist shifts into philosophical discourse, he or she ceases to function as an artist, except in the cases just illustrated, in which the artist is representing a person as philosophizing. On the other hand, the artist may well be convinced of the superiority of art to philosophy and so (to employ my previous terms) of the superiority of illumination and enrichment to explanation. But we do not write poems or novels in order to explain the superiority of art to philosophy. In this case the "demonstration" of the artist is a pointing out or exhibiting of an instance of the ostensibly superior genre. But something is still missing here, even for the artist: an explanation of the superiority of one genre to the other. And the genre of explanation is philosophy.

Let no one take me to be on the way toward an attempted demonstration of the unqualified superiority of philosophy to art. I do not doubt that art, understood broadly, has an essential role to play within the philosophical activity. My intention is rather to identify that role. Stated somewhat more abstractly, I want to discuss the relation between seeing and making in everyday life, in the hope of casting light on the question of whether we construct, or play an active role in the constitution of, what we discover. In other words, I ask whether the world is an artifact of human perception and cognition, and therefore an art-work, or instead possesses a nature independent of but accessible to our cognitive powers. And if it is an artifact, is it different for each of us or the same for all? This investigation will require me to say something about the nature of truth.

If we cannot ascertain the difference between truth and falsehood, employing these terms in their broad, not their narrow or propositional senses, then there is no difference between a wise or informative artifact and an arbitrary simulacrum. But in this case, there is no difference between philosophy and art, and none between good and bad works of art. In short, if there is no philosophy, there is also no art, because at bottom the truth of an art-work depends upon its philosophical significance. A true work of art expands and illuminates our experience by its own devices, but the discursive appropriation of this expansion and illumination, upon which depends the identification of the truth or genuineness of the work in question, is philosophical. Without philosophy, it would make no sense to speak of a "good" as distinct from a "pleasant" artifact. If there is no valid distinction between good and bad pleasures, or what comes to the same thing, if pleasure is held to be the good, then goodness disappears into neurophysiology. As Socrates pointed out in the Philebus, one must reason correctly, and hence speak the truth, in order to establish the principle that the good is the pleasant. In sum: without the truth, art has nothing to teach us. The successful defense of truth by philosophy is therefore in the best interests of art as well.

Perhaps the central thesis toward which the following remarks are directed is this: the distinction between truth and falsehood depends in turn upon the distinction between seeing and making. Even if it should turn out that we constitute the world by our cognitive activities, the result must be visible in a way that is accessible in principle to everyone. We must be in a position to see what we make, and hence to speak truly about it; and by "truly" is meant in a way that explains something about our common experience. Nevertheless, in keeping with my usual procedure, I do not believe it would be wise to begin with a strict definition of truth. In introducing the notion of truth, I have tacitly appealed to "what everyone knows," and in particular to the question of the difference between art and philosophy, something which perhaps not everyone knows but which can be ascertained without formal or rigorous definitions of the truth-predicate.

The truth-predicate applies to propositions within a formalized language. I am aware of attempts by philosophers to transfer the work of Tarski and others on the formal predicate of truth to the domain of ordinary language, but I cannot see any point to these ventures. To express myself with excessive brevity, the meta-statement that "'snow is white' is true if and only if snow is white" amounts to the assertion that the predicate "is true" adds nothing to the assertion of the statement itself, since obviously the expression on the right-hand side of "if and only if" is itself either an assertion or a discursive representation in thought of a perceived or assumed fact. In other words, the assertion "snow is white" has exactly the same meaning or force as the assertion "the statement 'snow is white' is true." I have no reason to doubt this. But as Tarski himself presumably granted, one must understand English in order to apply the general criterion to any particular English statement. And if we understand English, we know more about the word "true" than the very slender information conveyed by the criterion just noticed. It is correct that we use "is true" to characterize statements that we believe to convey a state of affairs. I note in passing that it looks very much as if Tarski is committed to a correspondence theory of truth here; if this is so, his criterion is subject to the further difficulty that we must know that snow is white, and so that it would be true to say that snow is white, prior to the enunciation of the criterion in this particular case. In other words, it looks as though we know what "true" is implicitly whenever we apprehend a state of affairs, and only because of this implicit or intuitive knowledge are we able to define the term.

More important for my purposes, however, is the fact that Tarski's truth-definition is not a satisfactory basis for constructing a doctrine of truth for ordinary language. The sentence "snow is black" might be true in a poetic sense even though snow is white. Or to take another example, I might utter the statement "it's a beautiful day" ironically when I actually believe that the day is quite unpleasant. There are, in other words, other meanings of "true" than those illustrated by the meta-statement or paradigm. What, for instance, of "true" as "genuine"? It seems to me that in order to follow Tarski's procedure in the case of ordinary language, we would require a truth-criterion that corresponded to every use of "is true" in ordinary usage. But even if all these criteria could be formulated, how would we apply them? We could apply the correct criterion if and only if we knew which criterion actually applied in the given case. But if we know this, then the formulae are themselves redundant. We are using the language correctly on the basis of our understanding, not only of the language, but of life, that is, of when it is appropriate to say something rather than something else. Someone could know all the rules and still not know how to apply them; there are no rules for the application of rules.

Examples like "snow is white" are especially misleading because it seems a simple matter to determine its truth. After all, either snow is white or it is not white but, say, blue or red; and everyone knows the colors as well as what snow is. But what about sentences like "Machiavelli is evil" or "the quality of mercy is not strained"? I dare say that the statement "the quality of mercy is not strained" is true if and only if the quality of mercy is not strained. But what is mercy, and what is it for mercy not to be strained? What is the point of this apparently tautological procedure? We surely do not wish to say that sentences are true if and only if they correspond to the state of affairs that is their content. As I have already noted, we must first know that the correspondence in question obtains in order to designate it by a true statement. But how do we know this? Not by uttering a statement that itself corresponds to the state of affairs, since again, we should first have to know that the state of affairs obtains in order to construct such a sentence. But this is trivial.

The interesting fact is that "true" is an equivocal term and none the worse for it. It has a range of meanings from which the normal speaker of a natural language is usually able to select the one that is appropriate to the linguistic situation. There are of course exceptions; sometimes we make a mistake.

But the mistake is easily identified and corrected. And the linguistic mistakes cannot be legislated out of existence in advance, any more than the circumstances under which the individual meanings of "true" obtained can be defined in advance or codified by rules of correct usage. I am, however, very far from suggesting that we should not think as carefully as possible about truth. I believe that we can take at least one step toward a conceptual elaboration of the meaning of "true" in its everyday, as opposed to its formalist, uses. And we can do so in such a way as to bring out the relation between seeing and making. If this is so, then we shall at the same time be able to acquire a better understanding of the difference between art and philosophy.

Very frequently, if not always, we say that something is a true instance of a kind if it renders wholly visible the essential nature of that kind. By "wholly visible" I do not mean "in its entire structure" but rather "visible as a whole, and so identifiable as what it in fact is." A true believer is one who displays enough of the properties of a believer to allow us to pick out believers from non-believers with great accuracy. And this is so even if we are unable to define with complete rigor the "concept" of the believer. This incapacity is rooted in the ambiguous and equivocal nature of all or most concepts of everyday discourse, which we employ successfully not thanks to rules but because of our linguistic tact. What I said above about the equivocity of "true" holds good for a wide range of other terms, perhaps for all of them. What is from a formalist's standpoint a terrible defect of natural language is from the standpoint of everyday life a tremendous advantage. It is absolutely false to say that, unless we employ formalist analyses of language, we do not know what we are talking about. Rather, the reverse is the case. We do know what we are talking about (and how to correct errors when we make them) in ordinary language; we cease to be talking about anything in particular when we shift to a purely formal language, and so it becomes literally true that we do not know what we are talking about, unless of course we are talking about the symbols and syntax of the formal language itself. But this, however impressive from a technical standpoint, is not very useful either to the average citizen or to the philosopher.

The ability to speak a natural language is not grounded in rules but rather in the innate mastery of equivocity. And this in turn is not grounded in the mastery of syntax but in the ability to see what needs to be said as well as to discern what it is that someone means when he or she says something. All rules are a posteriori or ad hoc. The philosophy of language, very far from explaining how we speak meaningfully, is itself a product of our ability to see what ought to be said. I would myself go one step farther and say that there is, in principle, no explanation of how we see what we or others mean, if to explain is to analyze, that is, to break unities or syntheses into their component parts, and these again into simpler elements, until we arrive at something that resists analysis and that exhibits easily intelligible properties which we believe can be transferred upward through the increasingly complex levels of structure until we arrive at the totality or whole. This entire procedure is a waste of time because the unity of our mastery of equivocity, that is, the living intelligence, is no more a property of some set of psychological or neurophysiological elements than the properties of mass, charge, motion, and direction that characterize atomic particles are properties of the activities of my lived body, that is, the episodes of my life.

To come back now to "true" in the sense of "genuine:" I am proceeding by calling up examples before the mind's eye of my audience, not by formulating rules or defining configurations of symbols. When I spoke just now of a true believer, every person of normal intelligence and experience understood what I meant; and this understanding, although of course impossible without our access to a common language and culture, is not explained by these but rather expresses itself—brings itself into actuality—by producing them. A true believer is not an arbitrary cultural artifact but a phenomenon of the human soul. In the last analysis, it is by the spontaneous light of the human soul that we understand what we mean by "true believer," and so by "true." If this is metaphysics, then so be it.

When I say that a kind is wholly visible in a true instance, I do not mean that every essential property of the kind is clearly and distinctly visible. In fact, I am hesitant to employ the term "essential" here because I regard it as possible that we are able to recognize true instances even if we should turn out to be incapable of defining essences—and even if there are no essences of an eternal or temporally unchanging nature. I know when I am in the presence of a true, that is, genuine, scoundrel, even though I cannot define the essence "scoundrel." It is probably more straightforward to define expressions like "a genuine diamond" or even "a genuine tiger." (Here, we neglect old-fashioned worries about how Aristotle would respond to a three-legged tiger. The answer is that he would call it a defective or deformed tiger, for tigers have four legs by nature.) We run into special trouble when we try to explain exactly what we mean in describing persons or actions. Not to make too great a fuss about it, let me just say that this is because Nietzsche was right to call man the not yet fully constructed animal. Not yet fully, but hence partly; animal, not vegetable or mineral. This extraordinary feature of our natures—namely, that we are so to speak always "half-baked" or require further cooking—is closely connected to our mastery of equivocity. If univocity and determinateness were indispensable for meaning, then we could say nothing whatsoever about ourselves and so, by extension, about our relations to other entities.

In general, there are no univocal terms in natural language. But this is essential to communication, because there are also no univocal experiences or uniquely valid interpretations of experience. The capacity to select the correct sense of a crucial word for a given context depends upon the aforementioned mastery of equivocation. However, it does not lead to a destructive regress of interpretations, because the equivocity of meanings allows us to select the appropriate interpretation, and the mastery of equivocity allows our discursive partner to see what is intended. Confusion and misunderstanding can of course arise from the equivocal nature of empirical sense, but it can also be corrected; in the language of traditional hermeneutics, to *subtilitas legendi* there corresponds *Einfühlung*.

My examples are intended to suggest that the wholeness of truth in its everyday sense is partly imagined or inferred from the appropriate presentation of properties. We can see an entity in its wholeness thanks to the ability of the speaker to pick out a property or set of properties that evokes in the auditor the correct picture. It is not even necessary for the property in question to be essential; successful communication frequently transpires on the basis of accidental predications. It is precisely *subtilitas legendi* that enables us to select the property that is appropriate to the given discursive situation. In some situations, reference to an essential property would not work, for example in technical contexts in which the auditor is ignorant of the official terminology. Rigid univocity would preclude the possibility of understanding in these cases.

This makes immediately evident a crucial point in the relation between philosophy and art. The perception of wholeness, or, somewhat more precisely, the success of identification, is not simply the discovery of what is given by nature but depends upon the imaginative or productive capacity of the observer. On this point the advocates of hermeneutics are entirely correct. Philosophy no more records in language the rigid structure of beings than art photographs or rigidly copies the forms or natures of psychic states. No more; but by this I do not mean "not at all." There is an element of recording or copying rooted in our apprehension of what we wish to interpret. We must see in order to make. The wholeness of intelligibility, that is, the capacity to see a form or a formal structure, or a pattern of events, or the character of a human being even if we cannot identify every element in these totalities, functions by production as well as discovery.

If this is so, then discovery and production cannot be simply juxtaposed as the sources of philosophy and art respectively. Seeing and making function jointly in both philosophy and art, which, if they are to be distinguished at all, must be distinguished by some other criterion. I have been advocating the distinction between the explanation of the totality of experience on the one hand and the expansion and illumination of it on the other. I claim further that the root of these two modes of productive discovery is one and the same. The root is the living intelligence which has been represented most importantly here as the mastery of equivocation. We select the appropriate senses of the elements of our experience by an act of interpretation that in the case of artistic production can be likened to the telling of a story and in the case of philosophical discourse to an explanation of stories. A novel, a symphony, or a poem are distinct but related types of stories about some aspect of human existence. A philosophical speech spells out the significance of the story with respect to the wholeness of human life, and thus to the order of its defining aspects or dimensions. To this I add that something analogous, but not precisely the same, holds good of scientific theories. A theory of space and time is an articulated model or story about the inner structure of spatial and temporal phenomena. But the explanation of the significance of that inner structure for the totality of human life is philosophical discourse.

The last several paragraphs have been necessarily rather abstract; I want to get back to the everyday. In order to understand the distinction between seeing and making, or the relationship between philosophy and literature, we must begin, not with philosophy and literature themselves, but with the everyday experiences that give birth to these activities. I need, however, to make one more professorial remark. Despite the extensive criticism that I have directed elsewhere against such postmodernist movements as deconstruction, I do not reject outright the contention that the world is a text. This should have been evident from my discussion of hermeneutics as the mastery of equivocity. The world is a weaving together of discovering and making; we therefore participate in the process by which the "world" or "whole" emerges as a concrete determination of the horizon of intelligibility. Even what the Greeks called "cosmos" is an ordering suitable for human habitation. As such, it cannot be strictly synonymous with "nature" because neither in the Greek phusis nor in the modern senses of the term is nature suitable for human habitation without modification by human labor. The whole is an artifact to the extent that it is made to be visible by and for human beings only.

But this does not mean that the whole is unintelligible or that the task of understanding it is blocked by a vitiating equivocity of the discursively accessible senses of its elements. Equivocity is grounded in the unity of being. The different senses that one can attach to a horse in its relations to human beings do not succeed in transforming the horse into a dog. And the senses are themselves discernibly different because each preserves its own identity. I can make the same point in the language of textuality. A text cannot be woven together from sub-texts which are themselves webs of sub-sub-texts, and so on indefinitely. To anticipate a later point, a text is a story or the content of a

potential story, and stories are not about an infinite regression of other stories. At each level of story-telling (and such a level is defined by the telling
of an intelligible story) there are fixed points—things, persons, purposes,
events, actions, values—the meaning of which within the given story may
depend upon an integration of sub-stories, but an integration culminating in
a totality that functions as an element within the whole of the story of the
particular world, or part of the world, under inspection.

A true account of the world would be one that tells the whole story. The
whole story contains more or less detail. If we could tell no whole story
about the world as a whole, however general, then we could never tell a whole
story about a part. Many would say that this is precisely our fate, but this is
because they adhere to an unnecessarily strict conception of wholeness. I
remind you of my previous remark to the effect that we can see something
as a whole, for example a thing or a person, thanks to the apprehension of
appropriate properties, even when we cannot grasp the complete set of essential properties of the entity, assuming that such a set exists. In other words,
we can identify a human being as distinct from a tree, a rock, a scarecrow,
or an ape, as a fixed point of reference for the construction of an interpretation or story. There is nothing to argue about here; all arguments about the
ambiguity of natures, the inaccessibility or non-existence of essences, the
puzzles of sense-perception, and the endless variety of interpretations of
sense, are arguments about individual beings of precisely this sort of fixed
identity that we can say of them: the stories that can be told about this entity
here—this man, this woman, this dog, this star—are endless and conflicting. If this were not true, there would be no experience, not even equivocal
or ambiguous experience.

The demonstration of equivocity is rooted in the antecedent fixity of identifiable entities. As such, these entities are wholly accessible to a story about
their role in our experience. I mean by "wholly accessible" that we can tell a
story about a horse without fearing that it is actually a dog (or nothing at all).
But to tell a story is to fit something into a larger context; in fact, it is the
larger context of the world, or an ordering, however equivocal, of everything
we come upon. Nor can the ordering be so equivocal as to prevent us from
selecting from among candidates to the whole story. To summarize: experience just is the identification of wholes as fixed units capable of identification and (as Strawson puts it) reidentification. But it is the world or cosmos
as context of the presentation of entities to be identified and interpreted that
makes these fixed units accessible. We do not have experiences of a person
or animal in a vacuum void of all reference to anything else, but always within
a horizon, the openness of which is again dependent upon a total ordering,
even if the structure of this total ordering is not itself totally accessible.

The whole story, then, is the story of the world or cosmos within which human beings tell their tales. One could say that the whole story is itself a part of the whole, and the most important part, since it is as it were the last touch to the process by which the whole becomes a whole. But the whole is not simply or entirely an artifact of story-telling, because we cannot speak without seeing what we mean. Even if we produced every element of the whole by discursive cognition, we would still have to identify what we had produced in order to interpret it. Seeing would continue to play a co-ordinate role with making in the philosophical or artistic or scientific account of the world.

My qualified acceptance of the metaphor of the world as text is related to the thesis that the meaning of the world is elicited in, although it is not merely, a story. This in turn leads me to introduce the doctrine of authorial intentionality, as I shall call it. I mean by this that regardless of all subsequent modifications, a story is told by human beings to other human beings in order to accomplish an intention or to fulfill a purpose by the communication of meaning. The purpose is to achieve wholeness, in the sense of a correct ordering of activities or capacities to act; and by "correct" I mean conducive to the best life, which the Greeks described by the word eudaimonia. The stories that interest me primarily are those by which we attempt to complete our lives by rescuing them from meaninglessness. Nor am I concerned in the slightest by those who hold that only words have "meanings," or still more radically, that there are no meanings but only words. Since life as a whole is a text, that is to say, a whole that includes its own explanatory story, it is entirely appropriate to refer to the meaning of life, and so too to its equivocity.

Just as there are no meaningless experiences, so too there are no unintentional stories. What is meaningless cannot be experienced but only encountered; it remains external to the web of existence that we weave by incorporating meanings into stories. What is unintentional is not a story but meaningless chatter. Even the desire to entertain or to play is intentional. When these intentions extend to other persons, they become co-authors of the text. To speak of the text as having its own intentions is merely to animate it, that is, to take it as representing the author. Whereas texts, like the world, may exhibit divine intentions, these become meaningful for human beings only when incorporated into stories that we have ourselves composed. That a text has a multiplicity of possible readings follows from the equivocity of the senses of the words of which the text is composed; but the range of equivocity is narrowed by the intention of the author, which the reader's mastery of equivocity enables him or her to determine. Otherwise put, the multiplicity of readings is itself determined and regulated by a primary intention, without which no story can be told. Whereas stories can mean more than we intend, they cannot mean less; and if the minimal or regulative intention is indiscernible, then the story is incoherent, which is to say that it is no story at all. Finally, if one denies intentions altogether to the text, or rejects them as irrelevant to the task of interpretation, this is a covert way of replacing the author's intentions with those of the reader, or in other words it is to replace reading by writing. In this case there is no reading, and so there can be no verifiable way of referring to texts. There is then no writing but only scribbling, to which corresponds the chatter of meaningless interpretation.

II

What is it about our lives that causes us to weave together texts, whether these be subsequently identified as philosophy or literature? The answer I have suggested is as old as Plato, but I do not propose to defend it by textual exegesis of the orthodox or philological type. There is no point in reading a Platonic dialogue if it is not a true story (as opposed to a set of true propositions). Nor could we determine the truth of a Platonic story simply by reading or analyzing it. The reading must occur within the context of an ongoing inspection of the process of story-telling. It is in this process that we are presently engaged. I am telling a story about story-telling, but there is no danger of a vicious circle here, because this is how we learn what it is to tell a story, namely, by the activity itself. There are no rules or principles independent of the activity from which its nature is deducible. There are no a priori stories.

I begin with an expansion of my preliminary remark about intentionality. This is a much-discussed topic but we cannot avoid going over some familiar ground. Our goal is not originality but truth. The first point I want to make is simple and in a way obvious even though not easy to state. The difference between random or chaotic flux and identifiable change is that the latter is defined by a terminus. This point has nothing to do with metaphysical or theological doctrines of teleology; it bears upon the structure of intelligibility. A terminus is intrinsic to, and is the organizing principle of, the structurally constitutive elements of the change it defines. Termini are things, persons, events, relations, and so on: identifiable and reidentifiable elements of experience that serve as nodal points in stories. In a traditional vocabulary, we may call them subjects and predicates or substances and properties. As Aristotle might say, they are "this somethings" of "such and such a kind."

A change is identifiable to an observer at some stage in its development, a stage that may or may not be predictable in advance and which varies from observer to observer. Persons with different experiences and educations may recognize at different moments the identity of a process: the blooming of a rose or the gestures of a mime. Often an observer is unable to identify precisely the terminus of the change, as, for example, that a certain bloom is a hibiscus. But the identification of the process as a flower suffices for the terminus to be further specified in the varying contexts, scientific, aesthetic, and so on, of everyday life. We may look up the flower in an illustrated textbook or ask a specialist to identify it. And what is true of things is also true of events, as in the case of the mime's gestures. It may seem that one could speak directly of things and events rather than introducing the vocabulary of termini. But I wish to avoid basing my argument on the assumption that there are things or static substances independent of processes and multiple hermeneutical perspectives. A terminus is the fulfillment of a process in the sense just defined: we act with and speak about them. And thus we interpret them.

Each person is of course free to construct private variations on the public identities of things and events in the communal world of everyday life. But this freedom is not entirely spontaneous; it is grounded in the identities or termini themselves. And when we speak about a process rather than a terminus, we treat the process as a terminus. If we could not identify changes, there would be no improvisations, because to improvise is to say something new or unexpected about something that has already been, or could have been, identified in a customary manner. A story about a rose may differ sharply from the tale told by the horticulturist, but it is intelligible to an audience only because the rose has a public identity, one that is the same for all members of the audience and that serves as the basis for specialized identifications. This identity is the terminus of the change constituted for every normal speaker of English as a flower and, for many of these, as a rose. One could say by a metaphorical extension of traditional terminology that the process of the change in question intends the rose as its shaping terminus. (In doing so, I do not mean to imply that the process is self-conscious).

Once again, traditional language is appropriate here, provided that one does not take umbrage at the ontological implications of substance terminology. Just as a conscious state is a state of a certain sort, and a thought is a thought of a more or less determinate content, so too a change is of the kind identified by its terminus (or that we identify by identifying the terminus). I have already referred to the Socratic maxim, common to both Plato and Aristotle, and intrinsic to our discursive intelligence, that to be is to be something of such-and-such a kind. Though I accept this maxim as indisputable, I have tried to arrive at the same result by honoring the anti- Platonist assumption that experience is constituted by change rather than formal structure. The anti-Platonist thesis cannot account for everyday life without smuggling the Platonist thesis back into the story, for the simple and obvious reason that change is of something. Formless changes play no role in our experience. Whether the forms that undergo change are ontologically separate will depend upon what we mean by "separate." Certainly the process known as a rose is, qua process, separate from the experienced rose. It really makes no sense to say that we are experiencing (nothing but) processes, when everyone knows that we are experiencing processes of such-and-such a kind. But the kind simply is not reducible to the process; we do not experience blurs. It is not my particular intention here to defend Platonism, but I do want to point out that there is an interpretation of the so-called doctrine of Platonic Ideas that is compatible with process-philosophy or the principle of comprehensive change. Changes have looks, and this allows them to look like other looks. But the Idea is the look.

By analogous reasoning, I think we can easily see that it is impossible to make sense of our experience, or even to have any, unless we refer to the "nature" of a look or terminus. First we must distinguish between two senses of "nature." In the first sense, it refers to the order of properties that make the look what it is. In the second sense, it is distinguished from "art" or "convention" and refers to what shows itself or comes into existence independently of human work. Even if we literally make every element in our experience, what we make must have a nature, just as, even if everything in the world is a process or change, these processes or changes have looks. If I make a pear, it is not also a refrigerator. This is the technical sense in which we employ the term "nature," and its validity is independent of the second sense of the term.

Nevertheless, a few words on the second sense are not out of place. What does it mean to say "I make the pear by perceiving it"? I might very well interpret the pear in a way that depends not only upon its identity but also upon my imagination or special scientific interests. But this interpretation depends upon the presence of a pear to my apprehension. I can imagine a pear, but this in turn amounts to the "re-presentation" in thought of something that previously presented itself to me directly. To a Kantian, the form of the cognized pear is a result of the functions of the transcendental ego; but this is a philosophical doctrine about ordinary experience, not an account immanent to ordinary experience itself. In our analysis of ordinary experience, we are looking for evidence that will enable us to decide whether to accept or to reject doctrines like Kantianism.

Kant's arguments on this point have nothing to do with pears or any other empirical object (although he speaks once or twice of dogs and trees by way of illustrating his account of perception). Indeed, if one criticizes Kant on the basis of how we actually perceive pears, he will soon be attacked by outraged champions of the sage of Königsberg for having descended from the transcendental to the ontic or even empirical level. I have written extensively on this point in several other places, and do not wish to repeat my entire argument here. But I must say that a transcendental explanation of perception that cannot explain how we perceive pears, dogs, or trees is not terribly impressive. I leave the matter open for a later analysis of transcendental accounts of perception. Here we need to say only that there are not and cannot be transcendental accounts within ordinary experience. And whatever may be true of synthetic a priori propositions (if there are any), causal connections, or the concept of necessity, there is nothing in everyday perception to sustain the thesis that we make pears by perceiving them.

All theoretical accounts of perception, scientific or transcendental, start with the everyday perception of pears, dogs, and trees. They must justify themselves by the properties of ordinary perception and the problems that these properties raise. I am not now contending that there are no problems associated with ordinary perception, but rather that it is rooted in termini of processes, some of which we make and some of which we do not make but discover. The ordinary distinction between nature and art can be easily illustrated. A seed develops under the proper natural conditions into a flower. But a gardener can modify the result of germination by taking various steps, and a geneticist can make still more radical changes in the result of germination. The modifications imposed by the gardener and the geneticist onto the natural process of germination do not themselves make the seed, nor in a fundamental sense do they make the flower. In order for the modified flower to bloom, there must have been a seed to be modified. If the geneticist does not make the seed but finds it in the soil, then he is modifying nature but not replacing or creating it.

Is it possible for the geneticist to make the seed? I have no idea, but I am sure that if he could, he would have to employ natural materials at some early stage in order to produce it. In general, the identification of nature is altogether less problematic than in the example just given. We know what we do not make because making is intentional. One cannot make a seed simply by looking at the ground in order to admire the landscape or just to see what is there. I understand that sometimes our actions result unexpectedly or spontaneously in the production of something, but this is not making. In order to make something, we require a pattern or blueprint or what we call an idea of what we intend to make, as well as materials, instruments, training, and so on. To make is to employ all of these in such a way that, by directing our intelligence and skills toward the pattern or idea and the material, we can bring them together in a way that is a terminus of a process, a terminus that did not previously exist.

The terminus of a natural change, whether with respect to a particular instance or to nature as a whole, does not satisfy human intentionality merely by allowing things or processes to fulfill themselves. Nature compels us to provide additional discursively constructed termini beyond those which it produces by its own activity. There is then a disjunction within the continuity of nature, of which human being is the locus. Though humanity depends upon, and individual human beings exemplify, the integrity of natural change, something more is required. This requirement manifests itself in both deeds and speeches, but primarily in speeches. In order to survive, human beings must cultivate the soil, alter the course of streams and rivers, make clothing and build shelters, and thereby modify natural change by the productive arts. But deeds are not sufficient; the human animal is compelled by nature to talk, and, in particular, to tell stories. As I am arguing, we cannot exist as human beings without telling, or attempting to tell, the whole story.

Most of our speeches are addressed to local ends, for example, to the acquisition of the necessities of existence; some few address generalized versions of these local ends, such as the need for survival. A still smaller—but nevertheless significant—number of speeches go beyond this, and are intended as justifications or evaluations of life as a totality. Such speeches attempt to tell the whole story, not in its every detail, but with sufficient detail to make the overall pattern evident. These stories are directed by termini not furnished by nature in the second of the two senses just distinguished. This is the main reason why students of nature so frequently regard the stories as empty or excessively vague. And yet, one cannot criticize stories of this sort for vagueness without implicitly telling another such story: the story of what we may call the scientific world-view. The scientific world-view is not verified by the results of natural science; on the contrary, it is the former that directs us toward the pursuit of the latter by persuading us of the ultimate value of scientific truth. The difference between the story and the positive results of science is rooted in the fact that nature does not tell us how to live. On the contrary, we tell nature how we wish to live. Where nature seems to demur, we can devote ourselves to changing her through the mastery of scientific technique.

Within nature, termini are intrinsic to the processes of change. In the case of human action, termini are produced or projected, not spontaneously or *ex nihilo*, but in response to a natural appetite, either in itself or as modified by custom and imagination, and so as naturally intended but not naturally furnished. To take an example, a cosmological myth is neither the direct fulfillment of a natural change, nor does it stand to the cosmos as an image to an original. The myth is intended to provide a supplementary or discursive completeness to the cosmos, a completeness that the cosmos, to the extent that it exists independently of human speech, does not itself require. The requirement comes from us, or from what Socrates calls our Eros. I should say here that the origin of Eros is somewhat ambiguous; although Eros is a function of the human soul, it comes from above and raises us up by taking possession of us. This is why Socrates calls it a god or a daimon. For our present purposes, it will suffice to say that Eros mediates between human desire and divine completeness. It is therefore an essential ingredient, even when it is not explicitly mentioned, in every attempt to tell the whole story.

Eros, one could say, is the artist who produces the variety of speeches elicited by our contemplation of the cosmos. This variety includes such types as myth, poetry, religion, science, and philosophy. Each element in the variety is subject to its own sub-variations and improvisations. One speech elicits another. *Homo sapiens*, the talking animal, is also *Homo faber*, who is in the process of constructing himself as the hero in a cosmological drama. Such a drama is true if it displays the speech-telling nature as a whole. Phil-osphy is that form of speech whose stories are, or intend to be, self-reflexive or self-explanatory. That is, they intend not merely to display, but to bring to full articulateness, the speech-telling nature as a whole. This was the claim made on behalf of his own speeches by Hegel, whose *Science of Logic* claims to provide the complete structure of the Concept, the speech of speeches.

Hegel is to my knowledge the only philosopher who ever attempted to furnish a fully explicit demonstration of his wisdom, and so to prove that the philosophical life is not merely the highest by nature, but that it culminates in the accessibility of wisdom and even, by way of participation, in divinity. This account would be defective if it could be shown to fail to explain adequately one fundamental mode or another of human discourse. It is worth pausing to ask how one could falsify or verify Hegel's claim to have told the whole story. It is easy to suggest that the claim is outrageous and that new speeches are constantly being elicited by historical development, or more specifically that Hegel failed to anticipate certain fundamental developments in, say, science. But a neo-Hegelian might very well defend Hegel by moving to a higher level of generality. One could contend, in other words, that Hegel's account of totality must be understood at a sufficiently high level of generality as not to be affected by the discovery of additional planets in the solar system, or by quantum mechanics, or by empirical events in world history.

The problem in understanding Hegel is that it is not clear what it is that he is attempting to explain. If we put to one side his popular lectures on the history of philosophy, religion, art, and the philosophy of history, and restrict our attention to the major works, in particular the *Logic*, then one could reasonably argue that Hegel is not describing the concrete events in history or the particular discoveries in science, and so on, but rather the general process by which all types of change organize themselves into intelligible structures—thanks to the development and interplay of categories and their moments—an interplay that furnishes the common "pulse-beat" (Hegel's own phrase) of thinking and being, and so overcomes the separation between them. Let us assume that this is a correct interpretation of Hegel. Is there in fact a pulse-beat in thinking and being that is independent of the speeches told by Hegel to invoke its actuality? If there is not, then Hegel would seem to have produced the pulse-beat by the particular story he tells. But if there is, then it must also be independent of the stories told by anti-Hegelians, for otherwise it would have no existence or nature of its own, and we would never be in a position to verify or falsify ostensible descriptions of it. And in this case, how could we ever describe it? For every description would be a story about the pulse-beat, and as such, subject to criticism by competing stories. There is no objective or "purely scientific" way of arriving at the thematic content of philosophical stories, and if there were, then of course philosophy would be superfluous.

The strongest case to be made on Hegel's behalf is that he does produce the pulse-beat by describing it correctly, because his story is itself the last stage in its self-manifestation. It is not Hegel's personal story but the voice of the Absolute as incarnated in his discourse. This is as far as I need to go in describing Hegel's peculiar attempt to tell the whole story. It is instructive as a kind of substitute for science that suffers from attempting to be too scientific. Differently stated, Hegel asks us to disregard our ordinary view that works of art, historical events, political actions, and the like are all susceptible of differing interpretations. A story about the whole will succeed to the extent that it is able to take into account the valid claim of late-modern hermeneutical doctrines about the multiplicity of perspectives, a claim, incidentally, that is implicit in the nature of the Platonic dialogue.

Please note that to say that the world is intelligible in various ways is very far from saying that the world is unintelligible. Furthermore, the same problem is discernible at the heart of all interpretations, however diverse the one from the other. We are attempting to make sense of the totality of our experience, to reconcile the interpretations and perspectives with one another, to rise to a level of generality sufficiently great that what we see there illuminates the existence and nature of all perspectives: on this point Hegel was undoubtedly right. But it is at the beginning rather than at the end of this process that we tell the same story. It is our ordinary experience that provides us with the common basis for subsequent diversity in our explanations of the totality of human existence. The more subtle and the deeper our accounts, the more they diverge. I would never say that there is no standpoint from which one cannot see the rank-ordering of these divergent accounts. My point is rather that there is no way in which to persuade those who do not see as we do that our vision is the best. Those who think otherwise have committed the error of identifying thought with speech. But even if everyone could understand the comprehensive and wholly true speech about the whole, one would still have to see the whole; one would have to see what the speech intends to say, what it means. And this vision is no longer a matter of speech; it is not a meta-discourse, a totally inappropriate notion that leads to an infinite regress or to mere chatter, and so, ironically, to a different kind of silence.

Every perspective, in order to do its work, must be determinate and intelligible. But the difference in each perspective, that which defines it as this perspective and none of the others, is the produced or fictional element contributed by the artistic root of human nature in response to the work of the root of discovery. In a very general sense, at the level of what I am calling "ordinary experience" or "everyday life," all human beings see the same world and thus share the same perspective. Unfortunately, our attempts to grasp this communal perspective in conceptual speech result in the functioning of the productive element of cognition, and so in the steady replacement of the communal perspective by individual variations. I am attempting to articulate ordinary experience, not as the last stage in the process of telling the whole story, or in a vain effort to duplicate Hegelian science, but rather in order to make clear the first step in philosophy. And I do this, not because I believe that everyone will see the truth of my analysis, but because I regard it as in principle possible to achieve agreement sufficient to establish the self-founding of philosophy, and hence to rescue it from charges that it is dead, or that it never did and never could exist, or that we have finished with it and now dwell in a post- philosophical epoch. I have no pretensions of being able to tell the whole story; but I do wish to attempt to explain why we are forced to tell the whole story. And perhaps that in itself is the whole story.[1]

8

The Relativity of Fact and the Objectivity of Value

CATHERINE Z. ELGIN

Catherine Z. Elgin is Professor of the Philosophy of Education at Harvard Graduate School of Education. She has taught philosophy at Princeton, Dartmouth, MIT, and Wellesley. Her scholarly work focuses on issues of epistemology, philosophy of art, and philosophy of science. She is the author of Considered Judgment, Between the Absolute and the Arbitrary, *and* With Reference to Reference, *and co-author (with Nelson Goodman) of* Reconceptions in Philosophy and Other Arts and Sciences.

Fact and value purport to be polar opposites: facts being absolute, material, objective, and impersonal; values relative, spiritual, subjective, and personal; facts being verifiable by the rigorous, austere methods of science; values being subject to no such assessment. The facts, they say, don't lie. So every factual disagreement has a determinate resolution. Whether barium is heavier than plutonium is a question of fact; and whatever the answer, there are no two ways about it. Values, if they don't precisely lie, are thought perhaps to distort. So evaluative disputes may be genuinely irresolvable. Whether, for example, a Van Gogh is better than a Vermeer might just be a matter of opinion. And on matters like these, everyone is entitled to his own opinion. Such is the prevailing stereotype.

I believe that stereotype ought to be rejected; for it stifles our understanding of both fact and value. Far from being poles apart, the two are inextricably intertwined: the demarcation of facts rests squarely on considerations of value;

113

and evaluations are infused with considerations of fact. So factual judgments are not objective unless value judgments are; and value judgments are not relative unless factual judgments are. I want to suggest that tenable judgments of both kinds are at once relative and objective.[1]

First, let us look at the facts. When we proclaim their independence from and indifference to human concerns, we forget that we are the ones who set and enforce the standards for what counts as a fact. We stipulate: "a thing cannot both be and not be," or "no entity without identity," or "whatever is is physical." In effect we decree that whatever fails to satisfy our standards hasn't got what it takes to be a fact.

At the same time, we arrange for our standards to be met. We construct systems of categories that settle the conditions on the individuation of entities and their classification into kinds. Thus, for example, we devise a biological taxonomy according to which a dachshund is the same kind of thing as a Doberman, but a horse is a different kind of thing from a zebra.

For all their clarity, scientific examples may mislead. We are apt to think that constructing a biological taxonomy is simply a matter of introducing terminology for what is already the case. Then prior to our categorization, dachshunds and Dobermans were already alike; horses and zebras, already different. The problem is that any two things are alike in some respects and different in others. So likeness alone is powerless to settle matters of categorization. In classing dachshunds and Dobermans together, horses and zebras apart, we distinguish important from unimportant similarities. That is, we make a value judgment.

The selection of significant likenesses and differences is not, in general, whimsical. It is grounded in an appreciation of why a particular classificatory scheme is wanted; and this, in turn, depends on what we already believe about the subject at hand. If our goal is to understand heredity, for example, it is reasonable to group together animals that interbreed. Then despite their obvious differences, dachshunds and Dobermans belong together; and despite their blatant similarities, horses and zebras belong apart.

More general considerations come into play as well. If our system is to serve the interests of science, the cognitive values and priorities of science must be upheld. Membership in its kinds should be determinate and epistemically accessible. There should be no ambiguity and no (irresolvable) uncertainty about an individual's membership in a kind. The classification should be conducive to the formulation and testing of elegant, simple, fruitful generalizations, and should perhaps mesh with other scientific classifications of the same and adjacent domains. In constructing a system of categories suitable for science, then, we make factual judgments about what the values of science are, and how they can be realized.

Science streamlines its categories in hopes of achieving exceptionless, predictive, quantitative laws. Narrative has quite different ends in view, being concerned with the particular, the exceptional, the unique. So schemes suited to narrative enterprises exhibit different features from those suited to science. Scientific vices—ambiguity, imprecision, immeasurability, and indeterminacy—are often narrative virtues.[2] The complex characterization of the emotional life that we find, for example, in the novels of Henry James requires a baroque conceptual scheme whose involuted categories intersect in intricate and subtle ways. Equally complex categories may be required to achieve the sort of understanding that biographers, historians, psychoanalysts, and serious gossips strive to achieve.

A category scheme provides the resources for stating various truths and falsehoods, for exhibiting particular patterns and discrepancies, for drawing specific distinctions, for demarcating conceptual boundaries. Purposes, values, and priorities are integral to the design. They constitute the basis for organizing the domain in one way rather than another. The acceptability of any particular scheme depends on the truths it enables us to state, the methods it permits us to employ, the projects it furthers, and the values it promotes. Together, these constitute a system of thought. A failure of the components to mesh undermines the system, preventing it from doing what it ought to do.

We design category schemes with more or less specific purposes in mind and integrate into the scheme such values and priorities as we think will serve those purposes. But the values that our schemes realize are not always or only the ones we intend to produce. Some are simply mistakes; others, inadvertent holdovers from prior systems; yet others, unintended byproducts of features we intentionally include. When pregnancy and aging are classified as medical conditions, they come to be considered and treated as diseases or disabilities—as deviations from a state of health. If Marx is right, the values of the ruling class are invisibly embedded in the social and economic categories of a society. And my students are convinced that a fundamental truth is revealed by the fact that witchcraft comes just after philosophy in the Library of Congress classification system.

As a first approximation, facts are what answer to true sentences. And different systems produce different truths. It is a truth of physics, not of botany, that copper is lighter than zinc. This alone does not lead to relativity, for such systems may complement one another, or be indifferent to one another. Relativity emerges when systems clash—when what is true according to one system is false according to another. Evolutionary taxonomy so groups animals that crocodiles and lizards are close relatives; crocodiles and birds, distant ones. Cladistic classification shows crocodiles and birds to be close; crocodiles and lizards distant. Each system divulges some affinities among animals and obscures others: neither invalidates the other. So whether it is a fact that crocodiles and lizards are closely related depends on a choice of system. According to a one system, any violation of the law is a crime; according to another, only serious violations—felonies—are crimes. So whether spitting on the sidewalk is a crime depends on which system is in use. According to one medical classification, health is the absence of disease; according to another, health is the absence of disease or disability. So whether a congenital defect renders a person unhealthy depends on which system is in effect. A single domain can be organized in a multitude of ways, and different schematizations may employ a single vocabulary. So under one schematization a given sentence—say, "Spitting on the sidewalk is a crime"—comes out true; under another, it comes out false. Truth then is relative to the system in effect.

Still, facts are objective. For once the system is in place, there is no room for negotiation. Events that are simultaneous relative to one frame of reference are successive relative to another. But it is determinate for each frame of reference whether given events are successive or simultaneous. Similarly, although some psychologistic systems consider neuroses to be mental illnesses and others do not, once a system is chosen, there is a fact of the matter as to whether a compulsive hand washer is mentally ill.

Such objectivity might seem spurious, if we can switch frameworks at will. What is true according to one framework is false according to another. So can't we just choose our facts to fit our fantasy? There are at least two reasons why we can't. The first is that rightness requires more than truth.[3] We need to employ an appropriate framework—one that yields the right facts. The fact that someone went to Choate, for example, neither qualifies nor disqualifies him for a federal judgeship. So a classification of candidates according to their secondary schools is inappropriate, even if it would enable us to choose the candidate we want. Correctness requires that the facts to which we appeal be relevant. Psychoanalytic categories are powerless to settle the issue of criminal insanity because they mark the wrong distinctions. People who cannot be held criminally liable for their actions are supposed to be, in some important respect, different from the rest of us. And the categories in question reveal no difference; for they characterize everyone's behavior in terms of motives and desires that the agent can neither acknowledge nor control. So the facts that psychoanalytic theory reveals do not suit the purposes of the criminal court; they do not discriminate the class of criminally insane. Rightness of categorization thus depends on suitability to a purpose. An aspiring lepidopterist whose collection consists of larvae seems to have missed the point. Lepidopterists concentrate on mature forms—they collect butterflies, not caterpillars. Although biologists class butterflies and caterpillars together, butterfly collectors do not. Rightness here requires fit with past prac-

tice. The fellow fails as a lepidopterist because he employs radically nontraditional categories in selecting specimens for his collection.

Moreover, even though we construct the categories that fix the facts, we
cannot construct whatever we want. If we take the notion of construction seriously, this will come as no surprise. Although we make all manner of inven-
tions, we can't make a non-fattening Sacher Torte, a solar-powered subway,
or a perpetual motion machine. And although we design programs that endow
computers with amazing abilities, we can't get a computer to translate a natural language, compute the last digit in the number π, or beat a grand master at chess.

Some of these incapacities are irremediable; others will eventually be
overcome. My point in mentioning them is to emphasize that construction is
something we do; and we can't do everything we want. Our capacities are
limited; and our aspirations often interfere with one another. So there is no
reason to think that we can convert any fantasy into fact by designing a suitable system. Plainly, we cannot.

In constructing a political system, for example, we'd like to maximize
both personal liberty and public safety. We'd like, that is, to arrange for as
many actions as possible to fall under the predicate "free to . . ." and as many
harms as possible to fall under the predicate "safe from . . ." But we can't
maximize both at once. The cost of security is a loss of liberty; and the cost
of liberty, a risk of harm. With the freedom to carry a gun comes the danger
of getting shot. So we have to trade the values of liberty and safety off against
each other to arrive at a system that achieves an acceptable level of both.

In constructing a physicalistic system, we'd like all the magnitudes of ele-
mentary particles to be simultaneously determinate and epistemically accessible. But this is out of the question. For although we can measure either the
position or the momentum of an electron, we can't measure both at once.

In building a system of thought, we begin with a provisional scaffolding
made of the (relevant) beliefs we already hold, the aims of the project we are
embarked on, the liberties and constraints we consider the system subject to,
and the values and priorities we seek to uphold. We suspend judgment on
matters in dispute. The scaffolding is not expected to stand by itself. We anticipate having to augment and revise it significantly before we have an acceptable system. Our initial judgments are not comprehensive; they are apt to be
jointly untenable; they may fail to serve the purposes to which they are being
put, or to realize the values we want to respect. So our scaffolding has to be
supplemented and (in part) reconstructed before it will serve.

The considered judgments that tether today's theory are the fruits of yes-
terday's theorizing. They are not held true come what may, but accorded a
degree of initial credibility because previous inquiry sanctioned them. They

are not irrevisable, but they are our current best guesses about the matter at hand. So they possess a certain inertia. We need a good reason to give them up.[4]

System-building is dialectical. We mold specific judgments to accepted generalizations, and generalizations to specific judgments. We weigh considerations of value against antecedent judgments of fact. Having a (partial) biological taxonomy that enables us to form the generalization "like comes from like"—that is, progeny belong to the same biological kind as their parents—we have reason to extend the system so as to classify butterflies and caterpillars as the same kind of thing. Rather than invoke a more superficial similarity and violate an elegant generalization, we plump for the generalization and overlook obvious differences.

Justification is holistic. Support for a conclusion comes not from a single line of argument, but from a host of considerations of varying degrees of strength and relevance. What justifies the categories we construct is the cognitive and practical utility of the truths they enable us to formulate, the elegance and informativeness of the accounts they engender, the value of the ends they promote. We engage in system–building when we find the resources at hand inadequate.[5] We have projects they do not serve, questions they do not answer, values they do not realize. Something new is required. But a measure of the adequacy of a novelty is its fit with what we think we already know. If the finding is at all surprising, the background of accepted beliefs is apt to require modification to make room for it; and the finding may require revision to be fitted into place. A process of delicate adjustments occurs, its goal being a system in wide reflective equilibrium.[6]

Considerations of cognitive value come into play in deciding what modifications to attempt. Since science places a premium on repeatable results, an observation that cannot be reproduced is given short shrift, while one that is readily repeated may be weighted so heavily that it can undermine a substantial body of theory. A legal system that relies on juries consisting of ordinary citizens is unlikely to favor the introduction of distinctions so recondite as to be incomprehensible to the general public.

To go from a motley collection of convictions to a system of considered judgments in reflective equilibrium requires balancing competing claims against one another. There are likely to be several ways to achieve an acceptable balance. One system might, for example, sacrifice scope to achieve precision; another, trade precision for scope. Neither invalidates the other. Nor is there any reason to believe that a uniquely best system will emerge in the long run.

To accommodate the impossibility of ascertaining both the position and the momentum of an electron, drastic revisions are required in our views about physics. But which ones? A number of alternatives have been suggested. We might maintain that each electron has a determinate position and a determinate momentum at every instant, but admit that only one of these magnitudes can be known. In that case, science is committed to the existence of things that it cannot in principle discover. Or we might contend that the magnitudes are created in the process of measurement. Then an unmeasured particle has neither a position nor a momentum, and one that has a position lacks momentum, since the one measurement precludes the other. Physical magnitudes are then knowable because they are artifacts of our knowledge-gathering techniques. But from the behavior of particles in experimental situations, nothing follows about their behavior elsewhere. Yet a third option is to affirm that a particle has a position and affirm that it has a momentum, but deny that it has both a position and a momentum. In that case, however, we must alter our logic in such a way that the conjunction of individually true sentences is not always true. That science countenances nothing unverifiable, that experiments yield information about what occurs in nature, that logic is independent of matters of fact—such antecedently reasonable theses are shown by the findings of quantum mechanics to be at odds with one another. Substantial alterations are thus required to accommodate our theory of scientific knowledge to the data it seeks to explain. Although there are several ways of describing and explaining quantum phenomena, none does everything we want. Different accommodations retain different scientific desiderata. And deciding which one to accept involves deciding which features of science we value most, and which ones we are prepared, if reluctantly, to forego. "Unexamined electrons have no position" derives its status as fact from a judgment of value—the judgment that it is better to construe magnitudes as artifacts of measurement than to modify classical logic, or commit science to the truth of claims it is powerless to confirm, or to make any of the other available revisions needed to resolve the paradox.

Pluralism results. The same constellation of cognitive and practical objectives can sometimes be realized in different ways, and different constellations of cognitive and practical objectives are sometimes equally worthy of realization. A sentence that is right according to one acceptable system may be wrong according to another.

But it does not follow that every statement, method, or value is right according to some acceptable system. Among the considered judgments that guide our theorizing are convictions that certain things—for instance, affirming a contradiction, ignoring the preponderance of legal or experimental evidence, or exterminating a race—are just wrong. Such convictions must be respected unless we find powerful reasons to revise them. There is no ground for thinking that such reasons are in the offing. It is not the case that anything goes.

Nor does it follow that systems can be evaluated only by standards that they acknowledge. An account that satisfies the standards it sets for itself might rightly be faulted for being blind to problems it ought to solve, for staking out a domain in which there are only trivial problems, for setting too low standards for itself. An inquiry that succeeds by its own lights may yet be in the dark.

So far, I have argued for the value-ladenness of facts. I developed a scientific example in some detail, because science is considered a bastion of objectivity. If scientific facts can be shown to be relative and value laden, there is a strong *prima facie* case for saying that relativity and value-ladenness do not undermine objectivity. Then, if the objectivity of normative claims is to be impugned, it must be on other grounds.

I want to turn to questions of value. Not surprisingly, I contend that value judgments are vindicated in the same way as factual judgments. Indeed, normative and descriptive claims belong to the same systems of thought, and so stand or fall together. Still, some systems seem more heavily factual; others, more heavily evaluative. For now, I will concentrate on the latter.

In constructing a normative category scheme, as in constructing any other scheme, we are guided by our interests, purposes, and the problem at hand. Together these factors organize the domain so that certain considerations are brought to the fore. In restructuring the zoning laws, for example, it is advisable to employ consequentialist categories. For we need the capacity to tell whether things would in fact improve if the building code were altered in one way or another. We need then the capacity to classify and to evaluate in terms of outcomes. If we are concerned with developing moral character, it may be advisable to use predicates that can be applied with reasonable accuracy in self-ascription; for the capacity for self-scrutiny is likely to be valuable in moral development.

For like cases to be treated alike, the evaluations yielded by a moral or legal system must be coherent, consistent with one another, and grounded in the relevant facts. Fairness and equity are demanded of such a system; arbitrariness and caprice are anathemas to it. So logical and evidential constraints are binding on evaluation as well as on description.

The problems we face and the constraints on their solution often have their basis in the facts. Whether, for example, we ought to perform surgery to prolong the life of a severely defective newborn becomes a problem only when we acquire the medical resources to perform such surgery. Prior to the development of the medical techniques, the question was moot. There was no reason to require a moral code to provide an answer. So a moral problem arises in response to changes in the facts.

Our previously acceptable moral code may never have needed, and so never have developed, the refinements required to handle the new case. Unanticipated facts can thus put pressure on a system, by generating problems it cannot (but should) solve, yielding inconsistent evaluations, or producing counterintuitive verdicts. Values that do not ordinarily clash may do so in special circumstances. Typically the physician can both prolong the lives of her patients and alleviate their pain. But not always. So a moral system that simply says she ought to do both is inadequate. It does not tell her how to proceed when the realization of one value interferes with the realization of the other. Our values then need to be reconsidered. In the reconception, previously accepted conclusions are called into question, competing claims adjudicated, a new balance struck. Our goal again is a system of considered judgments in reflective equilibrium. Achieving that goal may involve drawing new evaluative and descriptive distinctions or erasing distinctions already drawn, reordering priorities or imposing new ones, reconceiving the relevant facts and values or recognizing new ones as relevant. We test the construction for accuracy by seeing whether it reflects (closely enough) the initially credible judgments we began with. We test it for adequacy by seeing whether it realizes our objectives in theorizing. An exact fit is neither needed nor wanted. We realize that the views we began with are incomplete, and suspect that they are flawed; and we recognize that our initial conception of our objectives is inchoate, and perhaps inconsistent. So we treat our starting points as touchstones which guide but do not determine the shape of our construction.

Here too, pluralism results; for the constraints on construction do not guarantee a unique result. Where competing considerations are about equal in weight, different tradeoffs might reasonably be made, different balances struck. If any system satisfies our standards, several are apt to do so.

In child rearing, for example, we regularly have to balance concern for a child's welfare against the value of granting him autonomy. Responsible parents settle the matter differently, some allowing their children greater freedom, some less. A variety of combinations of permissions and prohibitions seem satisfactory, none being plainly preferable to the rest. It follows then that a single decision—say, to permit a child to play football—might be right or wrong depending on which acceptable system is in effect. Rightness is then relative to system.

But it does not follow that every act is right according to some acceptable system or other. It is irresponsible to permit a toddler to play with matches, and overprotective to forbid a teenager to cross the street. From the fact that several solutions are right, it does not follow that none is wrong. Some proposed resolutions to the conflict between welfare and autonomy are plainly out of bounds.

Nor does it follow that to be right according to some acceptable system is to be right *simpliciter*. Rightness further requires that the system invoked be appropriate in the circumstances. Although my freshmen's papers would rightly be judged abysmal failures if evaluated according to the editorial standards of the *Journal of Philosophy*, those are clearly the wrong standards to use. To grade my students fairly, I must employ standards appropriate to undergraduate work. (Then only some of their papers are abysmal failures).

Can we rest satisfied with the prospect of multiple correct evaluations? Disconcertingly, the answer varies. If the systems that produce the several evaluations do not clash, there is no difficulty. We easily recognize that an accurate shot by an opposing player is good from one point of view (excellence in playing the game) and bad from another (our partisan interest that the opposition collapse into incompetence). And there is no need to decide whether it is a good or bad shot all things considered.

In other cases, multiplicity of correct evaluations may be rendered harmless by a principle of tolerance. We can then say that what is right according to any acceptable system is right. Thus one parent's decision on how best to balance paternalist and libertarian considerations in child rearing does not carry with it the commitment that all parents who decide otherwise are wrong. And one physician's decision on how to balance the value of alleviating pain against the value of prolonging life does not carry with it the commitment that all physicians who strike a different balance are wrong.

Tolerance is an option because the prescriptions for action apply to numerically distinct cases. So long as parents decide only for their own children and both parents agree about that, they can recognize that other parents might reasonably decide the same matters somewhat differently. Pluralism does not lead to paralysis here because the assignment of responsibility is such that conflicting right answers are not brought to bear on a single case.

Tolerance seems not to be an option, however, when systems dictate antithetical responses to a single case. For we must inevitably do one thing or another. The problem becomes acute in socially coordinated activity. If the several parties in a joint venture employ clashing systems, their contributions are likely to cancel each other out, diminishing the prospect of success. Although nothing favors the convention of driving on the right side of the road over that of driving on the left, leaving the choice to the individual driver would be an invitation to mayhem. We need then to employ a single system, even if the selection among acceptable alternatives is ultimately arbitrary.

In such cases, then, we invoke a metasystematic principle of intolerance. Even if there are several ways of equilibrating our other concerns, we mandate that an acceptable equilibrium has not been reached until a single system is selected. The justification for this mandate is the recognition that unanimity or widespread agreement is itself a desideratum that is sometimes worth considerable sacrifice to achieve.

To be sure, an intolerant system remains vulnerable to criticism, revision, and replacement by a better system. The argument for intolerance is simply that where divided allegiance leads to ineffectiveness, a single system must reign. Successors there can be, but no contemporaries.

In the cases I've spoken of so far, both tolerance and intolerance look like fairly easy options. We readily agree to be intolerant about rules of the road, not only because we appreciate the value of conformity in such matters, but also because we recognize that nothing important has to be given up. It simply doesn't matter whether we drive on the left or on the right, so long as we all drive on the same side. And we readily tolerate a range of child–rearing practices, because so long as certain broad constraints are somehow satisfied, small differences don't much matter. The difference between a 10 P.M. curfew and a 10:30 one is unlikely to significantly affect a child's well-being. In such cases we can agree, or respectfully agree to disagree, precisely because no deeply held convictions are violated in the process.

Sometimes, however, conflicts run deep. For example, the abortion problem arises because in an unwanted pregnancy, the value of personal autonomy clashes with the value of fetal life. Neither is trivial. So to achieve any resolution, a substantial good must be sacrificed. Each party to the dispute achieves equilibrium at a price the other is unwilling to pay: the one maintaining that even fetal life cannot compensate for the loss of liberty, the other maintaining that even liberty cannot compensate for the loss of fetal life. Nor can the parties civilly agree to disagree. For each is convinced that the position of the other is fundamentally immoral.

Both parties to the dispute can adduce powerful reasons to support their position. But neither has the resources to convince its opponents. Nor has anyone come up with a compromise that both sides can in good conscience accept.

The existence of such seemingly intractable problems might seem to support a subjective ethical relativism. Having found no objective way to resolve such dilemmas, we might conclude that all morality is relative to system, and the choice of a system is, in the end, subjective.

Without denying the difficulty that such problems pose, I want to resist the slide into subjectivism. Our practice bears me out. Even in the face of widespread disagreement, we do not treat such issues as subjective. If we did, we would probably be more charitable to those holding opposing views. How do we proceed?

Sometimes we deny that the problem remains unsolved. We contend that one of the positions, although still sincerely held, has actually been discredited. The holdouts, we maintain, overlook some morally relevant features of the situation, or improperly weigh the relevant ones. This response may well be correct. Advocates of Apartheid, however adamant, are just wrong. And they remain wrong even if they are too ignorant, biased, or stupid to recognize it.

So the failure of an argument to convince its opponents may be due to defects in their understanding, not to weaknesses in the argument. This has its parallel in science. The inability of any argument to convince my accountant of the truth of the Heisenberg Uncertainty Principle does not discredit the objectivity of the principle; it discredits her claim to have mastered quantum mechanics.

Alternatively, we might concede that a question is unanswered, without concluding that it is unanswerable. We then take it to be an outstanding problem for the relevant field of inquiry. All fields have such problems. And if our current inability to solve the problem of the origin of life does not impugn the objectivity of biology, our current inability to solve the problem of euthanasia should not impugn the objectivity of ethics. What such disagreements show is that work remains to be done. This is no surprise.

The objectivity of ethics does not ensure that we can answer every question. Neither does the objectivity of science. If a question is ill conceived or just too hard, or if our attempts are wrong-headed or unlucky, the answer may forever elude us. That success is not guaranteed is just an epistemological fact of life.

Nor does objectivity ensure that every properly conceived question has a determinate answer. So perhaps nothing determines whether the young man whom Sartre describes ought to join the Resistance or stay home and care for his aged mother.[7] If the relevant considerations are in fact equally balanced, either alternative is as good (or as bad) as the other. The choice he faces then is subjective. But this does not make ethics subjective. For to say that personal predilections are involved in deciding among equally worthy alternatives is quite different from saying that personal predilections are what make the alternatives worthy. Subjective considerations function as tie-breakers after the merit of the contenders has been certified by other means.

I have suggested that factual and evaluative sentences are justified in the same way. In both cases, acceptability of an individual sentence derives from its place in a system of considered judgments in reflective equilibrium. Since equilibrium is achieved by adjudication, several systems are apt to be adequate. But since they are the products of different tradeoffs, they are apt to disagree about the acceptability of individual sentences. So relativism follows from pluralism. Something that is right relative to one acceptable system may be wrong relative to another.

Still, the verdicts are objective. For the systems that validate them are themselves justified. The accuracy of such a system is attested by its ability to accommodate antecedent convictions and practices; its adequacy, by its ability to realize our objectives. Several applicable systems may possess these abilities; so several answers to a given question, or several courses of action may be right. But not every system possesses them; so not every answer or action is right. The pluralism and relativism I favor thus do not lead to the conclusion that anything goes. If many things are right, many more remain wrong.[8]

9

Rethinking Progress:
A Kantian Perspective

MARC SCHATTENMANN

Marc Schattenmann is Associate Director of the Public Policy School Project at the University of Erfrot, Germany. He was a Visiting Fellow in the Department of Philosophy at Harvard during the 1999–2000 academic year. He is currently writing a dissertation on Kant's political philosophy.

Why think about progress? In this chapter, I try to show that we have good reasons to think about progress—if we do it the right way. I will defend this claim by examining Immanuel Kant's theory of progress. Kant dealt with the issue of progress in numerous writings, especially in *Idea for a Universal History with a Cosmopolitan Purpose* (1784), *What Is Enlightenment?* (1784), *On the Common Saying: 'That May Be correct in Theory, but It Is of No Use in Practice'* (1793), *Perpetual Peace* (1795), and the Second Part of *The Contest of the Faculties*, entitled "A Renewed Attempt to Answer the Question: Is the Human Race Continually Improving?" (1798).[1]

This chapter explores Kant's theory of political progress in order to show its systematic connection with his theoretical and practical philosophy and its importance for his normative philosophy of politics. In particular, I stress four points that have often been neglected or misrepresented:

1. Kant's theory of progress is an integral part of his philosophical system. (This claim is part of an argument among Kant scholars.)

2. Kant's view of progress is realistically utopian. (This claim is directed against the so-called "Realists" in political theory and international relations theory.)

3. Kant's notion of progress is essentially anti-deterministic. (This claim is directed against the followers of Hegel.)

4. The progress of humanity does not depend on the moral progress of individuals. (This claim is directed against the followers of Marx.)

1 The Role of Progress: Saving Morality

Kant's theory of progress has usually been criticized along two lines. One line of criticism considers Kant a prime example of the naive belief in progress supposedly typical of the Enlightenment. The other line maintains that, whatever its merits, Kant's theory of progress is not part of the critical enterprise undertaken by the *Critique of Pure Reason*, the *Critique of Practical Reason* and the *Critique of Judgment*. A representative of the first line of criticism is Paul Natorp, one of the editors of Kant's works for the Prussian Academy. In his 1924 book *Kant über Krieg und Frieden. Ein geschichtsphilosophischer Essay*, Natorp states that "the belief in the progress of humanity, which even the critically minded Kant had not yet given up entirely, has vanished almost to its last remains." Natorp concludes on a pessimistic note: "In the end, it was Kant's fundamental mistake that he . . . did not decide to discard the question: What may we hope of the future of mankind?"[2] The second line of criticism is embraced by Théodore Ruyssen in his 1962 article, "La philosophie de l'Histoire selon Kant." Ruyssen considers it "artificial" to regard Kant's smaller writings on history and politics as a corollary of his critical philosophy. He adds: "Commentators of Kant have asked themselves nevertheless in what measure his philosophy of history is connected to the critical system taken as a whole; a legitimate research, for sure, but one that, in regard of Kant, seems to us in vain."[3]

I will argue that both criticisms are mistaken. Kant's theory of progress is not the expression of a naive optimism. Furthermore, it is an essential and indispensable part of his moral philosophy. Kant is realistic enough to know that progress is far from being inevitable. But in order to save his moral philosophy from being imaginary, he has to show that progress is at least possible.

Although the word "progress" is not used in the *Critique of Pure Reason*, this work lays the ground for the theory of progress that Kant develops in his later writings. In a section entitled "On the ideal of the highest good, as determining ground of the ultimate end of pure reason," Kant writes:

All interest of my reason (the speculative as well as the practical) is united in the following three questions: 1. What can I know? 2. What should I do? 3. What may I hope? (C1 A, pp. 804f / B, pp. 832f)

He then goes on to explain briefly the meaning of those questions. About the third he says:

The third question, namely 'if I do what I should, what may I then hope?' is simultaneously practical and theoretical, so that the practical leads like a clue to a reply to the theoretical question. . . . For all hope concerns happiness, and with respect to the practical and the moral law it is the very same as what knowledge and the natural law is with regard to the theoretical cognition of things. The former finally comes down to the inference that something is (which determines the ultimate final end) because something ought to happen; the latter, that something is (which acts as the supreme cause) because something does happen. (C1 A, pp. 805f / B, pp. 833f; emphasis deleted)

This passage indicates the link between Kant's practical philosophy and his theory of progress that provides the key for an understanding of the latter. The link becomes clear through the way in which Kant rephrases the third question of reason. At first, it read simply: "What may I hope?" Rephrased, it reads: "If I do what I should, what may I then hope?" This new formulation makes clear that the third question is connected to the second question and somehow follows from it. But how exactly does "What may I hope?" (a question about the future) follow from "What should I do?" (the question of morality)? What is the nature of this connection?

At first glance, the connection might seem to be only psychological. As Kant says in *Religion within the Boundaries of Mere Reason*: "it is one of the inescapable limitations of human beings and their practical faculty of reason . . . to be concerned in every action with its result, seeking something in it that might serve them as an end" (*Religion* VI, p. 7). It is characteristic of humans that we are not content with knowing what we should do. We also want to know what will come of our actions if we do what we should, what gains and benefits we can expect. We want to know why we should try to live up to the standards of the moral law, and we want an answer more inspiring than, "because it's the law."

The problem with this psychological link between the demands of the moral law and our aspirations and hopes is that it may be too weak. Are we really justified in asking all those questions about the outcome of our moral actions? Are we not just acting like donkeys who won't start to run until they have a carrot dangling before their eyes? We certainly have a tendency to ask all those questions—but maybe we are just looking for a pleasant answer that hides an unpleasant truth about our lives.

Fortunately, we don't have to rely on this psychological connection. According to Kant, it is not only a psychological necessity but also an analytical truth, "indeed undeniable," that "every volition must have an object" (C2 V, p. 34). As volition (*Wollen*) must have an object, so must the will (*Wille*). Even the perfectly good will, that is, the will that is entirely determined by the moral law and not by some object, has an object: the idea of the highest good (C2 V, p. 122). To use the donkey metaphor again: Even if we don't run *because* of the carrot, there is nonetheless a relation between action and reward here, such that the carrot still is, in some sense, the "goal" of running. In abstract terms: If a specific formal procedure leads to a specific material end, this end is the object of the procedure, even if the procedure is carried out only for formal reasons. Thus, even if the moral law has to be followed only for its own sake alone, it still has an object. This object is called the highest good.

This conceptual connection between morality and its object gives us the answer to the third question of reason. If the answer to "What should I do?" is "You should follow the moral law!," then the answer to "If I do what I should, what may I hope for?" must be: "You may hope for the highest good!" But how can Kant say that? How can he say: "You may hope for the highest good?"

Kant's answer is based on the following chain of reasoning:

1. Morality can only require the possible: Ought implies Can.

2. The object of morality is the highest good.

3. Therefore: If morality is possible, achievement of the highest good must be possible too.

4. A fact of reason tells us that morality is possible.

5. Therefore: Achievement of the highest good must be possible.

6. Achievement of the highest good is possible if the conditions hold under which it is possible.

7. As achievement of the highest good must be possible (V. 5); the conditions must hold under which achievement of the highest good is possible.

Anyone familiar with Kant's moral philosophy will have recognized this type of reasoning: it is an argument for postulates of practical reason. By a postulate of pure practical reason, Kant understands "a *theoretical* proposition, though one not demonstrable as such, insofar as it follows as an inseparable corollary from an a priori unconditionally valid *practical* law" (C2 V, p. 122). Postulates of practical reason formulate the conditions under which a priori valid practical laws become meaningful. As the practical laws are intrinsically connected with the idea of the highest good, postulates of practical reasons are at the same time the conditions necessary for the achievement of the highest good. What are these conditions?

Before I can spell them out, I have to introduce a distinction concerning the term 'highest good'. As we have seen, the highest good is the object of morality. But according to Kant, morality has two branches: Ethics and Right. Ethics deals with individual morality, or virtue, while Right deals with public morality, or justice. In both branches of morality, the idea of the highest good is the focal point where the requirements of morality and the object of human aspirations converge. In Ethics, this is the convergence of virtue and happiness (C2 V, p. 110). In Right, it is the convergence of justice and peace. Kant develops the postulates of practical reason in the second *Critique* when he asks how the highest good of *Ethics* is possible. There, he identifies three such postulates: freedom, God, and the immortality of the soul (C2 V, p. 132).[4] This paper is concerned not so much with Ethics, but with Right. Therefore, we ask: How is it possible to achieve the highest good of public morality? How is it possible to achieve a state of perfect justice and peace? What are the conditions under which it is possible to achieve this state?

We can spell out the answer simply by analogy once we recognize the structural analogy that obtains between the two branches of morality. Three additional postulates of practical reason become necessary that exactly parallel the three postulates mentioned by Kant himself. In both cases, the first postulate is a claim about the agent subjected to the moral law—in Ethics, it is a postulate of freedom (especially internal freedom or freedom of the will), in Right it is again a postulate of freedom (especially external freedom or freedom of action). The second postulate is a claim about the structure of the universe that allows the convergence of morality and human aspirations—in Ethics, the structure is represented by the idea of God; in Right, the structure may be called 'Providence' or 'Nature' (this will be explained further in Section 3 below). The third postulate is a claim about the way from the current state of affairs to the ideal state. It is a claim about *progress* towards this ideal state. The content of progress is the gradual convergence of morality and human aspirations. Insofar, the third postulate is basically a dynamic version of the static second postulate. According to Kant, this progress is endless or a progress to infinity. Because our individual lives on earth are not endless, Ethics requires the postulate of the immortality of the soul. But Right is a different matter: the postulate of immortality is replaced by that of political progress.[5] Immortality is not necessary. The life of the species, of humanity, lasts indefinitely, maybe forever. And as long as there are human beings on earth, progress is possible.

To sum up: In order to save his moral philosophy from being imaginary, Kant has to show that progress is at least possible.[6] This is why he makes progress a postulate of practical reason. This is why he counts the question "What may I hope?" among the three questions of human reason in need of an answer. Natorp and others were wrong to condemn Kant for taking it up. The postulates of practical reason are not some superfluous or "metaphysical" adjunct to an otherwise sound theoretical edifice. On the contrary, they are an essential part without which the system as a whole would lack closure.

To be sure, critics may still argue that Kant's belief in progress, while systematically connected to his moral philosophy, is mistaken and naïve in the sense that it rests on an implausible belief in something utopian. It is to this argument that I now turn.

2 The Goal of Progress: Realistic Utopia

In order to defend Kant's political philosophy and the theory of progress it implies against the reproach of utopianism, it is useful to understand in which way a political theory can be called utopian. One way is to consider it an example of what one could call *surrealistic utopianism*. Here, an author lets his imagination run wild and dreams up an ideal world that he does not expect to come into existence ever. The word "utopia" is taken literally: it designates a nowhere place. Like Salvador Dali's pictures, surrealistic utopianism does not claim to be a statement about possible states of the world. Another version of utopianism can be called *realistic utopianism*, after John Rawls's use of the term 'realistic utopia' in his *Law of Peoples* (1999).[7] Here, the ideal state of the world is considered achievable in the sense that the nature of the world, and especially the nature of the social world, allows for its coming into existence. Realistic utopianism is a statement about a possible state of the world. Probably, some people will dispute this claim and dismiss the theory as *unrealistic utopianism*. In their view, realistic utopianism involuntarily ends up amounting to the same as surrealistic utopianism.

Kant wants his political philosophy and his theory of progress to be realistically utopian. In the *Contest of the Faculties* he writes: "[W]e must not expect too much of human beings in their progressive improvements, or else we shall merit the scorn of those politicians who would gladly treat man's hopes of progress as the fantasies of an overheated mind." (Contest VII, p. 92)[8] Despite this cautionary remark, there are critics who say that a theory like Kant's still expects too much. In their minds, any hope for progress towards a state of the world where politics is subject to the imperatives of justice is unrealistic. As a consequence, these critics like to think of themselves as "Realists."

One of the most powerful statements of Realism as it is commonly understood by its adherents is Machiavelli's *Il Principe*. Machiavelli's message is that belief in a better world to come may not only be a dream, but a dangerous one too:

> Many have imagined republics and principalities that have never been seen or known to exist in truth; for it is so far from how one lives to how one should live that he who lets go of what is done for what should be done learns his ruin rather than his preservation. For a man who wants to make a profession of good in all regards must come to ruin among so many who are not good.[9]

Machiavelli's impression has been shared and repeated by Realists over the centuries: the world is a bad place to be, and there is no hope of ever changing this in a fundamental way. There is no escape from the logic of power politics. Either there is hierarchy, or balance of power, or war. No progress towards a humane, peaceful, and just order of human affairs is possible.

With the rise and spread of the liberal state, Realism has lost much of its appeal as a theory of domestic politics. The modern democratic state seems a far cry from Machiavelli's Princedom or Hobbes's Leviathan. But Realism is still one of the dominant approaches in international relations theory. To many people, the structure of the present international system looks a lot like a Hobbesian state of war of all against all. E.H. Carr's attack on "utopianism," Hans J. Morgenthau's statement of "Political Realism" in his *Politics Among Nations*, and especially Kenneth Waltz's "neo-realist" *Theory of International Politics* are still very influential.[10] Even theorists who are not dogmatic Realists echo Realism's concern about far-reaching normative approaches such as Kant's. In "Liberalism and International Affairs," Stanley Hoffmann voices his skepticism thus:

> Some have not given up the quest for utopia and keep imagining schemes in which the logic of international politics would be finally abolished and replaced; . . . but they still have no answer to the questions: How are you going to achieve such a mutation? And how shall we go from here to there?[11]

What is the Kantian to make of the Realist's attack? Hoffmann's criticism shows the way. Those who have not given up the quest for a realistic utopia have to answer the question: How do we get from here to there?

Naturally, I cannot provide a detailed answer to this question here. However, I mention two points that underline the realism of Kant's theory. The first point is: We have come a long way. The second point is: We can go even further.

While the world still is far from perfect, considerable progress has been made towards a world order similar to the one Kant sketched in the three definitive articles of *Perpetual Peace*. For Kant, the goal of politics and therefore of political progress is a universal order of law and justice combining three constitutions:

(1) one in accord with the right of citizens of a state, of individuals within a people (*ius civitatis*), (2) one in accord with the right of nations, of states in relation to one another (*ius gentium*), (3) one in accord with the right of citizens of the world, insofar as individuals and states, standing in the relation of externally affecting one another, are to be regarded as citizens of a universal state of mankind (*ius cosmopoliticum*). (PP VIII, p. 349)

In all three respects, progress has been made since Kant's time. The liberal state is a reality in large parts of the world. In most of the other parts, it serves as the paradigm of statehood. International law has undergone significant changes since Kant's time. War has been outlawed; except in very limited circumstances, it no longer is a legitimate means of international politics. Human rights, while weakly enforced, have at least been affirmed by international declarations and treaties.

Probably the Realist would acknowledge the success of the liberal state but attribute it to the fact that it is a hierarchically ordered system. He or she would dismiss the changes in international law as surface phenomena. The logic of international politics, he would argue, was, is, and will be the logic of anarchy.

There are three things to say in reply. First, Realism was wrong before in its assessment of the domestic domain;[12] it could be wrong again in its assessment of the international domain. Second, one should not underestimate the importance of changes on the surface level of public declarations. It is already a sign of progress that even non-liberal states try to justify their actions using the concepts of democracy and human rights.[13] As Kant explains in the *Contest of the Faculties* with reference to the French revolution, changes in public opinion are crucial.[14] Third, and most important, we can suggest ways to transform the international system, ways "from here to there," ways of possible further progress. We have sophisticated theories of international politics that can explain a broad range of phenomena and at the same time confirm the Kantian hopes of progress. Alexander Wendt's *Social Theory of International Politics* is a case in point. In this seminal study Wendt outlines the possibility of historical progress from a "Hobbesian culture" of enmity, distrust, and fear, to a "Lockean culture" of rivalry, towards a "Kantian culture" of cosmopolitan co-operation or even "friendship."

What emerges from studies like Wendt's is that hope for progress is a belief that can survive reflection.[15] We cannot know that progress will take place. But we have good reasons to believe that it is possible. This is not the same as blindly believing in progress or being overly optimistic. This is only a refusal to let skepticism turn into cynicism and a self-fulfilling prophecy of doom. There lies the real danger of Realism: that it forecloses on the real possibilities we have and makes us settle for less than we can achieve. John Rawls fittingly quotes Rousseau's *Contrat Social* in his description of the concept of realistic utopia: "The limits of the possible in moral matters are less narrow than we think. It is our weaknesses, our vices, our prejudices, that shrink them."[16]

Kant does not claim that overcoming our weaknesses, vices, and prejudices will be easy. He knows that the transformation of politics from a game of brutal power to a system of law will take a long time, maybe an indefinitely long time. All he says is that he is talking about a *possible* state of the world and that there are ways to get from here to there (or at least close to there). Progress is possible, not inevitable. But that is the topic of the next section.

3 The Forces of Progress: Agents and Structures

The argument of this section can be put very simply: It is wrong to read Hegel back into Kant. Progress is not predetermined. It is a mistake to put a Hegelian spin on Kant's propositions. There is no materializing world spirit, no cunning of reason, no logic of history, no force independent of human action. Kant's vision of progress is essentially non-deterministic.

Unfortunately, it is quite easy to get Kant wrong on this point. The "First Supplement" of *Perpetual Peace*, for example, is entitled, "On the Guarantee of a Perpetual Peace." Kant writes:

> What provides this guarantee is no less than the great artist Nature herself, whose mechanical process visibly exhibits purposiveness to produce concord among men by means of their discord and even against their will. This design, if we regard it as a compelling cause whose laws of operation are unknown to us, is called fate. But if we consider its purposive function within the world's development, whereby it appears as the underlying wisdom of a higher cause, showing the way towards the objective goal of the human race and predetermining the world's evolution, we call it providence. (PP VIII, p. 360)

Some pages later, Kant asks:

> What does nature do in relation to the end which man's own reason prescribes to
> him as a duty, i.e. how does nature help to promote his moral purpose? And how
> does nature guarantee that what man ought to do by the laws of his freedom (but
> does not do) will in fact be done through nature's compulsion, without prejudice
> to the free agency of man? (PP VIII, p. 365)

Kant's answer:

> If I say that nature wills that this or that should happen, this does not mean that
> nature imposes on us a duty to do it (for that can only be done by non-coercive
> practical reason). On the contrary: Nature does it herself, whether we are will-
> ing or not ('the fates lead him who is willing, but drag him who is unwilling').
> (PP VIII, p. 365)

Passages like these have led numerous scholars to maintain that Kant
ascribes to Nature some kind of agency or that he believes in some sort of
Providence or Fate. Howard Williams, for example, claims in his book *Kant's
Political Philosophy*:

> Kant's optimism concerning man's historical development derives from his view
> that Providence has a hand in what occurs. Kant believes that behind the backs
> of individuals—leaders and ordinary citizens alike—there is a progressive his-
> torical purpose unfolding itself.[17]

In a similar vein, Wolfgang Kersting, one of the leading German Kant scholars, writes:

> History is understood by Kant not as a system of human actions and effects of
> freedom and side effects, but as a system of unmediated and mediated natural
> effects which are teleologically directed towards the realization of the ideas of
> republicanism and perpetual peace. . . . The progress in matters of right and jus-
> tice is not intended by men; rather, it happens behind the backs of men and is not
> at all the product of reason. It is the product of nature. Not man is the protago-
> nist of Kantian history, but a providential nature.[18]

I think that Williams and Kersting and others who have put forward similar interpretations are getting things wrong. Once again, I do not wish to
deny that it is possible to find apparent textual evidence in Kant for such an
interpretation. But I want to claim two things: (1) no picture of progress that
is deterministic in the sense that it relies on a non-human or super-human
agency such as Nature, Providence, or History could possibly fit the frame

of Kant's critical philosophy; (2) there is ample evidence in Kant's writings that he was aware of this. Even in the paragraph on Nature as the guarantee of perpetual peace, Kant says very clearly:

> We cannot actually observe such an agency in the artifices of nature, nor can we even infer its existence from them. But as with all relations between the form of things and their ultimate purposes, we can and must supply it mentally in order to conceive of its possibility by analogy with human artifices. Its relationship to and conformity with the end which reason directly prescribes to us (i.e. the end of morality) can only be conceived of as an idea. Yet while this idea is indeed far-fetched in theory, it does possess dogmatic validity and has a very real foundation in practice, as with the concept of perpetual peace, which makes it our duty to promote it by using the natural mechanism described above. (PP VIII, p. 362)

This description of agency brings back to mind an observation made in the first section: not only progress is a postulate of practical reason, but the providentiality of nature is one too. As Kant says in the passage quoted from the first *Critique*: hope finally comes down to the inference that *something is* which determines the ultimate final end *because something ought to happen.* We infer that "something" is—Nature, Providence, Fate—because we cannot imagine how else it should be possible that millions of different individual actions undertaken for a million different reasons should propel humanity forward to its highest goal.

But we should be careful here: we should not reify or personalize this something. As Kant says in the *Critique of Judgment*, it would be strange to think of Nature as a rational being (C3, p. 383); even the most complete teleology could not prove the existence of such a rational being (C3, p. 399).

Therefore we should interpret the postulate of providential nature as a *concept of structure*. The providentiality of nature is nothing but the fact that the circumstances of the world are such that they prompt people to devise institutions that lead towards justice and peace. Nature sets the stage upon which man has to play his part. An examination of all of the passages in which Kant talks about Nature as a guarantee for progress supports this interpretation. Take, for example, the guarantee section in *Perpetual Peace*. Kant starts:

> Before we define [the guarantee of perpetual peace] more precisely, we must first examine the situation in which nature has placed the actors in her great spectacle, for it is this situation which ultimately demands the guarantee of peace. We may next enquire in what manner the guarantee is provided. (PP VIII, p. 362f)

The answer to both inquiries can be summed up thus: Nature has driven people apart—by linguistic and religious differences, by war—but also has united them by their mutual self-interest in peace and prosperity. Kant concludes:

> In this way, nature guarantees perpetual peace by the actual mechanism of human inclinations. And while the likelihood of its being attained is not sufficient to enable us to prophesy the future theoretically, it is enough for practical purposes. It makes it our duty to work our way towards this goal, which is more than an empty chimera. (PP VIII, p. 368)

In Kant's philosophy, nature cannot be much more than a favorable background condition—the real work has to be done by human beings. "Guarantee," then, means a "possible underpinning" and not a "certain determinant."[19] It is true that progress is not necessarily the intentional object of human activity. But from the fact that progress may take place "behind our backs" it does not follow that Providence or Nature are the agencies of progress. Talking about Nature or Providence or History as agents is a figure of speech, a metaphor. It seems to me wrong to say, as Kersting does, that Kant sees history "not as a system of human actions and effects of freedom and side effects."[20] Kant's concept of the mechanism of Nature is closer to Adam Smith's "invisible hand" than to Hegel's "world spirit." And it seems highly problematic to claim that the market mechanism Smith identified is anything but "a system of human actions and effects of freedom and side effects." The market is not an actor, but only a framework for actions. It is true that it is a limiting framework that rewards certain courses of action and punishes others. But saying that the market, and not man, is the protagonist of economic history would seem odd. Those who reify the market or Nature confuse structure with process and especially with the agents of process.

It is true that the structure of the world may put pressure on humanity to progress in a certain direction—but it can never really force us in that direction. There is no inevitability. Any kind of determinism would be incompatible with Kant's doctrine of human freedom:

> Even if it were found that the human race as a whole had been moving forward and progressing for an indefinitely long time, no one could guarantee that its era of decline was not beginning at that very moment [and conversely] . . . For we are dealing with freely acting beings to whom one can dictate in advance what they ought to do, but of whom one cannot predict what they actually will do. (*Contest* VII, p. 83).

This understanding of structure supports Kant's claim of realistic utopianism. The world may at first be a bad place, just as the Realists claim, but something good may come of it. As Kant indicates in *Perpetual Peace*: the problem of setting up a state or any other public system of law can be solved even by a nation of devils as long as they possess self-interest and understanding. This claim leads directly to the argument of the next section: progress does not depend on the moral betterment of man but rather on just institutions.

4 The Basis of Progress: Individuals in Institutions

If the argument of the last section could be summarized by saying, "Don't read Hegel back into Kant," the argument of this one can be summed up by saying: "Don't mix up Kant and Marx!" I use Marx's name—as I used Hegel's—to refer to a certain philosophical position some scholars claim to have detected in Kant. In the case of Marx, it is both the belief that a new kind of consciousness can be the root of political progress and the belief that a significant and permanent change in human nature will occur once the right institutions are in place. The attempt to fuse Kant and Marx has been made both by Marxist scholars trying to claim Kant as a proto-Marxist and by Realist thinkers attacking Kant for his supposedly naïve belief in the malleability of human nature. In this section, I will argue that, in contrast to the socialist utopia of some Marxist theories, Kant's political utopia is not at all based on a belief in the malleability of human nature.

Marxist theorists—at least in the classical version of Marxism—believe it possible to transcend the state once the ideal economic and political conditions are in place. In the communist brotherhood and sisterhood of man, comradeship will replace citizenship. Political structures are no longer needed because all members of society have been delivered from the evils of capitalism. With the replacement of the "false consciousness" of bourgeois society by the "right consciousness" of classless society, greed for money and desire for glory have ceased to exist as a part of the human mindset.

In Kant's view, however, no significant change in human nature can be expected. Humans will continue to be what they are right now: probably neither entirely good nor entirely bad. But even if they were one of the two, the task of political philosophy and the perspective of progress would not change much. For Kant, political progress does not depend on the goodness of human nature or individual moral progress, but on the right set of institutions. On the one hand, the problem of setting up a state or any other legal system can be solved even by a bunch of devils as long as they possess self-interest and understanding. On the other hand, even a group of near-angels would still need a state.[21] Whatever the nature of man may be, the way to achieve political progress is the same. As Kant explains in *Perpetual Peace*, the problem of setting up a state can be generally stated as follows:

In order to organize a group of rational beings who together require universal laws for their survival, but of whom each separate individual is secretly inclined to exempt himself from them, the constitution must be so designed that, although the citizens are opposed to one another in their private attitudes, these yet check one another in such a way that the public conduct of the citizens will be the same as if they did not have such evil attitudes. (PP VIII, p. 366)

Kant then goes on:

A problem of this kind must be soluble. For such a task does not involve the moral improvement of man; it only means finding out how the mechanism of nature can be applied to men in such a manner that the antagonism of their hostile attitudes will make them compel one another to submit to coercive laws, thereby producing a condition of peace within which the laws have force (are in force). (PP VIII, p. 366)

This passage clearly supports my foregoing arguments. The establishment of a civil constitution represents significant political progress—and this progress does not "involve the moral improvement of man," and it does not depend on Nature acting on her own, but on the application of the "mechanism of nature" by men to men.[22]

Conclusion

In this chapter, I have tried to show that we have good reasons to think about progress if we think about it in the right way. In order to do this, I examined and defended Kant's theory of progress. Kant tells us that we need to believe in the possibility of progress if we want to believe that normative political philosophy makes sense, and he shows that both beliefs can be justified. Let me sum up his arguments.

1. Kant delivers a convincing theory of progress to save his political philosophy from being imaginary. The centerpiece of this theory is the postulate of progress as interpreted by Pierre Hassner: "Kant does not present the historical progress of intellect, culture, and politics as a fact but rather as the indispensable practical *postulate* for the moral subject. . . . Kant does not assert that men have a duty to believe in the attainability of the ends of progress; their duty is to act consistently with the desire for those ends as long as their unattainability is not certain."[23]

2. Kant's view of progress is realistically utopian. The goal of a universal order of law and justice set by Kant's political philosophy is not out of reach. Some progress has been made, most significantly in the domestic affairs of states. More

progress must and can be made, especially in foreign affairs. Contrary to the Realist's claim, there is no single "logic of anarchy." States may live in an "anarchical society," but that does not consign them to enmity. There are numerous ways to structure and govern the society of states. Anarchy is what we *make* of it.

3. Kant's notion of progress is anti-deterministic. While it is true that the structure of the natural and social world may propel us in a certain direction if we want to avoid self-destruction, that does not mean that our future is predetermined by dialectical processes beyond our control. If that were the case, the idea of freedom would be meaningless. Kant cannot want this: his critical philosophy is a philosophy of freedom. It puts the future in our own hands. History is what *we* make of it.

4. Political progress does not depend so much on the moral progress of individuals as on the right set of institutions. It depends more on what we actually do than on the reasons why we do what we do. It does not matter much if we do our duty because of external constraints, or out of respect for the moral law. Progress will be significant if and when institutions can make us do what we ought to do anyway.

Hints of all these claims appear in the closing paragraph of *Perpetual Peace*:

> If it is a duty to realize a state of public right (albeit by unending progress), and if there is also a well-founded hope of achieving this state, then perpetual peace...is no empty idea, but a task that is accomplished step by step and thereby comes steadily closer to its goal (since the times during which equal amounts of progress take place will, hopefully, become ever shorter) (PP VIII, p. 386).[24]

10

Philosophy as Hubris: Kierkegaard's Critique of Romantic Irony as a Critique of Immanent Thinking

HANS FEGER

Hans Feger is a research fellow at the Freie Universität, Berlin. Author of Die Macht der Einbildungskraft in der Ästhetik Kants und Schillers, *his interests include aesthetics, literary theory, and German Romanticism.*

When postmodern thinkers wish to communicate about the possibilities of contemporary thinking, they speak today about the disappearance of the difference between being and appearance. Human reality, according to them, has taken on increasingly the form of an artificial construction, so that traditional differences between reality and fiction, truth and simulation, or art and technology have more and more been leveled. Indeed, reality itself can be seen as no more than diminished forms of a metaphysical realism. Following upon the sad friends of the gay sciences, the rejuvenated gay human being as artist and creator of his own reality assumes the legacy and announces, full of pathos, but not without the ulterior motive of scientific hedonism:

> With us the adventure of becoming human has entered a new phase. We can see this most clearly in the fact that we are no longer able to differentiate between truth and appearance or science and art."[1]

Inherent in these diagnoses is the conceptual problem that even differences—when they disappear—require a conceptual criterion to explain their disappearance. The usual statement—that this reflects the general mainstream of history—does not suffice, but rather only displaces the need for an explanation. This then leads to a further claim: modern thinking "has since Kant moved closer and closer to the insight that the grounding of what we call reality is based on fiction. Reality proved increasingly not to be constituted as 'realistic' but as 'aesthetic'. Where this insight has been accepted—and it is widespread today—aesthetics loses the character of a specialized discipline and becomes a general medium for understanding reality."[2] These theses are problematic because aesthetics is no longer seen as part of a philosophical discipline that includes as well logic and ethics, all of which understand their object to be the practice of art. Rather aesthetics loses its object and in a general sense becomes a model of human life interpreted from the perspective of aisthesis. Thus constituted, aesthetics and its processes are to be reflected upon aesthetically. Yet, this only doubles the problem by inventing a (postmodern) reality and substituting it for the prior one. Hence, the very thinking that is to be critiqued becomes self-contented and isolating, an immanent thinking that is locked within the self-contentedness of aesthetic perception.

Nonetheless, there is something irrefutable about aesthetic perceptions—especially the postmodern variants expanded into a kind of hyperreality—once you begin to entertain the idea. From the world as experiential space to the simulation of virtual worlds, perceptual fields are opened that we can no longer deny. Since cognitive categories such as deception presumably no longer obtain here,[3] they reveal a condition of achieved freedom from moral orientations, a pluralism of convictions, a world cleansed of ideology, even a life without history. This certainly can function usefully. From this perspective such perceptions represent not only a diminished pressure from reality; they also create new realities. They express themselves both in superficial playfulness and in reflection that stimulates ever deeper thinking. One admits appearance, whether as myth, fiction, or simulation, and accepts it as reality. At the same time one enjoys the advantage of omnipotence: All decisions stay on hold, every truth may be considered a deception and relativized, nothing that exists must remain so; rather, anything can be repositioned in an infinite process or in an infinitely diverse chaos, even if it is only the familiar.

These advantages hardly feed the suspicion that the unreality in which we live could be a better or worse reality. Doubt disappears here like a blind spot. In totally aestheticized appearance truth must appear precisely as untruth, Adorno states. The world of art is its own world, one that does not allow for a consciousness that can criticize it. In this world you live more immediately, as if among a dizzying array of possibilities. The spectator is also a collaborator, not someone who looks back at the world as a fact to be explained. If you wish to criticize this world, you have to accept it and simultaneously maintain the consciousness that it is worthy of critique so that you can communicate within it what it actually would mean to relinquish reality.

Here it may be helpful to consider a theoretical tradition that in similar constellations resisted the tendency to aestheticize life. The early Kierkegaard confronted the not infrequently playful permissiveness of this aestheticization with the existential seriousness of moral decisions. A constellation that included both critics and supporters of such tendencies can be found in the tradition of Romanticism. In particular, the early Romantics in Jena reveal in their ironic relationship to the world a consciousness of intensified agility with which they believed they could master life's contradictions in an act of aesthetic dissimulation. That allowed them to appear at the beginning of the nineteenth century as highly postmodern and called forth besides Hegel's critique especially that of Kierkegaard, who recognized that the reverse side of this aesthetic gesture is in fact boredom and that both the expression and masking of reality hinder ethical behavior. The following will show how the early Kierkegaard formulated his critique of Romantic irony as a critique of immanent thinking.

I

Perhaps it would be plausible to imagine the postmodern philosophers of indifference to any metaphysical truth as being in the cheery garb of the early Romantic ironists—and Kierkegaard, who resists them as their conqueror through the passionate engagement of a self which stands its ground against disintegration and frees itself through an ethical decision. Indeed, that the early Romantics developed a style of thought that "questions all systematic and dogmatic fixations"[4] has been investigated by literary theorists with an eye toward the way in which it anticipates deconstruction's critique of subjectivity. But the view that the postmodern, with its "pyromaniacal cheerfulness of god expulsion by means of electrifying gags and coups,"[5] its plays on language and lively noncommittal paradoxes is simply the reflex of a new infantile society of Romantics, appears not yet in critical studies of deconstruction but already in Kierkegaard's view of early Romanticism. Torn between critique and sympathy, he recapitulates in his master's thesis *On the Concept of Irony* (1841):

> A cool breeze, refreshing morning air, blows through Romanticism from the primeval forests of the Middle Ages or from the pure ether of Greece; it sends a cold shiver down the backs of the philistines, and yet it is necessary to dispel the bestial miasma in which one breathed up to this point. The hundred years are over, the spellbound castle bestirs itself, its inhabitants awaken again, the forest

breathes lightly, the birds sing, the beautiful princess once again attracts suitors, the forest resounds with the reverberation of hunters' horns and the baying of hounds, the meadows are fragrant, poems and songs break away from nature and flutter about, and no one knows whence they come or whither they go. The world is rejuvenated, but as Heine so wittily remarked, it was rejuvenated by Romanticism to such a degree that it became a baby again. The tragedy of Romanticism is that what it seizes upon is not actuality. Poetry awakens; the powerful longings, the mysterious intimations, the inspiring feelings awaken; nature awakens; the enchanted princess awakens—the Romanticist falls asleep.[6]

This is an ambivalent evaluation, as was all of Kierkegaard's critique of the early Romantics. However, it carries within itself the possibility of a hermeneutic approach to the contradictory reception of the early Romantics. For Kierkegaard the decentralization of consciousness in a free poetic existence, which modern interpreters all too hastily construe as simply a disintegration into a play of signifiers, leads to a dead end. While their wish to transform life into a work of art[7] and to rescue it from the entanglements of the relative is plausible, it does not offer a way out of the contradictions of life. Instead, it dreams of its own world in which all consciousness of the ability to act is erased. The awakening that Romanticism promised was bought at the price of a complete denial of actuality. The *praise of nonsense* is not yet the conquest of uselessness, as one could suppose; it is not freedom from social constraints and the rational structures of this habitat, which constantly and ever more hastily strive for self-perfection. It simply grows out of an enthusiasm whose causes reside for the most part in self-isolation and self-dissimulation. The ironist[8] "does not, however, abandon himself to this enthusiasm for destroying" (p. 262). The *I* of the Romantic does not cease in its self-reassuring intentions, but rather is only "negatively free and as such is suspended, because there is nothing that holds him" (p. 262). As an ironic subjectivity, this *I*, rather than becoming a reality-giving principle, remains in empty immanence and leads, not to a utopian world, but to distraction. Thus, it only marks an interim state of utopian thinking that hasn't yet "grasped" reality, but instead—as Kierkegaard writes in his master's thesis—negates "all of historical actuality" (p. 275).

Kierkegaard's criticism is undoubtedly more plausible with regard to the *Romantic* aestheticizing of reality than to the postmodern celebration of difference, most likely because the aestheticizing of life that thinks itself to be postmodern is no longer dependent on the choosing of irresponsibility, as Kierkegaard maintains in *Either/Or* (1843), but rather has objectified and summed up this choice as the inescapable mark of the present.[9] The experience of powerlessness is then stylized only in the inexplicability of *différance*.

But this is already part of the technical inventory of deconstruction, which allows for the increase in the same myriad of interpretations that it had intended to tear down in order to expose the shaken foundations.[10] It is precisely this kind of immanent thinking, for which it has become impossible to grasp its own justification, that Kierkegaard's critique of irony attacks.

Decisive in Kierkegaard's criticism and more revealing for a deconstruction of the postmodern reception of the structure of irony is less the reproach that early Romanticism is merely escapism from an imperfect reality, but rather that it carries on a self-concealment in the existential insecurity of man, from which it can not withdraw. The aestheticization of life conveys—and Kierkegaard interprets this as utterly paradoxical—only the insight that there can be *no* conception of man's existence that is not itself aestheticized. In the enjoyment of aesthetic self-complacency, the view of the ironist's own freedom from obligation and existential insecurity is concealed. Instead of actualizing actuality, he rescues himself "from the relativity in which the given actuality wants to keep" (p. 263) him; and even worse, he falls into negativity, to destroy "actuality by means of actuality itself" (p. 262). The ironist cannot become aware of the negativity of his own situation, since he is constantly postponing its inconceivability and even ameliorating it in this thematization to an ironic form of execution. Exactly *because* one cannot, according to the edict of the early Romantics, discuss irony in any other manner than ironically, and poetry can "only be criticized through poetry,"[11] Kierkegaard as well as Hegel[12] subjects it to a critical revision. Ironic reflection as the establishment of a difference, or even—from a postmodern viewpoint—as "the effect of the play of *différance* itself,"[13] continues a contradiction that only leads to the bad infinity of an eternal recurrence. If one interprets this self-thematization of irony not as a strength, as for instance in the post-Fichtean sense of the intentionally paradoxical dealings with reflection's claim to universality, but rather as a weakness of the methodology, then the ironic reevaluation of existence only leads to a "dwelling in the realm of the subjective and the virtual. In that irony clings to the negative, it becomes itself negativity, despite having been conceived as its overcoming."[14]

Kierkegaard in any case introduces a critical caesura where the early Romantic ironists interpreted the constant alternation of reflection positively as a "floating of the imagination."[15] With this difference, he hopes to confront the carelessness that emerges from the ironist's discontinuous consciousness of life: "Irony is health in as far as it rescues the soul from the entanglements of the relative, it is sickness in as far as it can only bear the absolute in the form of nothing." Irony is justified for Kierkegaard only as dissimulation, in constructing an antithetical situation, "as the subject frees himself by means of irony from the restrain in which the continuity of life's conditions hold him" (p. 255n). Seen existentially, it is therefore not a question of "eternal" or even "divine freedom" (p. 279) but rather of boredom. For Kierkegaard, "boredom is the only continuity the ironist has. Boredom, this eternity devoid of content, this salvation devoid of joy, this superficial profundity, this hungry glut. But boredom is precisely the negative unity admitted into a personal consciousness, wherein the differences vanish" (p. 285).[16] Boredom is the basic mood of the aesthetician. Kierkegaard vividly described boredom in *Either/Or* with the example of the *Augenblicksexistenz*[17] ("existence for the moment") of the aesthetician. The ironist establishes his unstable happiness *in time* upon boredom's experience of indifference, which—constantly fleeing from emptiness—seeks redemption in ever new moments of enjoyment, even those of horror[18]—but that simultaneously calls forth boredom again and again as the basic mood of his existence. Only from the point of view of the ethicist, who does not make the mistake of taking a principle of his subjective moral action for a problem of a more general applicability, does this paradoxical relation to the self become evident.

As sweeping as this repudiation of ironic subjectivity at first sounds, it would be incorrect to accuse Kierkegaard of wanting to use it to persuade the Romantic ironist to relinquish the freedom granted by arbitrariness in order to make room for a *gravity of life* as it should emerge from what Kierkegaard calls the "stage of the ethicist." When he criticizes irony, it "by no means indicates that irony should now lose its meaning or be totally discarded" (p. 326). The ethical suspension of the aesthetic towards which Kierkegaard strives is not to be understood as a fundamental alternative to the ironist's aesthetic experience of life. Rather, this suspension remains dialectically related to experience. The ironic difference that supports the never-ending conflict of reflection remains much more the impassable horizon of Kierkegaard's dialectic of existence. It is precisely in its contradictoriness that ironic difference is not only negated by this dialectic but also interpreted as an upheaval that points beyond itself. The ironic perspective as the prerogative to a transcendence towards the ethical: this is Kierkegaard's perspective, even in the novel *Either/Or*. He deploys its poetic power in order to show that the aesthetic program of Romantic irony is only accomplished in the ethical.

This is above all the reason for inserting a critical caesura (Kierkegaard speaks of it in the figure of a surgeon's operation[19]) into the movement of Romantic irony as a whole that the Romantic existence is to take beyond itself. The immanent mode of thought of the early Romantics is to be broken up so that it has its "cause" (as Kierkegaard puts it) in view and so that it can be mindful of how ironic existence is indebted to a whole movement of thought that reaches beyond the ironist's immanent mode of thinking. The Romantic *I* is confronted with a mirror of the truth of a paradox by which its self-assertions, instead of succeeding, actually *fail* in order to gain access to itself as a fundamentally unhappy consciousness. It is confronted with the contradiction that thinking about one's own existence is *always* accompanied by the fact that it is *not* existence, since it merely remains on the level of representation and the idea. Paradoxically, it is precisely the failure in the attempt to bring about fruitful relationships with one's self out of finite relationships, the production of a reference that is to be brought about by infinite gravity. The ironist himself draws attention to this paradox, even if in so doing he runs completely contradictory to his purpose (namely "negatively" or "as the exact opposite of this"[20]) when he maintains that it is only because he "manages to be master over the irony at the time of writing he is master over it in the actuality to which he himself belongs" (p. 324). "The difficulty here", writes Kierkegaard in a Hegelian spirit, "is that, strictly speaking, irony actually is never able to advance a thesis, because irony is a qualification of the being-for-itself subject, who in incessant agility allows nothing to remain established and on account of this agility cannot focus on the total point of view that it allows nothing to remain established. . . . Ultimately the ironist always has to posit something, but what he posits in this way is nothing. But then it is impossible to be earnest about nothing without either arriving at something (this happens if one becomes speculatively earnest about it) or despairing (if one takes it personally in earnest). But the ironist does neither, and thus we can also say that he is not in earnest about it" (p. 269n).

With the formulation of the *infinite light playing with nothing or playing that is terrified of nothing*, Kierkegaard sums up his ambivalence vis-a-vis the idea that in the ironic assertion of identity only the experience of powerlessness is in the end given expression and that a successful self-relation can only be achieved by constantly deferring it as an unsolvable problem. "The more actuality is caricatured," Kierkegaard suggests, "the higher the idea wells up, but the fountain that wells up here does not well up into an eternal life. The very fact, however, that this poetry moves between two opposites shows that in the deeper sense it is not true poetry" (p. 305). A difference of experience is secretly established that does not transform reality poetically but rather turns it into a "total impression of unserious existence"[21] and, in so doing, ironically destroys it. The experience of the difference, of the crisis, and of one's own inadequacy folds back upon the Romantic consciousness. Instead of dispersing himself in the colorful variety of a poetic reality, the Romantic can conjure up successful relationships with the self only in an unsatisfied yearning that refuses him fulfillment. The difference between idea and reality only finds its disintegration in a fantastic reality, whose naive immediacy cannot turn into actuality. However, for Kierkegaard, the Romantic thus merely grasps one side of eternity, the annulment of time, but not the other, the introspection of time in eternity, and thus he remains in a *negative* freedom.

From the perspective of the ethical, the ambivalence of the ironic assertion of identity presents itself as a position of undecidedness, which continually betrays its own unsteadiness. The ironic sovereignty of the Romantic represents only *half* of the way: it is a not-choosing of the self, an impersonal, historical way of life. Behind the Romantic *desire* there always stands the unmastered potential of the self's *choice*; behind the Romantic arbitrariness there always stands the unmastered potential of the responsibility towards self-realization; and behind the Romantic inactivity there always stands the unmastered potential of the *act* in the ethical decision.

As much as Kierkegaard tries to burst open the empty immanence of ironic subjectivity by inserting a critical caesura in the early Romantic notion of irony (in order to keep the possibilities of a transcendental experience open), he does not abolish it, as Hegel does in his dialectic of ideas in a synthesis.[22] The establishment of a caesura itself is for him a deeply paradoxical undertaking, precisely in that it absorbs the conflict in the process of Romantic irony—rather than overcoming it—and hence turning irony against irony itself. The paradoxical claim of breaking through ironic subjectivity towards a human existence is itself based on the assumption of the surpassability of the ironic movement and so remains attached to it—even if negatively. In a certain way it is precisely the *ironic* reflection that—revealed as nonsensical—is meant to set free the requirements of possibility in order to surpass the aesthetic stage of the ironist and to set the ethical stage itself free.[23] In *The Point of View for my Work as an Author* Kierkegaard attempts to characterize succinctly the dialectical relationship of these stages to each other as a movement that continually negates itself, and in so doing he takes back the contradiction of ironic reflection.

This again, I say, is the dialectical movement, or is essentially dialectics, namely, in one's *action* to *counteract* oneself at the same time, which is what I call reduplication, and it is an example of the heterogeneity which distinguishes every true godly effort from worldly effort. To strive or to work *directly* is to work or to strive in immediate continuity with an actual given condition. The dialectical movement is the exact *opposite* of this, namely, by one's action to counteract one's effort at the same time—a duplication which is 'seriousness', like the pressure upon the plough that determines the depth of the furrow, whereas a direct effort is a slurring over, which not only goes more quickly and easily, but is by far a more thankful task, for it is worldliness and homogeneity."[24]

Decisive for an understanding of Kierkegaard's criticism of the Romantic notion of irony is the fact that he employs the same mode of thought that the ironists interpret as *positive* and uses it in revealing this interpretation as contradictory. Whereas the early Romantics define the essence of irony as a "floating alternation . . . in the eternal seeking and never-quite-finding,"[25] Kierkegaard's critical caesura directs attention back towards the internal disruption of this type of reflection and thus towards the process in which the ironist, by means of this internal disruption, apparently possesses an enormous power, "just as the ardor of despair gives rise to authentic strength" (p. 293). Whereas the early Romantics celebrate idleness as the highest form of reflection precisely because it embodies an attitude accepting that which should be achieved but cannot be achieved,[26] Kierkegaard counteracts this attitude with a position that directs attention towards the hidden powerlessness of this seeking. The determination to let fantasy alone prevail "exhausts and anesthetizes the soul and robs it of all moral tension,"[27] precisely *because* the power of imagination does not succeed in securing this poetical movement and positioning it in a simple, eternally moving image. And where finally the early Romantics hope to understand poetry as a *progressive* universal poetry[28] because it, as Schlegel says, "floats freely in the middle of all real and ideal interests on the wings of poetic reflection, thereby magnifying this reflection over and over and reproducing it as an endless row of mirrors,"[29] Kierkegaard draws attention to the state of being self-lost [*Selbstverlorenheit*]. Such an external consciousness believes itself to be in an endless progression, despite the fact that it always produces the same reflections. For Kierkegaard, irony must be controlled. It must be halted in the wild infinity into which it ravenously rushes. "As soon as irony is controlled, it makes a movement opposite to that in which uncontrolled irony declares its life" (p. 326). Only then does irony assume its proper meaning, its true validity.

Those who have understood the starting point of Kierkegaard's critique of irony can no longer view identity in Romantic reflection as the "effect of the play of *différance* itself"[30] but are directed, rather, to a dialectic that surpasses *yet again* the universal experiment of Romantic irony in the consciousness that this experiment has only gone half of the way. Indeed, the early Romantics did not want to draw attention merely to the "remaining difference of the between" that keeps the never-ending alternation of reflection in motion for the purpose of renouncing every metaphysical assumption. On the contrary, the Romantics, especially those centered in Jena, investigate with their concept of irony the *universal experiment* of an "eternal seeking and never-quite-finding,"[31] indeed, still with the awareness that precisely a feeling of *irresolvable* conflict between the unconditional and the conditional remains.[32] For this reason, their act of understanding, although it remains immanent and is not interrupted by interpretations, wishes to express a transcendental perception. Far from renouncing all transcendental reference in their poetic point of view (or even revealing the illusion of the "transcendental signified" in order to devalue it as a formerly metaphysical assumption into a play of signifiers that can be infinitely combined with and substituted for one another[33]), the early Romantics understand irony to be, as it were, "an epideixis [*Zurschaustellung*] of eternity."[34] This occurs not *despite* a bad finiteness, but rather *because* this finiteness is constantly relativized towards an outstanding lack.[35] The characteristic *floating* of positing, countering, and synthesizing of (poetic) reflection would in fact be groundless if the inconceivability of the absolute did not remain present within it. Kierkegaard may have found an interest in the Romantic fundamental figure of an "infinite lack of being" when he suggests that "there is in our days a prodigious enthusiasm, and, strangely enough, that which makes it enthusiastic seems to be prodigiously little" (p. 328). He too is influenced, especially through his Schelling studies, by a preliminary decision, "which is shared between Friedrich Schlegel and Novalis and the whole tradition of negative theology in the tradition of *Parmenides*, namely that of being able to encounter the absolute in no other manner but in the mode of transgression."[36] After all, he emphasizes in his criticism of Solger that, with the addition of middle-terms[37] in the Romantic concept of creation, there is still an adherence to an absolute—even if negatively severed—which can be perceived: "God has entered into nothing in order that we might cease to be nothing" (p. 316).[38] But Kierkegaard then questions whether the early Romantic fixation on the immanence of the self falls into a movement that, against its own claims, in its *actions* can no longer absorb a transcendental fixation and thus needs correction, which places the human agent *existentially* as well in a relationship with the absence of truth. Is the same never-ending *alternation* of reflection that, according to the self-understanding of the Romantics as well as of the poststructuralist conception of 'decentering', precisely does *not* aim at a fulfillment in the future, but rather wishes to leave this fulfillment in the present—is this not an encapsulation that suggests that there is "no ear for its whispering" but rather "a lack (eo ipso)" of "what could be called the absolute beginning of personal life?" (p. 326) The early Romantics and, with them, the adherents of non-linear or non-discursive thought forget in "their joy over the achievement . . . that an achievement is worthless if it is not made one's own. . . . Anyone who has a result as such does not possess it, since he does not have the way" (p. 327). One lives, then, in a lack of self-consciousness above one's own existential contradiction that, however, is impossible for an immanent thinking to grasp, and so one practices philosophy as hubris. It is exactly this contradiction with which Kierkegaard's inverse criticism of irony is engaged. For a *critical* irony, for which Kierkegaard strives, "brings the way, but not only the way whereby someone fancying himself to have the achievement comes to possess it, but the way along which the achievement deserts him" (p. 327n). Breaking down immanent thinking allows Kierkegaard to argue that the poetic is the very thing the early Romantics miss, "because true inward infinity comes only through resignation, and only this inner infinity is truly infinite and truly poetic" (p. 289). With regard to this immanent tragedy of poetic reflection, Peter Szondi has described the ironic consciousness very precisely:

> The subject of romantic irony is the isolated, alienated man who has become the object of his own reflection and whose consciousness has deprived him of his ability to act. He nostalgically aspires toward unity and infinity; the world appears to him divided and finite. What he calls irony is his attempt to bear up under his critical predicament, to change his situation by achieving distance toward it. In an ever-expanding act of reflection he tries to establish a point of view beyond himself and to resolve the tension between himself and the world on the level of fiction. He cannot overcome the negativity of his situation by means of an act in which the reconciliation of finite achievement with infinite longing could take place; through prefiguration of a future unity, in which he believes, the negative is described as temporary and, by the same token, it is kept and checked and reversed. This reversal makes it appear tolerable and allows the subject to dwell in the subjective region of fiction. Because irony designates and checks the power of negativity, itself becomes, although originally conceived as the overcoming of negativity, the power of the negative. Irony allows for fulfillment only in the past and in the future; it measures whatever it encounters in the present by the yardstick of infinity and thus destroys it. The knowledge of his own impotence prevents the ironist from respecting his achievements: therein resides his danger. Making this assumption about himself, he closes off the way to his fulfillment. Each achievement becomes in turn inadequate and finally leads into a void; therein resides his tragedy.[39]

II

If one looks back from this perspective towards the argumentation in the decisive second part of Kierkegaard's master's thesis *The Concept of Irony*, it becomes clear how Kierkegaard breaks down and reformulates historically the early Romantic concept of irony by taking a hermeneutic recourse to the Socratic concept of irony. Seen historically, the definitive caesura of both concepts is described in Fichte's *Wissenschaftslehre* (1794): "In Fichte, subjectivity became free, infinite, negative" (p. 275). But it was initially in the early Romantic reception of Fichte, especially in the surpassing of the productive activity of the transcendental *I* through the literary Romantics' ironic freedom of empirical subjectivity, that Kierkegaard recognized a weak point in the philosophical origin of Romantic irony. As a result, Fichte's principle of practical subjectivity is lost, for "in the first place, the empirical and finite *I* was confused with the eternal *I*; in the second place, metaphysical actuality was confused with historical actuality. Thus a rudimentary metaphysical position was summarily applied to actuality. Fichte wanted to construct the world, but what he had in mind was a systematic construction. Schlegel and Tieck wanted to obtain a world"* (p. 275). Finally, Romanticism allegedly counters Socratic irony by adopting a higher level of "ironic formation," in which the subject—aware of its own irony—flourishes in ironic freedom. With the early Romantics, "the intensified subjective consciousness…declares irony as its position" (p. 242). On this higher level of consciousness, which "corresponds to reflection's reflection" having "a subjectivity's subjectivity" as a precondition, is the "consciousness that finitude is a nothing is obviously just as earnestly intended as Socrates's ignorance" (p. 269). The preconditions, however, have been switched: "the Romantic ironist, who raises himself to a transcendental *I*, actually suspends concrete historical reality in the same way that he uses irony to create his own poetic reality as pure possibility (*kata dunamin*)" (p. 262).[40] "The ironist is the eternal *I* for which no actuality is adequate" (p. 283). Kierkegaard's polemics against Romantic irony, which strives to exchange infinite absolute negativity with a never-ending poetic freedom, begin here. He criticizes the modern manifestations of Romantic irony from the very different perspective of Socratic irony.

Socratic irony negates existing reality in order to allow subjectivity to come to the fore. But this "subjectivity's emancipation" that is "carried out in the service of the idea" (p. 263) does not question actuality at all but rather "was demanding . . . the actuality of subjectivity, of ideality" (p. 271). Socrates's irony endeavored to move his contemporaries from the confusing limits of custom to the true idea of the good as an object of ethical passion. His irony was obligated with respect to a new positivity beyond all negativity, a consciousness of subjectivity that inaugurated the historical development as pure possibility. Socratic irony was thus simply a vehicle, a stimulating power that was, according to Kierkegaard, "world-historically justified" (p. 271).

However, Romantic irony does not stand in the service of the world spirit, since it is not applicable here that "an element of the given actuality . . . must be negated and superseded by a new element, but it was all of historical actuality that it negated in order to make room for a self-created actuality. It was not subjectivity that should forge ahead here, since subjectivity was already given in world situations, but it was an exaggerated subjectivity, a subjectivity raised to the second power. We also perceive here that irony was totally unjustified" (p. 275). In contrast to Socratic irony, which works towards a positive ethical idea, aesthetic subjectivity of ironic-Romantic consciousness situates itself critically against *all* of reality. It relativizes not only ironic reality in general but also destroys existing reality [actuality] and, with it, all of historical existence in favor of a poetic life without history. Its sole positive expression regards reality as only vanity and pretense. The Romantics' total irony misses precisely that which "is constitutive in actuality, that which orders and supports it: that is, morality and ethics" (p. 283). This irony becomes a "seducer" through which existence is exchanged for the emptiness of pretense, which confuses life with a noncommittal existence in reflection and which is the halting of all historical actuality and thus an abuse of ironic sovereignty.

The arguments in Kierkegaard's harsh polemics against Romantic irony refer, in their hermeneutic approach, to Socrates, who has just shown that irony is only a "guide" (p. 327), an "excellent surgeon" (p. 328), but is not identical to the *idea*. Yet since Socrates has been "lacking in all positivity," he has, according to Kierkegaard's correction of Hegel's perspective, become the beginning of the initiation of all historical development: He is the beginning and therefore positive, but as *only* the beginning, he is negative.[41] Romanticism inverts this relationship of the higher reflection of irony precisely to its opposite. It can no longer be said about Romanticism, as it can about Socrates, that "his negativity virtually carries within itself, so to speak, the positivity of his historical consequences."[42] The gravity that stands behind the infinitely absolute negativity of Socratic irony like an "incognito," a "magnificent pause," (p. 198) a "turning point in history" (p. 200) and that finally, in contrast to Hegel's concept of morality, is broken down by Kierkegaard through a Christian anthropology, reveals itself against the backdrop of the existential abuse inflicted upon it by Romantic irony. The world-historical meaning of irony—according to the fundamental idea—is deduced from Socratic irony not only as paving the way for morality, but also—contrary to fact—from the injury that is inflicted by Romantic irony upon historicized morality. Christ as the salvation from negativity forms the caesura. After Christ, Socratic irony can only live on in a higher form as Romantic irony and thus becomes its opposite.

In this way, Kierkegaard's intention to overcome the Hegelian dialectic of concepts through a finally theologically interpreted dialectic of existence forms the background of his criticism of German Romanticism. The pathos of the position developed with regard to Socrates's method is revealed in the fact that precisely the renouncing of the knowledge of the truth (of existence) in the purely passionate *appropriation* of truth is the only truth there can be for one who exists. Seen in Johannine terms, the knowledge of truth is not a knowledge of the correct existence; rather, it is the true existence itself. The true existence that precedes all knowledge of reason is for Kierkegaard in the end only communicable through a religious experience. It is not attainable through reflection.[43] Reflection and contemplation of an original self lead precisely to the destruction of the unity of this self in antinomian powers that communicate themselves to the concrete individual as a fundamental contradiction in the feeling of fear and desperation. However, self-realization for Kierkegaard is "a consciousness about one's self, which is itself an action," and it realizes itself in the concrete existence of historical actuality. "What doubt is to science, irony is to personal life" (p. 326).

Kierkegaard's criticism of the ironic-Romantic form of life culminates in the accusation that it suspends the ethical. The suspension of a given reality and with it the conditions of historical existence, into pure possibility—the "emigration of actuality" (p. 297)—leads to chaos and confusion, to the destruction of all that is objectively given. It is a flight into a sham existence, which is propelled solely by the motivation no longer to be exposed to the existential experience of contradiction. The Romantic shuts himself in a fantasy world where he becomes intoxicated with the "infinity of possibilities" (p. 262) and believes to encounter in this infinity—"the enormous reserve fund of possibility" (p. 262)—*true* infinity but actually is intoxicated with bad infinity—an 'outer', or, as Kierkegaard puts it, "external infinity." "Even if he enjoys the whole world, the person who enjoys poetically nevertheless lacks one enjoyment, for he does not enjoy himself" (p. 297). The negative dialectic in Socrates's method is transformed here into a poetic progression that is meant to reach in the infinite. The enthusiasm of this ironic freedom lacks all existential gravity, because it does not possess anything higher than itself. It is not at liberty to command an ethical position. It lacks the 'negative moment' in the process of the dialectic of existence, which is precisely what characterizes Socratic irony. Socrates's path to truth becomes the truth itself in Romanticism—and is thus abused. The Romantic *exaggeration* of Socratic irony turns, according to Kierkegaard's criticism of, above all, Solger, "God's existence into irony" and thereby into "nothing" (p. 317n).

Thus, the life of the ironist, who is intoxicated by the interplay of "creating" and "annihilating" the poeticized and self-creating reality, also exists in actuality only in the *moment*. It breaks down into merely interesting details that, instead of existing in an actuality (or historical continuity), are gradual and occasional. "As the ironist poetically composes himself and his environment with the greatest possible license, as he lives in this totally hypothetical and subjunctive way, his life loses all continuity. He succumbs completely to mood. His life is nothing but mood" (p. 284). The only continuity of this "eternity devoid of content, this salvation devoid of joy, this superficial profundity, this hungry glut" (p. 285) is the selflessness of boredom, an emptiness that, as Kierkegaard writes in *Either/Or*, "rests upon the limitless infinity of change." Melancholy as "not to want deeply and introspectively," a flight from the world as the stepping out of temporality are the dark sides of ironic life, for which "no reality is suitable" but which is constantly stranded in reality. The turning point in the "summit" of Socratic irony—when "in that magnificent moment" the enthusiasm for destruction becomes Eros, "and Socrates became the beloved rather than the lover" (p. 190n)—transforms the Romantic irony in that empty moment[44] in which intoxication and desperation, melancholy and enthusiasm exchange each other without continuity. In positing irony as absolute, Romanticism revokes Socratic irony as its corrective.

Finally, Kierkegaard's attack on Romantic irony culminates in the reproach that the "poetic position taken by the writer" (p. 305) determines "the entire design" of the poetic work in such a way as to become a duplication of the poet's ironic freedom. Romantic poetry mirrors the inner strife of the Romantics' ironically transformed relationship to life: It becomes "poetic arbitrariness" and leaves behind as an overall impression "an emptiness in which nothing remains" (p. 305). Because "the writer himself does not enter into a true poetic relationship to what he writes," he "cannot enter into a truly poetic relation to the reader" (p. 305). The ironically transformed relationship to life increases itself in the relationship between poetry and the author's self-image. Precisely in this deficient sovereignty vis-à-vis irony as a poetic principle, Kierkegaard must have seen the most striking confirmation of the Romantic's inability to control irony (as a point of view) and his being controlled by it. Because it is one thing to let oneself be poetically composed and another to compose oneself poetically.

Thus, Romantic poetry for Kierkegaard is not autonomous but, rather, dependent on representation. It merely ironically caricatures reality to the point of the grotesque, destroying it in its most laughable moments without being able to supply a "true ideal:" "On the one side stands the given actuality with all its paltry philistinism; on the other the ideal actuality with its dimly emerging shapes" (p. 304n). The incommunicability of these opposites, the condition "that this poetry moves between two opposites shows that in the deeper sense it is not true poetry" (p. 305). The restlessness in the polemically surpassing play of irony, the negation of all content, the lack of continuity and the poetic arbitrariness, which becomes a "laboratory" of non-committal experimentation—all of this stands justified, viewed from Kierkegaard's critical standpoint, in a yearning for "poetic infinity" that is still only illusory, an eternity, which, "since it has not time," becomes a mere caricature. The strength of this poetry still remains at most only in the lyrical sphere, "because here mood—and mood, after all, is all-important—has absolute sway and is utterly free, since all content is negated" (p. 307). But ultimately "the musical element [in the lyric] isolates itself entirely" (p. 307) and becomes profane.

Kierkegaard bases his criticism of Romantic poetry on the example of Friedrich Schlegel's love story *Lucinde* and Ludwig Tieck's poetry. These reviews, which anticipate the later depictions of aesthetic life in *Either/Or*, pursue the goal of criticizing the poetic objectivizations of aesthetic forms of life by themselves. Romantic love—Schlegel's ideal of a poetic life—is discredited by Kierkegaard as a "catechism of love" (p. 291)[45] that proclaims "an infinitely cowardly life" (p. 298), an ahistorical "vegetating" and a "collapsing into aesthetic stupefaction" (p. 295)—which goes even to the point of the demonic nature of sensuality (p. 302)—and which therefore must be measured by the ethics of marriage, since it is there that romantic love first becomes historical. For Kierkegaard, the true poetic life lies in marriage, a poetry of life that cannot be represented but only lived. Not romantic love but marriage is the true poetic life—a poetry of life that cannot be represented in art. In this sense marriage is the testimony for the "wondrous paradox . . . that the highest and most beautiful things in life are not to be heard about, nor read about, nor seen, but may only be lived. Conjugal love is therefore more aesthetic than romantic love precisely because [!] it is so much more difficult to represent."[46]

Kierkegaard's criticism of Tieck's poetry and satirical dramas, on the other hand, reaffirms the accusation that they are mere puns, lyrical experiments, tone poetry, silly "childishness," and "poetic abandon," carried away to the point of "excessively ironic capering" (p. 302). Kierkegaard also makes clear that these forms of "poetic abandon," in so far as they exclude all contact with the real world, possess a historical justification. He recognizes this justification of Romantic irony as it becomes visible in Tieck's refreshing polemics against the "totally fossilized" (p. 303) Enlightenment. "The world was in its dotage and had to be rejuvenated. In that respect, romanticism was beneficial" (p. 304). However, this applies only to its shutting the self off from all reality. The more this principle is infringed upon, the closer such poetizing "becomes intelligible . . . through a break with actuality," the more "it forgets its poetic indifference" (p. 302) and collides with the experience of reality. That this collision is unavoidable in the end is due to the fact that the adventurous independence of fantasy, which has no central point, "never finds rest" (p. 306) in its strivings (p. 306); it does not instill trust in its figurations and even generates a "disquieting anxiety" (p. 306) in its absurd and shrill excesses. This fear most likely stems from the realization that the "infinitely light play with nothingness" does not encourage but rather injures "the identity of real temporality and even more real eternity, whose unity is first constituted in the entirety of reality."[47]

In his conception of a "controlled irony," Kierkegaard, in an final conclusion, attempts to show that irony as a poetic principle and means of expression is not to be wholly rejected, since it can also establish a positive relationship to existence. For Kierkegaard, this is paradigmatically achieved by Goethe, who ironically limits the Romantics' immediate aesthetic standpoint, absolute subjectivity, "to let the objective dominate" (p. 324). This restriction occurs because the poet relates "ironically to his writing...so that the irony is in turn ironically controlled" (p. 324). Only when irony itself is turned against its "prodigious enthusiasm" does its impatience become discipline. Only then does it find "the center of gravity in itself" (p. 324), to become a "controlled element," a "disciplinarian," an "excellent surgeon" (p. 328). This controlled irony "limits, finitizes, and circumscribes and thereby yields truth, actuality, content; it disciplines and punishes and thereby yields balance and consistency" (p. 326). In this way the form of controlled irony becomes the corrective of the Romantic aesthetician. To a certain extent, the higher form of Romantic irony is here turned against itself to such an extent that it appears, in poetry, to be Socratic in nature. In this manner the ironist stands above irony, controls it, can place it in the service of a "higher idea," and is immune to the abuse of its turning itself into an idea and a philosophy of life. Kierkegaard values this form of controlled irony, which overcomes the Romantic and moves towards a positive possibility, as being "extremely important in enabling personal life to gain health and truth" (p. 328). For Kierkegaard, Goethe's poetry is the fitting expression of a poetic life: "Here, then, irony is controlled, is reduced to an element. The essence is nothing other than the phenomenon; the phenomenon is nothing other than the essence. Possibility is not so prudish as to be unwilling to enter into any actuality, but actuality is possibility" (p. 325). Goethe's, like Shakespeare's, life was reconciled with actuality through an "irony's inner economy" (p. 325); or, "in other words, the poet does not live poetically by creating a poetic work...but he lives poetically only when he himself is oriented and thus integrated in the age in which he lives, is positively free in the actuality to which he belongs" (p. 326).

In the wake of Kierkegaard's work on irony, the conception of a *controlled irony* represents the utmost argument for the ability of the world-historical meaning of irony, in poetry, to be made fruitful for the artistic communication of existence. Here Kierkegaard's reflection on his own position takes place. The criticism of Romantic irony that Kierkegaard develops from the standpoint of Socratic irony and that from this point of view, furnishes proof of a perversion of its world-historical function, develops by its own criteria as to how poetry can be placed into the service of a true poetic life, that is to say of a historical existence. Through this hermeneutic approach Kierkegaard takes up another position, which he later changes with regard to the technique of representation in *Either/Or*. In the situation of the novel *Either/Or*, the aesthetic is indeed radically confronted with the ethical. This occurs, however, not in order to question the existential meaning of art, but rather in order to be able to follow the transformation of an aesthetician. At this point, Adorno's negative aesthetic and critical revision of Kierkegaard come into play. In Adorno's estimation Kierkegaard is the first theorist of modern art, who shows that the search for a true actuality starts, not even in ethics, but in an already determined aesthetics. In his *Construction of Kierkegaard's Aesthetic* (1933) he writes: "Not the hubris of grandeur with which the 'moralist' so scornfully reproaches the 'aesthete', but rather the reverse of the hubris of greatness is his best attitude. It is the cell of a materialism whose vision is focused on 'a better world'—not to forget in dreams the present world, but to change it by the strength of an image that indeed may be as a whole 'portrayed according to the abstract criterion *in general*' whose contours are concretely and unequivocally filled in every particular dialectical element."[48]

The aesthetic of a controlled irony is no longer the indication of an unstable form of living. Such an aesthetic does not understand the picture only on the manner of its subjective constitution but wants to show the transformation of the picture itself, "whereby eternity itself shines through as the content of transience" (p. 132). A picture, which can turn its face away—an image, which goes beyond all art but being itself an image—rescues the aesthetic even as the aesthetic is lost. This aesthetic does not form a sphere as an exception that has no part in life; it forms not even a self-sufficient experience in the form of a medium that coalesces with what it conveys (*à la* McLuhan's formula: the medium is the message). Rather than a depersonalization of life, it is a depersonalization of the living in which life, while passing away, yet breathes and rests free of sacrifice. From Adorno's point of view Kierkegaard's existential communication emerges from an art that deals with itself. It sounds like an attack on postmodern aestheticizing of reality, when Adorno formulates:

That which sets itself up against subjective idealism in the aesthetic sphere, the ontological character of a 'text', whose truth the individual means to secure as a mere sign; the depersonalization of the self from which a meaningful letter emancipates itself—this determines Kierkegaard's theological stage in the doctrine of objective despair. The parenthetical possibility, however, that ultimately the 'typographical error' itself would prove to be meaningful is the nonsensical caesura that brings hope into existence through its collapse. Existence, despair, and hope—it is with this rhythm, not the monotonous rhythm of the absolute 'I' and total sacrifice, that Kierkegaard's ontology must be measured, and it appears in the disparate images into which the abstract unity of existence is dialectically divided. (p. 133)

The 'typographical error' in the play of signifiers is the nonsensical caesura in a lost life, an exception that has no part in life but that breaks it through by its paradox. Adorno interprets Kierkegaard's attempt to insert a critical caesura into the movement of Romantic irony as the paradoxical attempt not only to understand aesthetic images and constructions but to make them accessible for an existential communication. Such disparate images into which the abstract unity of existence is dialectically divided show that there is something that cannot be represented in art and that we need not regret this. From Adorno's point of view Kierkegaard's aesthetic shows the course of a dialectic by which the translucence of semblance makes evident semblance itself.

In his pseudonymous essay *The Repetition* (1843), which is still utterly influenced by his early Romantic studies, Kierkegaard talks about an artistic representation that tries to demonstrate the limits of representation. By this method, the unreality in which we live can become visible and in the same moment eternity bends into time for the imagination. Adorno quotes a passage from this Kierkegaard essay, and it is striking how his view of Kierkegaard's criticism of Romantic irony anticipates the essence of modern art. Adorno writes:

> In his essay Kierkegaard talks about the old Friedrichstädter Theatre in Berlin and describes a comic actor named Beckmann by whose image he exactly and very realistically quotes the image of the later Chaplin. The sentences are:

> Not only can he go, he can also come as gone.[49] This coming as gone is something very special, and owing to this genius he improvises at the same time the entire scenic environment. He can not only act a strolling apprentice, he can come as gone in this figure of the apprentice so that you experience everything, you catch a glimpse of the friendly village beyond the dust in the road, you hear its muted noise, you see the footpath around the pond when you turn at the smithy's— when you see Beckmann come as gone with the small bundle over his shoulder, the cane in his hand, carefree and unflagging. He can come as gone onto the stage with street urchins behind him whom you don't see.[50]

The gone comer is Chaplin who, like a slow meteor, brushes the world, even where he appears to rest, and the imaginary landscape he suggests is his aura that collects here in the silent noise of the village as a transparent peace while he wanders on with his cane and hat, which suit him well.

11

Richard Rorty and the Ethics of Anti-Foundationalism

JON A. LEVISOHN

Jon A. Levisohn is Assistant Professor of Education and, by courtesy, Philosophy, at Brandeis University. This chapter is largely taken from the first chapter of his honors thesis at Harvard University, entitled Rorty, Relativism, and Responsibility. *His recent publications include "How to Do Philosophy of Religious Education,"* Religious Education 2005, *and "Patriotism and Parochialism: Why Teach American Jewish History, and How?"* Journal of Jewish Education.

The contemporary student of philosophy (and of its history) is confronted not only by the collapse of the metaphysical systems of the nineteenth century, but also by the slow demise of the empiricisms which struggled to replace them in the first half of the twentieth. Without a secure philosophical account of what is universal, what is absolute, what is transcendent of historical, political and social contingency—whether in the realm of our moral beliefs or, more generally, our knowledge of anything at all—all we are left with is a sometimes overwhelming diversity. We observe, even within our own society but certainly across sociological and historical boundaries, a dazzling diversity of opinions and beliefs, with no apparent independent or objective criterion at hand to help us distinguish between the good and the bad, between the true and the false.

One way to articulate the point is to say that "the enterprises for providing a *foundation* for Being and Knowledge . . . are enterprises that have disastrously failed."[1] For those who concur with this assessment, the alternative to the foundationalism which has characterized the philosophical tradition must be some form of anti-foundationalism—that is, consciously abandoning the pretense of philosophy to discover a secure basis, from which we might construct an independent, absolute, objective criterion for truth. But until anti-foundationalism is given content, relativism or skepticism may appear inevitable; certainly, the current proliferation of fashionable relativistic notions among philosophers and non-philosophers gives us little reason to think otherwise. The question remains: Is it possible to abandon the stable plateau of foundationalism for the slippery slope of anti-foundationalism, without sliding?

Richard Rorty, for one, confidently argues that it is indeed possible to walk a fine line between foundationalism and relativism. According to the book jacket of his *Contingency, Irony, and Solidarity*, Rorty has been declared by none other than Harold Bloom as "the most interesting philosopher in the world today."[2] Whatever else such a proclamation might mean, it should certainly indicate to us that Rorty is among the most *controversial* figures in contemporary intellectual circles, a situation which stems in part from the fact that some of his colleagues do not share his confidence.

In what follows, I offer a reading of the first two of Rorty's recently published collected papers, "Solidarity or Objectivity?"[3] and "Science as Solidarity,"[4] as points of entry into Rorty's philosophy. In these explicitly programmatic essays, Rorty deliberately avoids discussing the technical aspects of his views of truth and relativism in great depth and detail; so will I. Instead, I explain Rorty's program in his own terms, elucidating what Rorty means by solidarity and objectivity and why he advocates choosing the former over the latter. In the process, I emphasize the ethical underpinnings of Rorty's position, and show that Rorty himself admits (albeit infrequently) that there is some sort of mysterious "ethical foundation" which takes the place, or plays the role, of a metaphysical foundation. I also show, incidentally, that Rorty's vocabulary is surprisingly well suited to the articulation of an alternative position.

Solidarity versus Objectivity

In "Solidarity or Objectivity?" Rorty sets out the choice between the two options indicated in the title as an expression of his philosophical program, the program that he has pursued since the publication of *Philosophy and the Mirror of Nature*.[5] In that influential book, Rorty devotes the three hundred pages of Parts One and Two to exhaustively exposing the flaws in the traditional images of the mind as a mirror of nature, of knowledge as the perspicuous representation of or correspondence to a nonhuman, description-independent reality, and of philosophy as the discipline which evaluates the claims to knowledge of the rest of our culture. In the process, he surveys the history of epistemology from its Greek origins to its recent demise, as well as the history of its putative "successor subjects," empirical psychology and philosophy of language. Then in Part Three, he sketches an alternative picture of an "edifying" as opposed to a "systematic" philosophy, offering "hermeneutics" not in place of epistemology but merely as a name for how we might proceed without it. Thus, the tenor of his argument is that certain of the most fundamental aspects of our philosophical reflections are, in the end, merely optional.

Here, Rorty begins with the following proclamation: "There are two principal ways in which reflective human beings try, by placing their lives in a larger context, to give some sense to those lives" (p. 21). That is, Rorty perceives some human, existential need which demands satisfaction, and the two possible ways are the quest for solidarity and the quest for objectivity.[6] We tell ourselves stories of various sorts (according to Rorty's preferred terminology) in order to give meaning to our lives, in order to cope; for Rorty, the exercise of rationality, of thinking philosophically, theologically, historically, even scientifically, is to be considered in terms of coping with experience. And these stories do their work by establishing a community in the one case, and by invoking an "immediate relation to a nonhuman reality" (p. 21) in the other.

At first glance, if we were unfamiliar with Rorty's views, we might interpret his existential speculation as an analysis of essential human nature, as if to say, "Humans are not only Political Animals (as indicated by the desire for solidarity) but also Intellectual Beings (as indicated by the desire for objectivity)." This picture does, in fact, seem to reflect experience in a reasonably interesting, and perhaps justifiable, way. We do seem to be motivated to form communal associations, to find common agreement for our ideas and our aspirations, and we do seem motivated to search out objective justifications for those ideas and aspirations in theoretical terms; we are interested in politics and philosophy. Such a view would certainly not lack for precedent in the history of philosophical ideas.

But Rorty, of course, would deny that he is describing essential human nature, because he would deny that there is such a thing. Indeed, in his pragmatic view,[7] the concepts of "essence" and "human nature" are two products of the philosophy shop, two results of the neurotic obsession of the Western philosophical tradition with objectivity, as we will see. Instead, Rorty would presumably claim merely to be observing twin phenomena of human behavior, two deep and powerful social or psychological impulses which have

affected Western intellectual history. And he would advise us to keep reading, for that is where his account is leading.

According to Rorty, the philosophical tradition of the West has been dominated, since the Greeks, by a disproportionate emphasis on one method of
giving sense to our lives, namely the desire for objectivity. This desire arose,
he speculates, in response to an uneasiness with diversity, the diversity that
the Greeks began to notice as their consciousness of the world around them
expanded. Reacting to difference, they sought out commonalities, convinced
by Plato that "the way to transcend skepticism is to envisage a common goal
of humanity—a goal set by human nature rather than Greek culture" (p. 21).
That is, Rorty imagines that skeptical arguments about what in the world it
is possible to know, and how well we can know it, became fundamental to
self-conscious intellectual life in Greece (and subsequently thereafter in the
West) as a result of the new political circumstances. The antidote to the increasingly radical skeptical challenges seemed to lie in justification through increasingly expanded commonalities: universal, absolute, infallible, non-contingent
truths, both about human nature and about the world, which (it was hoped)
would serve as "common ground" for evaluating knowledge claims and differences of opinion. In this manner, truth—immediate and secure access to
moral and physical reality—became a virtue, and objectivity an ideal.

Moreover, Rorty argues, philosophy since the time of Plato has not merely
preferred objectivity, resulting in some kind of benign neglect of solidarity.
Rather, the search for truth has meant the "turning away from solidarity to
objectivity" (p. 21), because it has been bound up in the desire to articulate
the essence of human nature, to paint a picture of what an ideal individual
and especially an ideal society would look like. Just as we seek objective
knowledge about mathematics and about biology, so too we imagine an objective, universal "ultimate community":

> this [objectivist] tradition dreams of an ultimate community which will have tran-
> scended the distinction between the natural and the social, which will exhibit a
> solidarity which is not parochial because it is the expression of an ahistorical
> human nature. (p. 22)

We do care about solidarity with others—about community, about human
nature, about interpersonal morality—and we believe (or believed) that by
reducing it, by discovering the essence of human nature and ethics, we have
understood and accommodated our concerns, while avoiding the pitfall of
narrow-minded parochialism.

Rorty's analysis continues with his argument that the tradition, overly concerned with objectivity and willing to reduce solidarity to it, has had to con-

cern itself with metaphysics and epistemology, those fields which attempt to investigate the correspondence of ideas or beliefs to reality, the intrinsic nature of things. Once an unconceptualized, description-independent, metaphysically real world is posited, then it is appropriate to ask the question, "How does thought (or more recently, language) hook on to the world?" This has led to analyses of procedures of investigation and justification, and attempts to discover those elements of nature or of human nature which allow for this sort of objectivity. In short, every area of philosophy—from philosophy of science to political philosophy and ethics—has been gripped by the picture of knowledge as accurate representation of reality, and of truth as correspondence to reality, from Plato on.

Needless to say, Rorty views the tradition as a failure.[8] It failed in all its metaphysical and epistemological projects, as each one in turn stepped up to bat and struck out swinging. As Rorty exhaustively describes in *Philosophy and the Mirror of Nature*, the tradition itself has produced the criticisms which have undermined that objective ideal (and its corollary essentialism and representationalism) in the work of Quine, Sellars, Davidson, Kuhn, Putnam. And as he notes in this essay, "the best argument we . . . have against the realistic partisans of objectivity is . . . that the traditional Western metaphysico-epistemological way of firming up our habits simply isn't working anymore. It isn't doing its job" (p. 33). That is, from the late twentieth-century perspective, the tradition had not succeeded in producing a lasting, widely acceptable, independent or *external* philosophical justification for our desire for objectivity—or, for that matter, for any of our other moral, political, or intellectual "habits."[9]

But there have been pockets of resistance to this futile reductive endeavor, those who have recognized that solidarity—the agreement of community, or better, the role that community plays in determining those realities and those procedures for investigation and justification—cannot be reduced to objectivity. Among those hardy souls are the pragmatists, and they have no need and no desire for metaphysics or epistemology. Instead, according to Rorty, they abandon the quest for objectivity and take up the quest for solidarity with renewed commitment, confident that the justification of our habits lies with our fellow humans, not with correspondence to some objective ideal of the Good or the True. Instead of grounding solidarity in objectivity, they confidently reduce objectivity to solidarity. By this, Rorty intends the abandonment of the pretensions of the Western philosophical tradition to search for transcendent truth—and the conceptual baggage of "correspondence" and "representation" and epistemology and metaphysics in general—and the acceptance instead of the historical and pragmatic nature of truth. Instead of conceiving of truth as "correspondence to a nonhuman reality," truth is simply what it is better for us to believe, here and now.[10]

At this point, the picture has become a little muddled; before going any further into the pragmatist account of truth, the notions of objectivity and solidarity themselves require clarification. After all, Rorty began by considering them as human desires, social phenomena—not "natural" or "essential," to be sure, but at least relatively common and in some sense fundamental. However, they soon became transformed, in his account, into ideas or ideals, or maybe into values. Perhaps most importantly, in this transformation from social phenomenon to concept they seem to have lost their implied parallelism; instead, either solidarity is "grounded" in objectivity or objectivity is "reduced" to solidarity.[11] Rorty often refers to the pragmatists as "we partisans of solidarity," diametrically opposed to the objectivist tradition and the realists who have yet to escape it. So what started out as twin and compatible inclinations seem to have become entrenched as competitive, mutually exclusive ideals, and this transformation requires some explanation.

According to Rorty, the ideals of objectivity and of solidarity are mutually exclusive because each may be seen as appropriating the desire for the other, the value expressed by the other, to serve its own ends (so to speak). Thus, in grounding solidarity in objectivity, the realists transformed the desire for community into a "dream of an ultimate community," thereby attempting to explain away the values of community—of tolerance, mutual respect, even love—in terms of a transcendent community, "the expression of an ahistorical human nature" (p. 23). (This is the project of traditional foundationalist political philosophy.) And in their reduction of objectivity to solidarity, the pragmatists redirected the desire for objectivity to be "simply the desire for as much intersubjectivity as possible" (p. 23), explaining away truth without recourse to any notion of objective reality.

Two Versions of Rationality: Algorithm versus Ethic

In "Science as Solidarity," Rorty clearly sets out the opposing sides, in terms of the related question of rationality. He begins by confronting the familiar philosophical problem of the relationship between the natural sciences and the humanities, a problem which is bound up in our demand for rationality. Our Western, Enlightenment culture is gripped by a picture of the sciences as inquiring after objective truth, of corresponding to reality; indeed, the physical sciences are taken as the model of investigation into objective reality and therefore "scientific method" is taken as the epitome of rationality. The difficulty which then arises, given that the humanities (and even the social sciences) do not seem to accomplish quite so much, is a result of our slavish obsession with the "strong" sense of rationality. That is, we believe (according to Rorty) that to be rational and scientific means to adhere to prepared criteria, criteria established prior and external to the inquiry which we are currently undertaking and which are, therefore, not tainted by subjectivity or contingency. Science, then, is merely a matter of following the rules, simply and methodically; while this account will struggle to find a place for innovative creativity in the pursuit of science, it nevertheless gains by eliminating any subjective "value judgments" from the pursuit of objective, scientific truth. This, of course, is the popular algorithmic model of "the scientific method," a mysterious entity whose essence eludes philosophers and scientists, but which inevitably reveals itself, in all its splendor, exclusively to high-school science teachers.[12]

Instead, Rorty prefers the "weak" sense of rationality, where to be rational does not involve algorithmically following pre-existing guidelines, but rather merely being "reasonable" or "sane" or "civilized." That is, to be rational means to "eschew dogmatism, defensiveness, and righteous indignation," opting instead for "tolerance, respect for the opinions of those around one, willingness to listen, reliance on persuasion rather than force" (p. 37). Rationality is not a method in the sense of an algorithm, but rather a method in the sense of an ethic—though perhaps we should not bother to reinterpret the word "method," but should discard it altogether. In this way, the perceived (and problematic) essential distinction between the sciences and the humanities dissolves, since neither "corresponds to reality" but each can be pursued "rationally." Once we recognize that both the sciences and the humanities are equally rational, and that there is no essential epistemological difference between them, then we will feel free to differentiate on the basis of other factors—such as what we would like each to accomplish—without devaluing one or the other.[13]

As should be clear, the outmoded, problematic "strong" rationality is a product of the philosophical tradition, which (as we know) was gripped by the ideal of objectivity. The "weak" sense of rationality, on the other hand, is a reflection and an embodiment of the ideal of solidarity. At times, Rorty adopts the slogan "unforced agreement," instead of "solidarity," but in general, this paper abounds in familiar expressions of the choice which he is laying out.

Pragmatists would like to replace the desire for objectivity—the desire to be in touch with a reality which is more than some community with which we identify ourselves—with the desire for solidarity with that community. (p. 39)
    The desire for "objectivity" boils down to a desire to acquire beliefs which will eventually receive unforced agreement in the course of a free and open encounter with people holding other beliefs. (p. 41)

Differences in formulation notwithstanding—the desire for objectivity
is to be "replaced" in one metaphor, "boiled down" in the other—Rorty
clearly considers the dichotomy of solidarity and objectivity to be bound
up in two contrasting views of science, scientific method, and rational
inquiry. (Once we understand that Rorty intends to set the search for objective truth over against the ethics of solidarity, the distinctions among his
metaphors no longer seem confusing. Objectivity may be reduced to solidarity, because the old "strong" rationalism is supplanted by the new
"weak" rationalism. It may be reinterpreted as intersubjectivity, because
the desire for greater and greater degrees of justification gets expressed
as the desire for wider agreement. It may be dismissed as "scientism" (p.
26), since it implies a slavish worship of the false god of algorithmic, objective science. It may be considered to reflect the "fear of death" (p. 32),
since it demonstrates the desire to escape from the contingent to the absolute
and universal. Or it may simply be dropped altogether.) Thus, according
to Rorty's view of the traditional, metaphysically realist ideal of objectivity, rationality consitutes rigid adherence to a predetermined algorithm;
according to the pragmatist ideal of solidarity, it involves muddling through
towards intersubjective agreement on the basis of a non-foundationalist
ethic.

Why Should We Accept Rorty's Story?

There are good reasons to question Rorty's historical account, a device familiar from *Philosophy and the Mirror of Nature* but carried out here with a great
deal of haste.[14] For example, Rorty seems to neglect the role played by the
developing disciplines of mathematics and geometry in the evolution of Greek
metaphysics, so that he emphasizes the importance of the *immediacy* of knowledge: objectivity is the idea that one may be "in touch with the nature of
things, not by way of the opinions of the community, but in a more immediate way" (p. 21). But this reconstruction may not do justice to the Platonic
texts, where it seems that the growth of metaphysics, in particular the central
idea of true knowledge as more than mere opinion, owes a greater debt to the
apparent *security* of knowledge that had recently been demonstrated in those
new and blossoming fields.

Furthermore, Rorty casually jumps from the origins of the quest for objectivity in Greek thought to picking up the threads of the story with the Enlightenment, a familiar move but also a problematic one: aside from stressing the
development of modern science as the model of rational inquiry (and the scientist as the ideal intellectual), Rorty does not sufficiently differentiate the
contributions of the ancient and the modern periods to the story.[15] And it is

not clear exactly how the historical event of the emerging awareness of diversity and the corresponding "fear of parochialism" is supposed to have produced the desire for objectivity. According to Rorty, skepticism seems to be central to the story, perhaps forcing the Greeks to challenge themselves, provoking that existential need to give sense to their lives. But this explanation will not satisfy Rorty. After all, he wishes to explain the origin of only *one* of the ways that we give sense to our lives—namely, the desire for objectivity—not both.

However, the point of the account is not its historical "accuracy," which justifies, to a certain extent, Rorty's liberties in telling his story.[16] Rather, Rorty's purpose is to show how the quest for objectivity arose at a certain time and place. In this way, he devalues or undermines objectivity, by showing it to be not a natural or essential desire, but merely an optional and contingent one. Moreover, he is now free to argue, it is a *failed* option: "the best argument . . . against the realistic partisans of objectivity is that the traditional Western metaphysico-epistemological way of firming up our habits simply isn't working anymore" (p. 33).

So why choose solidarity? Apparently, because the desire for solidarity is more *fundamental* than the desire for objectivity. After all, in Rorty's account, it was the values associated with solidarity that gave rise to objectivity in the first place; this is why he emphasized the role played by the need "to envisage a common goal of humanity" and by the "fear of parochialism," while diminishing the significance of mathematics and geometry in the story. In Rorty's view, the emergence of the ideal of objectivity was inspired by ethical considerations which we retrospectively recognize as values associated with solidarity. The effect is to suggest that, from the very beginning, objectivity was simply solidarity gone wrong.

But what does Rorty accomplish by this line of argument? Even if we concede that solidarity is (in some sense) more fundamental than objectivity, there is no reason, in principle, why a similar story cannot be told about the historical, contingent development of solidarity as well. Given his thoroughgoing anti-essentialism, Rorty must certainly concede the point that solidarity can no more be an essential or necessary desire than objectivity can, that solidarity too is simply an option open to us. But if this is so, if both solidarity and objectivity are nothing more than options, then we should ask again: why choose solidarity?[17] At this point, Rorty must (and does, briefly) acknowledge a positive reason for his allegiance to solidarity. All along, he has claimed that his position is merely a negative one, but now he must come out from behind that shield; not surprisingly, this is his most vulnerable point. There is, in fact, a positive basis to Rorty's views—not a metaphysical basis, but an ethical one.

Ethical Anti-Foundationalism

From the very beginning of *Solidarity or Objectivity*, we may notice that
(what may be called) a concern for ethics is, obviously, fundamental to
Rorty's view. His discussion of the twin desires is cast in ethical terms; the
satisfaction of desires is a notorious source for the violation of ethical principles, whatever those principles may be, so we should have reason to beware.
Rorty points out the specific potential violations associated with solidarity and objectivity:

> Insofar as a person is seeking solidarity, she does not ask about the relation between
> the practices of the chosen community and something outside that community.
> (p. 21)

That is, the desire for solidarity—considered here as the concern with
maintaining the cohesion, structure, or even the very existence of a community, as well as preserving one's own membership within the community—
obstructs the potential inquiry into whether the practices (or standards, or
rules) of that community are *unjust*, as we might say. One imagines that Rorty
has in mind such examples as the phenomena of patriotism (in the political
realm) and peer pressure (in the psychological). The ethical problem, then,
is not the specific activities undertaken in pursuit of solidarity—again, here
the term is used in the fundamental sense in which it gives meaning to life—
for these may be justified by various arguments. Rather, the ethical problem
here is with the obstruction of inquiry, with the fact that the desire for solidarity may potentially blind and deafen the seeker of solidarity to ethical challenges, to the cries of the wounded from outside the community. Not every
challenge, not every wound, deserves to derail the search for solidarity, but
in the long run and on the whole, every challenge deserves to be heard.

So much for the potential ethical violations due to the desire for solidarity. Regarding the desire for objectivity, Rorty writes:

> Insofar as [a person] seeks objectivity, she distances herself from the actual per-
> sons around her not by thinking of herself as a member of some other real or
> imaginary group, but rather by attaching herself to something which can be
> described without reference to any particular human beings. (p. 21)

The first thing to note is that the potential ethical problem here does not
seem to involve other people, at least not initially. Rather, the seeker of objectivity seems to violate an ethical obligation to *herself*: by denying her own
membership within a community, she is denying her own humanity.[18] However, the reader already hears a hint of a further objection. Not only does this

scientist or philosopher "attach herself" to something non-human, but by doing so, according to Rorty, "she distances herself" from others. Thus, the ethical implications seem to involve not only herself, but others as well; by distancing herself in the independent pursuit of objectivity, she can no longer hear the ideas—or the cries—of others.

Thus, we might characterize the ethical problem with the pursuit of solidarity as the prior restriction of entitlement, suffrage or representation to those within the community, while the ethical problem of objectivity involves the prior restriction of ethical challenges, *in general*. The point here is that the two issues are not parallel: the problem with solidarity is specific, while the problem with objectivity is general. Moreover, Rorty views solidarity as fundamentally ethical, while objectivity is fundamentally non-ethical (although not necessarily unethical). That is, the ethics of rational inquiry— such as tolerance, openness, reliance on persuasion instead of force—are predicated on the value of community, the value of solidarity. In this light, the specific pitfall of restricted representation is a problem of the community not fulfilling its own ethic. The quest for objectivity, on the other hand, constitutes a denial of the value of community, and therefore does not support a non-foundational ethic (even though it may attempt to develop a foundationalist ethic, as it attempts to ground the desire for solidarity). The result is that, in Rorty's view, the former problem can be (and is) overcome, while the latter problem cannot be. As the two desires develop, objectivity becomes mired in its ethical flaw, formalizing its non-ethic into an amoral scientistic method.[19] But solidarity, on the other hand, acknowledges its own flaws (so to speak), abandoning this vulgar parochialism or base ethnocentrism. Picking itself up by its bootstraps, solidarity develops into a non-parochial ethnocentrism, an ethic of the community which is open even to those without.[20]

Therefore, Rorty casts the choice between objectivity and solidarity as the choice between an algorithm and an ethic, between a supposed (but in fact empty) "intellectual virtue called 'rationality'" and the actual "moral virtue" of the ethics of inquiry (p. 39). The mysterious positive basis for choosing solidarity is not a metaphysical foundation or justification, for Rorty repudiates metaphysics altogether. There is no positive position on metaphysics or epistemology lurking anywhere in the area. Nevertheless, Rorty acknowledges that he does have a justification for his views, an *ethical justification*.

Any description of justifications—or grounds, bases, or foundations— treads on thin anti-foundational ice, so Rorty is always careful to contrast his own view to a foundational one. Thus, he says that "the pragmatist's account of the value of cooperative human inquiry has only an ethical base, not a metaphysical or epistemological one" (p. 24). Or again:

The pragmatist suggestion that we substitute a "merely" ethical foundation for our sense of community—or, better, that we think of our sense of community as having no foundation except shared hope and the trust created by such sharing—is put forward on practical grounds. It is not put forward as a corollary of a metaphysical claim . . . nor of an epistemological claim. (p. 33)

What is this suggested "ethical foundation"? We know, pretty well, what it is not: it is not a *real* foundation, because it is not justified by any external or prior criterion. The tension over just what this ethical foundation is is evident: in this passage, Rorty suggests it as a substitute for a metaphysical foundation, but almost immediately wishes to retract the phrase and replace it with something less prone to misinterpretation.

The practical grounds that Rorty refers to here are the collapse of traditional metaphysics and epistemology, as he states explicitly at the (unquoted) beginning of the paragraph, so the pragmatist suggestion should be considered as the only alternative still open to us. But actually, that is not quite true. More precisely, Rorty considers solidarity to be the only option available "in order to avoid . . . *the bad side of Nietzsche*" (p. 33).[21] The contrast with Nietzsche is intended to confirm that, indeed, solidarity is optional. But if we desire to be ethical, to consider other people, to be tolerant and avoid cruelty—*if we desire solidarity*—then solidarity is the only option available. This circularity, common to anti-foundationalist philosophies, should not be taken as a criticism. It merely serves to indicate that, in the end, Rorty relies upon an intuition—his own intuition—about ethical obligations to others.[22]

Thus, metaphysically or foundationally speaking, Rorty's position is simply a negative one; in denying objectivity, he denies the search for metaphysical foundations. However, in affirming solidarity, he affirms the presence of a rationality without metaphysical foundation, and more importantly, an *ethic* without a metaphysical foundation. Instead, that "weak" rationality and the ethics of solidarity rely upon an intuitive, ethical foundation—which is to say, they rely upon themselves. His ethnocentric position is positive only ethically, and may be justified only non-foundationally. Solidarity may indeed be optional, contingent, an historical development, but it is the ethical option; in the absence of any satisfactory justificatory account, but in the presence of our intuitions, we should just be ethical.

12

Mirror and Oneiric Mirages: Plato, Precursor of Freud

SARAH KOFMAN

*Before her suicide in 1994, Sarah Kofman wrote over twenty books on phi-
losophy, literary analysis, and feminism. Her philosophical work, often broadly
syncretic, incorporates literary and psychoanalytic approaches. "Miroir et
mirages oniriques: Platon, précurseur de Freud," published in* Séductions:
de Sartre à Héraclite *(Paris: Éditions Galilée, 1990) and first appearing in*
La Part de l'Oeil 4 *(1988), is translated into English for the first time by Elizabeth Davis.*

Freud and Plato

In *The Interpretation of Dreams*, Freud cites Plato on two occasions. In the
chapter "The Moral Sense in Dreams," reviewing the various authors who
have expressed opinions on the subject, he writes, "Plato . . . thought that the
best men are those who only *dream* what others *do* in their waking life" (Stra-
chey, p. 99). On the last page of the book, Freud returns to the philosopher
to ratify him, and to cite him as evidence for the distinction between latent
meaning and manifest meaning, thereby invalidating all judgment which one
might bring to bear on dreams:

> I think . . . that the Roman emperor was in the wrong when he had one of his sub-
> jects executed because he had dreamt of murdering the emperor. He should have
> begun by trying to find out what the dream meant; most probably its meaning
> was not what it appeared to be. And even if a dream with another content had

had this act of *lèse majesté* as its meaning, would it not be right to bear in mind Plato's dictum that the virtuous man is content to *dream* what a wicked man really *does*? I think it is best, therefore, to acquit dreams. (p. 658)

This repeated allusion to, and nearly in the same words as, the famous passage from Book IX of *The Republic* (571a) is surprising, to say the least. If Plato, too, really believes that the dream is a sovereign route to knowledge of the unconscious—the desires "innate in each one of us, but repressed (κολαζόμενα) by laws and better desires . . . which reveal themselves during sleep"—he nonetheless does not distinguish between manifest meaning and latent meaning, but maintains that our dreams betray our desires, and thus permit our judgment. The good man does not fulfill these desires, even in his dreams, and there lies his superiority, for only the wicked man acts awake as asleep. If all men, even those who appear quite normal, possess "a species of terrible, wild, lawless desire . . . evidenced by their dreams," then some of them, sound of mind and body, experience the least possible disturbing visions during sleep, and there come in closer contact than ever with truth. The dreams of the wicked are the source of our knowledge about desires which are so well-repressed by reason in better people that they leave them in peace even during sleep; in any case, Plato says, they torment them less (ἥκιστα), since these disturbing (παρανόμοι) desires are entirely innate.

Freud thus seems to have read Plato in a rather rapid manner—a rapidity which would also explain why he neglects to cite him elsewhere when he discovers that the dream is the realization of incestuous and parricidal desires. Indeed, Plato writes: "You know that in this state (the state of sleep), the soul dares all, as if it were detached and disencumbered from all shame and reason (αἰσψύνης καί φρονήσερζ); it does not hesitate to attempt in thought to rape its mother, or any other, whether it be man, god, animal; there is neither a murder it shies away from, nor a food it abstains from; in short, it does not restrain itself from any madness or immodesty" (571d). It is an even more surprising silence concerning Plato that Freud, who corroborates his discovery only with Sophocles's *Oedipus Rex* and Shakespeare's *Hamlet*, complains in a note added later of the indignant outrage which his interpretation—and the unsupportable and dreadful revelation of incestuous and parricidal desires— provoked. And in the text itself he writes: "Like Oedipus, we live unconscious of desires which damage our morality, and from which nature constrains us. When we reveal these desires, we would rather avert our eyes from the scenes of our childhood" (229).

Could the effect of *Oedipus Rex* on Freud have been so powerful as to make him forget the text of *The Republic*, or did Freud turn his eyes away from Plato to Sophocles because the former anticipated too clearly

Freud's own discoveries, depriving him of his priority, of which he was so jealous?

In any case, Freud's repeated "error" in reading, his silences, and the return on the last page of Plato's name seem to me sufficiently significant incitement to regard the text more closely.

The Primal Scene of the Dream

It is upon examining the transition from the democratic regime to the tyrannical regime, or rather from democratic man to tyrannical man,[1] that Plato is led to appeal to dreams, in order to expose in them the sort of desires which dominate and characterize the tyrannical soul. Having analyzed the aristocratic regime and the corresponding type of soul, in which the intellect (the *noûs*) governs; the timocratic regime and timocratic man, in whom the *thumos* has the upper hand and ambition reigns; the oligarchic regime and oligarchic man, marked by the supremacy of desires (the *épithumia*)— among others, the desire for money; and the democratic regime and the democratic type of soul, in which the desire for liberty triumphs, Plato finally arrives at the last possible type of regime and man:[2] the tyrannical, the result of an excessive desire for freedom, which necessarily leads to servitude (the general law of regime-change[3] being a disturbance of the principle of motives grown excessive, each type of regime, governed by the desire for the good which is proper to it, being in general indifference to all the rest). Plato does not undertake his examination of different types of regimes and souls with a theoretical or descriptive objective, but rather a normative one. His (idealist) question is to discern which regime and type of soul is best able to procure for man the happiest life.[4] With this aim, his final examination of the extreme low turns out to be most important, for only a comparison of the two extremes—the most unjust man, the tyrant, and the most just man, the philosopher—will allow the choice of life and regime to be decided. What is really at stake is to refute the thesis of Thrasymachus, expounded in Book I, who decided in favor of the most unjust life—that of tyrannical man—which according to him is the happiest:

> When we have identified that which is most unjust, we will place it beside the most just, and thus we will be able to render an exact account of the effects of pure justice and pure injustice on the happiness or unhappiness of the individual and, consequently, we will either go along with the opinion of Thrasymachus and follow the route to injustice, or yield to the evidence which presses upon us and practice justice. (545a)

It would not have taken anything less than the ten books of *The Republic* to counterbalance this thesis, and the final myth of Er [Hera?] to respond to that of the ring of Gyges—this is the importance of the debate.

The analysis of tyrannical man demands consideration of a sort of desire, neglected until then, which had escaped the dichotomous division of desires conducted from 554a to 558d. This division was necessary in order to describe oligarchic man and democratic man; the first, after all, is led by necessary desires and pleasures, the second by superfluous desires and pleasures. Treating all these desires equally, tyrannical man permits complete anarchy and freedom to reign in his soul, and thus variegation, disorder, and injustice.[5] The sort of desires characteristic of the tyrannical soul had persisted unnoticed until then because the comprehension of other "psychic" and "political" structures did not require their display, and, moreover, because these were more difficult than others to discover; in fact, they were "repressed by laws and better desires" among most men. Indeed, this is what distinguishes them from the desires proper to democratic man, which, however superfluous, nonetheless are prohibited by neither social laws nor the laws of reason—they belong, one might say, to a superfluous "good . . ."

"Tyrannical" desires, superfluous *and* evil, are no less so for being natural, probably innate in everyone (κινδυνεύοθσι έγγίγνεσζαι παντί) and, because they are dangerous to the very existence of the society over which they loom, prohibited either by law and reason (in the case of the aristocratic or timocratic soul) or by better desires (in the case of the oligarchic or democratic soul). Their repression with the aid of reason can lead to their total extirpation in a small number of people, or their reduction in others—or, if reason does not interfere, their repression may fail in part, leaving them to subsist in number and in force.

Because tyrannical desires are thus more or less "inhibited," their existence is evinced above all in dreams, the "sovereign route" to knowing what law, reason or better desires censor in the waking state—during sleep, to degrees proportional to the strength or weakness of each person's repression, forbidden desires awaken as reason falls asleep. The mechanism described by Plato by which the inhibited returns anticipates Freudian description and metapsychology at every point. It is because, during sleep, the authority of supervision (Freud calls it the conscious mind or the superego; Plato, the careful, reasoning part of the soul, ready at the command: the intellect)—these sentinels and guardians of reason, known as good principles (cf. 560a and 591a)—slacken and rest; repressed desires are given free regin to satisfy their appetites; "the sleep of reason gives birth to monsters. . . ."

It is possible to overturn the hierarchy and mastery in favor of the wild and bestial part of the soul (the unconscious), which is more or less already stuffed, not with nectar and ambrosia[6] but with earthly—too earthly—food and drink.[7] The comparison, which has become classic, of superfluous and forbidden desires to the wild beast does not, however, escape Plato's notice. Indeed, earlier, at 563a, he shows that even animal savagery bursts out only when animals "imitate" man in their disorder, for instance in the democratic regime: "The same animals who are at the disposal of men are much more free here than elsewhere—to such an extent that one would have to see it to believe it. It really is true that dogs, as the proverb says, resemble their mistresses; that's why one sees horses and donkeys, accustomed to free and proud speed, strike down in the streets all the pedestrians who do not yield to their passage; and everywhere is the same excess of freedom." Dogs, donkeys, and horses are all animals domesticated by the reason of man, which, when it finds itself subordinated to its desires, cannot help but lapse into a wilder state. In the city, man alone is responsible for the disorder of the "beast" in himself and outside himself. Only the wild beast, whose freedom is not yet domesticated, serves as a metaphor for the savagery of tyrannical desires when these are no longer mastered—*bound* by laws, reason, or better desires. In fact they burst forth, no longer restrained by shame or modesty—the foundational virtues of social life, if one believes the *Protagoras*. In the scene of dreams—more of a simulacrum than the theater, where the laughter and tears of the best audience testify to their abdication of reason and their abandonment of all shame[8]—like the tyrant who ridicules all written and unwritten laws (cf. 563a), desires, delirious with freedom, dare all. *All*, Plato, awake and modest, says in the text, before clarifying—this time without mincing words, and right off the bat—incest with the mother (Μητρίτε γάρ ἐπιψειρεν μέιγνθσζαι), not without retreating immediately, obsessively, before its own audacity and oedipal horror,[9] to generalize the rape to "any other, whether it be man, god, animal," as if it does not allude to parricide and cannibalism, which are encompassed in a more general criminality, immodesty, madness, the result of a dispossession and generalized injustice.

Thus, dreams do not respect any of the three major forbidden components of humanity: no more than the tyrant (precisely whose desires dreams reveal) who, even awake, does not hesitate to eat his own children, kill his father or elder brother, or beat his father and mother to force them to serve his own wants and who, incurably mad, will suffer for his ignoble misdeeds an eternal punishment in Tartarus without the possibility of reincarnation (cf. the myth of [Hera]), if it's not being metamorphosed into a wolf or some other ferocious beast:[10] he will have transgressed all the laws of humanity; he himself will be always already transformed into a savage.[11]

However, the madness of dreams, unlike that of the tyrant, is only imaginary. The satisfaction of superfluous and forbidden desires in them, Freud would say, is hallucinatory. On this point, one should refer to the *Timaeus* (10c and sq.), which explains the possibility of such hallucinatory satisfaction by way of a peculiar device. According to Plato, the gods constructed for the nourishment of the body a sort of trough, between the diaphragm and the edge of the navel, and there they attached the appetitive soul, like a wild beast which must be fed if the human species is to survive. The gods lodged it there, as far as possible from the part which deliberates, in order not to disturb its deliberations on the common interests of everyone.[12] The appetitive part cannot hear reason; it simply lets itself be fascinated, *night and day*, by images and phantoms, simulacra, simple reflections of this mirror, the display of the liver, this other obscure cave, which reflects in the form of images the thoughts arriving from the intellect:

> To make use of this illusion, a god has erected before the intellect the display of the liver; he has placed it in its habitation and contrived it so that it is dense, sleek and bright, sweet and bitter; that way, the thoughts coming from the intellect are reflected in it as in a mirror which receives rays of light and offers images to view.

Dreams are one of these simulacra, one of these shadows which the appetitive, deluded soul mistakes for reality. However—and on this point Freud has not understood Plato—it is possible to control oneiric delirium, to escape the illusion and the brutish visions, so long as one knows how to master his desires during waking life. This requires, first of all, having a healthy body, and above all, a liver in good shape; for nothing is voluntarily wicked, but rather, "it is due to some vice of bodily constitution, or from the clumsiness of those who raised one, that the wicked man becomes wicked" (*Timaeus*, 87d). Thus the immoderate person is not blameworthy,

> for the disorder of lust derives, for the most part, from properties of a substance which the porousness of bones allows to stream through the body and inundate it, to the point of introducing a malady of the soul. And likewise nearly all the defects which one calls intemperance with respect to pleasures. (ibid.)

The second condition of mastering one's dreams, which thus depends so closely on the first, is temperance. The third is a sort of ritual of exorcism, which it is fitting to perform before being immersed in sleep; one endeavors to hold onto his waking soul, to nourish it with good thoughts and speculations, to turn it toward the best part of itself—towards the top rather than towards the base—so that even asleep, far from forgetting itself, the best principle continues to dominate the scene alone, all desires sleeping. The slumber of desires will leave the noble part of the soul in peace only if they have been calmed in accordance with a just measure of temperance, which demands neither fasting nor abundance:[13] in their excesses of dissatisfaction or satisfaction they could, in fact, trouble the soul, marry it to the body and to its sadnesses or joys, and prevent it from accomplishing its task. If the best part of the soul, before falling asleep, knew by the same token how to quash all anger, to appease the *thumos*—the heart, the intermediary part destined to assist it in containing the appetites[14]—then, paradoxically, it could accomplish its task of knowing even better than it could in the waking state: the state of sleep, one might say, prefigures the state of death, that ultimate state in which the exhausted soul, returned to its first divinity, freed from the body and the troubles it engenders, will finally be able to know the truth.

During sleep, in effect, the soul which has gone to sleep in perfect mastery of itself, in a just hierarchy of its parts, not only won't imagine any vision contrary to laws, but will be gifted with divination[15] of the past, the present, and the future—"will come in closer contact than ever with truth"; this is the only manner in which human infirmity can touch something true, the knowledge of which is reserved for the deity. In other words, dreams in themselves are not false illusions: the simulacrum, if it is "fabricated" by a well-trained soul, can be the bearer of truth. There are good and bad dreams, and the philosopher is a doctor who, capable of converting falsehood into a good dream, permits you to sleep in peace. The good man thus does not do, even in dream, that which the wicked do in reality. The dream scene, like the theater scene (Plato differs on this point from Aristotle, and from Freud, who relies on him), produces no cathartic effect. If one worries so much about sleeping and dreaming well, it is out of fear that he who is accustomed to killing his father or sleeping with his mother in his dreams, far from discharging these desires via hallucination, does eventually, by force of habit, really commit them—precisely like one who, believing himself to identify without risk with a mournful or laughable hero on the pretext that it is not he himself at stake, wails or cries without restraint at the theater and ends up behaving in daily life like a coward or a buffoon:

> Few people, I think, realize that the sentiments of others enter our hearts; for, having nourished and fortified our sensitivity to the pains of others, it is not easy to master our sensitivity to our own pains . . . Is it not so with the ridiculous? When you attend a theatrical representation . . . the desire to make others laugh which you had repressed, by reason, out of fear of looking like a buffoon, you now give free reign, and, having fortified it thus, you often let yourself get carried away, without thinking that you have become the joker. (*Republic*, Book Ten, 606b–c)

If the well-regulated soul can and should, asleep, bring forth good simulacra which alone are capable of divination and truth—supplements with
which the deity in its generosity has favored human infirmity—it is nonetheless only wakeful reason which is capable of interpreting dreams: Plato does
not grant the simulacrum, whatever good it does, the last word on the noble
part of the soul. By itself, the good simulacrum does not know how to speak
the truth; it can only captivate the hungry part of the soul and thus permit it
to sleep in peace. Upon waking, reason regains all its rights and mastery:

> Thoughts coming from the intellect are reflected in the liver, like a mirror which
> absorbs rays of light and presents images to the soul. Sometimes, the intellect
> terrifies the soul: using the bitterness which is in the nature of the liver, it adopts
> threatening and severe ways . . . Sometimes, on the other hand, completely oppo-
> site mirages appear on the liver by a peaceful inspiration issuing from the intel-
> lect; deigning neither to agitate nor to make contact with that which is of an
> opposite nature, it puts bitterness to rest; in order to have an effect on the organ,
> the soul uses its natural gentleness, and restores all of its parts to their proper
> positions, revives their sheen and their freedom; thus, it renders docile and tame
> the part of the soul rooted by the liver, which then enjoys well-regulated nights
> and takes pleasure in the sleep of divination. And this because the human species
> was made as perfectly as possible. Wanting to redress our weakness, and in order
> to touch, somewhere, upon the truth, our makers installed the organ of divina-
> tion in it. A sufficient proof that the deities have placed their gift of divination in
> the infirmity of human reason: no man with good sense achieves an inspired and
> veridical divination but that the activity of his judgment be fettered by sleep or
> by sickness or put off course by some kind of enthusiasm. On the contrary, it falls
> to man, in full reason, to assemble in his mind remembered words pronounced
> in dream or in the waking state by a divinatory power, to apply reason to his
> visions in order to extract what they might mean for the future, past or present,
> bad or good. As for those in a state of trance, it is not their role to judge that which
> appeared to or was proferred by them. (*Timaeus*, 71b and sq.)

If no man can escape dreams, the sign of his infirmity and its eventual
remedy, still all dreams are not alike: Plato, in contrast to Freud, would have
approved the Roman emperor who had one of his subjects executed because
the emperor dreamed the man had assassinated him, for our dreams judge us,
judge the violence of our superfluous and forbidden desires, our capacity or
not to master them; and, far from purging us of these desires, dreams work
to fortify them.

The peculiarity of the tyrannical soul is its incapacity to convert bad dreams
into good dreams. The tyrant never sleeps in peace — and his waking life is
itself a nightmare, since, without fearing punishment, he can satisfy without
restraint the wildest desires which dreams allowed him to reveal.

The Tyrant

How is such a man, at the very limits of humanity, possible? Plato locates the genesis of the tyrannical sort of soul at the "decay" of the democratic soul: as always, it is born of a division between desires, of a conflict between father and son. Democratic man had been born at the moment of conflict between necessary, useful desires—those honored by the father (of an oligarchic soul), the educator who inculcates in his son the principles appropriate to his parsimony, the sentinels and guardians of the law of the father in the soul of the son (his "superego")—conflict between these desires and the superfluous desires linked to luxury and to *mimesis*, to rivalry without law or measure, frustrated by the father and awakened in the soul of the son by the bad company of men for whom life is not regulated by need but by luxurious supplementarity (cf. 561a–c). Seductive principles capture him and frustrate the paternal principles, one model and *mimesis* replacing the other, the authority of the "second" father replacing that of the "first," not without imbuing in the son a certain guilt which keeps him in conflict: whence his adoption of principles midway between the two others, neither totally uncontrolled nor parsimonious; it is this middling, ultimate compromise which characterizes the democratic soul.

One turns from a democrat into a tyrant by the repetition of an analogous scene of seduction: the democratic father inculcates his mitigated principles in his son, who is drawn away from them by a model of life proposing, as its only principles, desires forbidden by law. These can seduce only—for no one is voluntarily wicked—by a magical operation of false exchange, of the falsification of names: this proposed deregulation, unchecked, is called *freedom*, a beautiful title which ratifies the anarchic equality of all desires, the absence of order and restraint in conduct (cf. 564d and sq.).

If the young man, however, resists the seduction of "freedom," an infallible plot to transform him into a tyrant—consisting of inciting his heart to love, the most tyrannical of desires, their boss and master (cf. 574c and sq.)— will drive him from extreme freedom to the deepest servitude. Though boss, love will not offer the soul a principle of hierarchical arrangement but will introduce, on the contrary, the same disorder as bile or pituitary in the body (546b), for it is the boss only of superfluous anarchic desires. Plato compares these desires, which do not need to work or expend much, to bees of various types. Thus at 552c, he writes: "A bee in a cell is the disease of the hive," and he distinguishes the winged bees without stingers, without sting, who end up beggars, and the two-footed bees, who have stingers and constitute the class of criminals. At 554c, he declares that "those with desires natural to bees restrain them with great effort." At 556a, the usurers are described as walking bees who injure with their stingers and increase their capital by a hundredfold; at 559d, "man delivered to his pleasures and desires is governed by superfluous desires," democratic man, is compared to a bee as against oligarchic and domesticated man, who is governed by necessary desires:

> When a young man raised as we have said, in ignorance and parsimony, has tasted the honey of bees, and he has frequented ardent and pernicious insects, able to indulge in various pleasures of all species and qualities, it is then, you can believe it, that his interior regime begins to pass from oligarchy to democracy. (559d)

Love has all the characteristics of a winged bee. It is the disease of the beehive, of which one is only the apparent master, for he will end in begging, in living at the expense of other superfluous desires which he subordinates and puts at his service but which, like the flatterers of the tyrant, end up in power. While Eros of the *Banquet* has, in order to leave the apories, more than one poros in its arc, tyrannical love has for its only poros a profusion of incense, perfumes, wreaths and wine: neither stinger nor sting. These are the flatterers who distend the stinger of unsatisfied desire. Such is, in effect, their strategy for conquest: rendering the other, the boss, literally mad with desire by expurgating in him all that could make him listen to reason (reason, but also the wiser, oligarchic and parsimonious desires, which, governed by the principle of reality, demand, by avarice, prudence in the seeking of pleasure). Just as the tyrant in the city exiles or exterminates all who try to return him to reason, and does not hesitate to kill father and mother (cf. 560 to 567c), tyrannical love, this "bad love"—which operates at the inverse of the philosophical catharsis of the true Eros—pulls all paternal principles up from the roots: one is not seduced this time by a principle contrary to that which up to now had guided him, by a false good which he would wrongfully have taken for the Good; he no longer even recognizes the value of the Good. This is the complete perversion of the tyrant, his dementia, his "becoming primal." Love, in its intoxication, thus leads to tyranny. And the tyrant, in his dementia and the absence of self-mastery, no longer recognizing human or divine law, undertakes to impose his law upon everyone.

    To the question posed initially—does the tyrannical life offer happiness or unhappiness? Is Thrasymachus right or not?—it is now easy to respond: tyrannical man can only be unhappy, and desperately so, since he is totally dispossessed of himself and of his own parents; he is captured by an incurable and limitless madness; no paternal guilting principle can check or put an end to his megalomania; awake or asleep, he behaves in the most savage and brutish manner, in the grip of the most terrible desires:

Previously, these ideas were only given free reign in dreams, during sleep, until the time when he again submitted to laws, to his father, and democracy reigned again in his soul; but once tyrannized by love, he will be constantly in a waking state what he was sometimes in dreams, and he will retreat before the horror of no murder, no food, no infamy. (574e)

Plato does not clarify whether the perfect tyrant continues to have bad dreams (could he, in his dementia, still distinguish dreams from waking life?). In any case, dreams produced during his democratic past will not be able to serve as catharsis; he will have probably even fortified them by nourishing his cannibalistic, parricidal, and incestuous desires.

If you want to sleep and live in peace, it is thus far better, instead of—like this incense of which the myth of [Hera] speaks—rushing toward the tyrannical life, to choose a philosophical and regulated life. For if these terrible desires exist in you, as they do in us all, it will be better to psychoanalyse them in order to recognize them. Waiting, Plato stands guard; sleep tight, and sweet dreams.

13

Schleiermacher's Hermeneutics: Some Problems and Solutions

MICHAEL N. FORSTER

Michael N. Forster is Professor of Philosophy and Chairman of the Philosophy Department at the University of Chicago. His research interests include the philosophy of language and topics in epistemology. His books include Wittgenstein on the Arbitrariness of Grammar *and* Hegel's Idea of a Phenomenology of Spirit.

Friedrich Schleiermacher is widely regarded as the father of modern hermeneutics, or interpretation theory. That title may in the end more properly belong to his predecessor Johann Gottfried Herder. But whichever of them deserves the greater credit (a question I shall set aside here),[1] the theory which they both develop is arguably not only the ancestor of, but also philosophically superior to, its more metaphysically pretentious descendant in Heidegger and Gadamer, and is of great intrinsic interest.[2]

The purpose of this chapter is to explore some central aspects of Schleiermacher's hermeneutics and to suggest how they should be interpreted and assessed.[3] My general strategy will involve pointing up rather than playing down certain inconsistencies and other problems in his position, in part simply because I believe that they are there and that exegesis therefore ought to recognize them, but also in part because reflecting on them seems to me philosophically fruitful. The interpretive and philosophical suggestions which I will be offering are provisional and tentative in spirit.

Philosophy of Language

Schleiermacher's hermeneutics rests on several important principles in the philosophy of language.

(1) Herder had already advanced a doctrine that thought is essentially dependent on and bounded in its scope by language—that is, one can only think if one has a language, and can only think what one can express linguistically.[4] This doctrine is very important for interpretation, because in a sense it guarantees that a person's use of language is a reliable indicator of the nature of his thought. Schleiermacher takes over this doctrine and makes it fundamental to his hermeneutics.[5] However, he is also tempted to make it bolder in a certain way: Sometimes he merely advances it in the form just stated.[6] But often he instead elevates it into a doctrine of the outright *identity* of thought and language,[7] or of thought and inner language.[8] Commentators have commonly approved of this—for example, Kimmerle seems to like the identification with language,[9] Niebuhr and Frank that with inner language.[10] But it is philosophically untenable in either version. For I can think something without expressing it linguistically; and I can express something linguistically without doing any corresponding thinking (for example, if I happen not to understand the language that I am using). And likewise, I can think something without using language internally (for example, having been told to expect John home before Mary, I hear the door open and footsteps mount the stairs, Mary appears and I say quite truthfully, "I thought it was John," even though no such little formula ran through my head, merely a feeling of unsurprise), and I can use language internally without doing any corresponding thinking (once again, if it happens to be a language I do not understand, for example). So Schleiermacher should have stuck with the more cautious Herderian formulation of the doctrine (here, as elsewhere, he has *implausibly overspecified* a plausible position which he has inherited from Herder). On the other hand, rather to his credit, in his later work he seems at least somewhat inclined to retreat from the identity-versions back towards that superior formulation.[11]

(2) Some further important positions concern the nature of *meaning*. Ernesti, Herder, and Hamann had collectively moved away from traditional philosophical theories which took meanings to be items in principle independent of language—such as the referents involved, Platonic forms, or empiricist ideas—and towards identifying them rather with *word usages*, or *rules of word use*.[12] It follows from this move that interpretation essentially involves pinning down word usages, or rules for the use of words. Schleiermacher adopts this whole position. Hence, for example, one finds him saying that "the[. . .]meaning of a term is to be derived

from the unity of the word-sphere and from the rules governing the pre-supposition of this unity."[13]

(3) However, Schleiermacher eventually attempts to combine with this position a further one which entails that a capacity to have *images* plays an essential role in meaning as well. Specifically, he tries to explain meaning in terms of Kantian (empirical) schemata: rules for the production of images.[14] This combination of positions is again in a way continuous with Ernesti and Herder, who had somewhat similarly combined with their emphasis on the role of word usage in meaning an essential role for empiricist ideas (Ernesti) or sensations (Herder). Such combinations are likely to seem unhappy to us at first hearing, but they may not be. Here are some prima facie problems: (a) Explaining meanings in terms of such mentalistic processes as having images might sound incompatible with equating meanings with word usages because it might seem to make words and their usages *inessential* to meanings. They actually *were* in Kant's own version of the doctrine of schematism, and it must be admitted that Schleiermacher's formulations of the schema-theory some-times take over this unfortunate feature.[15] However, such a theory *need not* do so; instead it can be thought of as specifying a *further* essential aspect of meaning (or perhaps—to anticipate my next point—one already implicitly included in the relevant concept of word usage). (b) Another way in which there might seem to be an incompatibility between the two doctrines is this: if we equate meanings with word usages, then does that not preclude any essential role in meaning for the capacity to have images? The answer is, again: not necessarily. For a usage of anything always involves some *context* or other, and that context might well in this case essentially include having images. (c) Anglophone philosophers are likely to be prejudiced against such a combination of positions by more recent and familiar versions of the "mean-ing as word usage" doctrine, in particular the later Wittgenstein's. Wittgen-stein purports to show, by examining our actual criteria for ascribing conceptual understanding to people, that having images and similar mental processes is neither sufficient for conceptual understanding nor necessary for it.[16] His arguments for the former conclusion are extremely compelling, but his argu-ments for the latter seem much less so. We may certainly grant Wittgenstein that our linguistic intuitions do not require that in order properly to ascribe conceptual understanding to someone on a particular occasion he must, in addition to using words with external competence, have images *actually occur-ring* as well. But would our linguistic intuitions really sanction ascribing con-ceptual understanding to someone who, for example, had (by some science-fictional means or other, say the implanting of a device in his brain) arrived at an external competence for the word "red" without ever having had sensations of redness (contra Herder) and without now even being *able* to

generate any image of it (contra Schleiermacher)—to someone whose external competence was (to put the point a bit tendentiously) merely *robotic*?[17] The answer seems to be No. In short, some version of the sort of combined position to which Schleiermacher (like Ernesti and Herder before him) is attracted may well be both self-consistent and philosophically defensible.

(4) Although Schleiermacher does not himself make this point, note that doctrine *(2)*, the doctrine that meanings are word usages, promises an explanation and justification of doctrine *(1)*, the doctrine of thought's essential dependence on and boundedness by linguistic competence. For, uncontroversially enough, thought is of its very nature articulated in terms of concepts, or meanings, but then if meanings turn out to be *usages of words*, one can see immediately why thought would be essentially dependent on and bounded by a thinker's linguistic competence.[18]

(5) There remains here, however, an important further question which leaves the exact force of doctrines *(1)* and *(2)* in some doubt: must thought and meaning be articulable by a thinker in language in the usual sense of "language" (let us call such a position "narrow expressivism"), or can other symbolic media play this foundational role for thought and meaning as well, for example sculpture or music (let us call such a position "broad expressivism")? Schleiermacher's commitment to doctrines *(1)* and *(2)* might seem already to imply the former answer to this question. But it really does not, or at least not clearly. For the terms *language* and *word* in those doctrines might be bearing unusually broad senses.[19] Indeed, they actually *had* done in Hamann's version of the same doctrines in his *Metacritique*. And Schleiermacher himself on occasion includes such media as instrumental music under the term *language*.[20] Perhaps the best place to look for Schleiermacher's considered answer to this question is his lectures on Aesthetics. The lectures on Aesthetics set out to develop a position on art that would imply narrow expressivism, or the fundamentalness of language (in the usual sense) to thought and meaning, and they do so in an extremely simple way: (a) Arts, such as sculpture and music, which are not linguistic (in the usual sense) do not express thoughts *at all* (for instance, music expresses physiologically based *Lebenszustände* but not representations or thoughts). This theory is quite untenable, however. And Schleiermacher abruptly realizes this in the course of developing it when, discussing sculpture, he suddenly recalls Pausanias's account that the very earliest Greek sculptures were merely crude blocks whose main function was to serve, precisely, as symbols of religious ideas (oops!).[21] At this point Schleiermacher changes tack, acknowledging now that such non-linguistic arts *do* at least sometimes express thoughts after all, and he then vacillates between two inconsistent explanations of this: (b) They do so in such a way that the thoughts are (at least sometimes) not (yet) lin-

guistically articulable (for example, Schleiermacher suggests that the early Greek sculpture just mentioned expressed religious ideas which only *later* got expressed linguistically).[22] (c) They do so but in virtue of a pre-existing linguistic articulation of the same thoughts in the artist (actually, Schleiermacher only says in virtue of "something universal," "a representation," but the dependence on language seems clearly implied).[23] In the end, therefore, having rightly rejected the clearly untenable position *(a)*, Schleiermacher is left torn between two more sensible positions which, though, give contradictory answers to our question: position *(b)*, which entails broad expressivism (a position that had already been taken by Hamann, and that was also adopted by Hegel and the later Dilthey); and position *(c)*, which entails narrow expressivism (a position that Herder had eventually arrived at).[24] Both of these positions deserve to be taken seriously, philosophically speaking. But Schleiermacher does not decide between them, and he thereby also leaves the exact force of doctrines *(1)* and *(2)* uncertain.

(6) As we already saw in passing, Schleiermacher advances a thesis of "the unity of the word-sphere."[25] The force of this thesis seems to be that there is something like a *single meaning* common to all the uses of a word in a language.[26] Consequently, the interpretation of a word is for Schleiermacher roughly a two-stage process: first, one infers from the known actual uses of the word to particular usages, or rules for use, and then one infers from the latter to a single, all-embracing rule for use which covers them all.[27] At first sight, this thesis seems to take sharp issue with Ernesti, who had stressed the *multiplicity* of a word's usages, and hence meanings.[28] It also seems to conflict sharply with our usual way of thinking about these matters, according to which, for example, the various different entries for a word in a dictionary give *different meanings*. Indeed, at first sight, the thesis seems to involve a hopeless coarsening of our usual criteria of meaning-identity—hopeless not only in that, as just noted, it would force us to override our strong common-sense intuitions that the same word often bears different meanings, but also in that it would force us to endorse contradictions (for example, suppose that "Smith is sitting on a [river] bank" is true and "Smith is sitting on a [financial] bank" is false; will we not by this thesis have to say that the *same proposition* is both true and false?). Can anything be said in Schleiermacher's defense here? There is, I think, one rather small class of cases for which a form of the objection that he is unacceptably violating our common-sense intuitions about meaning does in fact hold up in the end: cases which we would normally classify as ones of *sheer* polysemy (*bank* is a plausible example; such cases often arise when two or more unrelated etymologies lie behind a word). He should probably just concede that there are such exceptions to his thesis.[29] But his thesis is really concerned with the much more common

cases in which we would intuitively want to say that, although there are different meanings involved, they are in some degree related (for example, *impression* in "He made an impression in the clay," "My impression is that he is reluctant," and "He made a big impression at the party"). And our common-sense intuition of a diversity of meanings, and also our need to preserve consistency, in such cases are in fact amply *respected* by Schleiermacher's thesis. This is because he in effect distinguishes between two sorts of "meaning," allowing that against the background of the single meaning1 postulated by his thesis a word may indeed have several different meanings2.[30] Hence the charge of hopelessly coarsening our criteria of meaning-identity turns out to be mistaken. Indeed, it turns out that the upshot of Schleiermacher's thesis is in fact exactly the *opposite* of that. For his thesis involves a *holism* to the effect that the meanings2 of a word are always dependent for their exact character on the single overarching meaning1 which they together compose.[31] Consequently, if the overall pattern of particular usages is altered in any respect, this modifies each of them, each meaning2. And this makes for extremely *fine-grained* criteria of identity for meaning2.[32] Accordingly, Schleiermacher claims that, contrary to common assumptions, there are never any real synonyms in a language,[33] or between two different languages.[34]

(7) Finally, a more general observation about Schleiermacher's theory of meaning and conceptual understanding: Such features of his theory as his inclusion of the meaning-holism just mentioned do arguably still transcend or even conflict with our usual criteria for meaning-identity and conceptual understanding, albeit not in the crude way in which the doctrine of "the unity of the word-sphere" initially seemed to. After all, in the case in question my expression "extremely fine-grained" implied *more fine-grained than we would usually accept*. This will no doubt still seem objectionable if one assumes a certain picture (fairly widespread in recent Anglophone philosophy) about the nature of meaning and our cognitive relation to it: that meaning is a sort of single natural kind whose character can be distilled consistently and determinately from our usual linguistic intuitions concerning it. However, such a picture is in fact pretty implausible.[35] A better way to think about the concept of meaning is as a concept or a range of concepts constituted by pre-given linguistic intuitions which are sometimes inconsistent, sometimes indeterminate, and no doubt inadequate in other ways as well, a concept or range of concepts which we therefore may and should refashion more consistently, determinately, and otherwise adequately in order to serve our various purposes, doing which will indeed sometimes involve transcending and even contradicting those pre-given linguistic intuitions. From this perspective, such features of Schleiermacher's theory escape the sort of objection envisaged, and can indeed begin to look quite attractive (for example, developing more

fine-grained criteria of meaning-identity than we currently employ might serve our purposes very well).[36]

Misunderstanding Occurs as a Matter of Course

Schleiermacher famously holds that, contrary to a common assumption that "understanding occurs as a matter of course," "misunderstanding occurs as a matter of course, and so understanding must be willed and sought at every point."[37]

What is the basis of this position? The points just made suggest that part of the answer to this question may be that Schleiermacher presupposes a certain (arguably justified) "raising of the bar" of our usual criteria for meaning-identity, and therefore for exact conceptual understanding, which he has effected. There is some truth in this. However, he clearly conceives the position in question as more a discovery than merely a byproduct of his own conceptual innovations. So wherein lies the putative discovery?

Schleiermacher has two very different lines of reasoning underpinning this position, one of them a priorist, the other empirical. (Officially, he wants to overcome the very distinction between a priori and empirical knowledge.[38] But in this case at least, what he ends up with is rather a vacillation between the two than a synthesis.)

The a priorist explanation is dominant in the lectures on hermeneutics and has been heavily stressed by Dilthey and Frank. As Dilthey observes,[39] in the *Ethics* Schleiermacher argues in an a priori fashion that all living reason combines identity with *difference*. Similarly, as Frank notes,[40] in the *Dialectics* Schleiermacher argues in an a priori fashion that all meaning and understanding involves, along with a universal aspect, an *individual* aspect coming from the subject. These positions entail that whenever an interpreter attempts to understand another person there is *always and ineliminably* an obstacle of difference or individuality present.

On this line of reasoning, then, the problem of misunderstanding is *entirely general*. In particular, it is not especially due, and is not restricted, to cases of historical or cultural distance, as Schleiermacher indeed explicitly says at one point in his hermeneutics lectures.[41] Moreover, on this line of reasoning, it is impossible for exact understanding of another person *ever* to occur; understanding of another person can only ever be *approximate*, as Schleiermacher again says explicitly at points.[42]

The contrasting *empirical* line of reasoning occurs especially in Schleiermacher's classic 1813 essay *On the Different Methods of Translation*. According to this essay, there are two common sources of conceptual incommensurability between an interpreter and the text he interprets, and these are especially troublesome when they both occur together: (1) historical or cultural distance, which causes the standard conceptual resources of languages to diverge;[43] and (2) an author's own conceptual innovations.[44] (Ernesti and Herder had both already stressed these two sources of difficulty for the interpreter.)

On this second line of reasoning, it may indeed be the case that the obstacles in question occur more frequently than is commonly recognized—for example, Schleiermacher would say that interpreters dealing with distant periods or cultures confront conceptual divergence more commonly than they realize;[45] and furthermore, he thinks that conceptual innovation by authors is a less rare phenomenon than we often suppose (to the point, in the essay mentioned, of actually considering it a sine qua non of great literature or philosophy, literature or philosophy that is worth hearing beyond its own time and place).[46] But they will not *always* be present. Indeed, the essay in question argues that there is one whole area of language where historical and cultural distance *never* generates conceptual incommensurability, namely everyday referring and descriptive language concerning items of sensory experience (as heavily used in commercial contexts, travel literature, and so forth),[47] and the essay certainly sees authorial conceptual originality as something exceptional, not ubiquitous.[48] Again, on this second line of reasoning, there is no question of exact understanding being *impossible* (not only because, as was just mentioned, there are cases where the obstacles do not arise at all, but also because when they *do* arise they can often be overcome by careful interpretation).[49]

I would suggest that Schleiermacher's empirical line of argument is far superior to his a priori line of argument. For (1) the a priori line of argument rests on very dubious a priori theories about the nature of reason or the subject (dubious both in their a priori status and in their specific details), and (2) the a priori line of argument's consequence that exact understanding of another person is always strictly impossible is radically counterintuitive.

If we do read Schleiermacher's position on the difficulty of understanding in the empirical way that I am advocating, then certain further issues take on importance. As was mentioned, *On the Different Methods of Translating* implies that there is one area of exceptions to conceptual variation: referring and descriptive language concerning sensory items. However, at other points Schleiermacher seems to align himself rather with a (Herderian) position which stresses the *variability* of sensory experience and its language.[50] And of course his official a priorist position that we *always* conceptualize in an individual way would also imply that there are no real exceptions here. In his *Dialectics* he identifies a second area of putative exceptions as well: everyone shares the same concept of *being*.[51] However, he is again somewhat ambivalent about this. Thus the *Dialectics* virtually retracts it by adding the qualification that this is not strictly a case of "thought." And in a more straightforward way *On the Different Methods of Translation* questions whether this case constitutes an exception as well.[52] Also, Schleiermacher's official a priorist position that we always conceptualize individually would of course again preclude any real exception here.

Now I would suggest that Schleiermacher should have *dropped* this whole idea of exceptions. As a matter of philology, sensory discourse, far from being an area of exceptions, arguably turns out to be a *paradigmatic* locus of conceptual variations.[53] And in light of Charles Kahn's work on the verb *to be* in ancient Greek, even the concept of *being* looks variable.[54]

A further issue is this: the philosophically superior empirical strand of argument which I have been highlighting (in opposition to its neglect by the secondary literature) coheres with an admirable empirical approach in several other key areas of Schleiermacher's theory as well (where it has similarly been neglected or denied by the secondary literature). Here are two examples:

(1) Dilthey and Gadamer hold that Schleiermacher's basic method of interpretation is a sort of empathetic self-projection onto texts, that it is in that sense at least a priorist rather than empirical. Schleiermacher on the contrary explicitly rejects a priorism both on the linguistic (or grammatical) and on the psychological (or technical) sides of interpretation: "Grammatical [interpretation]. The elements of a language as presentations of a specifically modified capacity for intuition cannot be constructed a priori, but only recognized via comparison of a great number of individual cases. In the same way on the technical side, one cannot construct the differing individualities a priori."[55] His position is instead that one proceeds "bottom up" from empirical evidence, in linguistic interpretation beginning from the examples of a word's actual uses, classifying these into particular usages, and then looking for their all-embracing unity; and in psychological interpretation starting with the (linguistic) evidence furnished by the author, and then inferring from that a psychological portrait of the author.

(2) Dilthey and Kimmerle say that Schleiermacher excludes consideration of a text's *historical context* from interpretation.[56] This is an extraordinary misunderstanding of his position. He does indeed say that the consideration of a text's historical context must precede interpretation proper.[57] But the force of that is not to imply that interpretation should *dispense* with it, but on the contrary to insist that it is *absolutely indispensable* to interpretation, a sine qua non of any interpretation worthy of the name taking place at all.[58]

Linguistic versus Psychological Interpretation

Schleiermacher famously distinguishes between two essential sides of all interpretation: on the one hand, linguistic (or grammatical) interpretation, and on the other hand, psychological (or technical) interpretation.[59]

There has been a long debate in the secondary literature concerning this subject which should be addressed here briefly at the outset: Dilthey and Gadamer characterized Schleiermacher's theory as fundamentally psychologistic and empathetic. Kimmerle then, on the basis of a detailed investigation of the hermeneutics manuscripts, argued that this was only true of the later Schleiermacher but that the earlier Schleiermacher had believed in the identity of thought and language and had made interpretation focus on language. More recently, Frank and Bowie have argued that there is really no great change here: both early and late Schleiermacher give roughly equal weight to language and psychology.

I basically agree with this last view. The Dilthey-Gadamer account is hopelessly one-sided and misleading. But nor is Kimmerle's view correct. For (1) the later Schleiermacher continues to assume at least the dependence of thought on language,[60] and continues to devote roughly as much space to linguistic (or grammatical) as to psychological (or technical) interpretation;[61] and (2) Schleiermacher's earliest manuscripts already stressed psychological (or technical) interpretation as well as linguistic (or grammatical).[62] (It is worth noting in connection with *(2)* that this earliness of Schleiermacher's commitment to complementing linguistic with psychological (or technical) interpretation seems much less surprising once one realizes—as commentators almost invariably fail to—that he did not himself invent the idea of doing so but instead inherited it from Herder.[63])

What is Schleiermacher's rationale for his distinction between the linguistic and the psychological sides of interpretation? One rationale which is prominent in the texts is the following:

(1) This distinction corresponds to Schleiermacher's distinction between the *identical,* or shared, and the *individual*, or idiosyncratic, aspects of a text (whether the latter distinction is grounded in the a priori or in the empirical way discussed above). What is shared in a text's use of language, especially what is shared conceptually, is to be investigated by linguistic interpretation (using a predominantly "comparative" method); what is individual in a text's use of language, in particular individuality in concepts, is to be investigated by psychological interpretation (using a predominantly "divinatory" method). This rationale has been stressed by Frank,[64] and it is indeed prominent in Schleiermacher's texts.[65]

More specifically, a central part of this rationale seems to be the following: Recall Schleiermacher's conception that meanings are rules for the use of words, and that accordingly the fundamental task of interpretation is to infer from observed actual uses of words to the underlying rules which are guiding them. Now in the case where an interpreter is attempting to discover the meaning that a word bears in a common language—the task of linguistic interpretation—there will typically be a large number of examples of the word's use in a rich variety of contexts available to serve as the evidential basis from which to infer the underlying rule. Accordingly, in such a case all the interpreter usually needs to do in order to arrive at a reasonably certain and accurate estimation of the underlying rule is to gather these examples and infer directly from them the character of the underlying rule which is guiding them by means of a "comparative," or in other words a plain-inductive, method. However, in cases where an interpreter is trying to discover the novel usage or meaning which a conceptual innovator has conferred on a word, the task is typically much less simple. For in such cases the number of actual examples of the usage in question which are available will usually be much smaller,[66] and the variety of contexts in which they occur much more limited.[67] Consequently, merely collecting and "comparing," or doing plain-induction on, the examples will usually not by itself be enough to enable the interpreter to pin down with any confidence or precision the underlying rule in accordance with which the author is using the word. What, therefore, is the interpreter to do in such a case? Schleiermacher notes, sensibly, that he should first examine the common background language (since, for one thing, the author will typically be *modifying* a pre-existing rule for the word, rather than wholly departing from it or coining a sheer neologism).[68] But that only minimizes the original problem rather than solving it. Schleiermacher believes that what is needed in addition is a knowledge of the innovative author's *psychology*, that knowing his psychology can facilitate the task of estimating his new rule for the use of the word from the meager evidence available of how he has actually used it. This idea is at least somewhat plausible. For example, suppose that an author has gone as far as to coin a new term, which he uses on only three occasions in extant works, each time with reference to women. In such a case, the knowledge that he was a *misogynist* might be of considerable help towards more closely determining what the term was likely to mean. In particular, such knowledge would more or less exclude the possibility that it connoted a virtue, and make it likely that it connoted a vice.

However, it would not be satisfactory for Schleiermacher to make this first rationale *the* rationale for the distinction between linguistic and psychological interpretation. For one thing, as has been mentioned, he often acknowledges that conceptual originality occurs only *sometimes*, and moreover this *should* be his position. But in that case, if this rationale were *the* rationale for psychological interpretation, how could psychological interpretation *always* be required, as he says it is? For another thing, even where conceptual originality does occur, it is hard to believe that recourse to authorial psychology in the manner of the imaginary example just given is going to be necessary and helpful *in all cases*, and this still further diminishes the range of cases for which this rationale would justify psychological interpretation.

There are, though, also at least two further rationales for psychological interpretation in Schleiermacher:

(2) He sometimes indicates that (as their very names might suggest) linguistic interpretation is oriented to *language* whereas psychological interpretation is oriented to the underlying *thoughts* conveyed by language.[69] This may seem unhelpful at first sight, but is arguably not. For one thing, does it not violate Schleiermacher's doctrine of an intimate connection between thought and language? The answer is: not once the crude "identity" version of that doctrine is rejected, as it must be anyway. For another thing, is not determining thoughts something that linguistic interpretation *already* does in determining the *meanings* of words and sentences? Here the answer is that Schleiermacher has *further* aspects of "thought" in mind. As Quentin Skinner has recently stressed, in order fully to understand an utterance or text one needs to do more than just determine its linguistic meanings; one needs in addition to pin down authorial intentions. To borrow an example used by Skinner, if one encounters a stranger by a frozen lake who tells one, "The ice is thin over there," one may understand the linguistic meaning of his utterance perfectly, but yet still not fully understand the utterance, because one remains uncertain as to what he intends to do with it—simply inform one?, warn one?, threaten one?, joke (by stating the obvious)?, and so on. This, I suggest, is part of what Schleiermacher is getting at when he writes that "the possession of the whole spirit of the utterance is only achieved via the technical; for dealt with merely grammatically the utterance always remains just an aggregate" and that "every utterance corresponds to a sequence of thoughts and must therefore be able to be[. . .]understood via the nature of the utterer, his mood, his aim[. . . .] [This] we call technical interpretation."[70]

(3) In addition, Schleiermacher suggests a further rationale for complementing linguistic interpretation with an appeal to authorial psychology. Skinner tends to write as though one can fix linguistic meaning prior to establishing additional authorial intentions. That may be so in *some* cases—for instance, in that of the frozen lake example just given. But is it *generally* so? Schleiermacher, very plausibly, implies that it is not, because in order to fix the linguistic meaning of words and sentences one often needs to address problems of semantic and syntactic *ambiguity*, and that can only be done by appeal to

conjectures about authorial psychology (for example, about the subject matter which the author intends to treat). This, I take it, is Schleiermacher's point in the following passage: "The technical side is presupposed for the completion of the grammatical side. For in order to determine what is grammatically indeterminate, knowledge of the whole . . . as a sequence of thoughts . . . is presupposed. And in the case of ambiguity the sequence of thoughts is always one of the determining factors, even in relation to details."[71]

I would suggest that rationales *(2)* and *(3)* constitute much better fundamental rationales for always complementing linguistic with psychological interpretation than does rationale *(1)*. For, unlike the task identified by *(1)* of dealing with conceptual innovation, a task which seems very restricted in scope, the tasks identified by *(2)* and *(3)* can plausibly claim to be more or less *ubiquitous* in interpretation. And unlike the former task, they can plausibly claim to require an appeal to authorial psychology for their solution not only sometimes but *always*.

However, it would be a mistake to exaggerate the opposition between these rationales. For rationale *(1)* can certainly stand as a *further* part of Schleiermacher's full case for complementing linguistic with psychological interpretation.

Indeed, there are arguably additional, similarly subordinate (that is, less-than-universally-applicable) rationales as well. To give one example:

(4) Schleiermacher's friend and colleague F. Schlegel had made the very important point that a text will sometimes communicate thoughts over and above those which it expresses explicitly, but via the latter and the way in which they are put together to form a whole.[72] And Schleiermacher himself arguably retains a version of this very plausible idea in his (otherwise rather dubious) doctrine of a "seminal decision [Keimentschluß]" that underlies and unfolds itself in a necessary fashion through the whole of a text (on this doctrine, more in a moment).

Actually, the idea of complementing linguistic with psychological interpretation and even the several rationales for doing so which have been distinguished above were not really new with Schleiermacher, but can already be found in Herder, especially in his *On Thomas Abbt's Writings*, his *On the Cognition and Sensation of the Human Soul*, and his *Critical Forests*. Unlike Herder, however, Schleiermacher also develops the theory of psychological interpretation in certain more specific ways which are unhelpful. The following are two examples.

Herder had included among the evidence on which an interpreter should draw for psychological interpretation both an author's verbal and his *non-verbal* behavior. Schleiermacher occasionally implies the same—for example, when he refers to "the totality of the person's acts."[73] But more usually he implies that the evidence adduced should only include verbal behavior, or even only writings.[74]

The former, Herderian position seems clearly the correct one. For example, in our imaginary case of the misogynist, his record of nasty *deeds* against women might be the only or the best evidence for his misogyny. And of course, a restriction to written evidence would make no sense at all in many contexts of interpretation (for example, when one is interpreting a preliterate culture).

However, *something* can perhaps be salvaged from Schleiermacher's more standard view: he sometimes implies that, although there is indeed no *universal* requirement that an interpreter restrict himself to verbal or written evidence, there is an important subset of cases for which this is at least generally advisable, namely that of *ancient* texts, where we usually lack reliable biographical evidence beyond what is supplied by the author's own texts.[75]

Another respect in which Schleiermacher develops the theory of psychological interpretation more specifically and unhelpfully concerns the doctrine, recently mentioned, of a "seminal decision" made by an author from which his text unfolds in a necessary fashion (at least in its main lines), and which it is the interpreter's job in psychological (or technical) interpretation to identify and trace in its necessary development.[76] This doctrine was absent from Schleiermacher's earliest version of his theory of psychological (or technical) interpretation, but eventually acquired a central role in it.[77]

This seems to me another example of Schleiermacher's implausible overspecification of a very plausible position inherited from Herder. The doctrine of the seminal decision faces at least three prima facie problems. (1) As Dilthey points out, the doctrine was originally inspired by Fichte's theory of the necessary generation of the world of experience out of the self's original act of self-positing.[78] Such an extravagant and implausible metaphysical theory is surely an inauspicious birthplace for a doctrine about the nature and interpretation of texts. (2) Schleiermacher's doctrine is from the start afflicted by an ambiguity between two models of *generation* which were competing in biology at the time: the preformationist model (according to which all the parts of a mature organism are already present in the seed in microcosm) and the primitivist model (according to which they are not, but only develop subsequently). In the *Introductions to the Dialogues of Plato*, where Schleiermacher applies the theory of the seminal decision to the Platonic corpus as a whole, he goes back and forth between these two models. Clearly, however, they would entail very different versions of the doctrine (not only with respect to the nature of the seminal decision itself but also with respect to the nature of the supposed "necessity" of its further development in a text), with very different consequences for interpretation. Moreover, each alternative has drawbacks. It looks very unlikely that a version of the doctrine based exclusively on the preformationist model would be generally applicable.[79] And the primitivist model has the disadvantage that it leaves the nature of the supposed "necessity" of the further development involved quite obscure. (3) Most importantly, *whichever* of the two models of generation is in question, the doctrine of the seminal decision is surely very implausible as a general doctrine about how texts arise and function. For texts often arise through *multiple* decisions—often, moreover, ones made at *different stages* in the process of composition, and often with a lot of *serendipity* influencing the process along the way as well. Something like Schleiermacher's picture may *occasionally* apply to texts, but surely not very often, let alone always.

In fairness, it seems to me that Schleiermacher eventually in a way recognized that the doctrine faced problems of these sorts. They should really have caused him to abandon it, or at least demote it to the status of a subordinate principle with only limited application (a further subordinate rationale to add to those already mentioned), but instead he clung to it doggedly and tried to qualify it in ways which would enable it to cope with them. Thus, in partial recognition of and answer to problem *(1)*, the 1832 version of the hermeneutics makes an effort to confront, and reconcile, the doctrine with the empirical character of various sorts of texts.[80] (But the reconciliation is not effective.) In partial recognition of and answer to problem *(2)*, the 1832 version of the hermeneutics in effect says that the seminal decision is sometimes more of the preformationist sort and sometimes more of the primitivist sort.[81] (But this leaves the doctrine extremely vague, and it still leaves the nature of the supposed "necessity" in the primitivist cases quite obscure.) And in partial recognition of problem *(3)*, the 1832 version of the hermeneutics acknowledges that multiple decisions at different points in the process of composition are sometimes involved,[82] that serendipity often plays a role in the process of composition,[83] and more generally that works do not always contain everything essential in a seminal decision[84]—but it attempts to hold on to the doctrine of the seminal decision in the face of these concessions by implying that when multiple decisions are involved they somehow *follow from* a seminal one,[85] that the results of serendipity are merely *secondary* thoughts,[86] and that when there is no containment of everything in a seminal decision the work is *imperfect* [unvollkommen].[87] (However, these qualifications are surely very dubious and ad hoc.)

The Comparative and Divinatory Methods

Schleiermacher holds that a "comparative" method dominates in linguistic interpretation's inferences from actual word uses to the rules which govern them, but a "divinatory" method dominates in psychological interpretation's inferences from linguistic (and perhaps other) evidence to the psychological traits of the author. However, he also allows that the "comparative" method plays a role in psychological interpretation and that the "divinatory" method does in linguistic interpretation.[88] His idea in the latter case is that this happens especially when the available evidence consisting of a word's actual uses is relatively meager in amount and in contextual variety, as for example when the interpreter is a young child first learning a language[89] or when the subject interpreted is a conceptual innovator.[90]

What does this distinction between methods mean? As I have mentioned, Schleiermacher essentially conceives the "comparative" method as a method of *plain induction* (this first a is F, this second a is F, this third a is F . . . therefore all a's are F), whereby one infers from a collection of a word's actual uses to a general rule governing them (for instance, one perceives the word *rouge* applied on multiple occasions to red things, without exception, and one infers that the rule governing its use is that it applies to all and only red things).[91]

But what does Schleiermacher mean by a "divinatory" method? There are several possible answers. (1) Dilthey and Gadamer understand this to consist in a sort of psychological self-projection by the interpreter onto the person interpreted (or his texts).[92] There is indeed some textual evidence which seems to support such a reading: (a) Schleiermacher writes that the "divinatory" method "depends on the fact that every person, besides being an individual himself, has a receptivity for all other people. But this itself seems only to rest on the fact that everyone carries a minimum of everyone else within himself, and divination is consequently executed by comparison with oneself."[93] And (b) he also commonly speaks of the interpreter "put[ting] himself 'inside' the author" or "in the position of the author."[94] However, I would suggest that these passages should really be understood in the following way. As *(a)* shows, Schleiermacher does believe that interpretation by divination involves psychological self-projection to this extent: it involves presupposing that the people whom one interprets share *something* in common with one mentally. However, that is a fairly modest and uncontroversial claim (after all, interpretation surely at least requires that the interpreter presuppose that, like himself, the people whom he interprets *think* and *mean* things). The important question is whether Schleiermacher also means to be advocating more ambitious forms of psychological self-projection, for example a projection of one's own concepts and beliefs. I think that the answer is No. Talk of the interpreter "put[ting] himself 'inside' the author" or "in the position of the author" might seem to suggest this. However, this cannot be Schleiermacher's considered position, and it would not be a defensible position. For Schleiermacher, very plausibly, identifies such assimilation of texts to one's own manner of thought as the deepest source of *misunderstanding* and strictly *prohibits* it: "Misunderstanding is either a consequence of hastiness or of prejudice. The former is an isolated moment. The latter is a mistake which lies deeper. It is the one-sided preference for what is close to an individual's circle of ideas and the rejection of what lies outside it. In this way one explains in or explains out what is not present in the author [*sic*]."[95] I would therefore suggest that when Schleiermacher speaks of the interpreter "put[ting] himself 'inside' the author" and the like, this should really be understood as little more than a metaphor for a not-thereby-more-closely-specified process of interpretation.[96] Indeed, one can sometimes see that this is the force of such remarks from the fact that he goes on to explain them in terms of a complex process of interpretation having nothing to do with self-projection.[97] And it is also significant in this connection that alongside such metaphors of an interpreter's self-transposition into the author Schleiermacher just as often uses metaphors of an interpreter's self-*effacement* and self-*transformation*—for example, the interpreter should "step outside of [his] own frame of mind into that of the author," he should "transform himself, so to speak, into the author."[98]

(2) Another possibility is suggested by the Latin etymology of the word *divination* (*divus* [n.], a god; *divinus* [adj.], of a god, divinely inspired, prophetic; *divinus* [n.], a prophet), which might lead one to infer that Schleiermacher means *prophecy*, that is, some sort of immediate insight having a religious basis and perhaps also infallibility. Schleiermacher does sometimes write in ways which encourage such a reading. For example, at one point in the hermeneutics lectures he initially wrote *prophetisch* before substituting *divinatorisch*.[99] However, this would obviously again be a very unattractive position philosophically. Moreover, it clearly does not reflect Schleiermacher's considered view. For one thing, he is in fact strongly opposed to any interpretation of texts (including sacred texts) which relies on a supposed divine inspiration.[100] For another thing, he stresses that "divination" is based on scrutiny of available evidence, and is fallible.[101] His main reasons for evoking a kinship with prophecy here are merely that he thinks that "divination" radically transcends the available evidence, and that the sort of grasp of a person's psychology at which it aims includes hypothetical and predictive knowledge about how the person would or will behave in such-and-such circumstances.[102]

(3) A more helpful etymological clue is the French verb *deviner*, meaning to guess or conjecture.[103] For Schleiermacher's considered conception of "divination" does in fact turn out to be a (perfectly secular) process of guesswork, conjecture, or hypothesis, based on close scrutiny of the available evidence, but also going well beyond it, and hence open to either additional support or falsification by further evidence. Thus at one point he writes that

divination is required in order to construct "a complete image of a person from only scattered traces," noting that "we cannot be too careful in examining from every angle a picture that has been sketched in such a hypothetical fashion. We should accept it only when we find no contradictions, and even then only provisionally."[104] This is Schleiermacher's considered conception of "divination," and it is obviously a far more philosophically attractive one than either of the two preceding alternatives.

It is worth noting here that Herder had already advocated the use of a method of "divination," especially on the psychological side of interpretation, and that he too had fundamentally conceived this as a process of fallible hypothesis from meager empirical evidence.[105]

Is Interpretation a Science or an Art?

There are two important points of similarity between interpretation and natural science which Schleiermacher would certainly concede: (1) He assumes (as did virtually everyone else in this period) that interpretation, in its attempts to discern what an author means in his text, is as much concerned with the discovery of *objective facts* as natural science is in it attempts to discern the workings of physical nature. There has been some controversy about this in the secondary literature, some scholars reading Schleiermacher in this way (for example, Gadamer, Betti, and Hirsch), but others instead seeing him as anticipating Gadamer in conceiving meaning as something constructed in interaction with an indefinitely expandable audience of interpreters (for example, Frank and Bowie).[106] However, the latter reading is without textual justification[107] and is anachronistic.[108]

(2) As one can see from his position that misunderstanding is the interpreter's natural condition and from his development of an elaborate hermeneutical methodology to cope with this problem, Schleiermacher believes that interpretation is, in many cases at least, a very *difficult* undertaking, requiring *methodologically informed* and *laborious* solutions—just like natural science.

Nonetheless, Schleiermacher famously infers from the central role of "divination" in interpretation that interpretation is an *art*. And the main force of this position is precisely to say that it is *not* a science. That this is so can be seen from the fact that this position arose in response to a question posed by F. Schlegel: Is interpretation an art or a science?[109]

I think that Schleiermacher is quite right to stress the role of "divination," qua hypothesis, in interpretation, but that he should have been moved by this towards precisely the opposite conclusion on the art versus science question: this again makes interpretation very much *like* natural science. For since the work of Poincaré and Popper, we have come to see this sort of method as *par-*

adigmatic of natural science.[110] I suggest that Schleiermacher gets seduced into his error here by an assumption—common at the time, but mistaken— that the method of natural science is one of plain induction (this first a is F, this second a is F, this third a is F . . . therefore all a's are F).[111] Had he not made this mistaken assumption, he might well have been moved to draw the correct conclusion.[112]

In sum, ironically enough, we can extract from Schleiermacher himself at least three good reasons for *resisting* the sort of sharp distinction between interpretation and natural science that he himself argued for and that he perhaps did more than anyone else to establish in the subsequent German tradition, where it became and has remained virtually a knee-jerk assumption.[113]

14

Bentham's Philosophical Politics

JAMES E. CRIMMINS

James E. Crimmins is Professor of Political theory at Huron College, Ontario. His publications include Secular Utilitarianism: Social Science and the Critique of Religion in the Thought of Jeremy Bentham, Religion, Secularization and Political Thought: Thomas Hobbes to J.S. Mill, Utilitarians and Religion, Bentham's Auto-Icon, and Related Writings, *and* On Bentham *in the Wadsworth Philosophers series. He is currently researching the writings of American utilitarians and critics, and working on a multi-volume collection of death penalty tracts in Britain and America, 1925–1867.*

Jeremy Bentham (1748–1832) is most well-known as a utilitarian legal philosopher. However, he is often encountered in the history of ideas as a radical democrat, a political theorist and reformer of consequence. It is commonly remarked that though Bentham wrote extensively in the area of political philosophy, he did not write one single work—like Hobbes's *Leviathan* or Rousseau's *Du Contrat Social*—that encompasses all the primary features of his political thought. Rather we find interesting material scattered in voluminous published and unpublished writings, produced at various times through a long, industrious, and extraordinarily productive career. My subject is the "political" Bentham—the political thinker, political actor, and agitator for reform, the theorist of politics, government and its attendant institutions and the insatiable public policy enthusiast. My purpose is to suggest a more appropriate conception of Bentham's politics than is generally held, and to indicate a problem at the heart of our understanding of his political thought.

One potential problem can be dealt with at the outset: what did Bentham understand by "politics"?[1] It is a moot point whether Bentham had a very distinct category of "politics" in the manner we usually associate with the canon of political theorists in the western philosophical tradition. Certainly, he commonly employed the adjective "political" when referring to particular contemporary institutions and practices. Yet, at the same time, when he shifted from theory to practice the categories he most frequently invoked were essentially jurisprudential. So, for instance, his theory of the state (*contra* Rosenblum)[2] is, in the main, really a theory of constitutional legislation, and when he spoke of policing, punishment, and the maintenance of order he wrote of "indirect legislation," the laws of evidence, judicial administration, and penal law. There is a sense, therefore, in which politics as such is a residual category for Bentham and this has the effect of extensively broadening what is to count as "politics" and "political" when analyzing his writings.

The conventional account of Bentham's political convictions usually begins by assuming that he was *a*political for much of his life. For instance, in an extremely important essay on Bentham's politics the late John Dinwiddy denied that Bentham was converted to democracy as a result of the French Revolution, as some have held.[3] On the contrary, replied Dinwiddy, Bentham's "revulsion against popular government in the early 1790s was deeply felt"; "he could denounce Jacobinism with almost Burkean vehemence." In Dinwiddy's account, it was only after the beginning of his friendship with James Mill in 1808 that Bentham was persuaded to advocate democratic institutions in earnest, that "the really fruitful turning-point in the development of his political thought came in 1809".[4]

This interpretation can be challenged in two ways—the first commands us to scrutinize the evidence directly relevant to Dinwiddy's interpretation; the second invites us to look beyond this evidence to the underlying philosophy that gave shape to Bentham's politics. In the first approach the disputed evidence is: (1) the nature of Bentham's political writing of the years 1788–90; (2) the apparent retreat from political reform sketched out in manuscripts dated 1793–95;[5] and (3) the character and import of the Mill-Bentham association of 1808–09. Further inquiry has suggested that Dinwiddy's view cannot be sustained, that Bentham had indeed worked out the logic of democratic reform inspired by the upheaval in France, that in the furor of the post-revolutionary years he decided to put aside his recommendations until more propitious times, but that the essential components of his democratic theory had not changed when he joined with James Mill and others in the general agitation for reform in the 1810s.[6] However, while this is useful for plotting the chronology of Bentham's political development, it is limiting as a method for arriving at a comprehensive view of his politics. The second approach is more fruitful in this regard.

My starting point is to submit that Bentham's politics cannot be adequately explained in terms of responses to historical events, but were rather the product of the general premises of his overall approach to social questions. Here I am not concerned with the chronology of Bentham's political development, but with the nature of his philosophy. And, when we speak of his philosophy, I mean by this more than just the expression he gave to the principle of utility and its subordinate principles (security, subsistence, abundance, and equality). For, in and of itself, "utility" does not determine any one particular set of political prescriptions. As I have said before,[7] in the century before Bentham's influence began to be felt, and for some time after, utility was most often the ally of religious orthodoxy in England and (with few exceptions) employed in the defense of the status quo religious and political establishment.

What this suggests is the contingent nature of the relationship between the doctrine of utility and the commitment to particular political positions. In other words, Bentham's adoption of the principle of utility (in 1769 after reading Helvetius's *De l'ésprit*) was not sufficient to convert him to "radical" politics, in whatever form this might be construed. This suggests a commonplace distinction made by philosophers of causality—between, on the one hand, those conditions *necessary* for something to occur (in this case the development of an attitude toward public institutions) and, on the other hand, those conditions *sufficient* (including that which is *necessary*) for something to occur. Utility, as the governing principle of Bentham's philosophy, was a *necessary* component of his views on economics, the law, penology, education, religion, and so forth, but it was not of itself *sufficient* to cause him to mount his numerous attempts to introduce utilitarian reforms, nor can it explain all the specific characteristics of his social and political philosophy. For this we have to look elsewhere.

The argument here is that Bentham's radicalism was profoundly rooted in a general philosophy in which utility functioned as a connecting link between, on the one hand, his materialist metaphysics with its attendant empiricist epistemology and nominalist science of meaning and, on the other hand, his various prescriptions for improvement over a vast range of social, juristic, political, economic, and religious questions.

What requires special attention, therefore, are the theoretical principles which together constitute Bentham's philosophy. Moreover, this was not a late development in Bentham's thinking, but was a central feature of his early career as a social and legal theorist, during the 1770s, when he embarked upon a far-reaching attempt to define the "fundamental terms of Universal

Jurisprudence" in a collection of manuscripts (some 614 pages) variously titled "Crit[itical] Jur[isprudence] Crim[inal]" and "Preparatory Principles".[8] These manuscripts still await publication; they contain a collection of definitions, distinctions, axioms, and aphorisms which define Bentham's empirical epistemology, materialist metaphysics, nominalist ontology and referential theory of language.

For Bentham these were the appropriate "tools" for clarifying or demystifying the "fictions" of current legal practice and conventional modes of legal theorizing. In sum, what we find in these manuscripts is an analytical methodology which is unequivocally "radical" (in the adjectival sense of that term), an approach that served to encourage Bentham's general inclination to adopt a critical perspective when dealing with established opinions and institutions of whatever kind. From this standpoint he consistently adhered to an all-encompassing attempt to structure a philosophy that integrated within itself all the required premises to analyze the complete range of social, religious, economic, legal, and other public issues that came before him, and to suggest alternative policies based upon the principle utility. Whether and when such analyses and alternative policies were committed to print and publication depended at least in part on tactical considerations, but this should not distract us from the systematic nature of the relationship between Bentham's analytical "methodological radicalism" and his social, legal, economic, and political prescriptions—in short, what we might call his substantive radical proposals for reform.

This essential relationship between philosophy and politics in Bentham's thought is clearly displayed in his distaste for natural law discourse. He attacked the American revolutionaries (and subsequently their French counterparts) not because they were inherently evil, but because they had been led astray by the metaphysics of inalienable natural rights ("fictions" of the political imagination providing a tendentious foundation for a new state). Once natural rights theory had been exposed as hollow and dangerous rhetoric, utilitarian doctrine demanded that it be rejected. The relationship between philosophy and politics is also seen in Bentham's early jottings on religious issues dating from 1773–74,[9] and, as one might expect, it is most evidently conspicuous in his positivist jurisprudence, to which he devoted most of his energy in the first decade of his intellectual activity.[10]

From the mid-1770s forward Bentham began to critically analyze the legal structure as it then existed in England and to systematically set about the business of constructing a codified substitute to replace it. Ultimately, he conceived this task as ranging from civil and penal law and the judiciary, to financial matters, education, political economy, public administration, and religious institutions. In each and every facet of this vast prescriptive social science the central, fundamental—one might say, "radical"—tenet was "to rear the fabric of felicity by the hands of reason and law".[11]

However, that a rift sometimes occurred between Bentham's theoretical constructs and his practical proposals suggests the difficulty of the enterprise, and defines a focal problem for students of his work. Ever since Elie Halévy described Bentham in his later years as a convert to "democratic authoritarianism" commentators have sought to stitch together apparently disparate elements of his thought.[12] As more of Bentham's writings have become accessible over the past twenty years this task has become perceptibly more difficult, with scholars increasingly divided in their understanding of his thought and its application to practice. There are those who, in one way or another, emphasize Bentham's legal positivism and his tendency to advocate statist or managerial solutions to particular social, economic and political problems. They detect "authoritarian" tendencies in his thought, with his system variously described as "behaviouralist", "constructivist", "totalitarian", "interventionist", and "collectivist".[13]

Commentators of a very different persuasion, while allowing that legal positivism is characteristic of Bentham's utilitarianism, tend to emphasize the individualist premises of his thought (especially the use of law to enhance the individual's security of expectations), and prefer to found a general account of his utilitarianism on an exposition of the central legal works or the "mature" constitutional writings of his later years.[14] On this basis—and not without good reason—they claim Bentham as one of the intellectual forebears of modern liberalism. But can both schools of interpretation be correct?

This is not an easily answered question, for I do not think it could be said of any of these commentators that they have simply misunderstood Bentham. In part, the problem is that Bentham had a long and prolific career that ranged far and wide over an extensive realm of theoretical and practical issues, making it difficult within the confines of a single study to account for all that he thought and wrote. It is also the case that commentators on Bentham's thought are usually at pains to elucidate *one* particular feature of his work, and there is a tendency to take the particular for the whole. Reflecting, for example, on the accounts we have of Bentham on liberty, on administration, or on the Common Law,[15] it is perhaps reasonable to conclude that both the "authoritarian" and "liberal" views I have outlined above have a place in a complete and comprehensive interpretation. But if this is so, then we should not be surprised if we discover that Bentham's system is less systematic than he pretended and than has often been supposed since.

In short, there may well be a disjunction in Benthamic praxis, between the individualist principles which are generally held to characterize his utilitarianism and the interventionist practice to which he was occasionally prone when advocating specific public policies. If this is true, then it seems entirely possible that both schools of interpretation, by degrees, are guilty of what Quentin Skinner has dubbed "the mythology of coherence",[16] maintaining that a coherency between theory and practice in Bentham's thought can be established where, despite the exhaustive pains that Bentham often took to clearly express his ideas, it is entirely conceivable that it does not exist.

15

Undocumented Persons
and the Liberal State

JOHN S.W. PARK

John S.W. Park completed his Ph.D. in Jurisprudence and Social Policy, in the School of Law at the University of California at Berkeley. His dissertation explored justifications for immigration restrictions, both in Anglo-American political theory and in American public law. He received a Master's in Public Policy from the Kennedy School of Government, and Bachelor of Arts degree from the University of California at Berkeley. He served for two years (2000–2002) as an Assistant Professor of American Studies and Asian American Studies at the University of Texas at Austin, and is now serving as an Assistant Professor of Asian American Studies at the University of California at Santa Barbara. His books include Elusive Citizenship *and* Probationary Americans.

Societies, multiplying or spreading rapidly, soon covered the entire surface of the earth; and it was no longer possible to find a single corner of the universe where one could free oneself from the yoke and withdraw one's head from the sword, often ill-guided, that every man saw perpetually hanging over his head. Civil rights having thus become the common rule of citizens, the law of nature no longer operated except between the various societies, where, under the name law of nations, it was tempered by some tacit conventions in order to make intercourse possible and to take the place of natural commiseration which, losing between one society and another nearly all the force it had between one man and another, no longer dwells in any but a few great cosmopolitan souls, who surmount the imaginary barriers

that separate peoples and who, following the example of the sovereign Being
who created them, include the whole human race in their benevolence.

—Jean-Jacques Rousseau,
Discourse on the Origin and Foundations of Inequality Among Men

In the months leading up to the November elections of 1994, the issue of
undocumented immigrants spread across the borders of California. The state's
ballot included a controversial law that would deny public education and public health benefits to the estimated 1.6 million undocumented immigrants
residing in the state. Under Proposition 187, all government agencies and
officials would also be required to report to the state Attorney General and
to the INS those "suspected of being present in the United States in violation
of federal immigration laws." The INS would then deport those found to be
illegally present.[1] Despite these harsh provisions, or perhaps because of them,
an overwhelming majority of voters formally approved Proposition 187.

But the passage of that law did little to settle the controversy about undocumented immigrants, and about their proper "place" in American society. On
the one hand, undocumented persons clearly arrive in this country without
any legal permission, and as such, they are law-breakers by definition. On the
other hand, the plight of undocumented immigrants often deserves sympathy. Many citizens recognize that one need not "do" anything to be undocumented. In other respects, these immigrants look, speak, act, and work just
like American citizens, and they usually come here simply to live a better life.

But their condition and presence raise some obvious, but neglected, problems for liberal theorists. In the first part of this chapter, I outline more precisely why undocumented aliens pose such a problem for liberal political
theory at all. In the second, I present and then critique a consensualist approach
to solving the problem in liberal societies, an approach proposed by Peter
Schuck and Rogers Smith in their book *Citizenship Without Consent*. In the
third part, I offer and then critique yet another approach, this one suggested
by several other theorists, including Yael Tamir. Finally, at the end of this
essay, I explore whether liberals can legitimately defend nations against outsiders without compromising important liberal values. I myself do not provide a positive answer to that question in this chapter, either from within
liberal theory or otherwise; but certainly, in a world in which the distinction
between "member" and "stranger" increasingly matters, this is no easy matter, and principled solutions are exceedingly difficult.

I. Undocumented Aliens and Liberal Theory

In *A Theory of Justice*, John Rawls tells us that the well-ordered liberal society is one where all persons are equals, where everyone has the same rights

as everyone else and the same opportunities to take advantage of those rights.[2] In such an ideal society, persons live by principles of equality which compensate for "contingencies that are arbitrary from a moral point of view," such that no one, based on a "contingency," is "worth" more than another; in a liberal society, persons are committed to "treat one another not as means only but as ends in themselves" (pp. 510–511, 179). If economic or social inequalities are to exist at all among these equals, they must do so under a principle of justice where these inequalities are "attached to offices and positions open to all under conditions of fair equality of opportunity," and structured in a way that they are "to the greatest advantage of the least advantaged" (p. 83). For Rawls, the well-ordered society is not just one where persons are equals and have equal liberty; it is also a place where persons have profound commitments to principles that account for the least well-off among them.

The presence of 1.6 million undocumented persons threatens, and challenges, this liberal ideal in several ways. First, whether they *should* be treated as equals or not, undocumented aliens *are not* equal to legal residents and citizens in a number of fundamental areas. They are without certain basic rights, as the debate around Proposition 187 made clear. Because they are here illegally, revealing any presence is an occasion for detention or deportation. Thus, unlike legal residents, undocumented aliens are without a "right" to speak; in a matter that directly impacts their lives, "the more visible [they] became, the more difficult [it was] to beat Proposition 187."[3] Persons spoke for them, but no one claimed to be speaking as an undocumented person, and for obvious reasons. The specific provisions of the new rule also suggested that undocumented aliens had no right to privacy. By ordering all government units to report any information that could reveal illegal status, regardless of whether such information pertained to immigration, Proposition 187 directly contradicted federal rules designed to protect privacy.[4] But no one spoke as though undocumented aliens had a "right" to privacy, while many did warn of how the new rule could impact the privacy rights of *citizens*.[5] Thus, even if the right to speak and the right to privacy are crucial to a set of liberties that all persons in a liberal society ought to share, not all persons in this liberal society share them.

Secondly, other provisions of Proposition 187 obviously suggest that undocumented aliens have no "rights" to public health or education. Prior to the new rule, undocumented persons were already ineligible for most forms of government assistance; nevertheless, the new rule further underscores the idea that undocumented persons have no claims to society's help. Governor Pete Wilson, in speaking for Proposition 187, said, "Illegal aliens do need health care and education. But it is the government in Mexico, not in Washington or Sacramento, that should provide them."[6] And even when it had defended undocumented children against a Texas law that would have deprived them of public education, the Supreme Court in *Plyler v. Doe* said that those children had an "interest" in education, but not a "right."[7] Indeed, most commentators consistently speak of undocumented persons as though they have no entitlement to society's resources, even though they acknowledge that undocumented persons *are* in fact among the least well-off in American society.

Yet, that these immigrants are treated as such pariahs is problematic for at least two reasons. First, almost everyone can acknowledge that in many cases, undocumented persons are often not responsible for their illegal status. In particular, undocumented children who come to this country with their parents do not come willingly, but are nonetheless treated as wrongdoers. Justice Brennan had recognized this problem in *Plyler*, and he had struck down the Texas law in question partly on the grounds that "[it] imposes its discriminatory burden on a legal characteristic over which children can have little control."[8] Similarly, opponents of the proposed California law had said that "[it makes] kids victims because adults haven't enforced existing laws."[9]

In addition, many citizens do notice that undocumented persons are like themselves in important ways. In the debate around 187, conservative columnists had characterized them as "hard-working, tax-paying, minimum-wage gardeners and nannies."[10] Entrepreneurs in the multi-million-dollar garment and agricultural industries had claimed that undocumented workers were an indispensable part of their labor force, and many had vowed to ignore 187 once it passed.[11] In fact, throughout California's history, undocumented workers have been a critical source of cheap labor; they have always had a presence here.[12] And most undocumented persons in California have settled in local communities where they share the same ethnic and cultural ties to the legal residents who are already there. Given this fact, both opponents and proponents of 187 had worried whether officials could accurately discern legal resident from alien.[13] Overall, because of their contributions to society, their continued presence here, and their cultural similarities to legal residents, some had argued that the "illegal" status of undocumented persons should be treated as a morally arbitrary, and thus legally irrelevant, characteristic.[14]

II. The Consensualist Approach

Sovereignty and Consent

Few liberals, however, argue for abandoning the idea of national boundaries, or with it, the distinction between citizen and stranger. Rather, in their book *Citizenship Without Consent*, Peter Schuck and Rogers Smith offer a "principled way" to protect U.S. boundaries, specifically against illegal immigrants.

Unlike some, Schuck and Smith phrase the problem as a serious threat to the nation. They warn that "the existence of a large, discrete population that is present within the political community but is ineligible not only for membership but also for many lesser forms of political participation in social life cannot fail to provoke continuing political turbulence."[15] But while they argue that undocumented aliens are a threat, they acknowledge the morally arbitrary nature of the Constitution's Birth-Right Citizenship Clause. Under the Fourteenth Amendment, "one's political membership is entirely and irrevocably determined by some objective circumstance." By being born within US jurisdiction, one automatically becomes a member. "Human preferences do not affect political membership; only the natural, immutable circumstances of one's birth are considered relevant." Against prevailing law, which does seem to discount persons' own decisions, Schuck and Smith offer an "essentially consensual ideal of citizenship" (p. 4).

Schuck and Smith begin their argument with a detailed history of the Birth-Right Citizenship Clause. They tell us that prior to the Civil War, citizenship rules were understood to embody notions of consent, much as in English common law. Officials and citizens in the United States commonly believed that "to be born a citizen, one must belong to a class eligible for naturalization" (Chapter 2, p. 68). This formulation which consciously excluded Native Americans and blacks, illustrates the then-prevalent idea that white men would consent to accept only other white men as free and equal citizens. The "dependents" of white men, white women, could "partake of citizenship," even though it was commonly understood that this would not mean full membership. Generally, though, white men agreed only to accept other white men as citizens. Here, by showing how a dominant class of members deliberately withheld membership from various other classes of persons, Schuck and Smith claim that the process of granting citizenship has always had within it important elements of political consent.

Furthermore, Schuck and Smith insist that after the Civil War, federal officials were more concerned with finding an expedient way of absorbing and protecting newly freed blacks than with delineating more carefully the vague principles that had once restricted membership to whites. Fully aware of the tension between state and federal powers, they settled on birth within national borders as the ground for determining membership. This rule would effectively undermine the Southern states' claim that *state* citizenship should determine whether one was a U.S. citizen, and thus it would quickly guarantee political membership to a new class of persons—freed black slaves— whose fate was dangerously uncertain within the Southern states. Still, Schuck and Smith say that "the debates . . . establish that the Citizenship Clause had no intention of establishing a universal rule of birthright citizenship." They argue that despite the language of the clause, the framers intended just the opposite:

> The framers intended to limit the scope of birthright citizenship. The essential limiting principle was consensualist in nature. Citizenship, as qualified by this principle, was not satisfied by mere birth on the soil or by naked government power or legal jurisdiction over the individual. Citizenship required in addition the existence of conditions indicating mutual consent to political membership. (p. 96)

Since the framers intended to facilitate *only* the political integration of freed blacks, Schuck and Smith claim that the Citizenship Clause was never intended to favor "objective circumstances" above political consent. Under the Fourteenth Amendment, the nation-state consented to accept *one* class of persons as members; but the framers did not, according to Schuck and Smith, intend to accept just anyone born within the territory, notwithstanding the language of their own rule.

Schuck and Smith then argue that under this reading of American history, undocumented immigrants pose a problem because they enter without the explicit permission of the pre-existing political membership. The fact that they are here violates a right that the nation-state has always had. Schuck and Smith argue that by having a fairly coherent idea of just who can be a member by birth, and by enforcing a strict naturalization law, the nation has been committed to accepting outsiders in a very deliberate fashion (pp. 92–94). Undocumented immigrants, then, are "poorly situated, morally speaking, to contest that policy choice" (p. 99). As a further step to reclaim notions of consent, Schuck and Smith advocate the outright repeal of the Birth-Right Citizenship Clause, expressly to deny formal membership to the *children* of undocumented aliens. They write that "if mutual consent is the irreducible condition of membership in the American polity, it is difficult to defend a practice that extends birthright citizenship to the native-born children of illegal aliens. . . . If society has refused to consent to the membership [of undocumented aliens], it can hardly be said to have consented to that of their children who happen to be born here while their parents are in clear violation of American law" (p. 94).

Finally, to make rules of citizenship truly consensual, Schuck and Smith advocate a policy by which those born within U.S. territory are not automatically granted membership. All persons born to legal residents would be "provisional" citizens, "in the sense that they would have the opportunity upon attaining majority to renounce the citizenship if they so desired" (pp. 117–18). When they come of age, all prospective members would have to declare formally their intent to become a member. Citizenship would become an "option guaranteed to all children of an American parent, whether born in or out of the United States." No one would be forced to join. Thus, Schuck and Smith suggest that by making the decision available, membership would have greater moral weight; the occasion would allow all prospective members to express explicitly their loyalty and commitment, both of which are important to the survival of the liberal state (pp. 139–140).

Accidents of Birth

For some liberals, the approach suggested by Schuck and Smith looks very appealing. Particularly for those who "reject the notion that one can find one-self with special responsibilities without having done anything at all to incur them," Schuck and Smith's scheme is especially interesting.[16] Given some of the demands that liberal societies make on their members—including obedience to a particular system of law, or the possibility of being drafted for military service—many persons here might welcome the choice to be a "non-member." Also, Schuck and Smith make an argument for excluding undocumented immigrants and their children that some liberals might find compelling. Indeed, if we think of our laws as originating from a government by consent among free and equal members, it does seem as though we are not bound to tolerate, nor to help, any person who enters in violation of our settled, known will.

But in spite of these strengths, the consensualist approach to citizenship has its flaws. First, the approach simply moves the source of moral arbitrariness associated with citizenship rules from one site to another. Instead of territory, Schuck and Smith link prospective membership with parentage. But to be born to one set of parents—who happen to be legal residents or citizens—rather than another would still seem morally arbitrary. For a child to be born of American parents would give that child, according to Schuck and Smith, a special choice later in life to become a citizen of American society. Another child born in Mexico, or in Korea, does not have that choice for reasons that Schuck and Smith do not establish. One can glean that this has something to do with American parentage, and thus, with pre-existing connections to the nation; however, it hardly seems fair to allow one child a choice and deny it to the other, particularly when neither "did" anything to be born to one set of parents rather than another. Though they acknowledge the moral arbitrariness of birthright citizenship, Schuck and Smith still tie political membership to accidents of birth.

Moreover, the consensualist approach says nothing about another type of objection to formal arrangements of national membership. Even though members in a self-contained, well-ordered society might truly agree to pledge allegiance to one another, those who are not parties to the agreement may still question their moral commitments. For instance, while the leaders of the United States express commitments to human rights and to global justice for all, they also exhibit a certain willingness to fence in the nation, to protect its borders from those who seek protection for reasons of human rights, or justice, or just a better way of life. When the United States "gives the interests of [its] associates priority of various kinds over the interests of other people," those who are not associates, not citizens or legal residents, can legitimately wonder why the nation should act like such an exclusive club:

> [This] distributive objection sees associative duties as providing additional advantages to people who have already benefited from participation in rewarding groups and relationships, and it views this as unjustifiable whenever the provision of these additional advantages works to the detriment of people who are needier, whether they are needier because they are not themselves participants in rewarding groups and relationships or because they have significantly fewer resources of other kinds.[17]

Certainly, many undocumented immigrants are as destitute or as desperate as the worst-off American citizen. For these immigrants, Schuck and Smith do not provide any account of why their interests should count so much less than the interests of members. Moreover, this arrangement seems more unjust *within* the liberal state in light of some of the contributions many "non-members" make to *this* society; it hardly seems fair to claim that all of them deserve expulsion, or exclusion, when what they really want is to share what all "members" have a right to share unproblematically.

Not surprisingly, perhaps in answer to these objections, and perhaps to make membership more consensual than Schuck and Smith have proposed, some theorists have suggested something close to a policy of open borders. For example, like Schuck and Smith, Bruce Ackerman expresses a similar commitment to notions of consent, although Ackerman certainly expands the range of possible participants. He argues that what is distinctive about liberal states is that within their borders, citizens are committed to a set of common values and beliefs and that they pledge to engage in a continuing dialogue based on those shared principles. Thus, "in an ideal theory, *all* people who fulfill the dialogic and behavioral conditions have an unconditional right to demand recognition as full citizens of a liberal state." This scheme might not fully satisfy the distributive objection; non-liberals might still protest. But Ackerman's theory does not rely at all on accidents of birth. Under this "super-consensualist" view, thousands of immigrants could make a moral claim to live within US borders, provided that they consent to a set of principles, and express allegiance to "the national project."[18]

And yet, many liberals, and many others who are not so liberal, might find this too objectionable, and their objections have more to do with protecting a national *culture*, rather than the nation per se.

III. The Cultural Approach

Liberalism and Culture

In her book *Liberal Nationalism*, Yael Tamir writes that with respect to maintaining the integrity of nations, liberals have a "hidden agenda." Tamir notes that while they do express universal commitments to the moral worth of all persons, liberals maintain that nation-states have the right to control admissions and to treat their members with "favoritism." But instead of using universalist principles to reject the moral foundations of particularist, national obligations, Tamir endorses an approach that *justifies* nationalist obligations by conceptualizing the nation-state as a kind of community.

On her first point, though, liberal commitments to culture seem hardly "hidden." For instance, Neil MacCormick and Joseph Raz offer two similar accounts that underscore the relationship of nation and culture. MacCormick argues that "nations are constituted by a form of popular consciousness, not by a mode of legal organization":

A nation is constituted by a relatively large grouping of people who conceive themselves to have a communal past, including shared sufferings and shared achievements, from which past is derived a common culture which represents a form of cultural continuity uniting past and present and capable of being projected into the future.[19]

MacCormick further says that "exclusionary sentiments"—such as those against undocumented immigrants—are not necessarily evil because, in excluding outsiders, members are not so much denying moral equality as affirming the possibility for associates to have meaningful commitments to each other, which in turn makes *universal* commitments possible. "It is . . . those who have a decent and moderate love of their own family, country, colleagues, co-religionists or whatever who can alone recognize as equally legitimate the love others bear for their own" (p. 253).

Moreover, acknowledging these particularist loyalties might be important for other liberal values. First, if liberals are committed to the full development of persons, perhaps they must give all persons a comprehensive framework in which to make meaningful choices. Thus, Joseph Raz writes that "individuals find in [encompassing groups and nations] a culture which shapes to a large degree their tastes and opportunities, and which provides an anchor for their self-identification and the safety of effortless secure belonging."[20] Protecting a national culture can mean, then, protecting the grounds upon which persons become free and autonomous.

Yael Tamir echoes all of these claims.[21] She writes that "the terms of membership set by the liberal state thus reinforce the view of the state as a distinct historical community rather than a voluntary association" (p. 124). In addition, she underscores the need for "communal membership," so that members can see "fellow members as partners in a shared way of life, as cooperators they can rely on." She suggests that the sense of belonging is indispensable for liberal society:

> Having developed this attitude, they cannot but care for other members, wish them well, delight in their success, and share in their misfortune. These feelings provide individuals with a reason to attend first to the needs and interests of their fellows. If the moral force of such feelings is denied, ruling out any special attention to fellow members, the social structure might collapse and we shall be left with isolated individuals and an abstract humanity. (pp. 115–16)

What Tamir fears might be a "total isolation and indifference among the various subgroups" that would compose a multi-fragmented nation, a place *without* a common culture (p. 110). Other liberals seem to agree that, conversely, without particularist commitments to help sort through "the abstract humanity," everyone threatens to be overwhelmed by a sea of duties.[22] Neither nations nor persons could function coherently.

For Tamir and other liberals, this last concern is directly related to another commitment important to liberalism. By granting priority to fellow countrymen, persons can begin to learn to care for, and to help, others in need without being overwhelmed. Tamir writes that "communal solidarity creates a feeling, or an illusion, of closeness and shared fate, which is a precondition of distributive justice." Tamir suggests here that although the solidarity might be an "illusion," liberals should recognize it: "The community-like nature of the nation-state is particularly well-suited, and *perhaps necessary*, to the notion of the liberal welfare state."[23] In other words, without "feelings of solidarity and fraternity," persons would be hard- pressed to find reasons for reaching out to anyone (Tamir, p. 124).

Thus, Tamir concludes that for both moral and for practical reasons, liberals are justified in making distinctions between member and stranger:

> Assuming that individuals have a right to preserve the uniqueness of their communal life, it would make sense to place some restrictions on membership and

claim that we, who already belong, should do the choosing "in accordance with our own understanding of what membership means in our community and of what sort of a community we want to have."[24]

For Tamir, given their own values, liberals ought to be liberal nationalists.

Multiculturalism, Nationalism, and History

Whether Tamir or other liberals would condone the provisions of Proposition 187 and other anti-immigrant initiatives around the world, one can only guess. Although many liberals did openly oppose the measure, many did not. But whether they actually did or not, the idea of liberal nationalism does explain to a large degree the appeal of various arguments to curb immigration generally and undocumented immigration in particular. The experiences of the last election are again an example.

About three weeks before the November vote, thousands of people held a mass demonstration in Los Angeles to oppose Proposition 187. The display of red and green flags, the speeches delivered in Spanish, and the enormous size of the crowd made some feel that "American values are over-run by an uncontrolled influx of Third World citizens."[25] "To proponents of 187 . . . the march was an outrageous display of Mexican nationalism that bolsters the case for reducing immigration." A co-author of the initiative said that "any time they're flying Mexican flags, it helps us."[26] To many, the march indicated that for some persons here, political or patriotic allegiances lay elsewhere. Also, partly in response to the demonstration, proponents of 187 characterized undocumented immigrants as bearers of an outlaw culture, not just because they came illegally, but because "illegals do not work at all," but "burglarize our homes, sell dope, and steal and chop automobiles or send them across the border to be used as Mexican officials' personal cars."[27] Exaggerations aside, proponents of 187 suggested that if American "cultural" values included respect for law, for hard work, for honesty, for a commitment to this nation and its symbols, or simply for personal property, undocumented immigrants were truly unworthy strangers. As formal members of the nation, proponents of 187 portrayed themselves as citizens of "a community struggling to preserve its distinctive character" (Tamir, p. 127). Tamir's theory explains much in this regard.

But it, too, has normative problems. First, the cultural approach is vulnerable to both voluntarist and distributive objections. Consensualists like Schuck and Smith might argue that although members of liberal communities might feel strong attachments to one another, largely on the grounds of a common political or social culture, no one performs a conscious act to accept political obligations. To this argument, "liberal nationalists" like Joseph Raz might propose a right of exit: "people may migrate to other environments, shed their culture, and acquire a new one" (Raz, p. 444). Raz does not suggest, however, where such persons could go. On the other hand, for those who want to migrate to *this* culture, away from their own, Raz suggests that the right to protect culture against outsiders should have considerable weight: "the interests of members of an encompassing group in the self-respect and prosperity of the group are among the most vital interests" (Raz, p. 461). Here, protecting culture could outweigh individual choice.

To other distributive objections, liberal nationalists seem more ambivalent, and more vulnerable. That one is born into a fulfilling cultural group or nation serves as the grounds for a right to enjoy the benefits of that culture or nation. For those *not* born into such circumstances, the liberal nationalist has little to say. Tamir says that "the morality of community justifies favoritism," and that "liberal nationalism... justifies support for the right of individuals to prosper within their own communities."[28] Therefore, if "membership is a matter of belonging, not of achievement," and if the members of the community do not wish to recognize certain outsiders as associates, then the strangers have no claim to partake of a culture that is not originally theirs, despite their desire to benefit from that association.[29] Again, to protect culture, a liberal nationalist can reject "people who are needier."

But this position leads to another set of concerns, when thinking about how the theory of liberal nationalism might apply to the specific problem of undocumented immigration in California. First, this is because, as I noted earlier, most undocumented immigrants in this state usually settle in local communities where they are *not* a cultural minority and where they are often gladly accepted and recognized as members. Given how diverse California is, that is hardly surprising; given that California will soon no longer be predominantly Anglo, no one should expect that to change. If undocumented persons come into contact with citizens who are not culturally similar to them, it is often because the citizens employ them as "minimum-wage gardeners and nannies."[30] But for the most part, that 1.6 million undocumented persons can live in California—and largely remain undetected—speaks to the degree to which they are just like us.

In other aspects of "culture," undocumented persons do not appear to act much more differently than legal residents and citizens: in reality, these persons *do* work (usually in undesirable, low-wage sectors of the economy), and they *do* obey the law (with one exception). In fact, most commentators agree that the rates of employment, criminality, and reception of public assistance for undocumented aliens who settle here are *lower* than for the general population.[31] Although the extent to which they strain public services is debatable, many studies strongly suggest that they do not consume more in public services than they pay in taxes.[32] Thus, even if a liberal state needs communal ties to facilitate commitments to distributive justice, undocumented immigrants may not be the ones who unduly strain either the ties or the haphazard system of "re-distributive justice" that we have.

And if undocumented immigrants and others occasionally express pride in their cultural heritage, it is not clear why that should be such a problem for a society purportedly committed to multiculturalism. In a way, those who oppose the presence of undocumented immigrants seem as though they are not concerned with protecting "culture" per se, but with protecting — desperately — one particular culture, in a state that has many. This is clearly impermissible for a liberal nation committed to multiculturalism. Joseph Raz tells us:

> Multiculturalism requires a political society to recognize the equal standing of all the stable and viable cultural communities existing in that society. . . . A political society, a state, consists—if it is multicultural—of diverse communities and belongs to none of them.[33]

But if *cultural* borders are the ones that should count, as Tamir and other liberal nationalists suggest, then perhaps most undocumented immigrants *should* be allowed to remain in the United States, and most of their friends back home should also come. To avoid this possibility, liberal nationalists might suggest that the dominant cultural group within a multicultural society has a right to control, through immigration restrictions, their very own hegemonic culture. Fortunately, such an option is not one that most theorists would be willing to accept. To be fair to Tamir, she does address the xenophobic and racist tendencies that some critics might attach to her theory, and she disavows them.[34] Still, whether liberal nationalists can adequately address the particular problem of "borders" in such multicultural societies remains questionable, especially in a place with a history of one cultural group dominating others.

Finally, one last concern that further complicates the cultural approach is history itself. In some parts of the world, culture and territory are somewhat synonymous: we think, for example, of Irish culture as rooted in the landscape and history of Ireland. In such places, one might say, perhaps in sympathy with the liberal nationalist, that the culture and people "belong" there. But in places like California, where culture and territory have not been fixed, things become more complicated. In reality, most of the state's undocumented immigrants are Mexican nationals. About a century ago, though, California was indisputably Mexican territory, acquired through a war of conquest. Of course, prior to belonging to Mexico, California was Spanish, and prior to that, Native Americans lived here. In large part, the history of California has been "indelibly tainted with past unjust conquest, genocide, colonialism, and enslavement."[35] Here, as in other parts of the world, it is difficult to fix which culture rightfully "belongs" to this territory, given its history. Moreover, it does seem morally arbitrary, and strange, to solve this problem by privileging the culture that happens to have conquered the territory most recently. Whatever the "solution" may be, the problem is certainly an important one for liberals, including liberal nationalists.[36] But while they acknowledge the problem, and its importance, they rarely seem to address it at the level of theory. Very few do.

In his bid for re-election, Governor Wilson ran television ads showing undocumented immigrants running frantically across the state's border; and in these ads, the narrator described the influx of these immigrants as an "invasion." To appreciate the irony here, one does need an historical context.

IV. Liberalism and Borders

"An Unruly Set of Values"

In the end, the problem of undocumented immigrants remains a pressing and unsolved one for politicians, for citizens, for the "strangers" themselves, and for liberal theorists. For the last group, the problem is particularly odd. In spite of their general commitments to be sensitive to morally arbitrary characteristics, both consensualists and liberal nationalists rely heavily on arbitrary factors to limit an incredibly important part of modern life: political membership. To be born on a particular part of the Earth, to a fortunate set of parents, or to a specific culture "is no deed of him who is born."[37] Yet, in one way or another, all these theorists make much of it.

Liberal commitments to autonomy, and to choice, are also implicated in this problem. As far as political membership is concerned, consensualists may not be consensual enough, while liberal nationalists don't seem too preoccupied with consent at all. If someone wants to leave her native culture or nation to travel to another, both consensualists like Schuck and Smith and liberal nationalists like Raz and Tamir might leave her fate to the discretion of the nation-state to which she wishes to settle. She can choose another nation-state, but that nation-state need not choose her, even if she is, culturally and in other respects, similar to the people she wishes to join—or at least, similar to some of them. And neither consensualists nor liberal nationalists seem to answer this variant of both voluntarist and distributive objections— "why can't she choose to be a member?"

Finally, in a more fundamental way, the problem of citizenship is complicated here by the peculiar history and circumstances of California, and the nation, which further challenge liberal commitments to equality and fairness. As Schuck and Smith point out, full membership in America has been, for most of American history, the monopoly of one socio-cultural group: white men. They consented to accept each other as members, while excluding others. In California, we have a history of conquest, genocide, and colonialism culminating in the establishment of a dominant white culture that exists, despite the best efforts at exclusion and expulsion, in the presence of other cultures. Yet members of that dominant culture were not always "members" or "dominant." Strange, then, that so many of them should now claim that these new "invaders" don't belong, while never examining why they do. Liberal theorists like Schuck and Smith do not really acknowledge these particular problems of history; liberal nationalists like Tamir recognize these problems, but do not address them. These omissions are troubling, especially if liberal societies are committed to fairness between nation-states, as well as within each one. In the end, it may be true that "liberalism may not yet have found the most satisfactory way of accommodating an unruly set of values, none of which we are simply willing to abandon."[38] Still, the degree to which some liberals take leave of their own values is surprising, especially at the border.[39]

16

A New Interpretation of Plato's Socratic Dialogues

CHARLES H. KAHN

Charles H. Kahn is Professor of Philosophy at the University of Pennsylvania. He has published The Art and Thought of Heraclitus, The Verb 'Be' in Ancient Greek, *and* Pythagoras and the Pythagoreans, *as well as his first book,* Anaximander and the Origins of Greek Cosmology. *The present article reflects the views developed in his* Plato and the Socratic Dialogue *(1996).*

Despite the fact that he perfected the form, Plato did not invent the Socratic dialogue. In the years following Socrates's death, a number of his former associates wrote short dialogues in which Socrates was the principal interlocutor. Aristotle in his *Poetics* recognizes the *sokratikoi logoi*, or "Conversations with Socrates," as an established literary genre. One of the innovations in my interpretation of Plato is to attempt to situate his early work in the context of this literary genre.

In some fields, and particularly in Biblical scholarship, genre studies have been dominant for a generation or two. Students of the Gospels, for example, have shed new light on their subject with interpretations that focus on the literary form of the narrative and speeches reported in each Gospel. It is a striking fact that, as far as I can see, there has never been a similarly genre-oriented study of Plato's dialogues. So I want to direct your attention to certain generic features of the Socratic literature that can be of considerable importance for the understanding of Plato's work.

It is fascinating to see how many authors dealt with the theme of Socratic *eros*, that is, the theme of love in the context of Socrates's philosophy. We know of at least five or six. Aeschines is the best preserved of these (in addition to Plato and Xenophon). So Plato's *Symposium* does not stand alone. For example, the figure of Diotima, who serves as Socrates's teacher on the subject of love in the *Symposium*, is paralleled in Aeschines's dialogue *Aspasia*, by the figure of Aspasia herself, the semi-legal wife of Pericles and the most famous—or notorious—woman in Athens in the Periclean age. Aspasia was a real historical person, but the treatment of her in Aeschines's *Aspasia* and also in Plato's dialogue *Menexenus* is pure fantasy. The comic poets had represented her as a woman of low morality and the manager of a brothel. But in Aeschines's dialogue, Socrates recommends Aspasia as a teacher of virtue. In the *Menexenus* Socrates delivers a funeral oration that he claims was composed by Aspasia "from the leftovers of the Funeral Oration that she wrote for Pericles!"

I mention this aspect of fun-and-games in the genre of Socratic literature because it points to what I take to be the most important lesson to be learned from a study of the Socratic genre: namely, that these dialogues are essentially works of fiction, products of the author's imagination, even though the characters in the dialogues are usually historical personalities. Hence, although the Socratic dialogues have some biographical features, they are not works of biography in our sense. As the historian Arnoldo Momigliano pointed out in his study of the *Development of Greek Biography*, "the Socratics experimented in biography, and the experiments were directed towards capturing the potentialities rather than the realities of individual lives. Socrates . . . was not so much the real Socrates as the potential Socrates . . . the guide to territories as yet unexplored" (p. 46).

It is essential to see, then, that the Socratic literature, despite its historical framework, is a literature of fiction and often of fantasy. This essential feature tends to be disguised by the unique greatness of Plato's achievement, in creating what we may call the "realistic" historical dialogue, a work of art designed to give the literary impression of a record of actual events, like a good historical novel. Since Plato's art is so uncannily successful, we have the feeling that we have as it were overheard an actual conversation, in which the historical Socrates is developing his ideas in discussion with a real interlocutor. This is no less true when the interlocutor himself is a creature of Plato's imagination (as seems to be the case with Callicles in the *Gorgias*) or someone that Plato could never have met (like Protagoras, who died when Plato was a child). The dialogue *Protagoras* is not only fictitious; its fictitious date is located in a period before Plato's birth, when of course there were no video cameras and no tape recorders. Nevertheless, as readers of Plato's *Pro-*

tagoras, we feel that the dialogue has the absolute ring of history about it. And professional historians have in fact reconstructed Protagoras's theories on the basis of Plato's text. I believe, of course, that they were simply taken in by Plato's art.

This impression of total verisimilitude is what I call the optical illusion of the dialogues: the fact that these works of fourth-century imaginative literature can be, and often have been, read as if they were documents of fifth-century intellectual history, as if they belonged to the age of Socrates rather than to the age of Plato.

The importance of this fact for the interpretation of Plato's work will become clear if I first summarize what I take to be "the state of the question."

The interpretation of Plato's thought poses a unique problem. There is no real parallel for any major philosopher. This is partly a function of the fact that Plato is the only philosopher of the first rank who was also a supreme literary artist. But the problem derives not simply from Plato's artistry, but also from the specific literary form he chose (namely, the Socratic dialogue), and from the manner in which he exploited this form.

There is first of all the anonymity of the dialogue form, in which Plato's own voice is never heard. It would have been natural for us to expect him to appear in the *Phaedo*, where the inner circle of Socrates's followers are gathered around the master on his last day, before he drinks the hemlock. Phaedo, the narrator of the dialogue, begins by listing the disciples who were present that day in Socrates's prison cell. When he comes to Plato's name, Phaedo hesitates: "Plato, I believe, was sick." Never was malady more convenient!

Since Plato himself does not appear, we fall back on Socrates. But does Socrates always speak for Plato? Or does he sometimes speak for Plato, sometimes not? Or does he never speak for Plato directly? And how are we the readers supposed to tell?

This difficulty is aggravated by the discrepancy between the views ascribed to Socrates in different dialogues. Probably the most dramatic example of such discrepancy is the contrast between the attitudes toward pleasure in the *Gorgias* and in the *Protagoras*. In the *Protagoras* Socrates defends an identity between pleasure and the good which he systematically refutes in the *Gorgias*. Has Plato changed his mind? Or consider the variation in regard to Recollection, where the differences are less dramatic but scarcely less significant. In the *Meno* we have the doctrine of Recollection without metaphysical Forms; in the *Phaedo* we have Recollection with the Forms as objects recollected; in the *Republic* we have the doctrine of Forms without Recollection; in the *Phaedrus* we have *both* doctrines again. What are we to make of such variation?

In the history of Platonic interpretation, there are three recognized possibilities:

1. *Pluralism*, the interpretation defended by George Grote, the great historian of Greece. According to Grote, Plato has no fixed or stable dogmas. He is an honest inquirer, following the argument wherever it leads. Plato can always see more problems than solutions. So contradictions between the dialogues are not to be eliminated.

2. The *developmental* view, as represented by mainstream scholarship in English. (Guthrie's *History of Greek Philosophy* is a standard example.) According to this view Plato moves from an early Socratic period, under the predominant influence of his master's philosophy, where the dialogues are typically aporetic or inconclusive, into the middle period where he develops his own mature philosophy. (According to this story, there is also a later, "critical" period, which does not concern us here.) The middle period, best represented by the *Phaedo* and the *Republic*, is characterized by the metaphysical doctrine of Forms. (The interpretation given by Gregory Vlastos in his book on Socrates is an extreme example of this developmental view, since Vlastos claims that the earlier, Socratic philosophy is not only distinct from but actually opposed to Plato's mature position.)

3. The *unitarian* interpretation, going back to Schleiermacher, which tends to see a single philosophical view underlying all or most of the dialogues. According to Schleiermacher, the order of the dialogues is the order of a philosophical education. According to the contemporary Tübingen School, the order does not matter, since the esoteric message is always the same: all or most of the dialogues allude to the "unwritten doctrines," the so-called doctrine of First Principles. The most distinguished American representative of the unifying tendency was Paul Shorey, who wrote a book entitled *The Unity of Plato's Thought*. (Shorey's view, however, was quite different from that of the Tübingen school.).

We come now to my own view, which is "none of the above." But if I have to be classified, I am certainly more in sympathy with the unitarian tradition. There is of course an unmistakable change between the aporetic (inconclusive) dialogues, on the one hand, and the *Phaedo* and the *Republic* on the other. But I am inclined to see this as a development of Plato as a writer, as marking different stages in his literary career rather than different stages in his thinking. (There is a different kind of change in his political thinking between the *Republic* and the *Laws*. But I am not here concerned with any dialogues later than the *Republic* and the *Phaedrus*.) We probably have some dialogues that were written before Plato's metaphysical thought is fully formed. (My guess would be that this is true for five works: *Apology*, *Crito*, *Ion*, *Hippias Minor*, and *Gorgias*.) But this does not correspond to the usual notion of Plato's "Socratic period." In my view, some seven typically "Socratic" dialogues are in fact to be read *proleptically*, that is to say, as deliberately anticipating and preparing the way for the middle dialogues. These proleptic dialogues include the *Laches*, *Euthyphro*, *Protagoras*, and *Meno*.

I will illustrate what I mean by proleptic writing in a moment. But first let me make clear that the theme of my interpretation is double: both negative and positive, both deconstructive and reconstructive.

First the moment of deconstruction. This aims to undermine the "standard view" of a period in Plato's early work when the philosophy expressed was essentially the philosophy of Socrates; and I aim also to challenge the authority of Aristotle, on which this view ultimately rests. The standard result is a pseudo-historical account of the philosophy of Socrates and an interpretation of the dialogues that offers a hypothetical account of Plato's intellectual biography.

It is clear that Aristotle, for purposes of his own, identified the philosophy of Socrates with the search for definition in dialogues like the *Laches* and *Euthyphro*, and with the denial of *akrasia* (weakness of will) in the *Protagoras*. But Aristotle is not a reliable historian of philosophy. It is well known that Aristotle forces the development of Presocratic philosophy into his own conceptual scheme of the four causes. And he is even less reliable on Socrates, who left nothing in writing.

We must remember that Aristotle arrived in Athens as a youth of seventeen, more than thirty years after Socrates's death. He was separated from Socrates by a whole generation of Socratic literature, of which the dialogues of Plato were obviously the most important philosophically. The oral tradition of the Academy could assure him that the doctrine of Forms belonged to Plato, not to Socrates. Beyond that, Aristotle was on his own. So he recognized the philosophy of Socrates in the earlier dialogues of Plato, and the Stoics later did the same. Now Aristotle and the Stoics were interested in philosophy, not in history as such; for them the figure of Socrates served to define a certain position in a theoretical debate. But the modern scholars who follow in their footsteps claim to be writing history. And since they treat Plato's literary creations as if they were historical documents, the result is a pseudo-historical account of the philosophy of Socrates.

Even more unfortunate, in my opinion, are the consequences for our understanding of Plato's own work. Scholars who believe they can identify the philosophy of Socrates in Plato's earlier dialogues proceed then to interpret the various dialogues as stepping-stones along Plato's path from Socratic discipleship to his own independent position as an original philosopher. But this account of Plato's development is purely hypothetical: it is not based upon any independent documentation. In my alternative interpretation, what we trace in these so-called Socratic dialogues is not the evolution of Plato's thought but the development of a literary project and the unfolding of his pedagogical strategy, in composing a series of dialogues carefully designed to attract readers into philosophy and to prepare the minds of his readers for a sympathetic understanding of his new and radically unfamiliar vision of reality—a vision that he was eventually, gradually, and only partially to expound in his literary work.

In order to do justice, then, to Plato's genius as a philosophical writer, we must first free him from the shadow, or rather from the phantom, of the historical Socrates. That is why a study of the Socratic genre and its fictional character is so important. As a recent writer (Andreas Patzer) put it, summarizing the results of a generation of Socratic scholarship: "The historical Socrates disappears from view; in his place appears a multiformed literary creation, the Socrates of the Socratics."

Hence, in my opinion, we know very little about the philosophy of Socrates, beyond the paradox that no one voluntarily does wrong (or that no one is voluntarily bad). What little we know has to be found in Plato's *Apology*, the one Socratic document which is not a fictional dialogue but the literary record of a public event, the trial of Socrates. This is an event at which Plato was personally present, together with hundreds of other Athenians. Consequently, there are historical constraints on Plato's presentation of Socrates in the *Apology* that do not apply to any of the dialogues. The dialogues are mostly private conversations, and Plato is free to make them up as he pleases. From the parallels in the works of Aeschines, Phaedo, and Xenophon, we can see that historical accuracy, or even chronological possibility, was not a feature of the genre.

The moral stance of Socrates and his willingness to face death rather than commit an unjust act were certainly of the greatest importance for Plato. But we possess no reliable account of the philosophy of Socrates that can provide us with a clue for understanding Plato or interpreting his early work.

So much for the deconstruction. Now for the more constructive moment. I want to sketch an interpretation in two phases: first, the philosophical approach, and second, the literary approach.

To begin with philosophy. What is Platonism (with a capital "P")? It is not a doctrine about universals—that is Aristotle's perspective. It is not a doctrine about abstract objects (sets or numbers)—that is modern platonism with a small "p." It is only incidentally a distinction between properties (such as equality) and the things that have properties (such as sticks and stones). That is one of the aspects of Plato's work that may be most attractive for some contemporary philosophers. But that is not the central issue for Plato.

Plato's philosophy is essentially an otherworldly view about the nature of reality and the place of the human psyche: a view according to which the "real world" is an invisible realm that is the source of all value and the source of all rational structure. That is why Socrates in the *Phaedo* can describe philosophy as the practice of death. For death means the escape of the soul from the body, and hence its potential return to the blessed realm of all goodness, truth, and beauty.

The *Phaedo* is Plato's strongest statement of this view. But the same view is echoed much later, for example in the *Theaetetus* (176A): "It is impossible for evils to disappear. There must always be something opposite to the good. But evils have no seat among the gods; of necessity they must circulate in this region and in mortal nature. Therefore we ought to try to escape from here to there as quickly as possible. To escape is to imitate the divine, to assimilate to the divine as far as possible. The assimilation is to become just and pious with wisdom."

Thus the *Theaetetus* repeats the conception of the *Phaedo*. Both moral virtue (as represented by the ethical stance of Socrates in the dialogues) and philosophic wisdom (as represented in the dialectic concerned with defining essences) are conceived as the path that leads the human soul to the supersensible realm, to the divine realm where there is no evil.

Now this is essentially the world view of Eastern mysticism or of Plotinus and the Neoplatonic tradition. However, it is not clear that "mysticism" is the right word for Plato. The fundamental *rationality* of his conception is guaranteed by the role of mathematics, as the privileged means of access to reality. The central importance of mathematics for Plato is that it leads us away from the sensible realm, but not too far away! It does not lead to magic or to nonrational revelations, as in later Neoplatonism.

I want to suggest that this otherworldly sense for meaning and truth, this conception that everything good and real is located in the realm of the supersensible, is the core of Plato's philosophy. The doctrine of Forms and the metaphysical distinction between Being and Becoming have to be understood as the rational articulation of this otherworldly view. One misses the point if one *begins* to understand Plato as offering a solution to the problem of abstract entities, or to problems in the philosophy of language or the philosophy of mind—a theory of concepts or a theory of terms. It is even a mistake to think of him as beginning from ethics as ordinarily understood.

Of course Plato is a total philosopher, and as such he is interested in *all* of these topics and in politics as well, in politics above all. Plato's lifelong concern with politics and with moral reform in the city (reflected in the *Gorgias*, *Republic*, *Statesman*, and in his final work, the *Laws*) is perhaps the only driving motive in his philosophy that is essentially independent of the otherworldly concern. The dominating position of the *Republic* as Plato's masterpiece may be misleading for a balanced understanding of his philosophy. The *Republic* is very this-worldly, in its intense concern for the just individual and the just society. We might be tempted to think of Plato as a split personality: a metaphysical visionary alternating with a social reformer and a would-be politician and legislator. But even in the *Republic* the philosopher-king is there to establish the junction between the two realms: between the world of Forms and the world of the city.

Plato's metaphysical vision, the primacy of the supersensible, is partially expressed in a very short passage in the *Symposium*, at the end of Diotima's lesson of love (as we shall see in a moment). But it is fully expressed for the first time in the *Phaedo*, in the discussion of immortality and the afterlife. The death and sanctification of Socrates are chosen by Plato as the occasion for revealing his deepest view. And it is no accident that the *Phaedo* also gives us the first *systematic* statement of the doctrine of Forms. Plato's metaphysics can be seen as his own understanding of the meaning of Socrates's life and death.

Now Plato's view of the primacy of the unseen world is the metaphysical counterpart to the Orphic-Pythagorean doctrine of the soul, with its promise to the initiate of escape from the cycle of rebirth. These "weirdos," the eccentric cults of Pythagorean or Orphic inspiration, would be Plato's only spiritual allies in the very materialistic, competitive world of Athens in the fifth and fourth centuries B.C.—the world of Aristophanes, Thucydides, and the orators. It was not a hospitable social environment for such an otherworldly view, not at all like the age of Plotinus. It is in this perspective, in view of the tension between Plato and his *Zeitgeist*, that we have to understand Plato's caution as an author. This awareness of a potentially hostile or unreceptive audience helps us to understand the strategic-rhetorical motivation for his use of indirect statement and the device of myth-making, his holding back and then his gradual, ingressive exposition of the otherworldly metaphysics.

And that brings us to the second contructive aspect of my interpretation: the literary approach.

This is not the occasion for studying in detail the seven proleptic dialogues in which Plato makes use of the aporetic form to prepare his audience for a more sympathetic response to his central metaphysical vision. From this group I can refer only to the *Meno*. But first I want to look briefly at the two dialogues which Plato composed for the introductory exposition of his core doctrine: the otherworldly vision and the theory of Forms.

These doctrines are presented to the world for the first time in two of the most dramatic and powerfully written of all the dialogues: the *Symposium* and the *Phaedo*. Together they form a pair, or a diptych. The scene of the *Symposium* is a drinking party, celebrating Agathon's victory in the tragic competition at the Dionysiac festival: here we meet Socrates in the midst of life. In the *Phaedo* we find him in prison, in the shadow of death, in a final conversation on immortality, just before his own life comes to an end.

At Agathon's victory party there are a series of speeches on love. Socrates's speech consists of the lessons on *eros* that he heard from an unknown priestess named Diotima. In the last few paragraphs of this speech, Diotima reveals the final mysteries of love, into which Socrates himself is perhaps not ready to be initiated. This final revelation is presented as a ladder of love, at the climax of which comes the beatific vision of Beauty itself. "There (says Diotima), if anywhere, is life worth living for a human being, beholding Beauty itself." Here we have not the doctrine of Forms (in the plural) but the magnificent vision of a single metaphysical object, the Beautiful as such. A moment afterwards, the drunken Alcibiades enters the party, and we hear no more of metaphysics. (There was only a brief glimpse of the vision.) Furthermore, there is not a word spoken about an immortal psyche. Talk of transmigration would not be taken seriously in this worldly company of high society. Plato's exposition is carefully adapted to his fictive audience.

In the *Phaedo*, on the other hand, the atmosphere is completely different. Here we have an intimate circle of Socrates's closest associates. The entire dialogue is a philosophical discussion of the destiny of the soul, and the full doctrine of Forms is systematically presented. It is here that philosophy is described as training for death, that is, for the future state of the disembodied psyche, in contact with the transcendent reality represented by the metaphysical Forms.

I suggest that this carefully crafted staging for Plato's introduction of his core philosophy, in the *Symposium* and *Phaedo*, must be viewed as the product of a deliberate artistic plan. There is no reason whatsoever to suppose that these two dialogues reflect a recent experience of conversion on Plato's part. It is more reasonable to suppose that he has been preparing this for some time!

In fact there are many hints of what I am calling the core philosophy in earlier works. For example, in the *Gorgias* Socrates quotes from Euripides: "Who knows if life is really death, and death is recognized as life in the world below?" This is a clear allusion to the otherworldly view of the soul. But in the *Gorgias* there is no trace of Forms nor of the metaphysics of Being.

The most important example of proleptic writing and doctrinal anticipation is in the *Meno*. In the *Meno* we clearly have a partial revelation of Plato's core position in the doctrine of learning as Recollection. The doctrine of

Recollection presupposes immortality for the soul (which is not at all a traditional Greek idea), and it attributes a priori knowledge to the transmigrating soul. But there is no reference to Forms in the *Meno*. We have to wait for the *Phaedo* to tell us that the metaphysical Forms are what is recollected.

On the developmental view, Plato would have worked out the doctrine of Forms *after* he wrote the *Meno* and before he wrote the *Phaedo*. But this assumption would be quite arbitrary. If we look closely at the argument of the *Meno*, we will see that the Forms, though not mentioned, are definitely entailed.

In the *Meno* Recollection is introduced as a response to Meno's paradox. And Meno's paradox is provoked by the principle of priority of definition. The priority of definition is the principle that you must first know *what-X-is*, in order to know anything about X. But how are you going to get started? At this point we get Meno's paradox of inquiry: you can't even begin to inquire, because you don't know what to look for; and furthermore, you won't know how to recognize it even if you find it.

Socrates's solution is Recollection: you already know *what-X-is*, because you have already learned everything in a previous existence. Hence you only need to be reminded. But just how does that help? How is Recollection supposed to be a solution to the paradox of inquiry? How did you learn anything in a previous life? If the previous life was like this one, the paradox is simply deferred. We get a regress, not a solution.

If Recollection is to provide a solution, then the previous existence was not an ordinary human life, but the experience of a disembodied psyche in direct cognitive contact with a priori essences. So the objects of Recollection, to avoid Meno's paradox, must themselves be transcendental, incorporeal essences: in other words, Platonic Forms. Hence Plato's metaphysics and epistemology are entailed by, but not directly expressed in, the argument of the *Meno*.

If we were inclined to doubt that Plato could write in such an indirect way—that he could intend in the *Meno* this conclusion that he will formulate only in the Phaedo, we can be reassured by a suggestive parallel in the *Meno* itself. Recollection is illustrated by a geometry lesson, in which an untutored slave boy learns (or "recollects") how to double the area of a square. Socrates shows him that you can double any given square by constructing the square on the diagonal. Now this construction also illustrates two important mathematical results: (1) the Pythagorean theorem (that the area of the square on the hypotenuse is equal to the sum of the areas of the squares on the other two sides), and (2) the existence of incommensurable magnitudes, or what we call irrational numbers, since the length of the diagonal of a unit square is the square root of two.

Why does Plato make no mention of these important mathematical truths? Clearly, he is writing for a double audience: he expects his more intelligent and better informed readers to do some thinking on their own. The case is similar for the link between Recollection and the Forms. Just as anyone trained in geometry will see what is involved in doubling the square, so anyone familiar with Plato's metaphysics will see what the objects of Recollection must be.

This incomplete, tantalizing, discussion of Recollection in the *Meno* may serve as one example of what I call proleptic writing in the pre-middle, or threshold dialogues.

Let me conclude by summarizing the advantages of my approach over the traditional, developmental view of the early dialogues.

1. The negative advance is to get rid of some unsubstantiated history: the pseudo-historical account of the philosophy of Socrates and the undocumented account of Plato's intellectual development.

2. The positive contribution is twofold.

First, we get a more unified view of Plato's philosophy. Despite some readjustment and refinement in the theory of Forms, the metaphysical-otherworldly vision remains central in Plato's later work as well. (I have quoted the passage from the *Theaetetus* on escaping from evils by assimilation to the divine. The otherworldly view is even more prominent in the *Timaeus*, with echoes in the *Sophist* and *Philebus*.)

Secondly, we achieve a much more subtle understanding of Plato's artistry in composing dialogues. After all, Plato had a problem. On the one hand he was a gifted dramatist, one of the greatest writers the world has ever seen. On the other hand he was a follower of Socrates, who wrote nothing himself but philosophized with every word and every breath.

Plato was himself acutely aware of the difficulties and disadvantages of communicating philosophical thought in written form. In the *Phaedrus* he compares the book to a statue, which looks alive but always gives the same answer if you ask it a question. And so he insists that the serious philosopher will never take his written work seriously.

So this is Plato's problem. How could he use his extraordinary literary gifts and change the world by communicating with a larger audience—and carrying his message into the future—while at the same time remaining loyal to his sense of philosophy as the living exchange of ideas in conversation, with questions and answers, arguments and objections? Providentially, he had available to him the Socratic dialogue form as a popular genre. Plato—and Plato alone—transformed this minor genre ("conversations with Socrates") into a major art form and the expression of major philosophical thought. But Plato remained loyal to his Socratic heritage by writing *only* dialogues, and by designating the highest form of philosophy by a term that he invented: *dialektike*, "dialectic", which literally means "the art of conversation."

17

What Is Postmodernism?

EVA T.H. BRANN

Eva T.H. Brann was Dean of St. John's College, Annapolis, from 1990 until 1997. She is the author of a trilogy, The World of the Imagination, What, Then, Is Time?, *and* The Ways of Naysaying. *Her latest book is* Homeric Moments: Clues to Reading the Odyssey and the Illiad. *She is currently teaching at St. John's.*

The question proposed is: "What is Postmodernism?" What kind of question is it? We may ask: "What is a human being?", for there *are* natural human beings, and the question invites us to define their essence or to analyze their existence or to describe their characteristics. It is a question worth asking because our lives depend on the answer. We may ask: "What is a work of art?", for we can point to an example and meet rational opposition: "That's not art, it's . . ." That question has recently acquired even a cash interest, since some members of Congress want public funding to go only to those who produce acknowledged works of arts.

Postmodernism, however, is not a *natural kind* nor a *material artifact*. It isn't even a *theory*, that is to say, a work of intellectual architecture, free-standing and well-founded. Instead it bears the signature of an intellectuals' movement: the "ism" ending. We speak of the Theory of Relativity, and then again we speak of Relativism. That pair exemplifies the distinction I mean.

Hence when we are asked about "Postmodernism" we are asked not about an object of thought but about what a number of people are thinking.

Probably only some are thinking while others are following the trend by repeating language, that is, by letting their vocabulary do their thinking. In such cases the "What is it?" question seems to me to have three profitable approaches. We may go to the writings of the masters of the movement and ask what the texts mean. Then we may ask what the wider implications of the chief of these are. And at some point we must ask whether the thought-complex is invented or discovered, created or found, constructed or contemplated. In the old days invention was the business of rhetoric and discovery the part of philosophy. Since we are said to live in an era of when rhetoric has absorbed philosophy, we may suppose that Postmodernism is a construct.

If it is a construct, and if it is well-named, then to deconstruct the name should be helpful. It is tripartite: Post-modern-ism.

The ultimate element is the above-mentioned "ism" or the personal form "ist." It is a Greek and Latin ending, connoting the adoption, often perverse or specious, of the habits of a group. For example, barbarism is behavior like that of those who babble inarticulately, and a sophist is one who looks like a wise man, a *sophos*, without having or loving wisdom, in opposition to a *philosophos*. Whether for good or ill, "ism" connotes running in droves, and an 'ist' is an intellectual assimilationist.

The penultimate element, "modern," is a coinage of the sixth century A. D. It comes from the Latin word *modo*, "just now, this moment."[1] It is a word needed, now as then, when an epoch is felt to have been superseded by the present, the up-to-date. It betokens a sense of having left something behind and of being on the cutting edge of time. It is a term of temporal self-location.

There have been many modernisms: theological, national, esthetic, literary, architectural. In fact, one might say that modernity is the propensity to modernisms; I mean the urge of elites not only to be continually displacing the late by the latest, but to induce "movements," that is, tendentious drift, in followers.

One modernism important to the shaping of Postmodernism was articulated by the literary Modernists, among them Proust, Joyce and Eliot, particularly in their avoidance of the linear temporality, the straight, progressive narrative, of Realist writers. The Modernists were in rebellion against all sorts of determinism, and they subverted the simple temporal causality of physical time by using flash-backs, by cutting back and forth, by introducing timeless revelatory moments. The effect sought was a panoramic mythical temporality. It was sometimes criticized as ahistorical, but it was really rather panhistorical: All times were available in their atemporal essence.

The modernism most immediately relevant to Post-modernism was architectural.[2] Architectural Modernism meant an incessant search for the new by a creatively original architect striving to find universal, technologically valid rules. This Modernism was indeed more than ahistorical, it was on occasion overtly antihistorical. It trashed the past.

Both literary and architectural Modernists eventually came under attack for their personal elitism as well as their intellectual universalism. It was in architecture that the term Post-modernism first gained currency.

The first—and my final—element of Post-modernism is its first syllable, "post." "Post" in this context does not mean simply "after" in time, as period prefixes often do. Think, for instance, of the designation "Presocratic." The "Presocratic" Heraclitus, for example, is not essentially a precursor of Socrates; in fact a claim has been made that he still had access to something Socrates had lost: the *Logos*.[3] If that is so, Heraclitus is not working "up to" Socrates. "Presocratic" is a merely chronological term.

Not so "Postmodern." The "post" in this term, says Lyotard, one of the leading definers of the movement, intends the Greek preposition *ana*, which as a prefix can mean "back again," as in *anamnesis*, re-collection.[4] Recollection is not mere recall, but effective reappropriation of memory. Lyotard goes further. "The *post modern* would have to be understood according to the paradox of the future (*post*) anterior (*modo*)."[5] He means that in a postmodern work the future comes "after" the "just now" in the sense that such a work is not composed in accordance with any previous universal rules, or, as he calls it, any metanarrative. It has no antecedently present conditions. "Simplifying to the extreme, I define postmodern as incredulity toward metanarrativies." This definition is made with reference to the term "modern" which designates "any science that legitimates itself with reference to a metadiscourse—such as the dialectics of spirit, the hermeneutics of meaning," or, I might add, the shared rationality of minds (Ibid., pp. xxiii–iv). Thus the "post" makes reference both to the readmission of history by anamnesis and to the definitive exclusion of metaphysics and its derivatives.

The sawing through of the perch we sit on, the undermining of the structures we rely on, is to be taken in the most total sense: Nothing is to support anything. In the realm of the imagination, for example, this regime has the most drastic results. Traditionally the peculiar product of the imagination, the image, is in its very being derivative from an underlying original.[6] The Postmodernist image is regarded as entirely cut off from any original, from any supporting base. Images image images. Like facing mirrors, they reflect nothing but each other. Their infinite play expresses nothing. They are without any "referential depth."[7] Andy Warhol's seriograph of twenty-five Marilyn Monroes is emblematic: The cumulative effect of the mechanical iteration is meant to obliterate the sitter.

This definition of postmodernism need not be written with a capital P. Just as there is Romanticism, a movement of the late eighteenth and early nineteenth century, and romanticism, a disposition that can show up at any time, for example in the hazy distances of Pompeian wall paintings, so there is postmodernism, the fundamental disposition—Lyotard discerns it in Montaigne's essays—to let the rules be emergent from the work rather than to work to antecedent standards.

The recall of history is intended to cancel the antihistoricism of Modernism and its rage for the New. In fact, one might say that postmodernism has to modernism a relation similar to that which every romanticism has to its ever-anterior rationalism, a relation of reaction and return. However, the particular modes of this round of Postmodernism are dictated by the particular Modernism which it sublates. As the technological universalist Esperanto is superseded by a folksy local vernacular, the Postmodernist work becomes, "radically eclectic."[8] This eclecticism treats the past as a flea market where one can easily acquire old functionless things: *Bricolage* is the technical term for this browsing in the Postmodernist literature. We engage in it all the time, as when we buy an old inoperative Singer sewing machine as a piece of decoration. So did the ancients. In late antiquity the great monuments of the past were taken apart for small present purposes. And even then this parasitism was not always felt as a sign of meager times. It must be said that bricolage is the most effective kind of preservation available, and a lot better than another late ancient habit, that of throwing antique marbles into the lime pit to make plaster for new hovels—a habit whose modern analogue is the wrecking ball.

There is of course a dissonance between Postmodernism (capital P) and postmodernism (lower case). If postmodernism is a universal human disposition—the propensity for now and then knocking away all given supports and for finding compensation in raiding the past—then Postmodernism loses some of its force as the singular apocalyptic vision for which it takes itself. It is, after all, so named as to make a next epoch unnameable (though I have heard "Postpostmodernism"). What can possibly come after the time when the "just now" has itself been pushed into the past, when we are said to be already living ahead of our own present?

Perhaps such namings are attempts to tempt fate, or rather to propitiate history, to turn her whimper after all into a bang. They are perhaps whistlings in the dark, creative construals of neediness into glamour. I mean this: In the straight talk of *ex post facto* history, an epoch that defines itself against its predecessor is called reactionary. An epoch that is sawing off the branch on which it sits and digging a hole beneath itself is called perverse. An epoch that has no originals for its images is called antic and untethered. An epoch that is bored by what is established is called ephemeral. An epoch that lives off borrowings is called indigent. An epoch suffering from acute cultural fatigue is called decadent. But an epoch that legitimizes all these tiring torments and takes then to its bosom may be said to be whistling in the dark, to be turning to sophisticated theory to fill the empty throne of substance.

But I should be ashamed of talking as if epochs did and suffered things. A time, a culture, a society, a movement are and do nothing. All there is, is people believing things about their temporal location and persuading others. The question proposed, "What *is* Postmodernism?", runs the danger of positing as a being what is only a movement—and movements are to the human intellect what inertia is to material bodies, a relative motion without an innate force.

What each human being reports as a personal conviction is always to be taken seriously. When anyone speaks impersonally of intellectual happenings or uses a collective "we" about thought, an inquiry into the meaning of that companionable pronoun is called for. "The idea that we are in a 'postmodernist' culture has been a commonplace since the mid-seventies" says a commentator.[9] Who here is a "we"? The same author says: "Picasso is no longer a contemporary or a father figure; he is a remote ancestor, who can inspire admiration but not opposition. The age of the New, like that of Pericles, has entered history." For whom? Go see the painting; read Thucydides. Picasso may not be a toothless lion to you, and Pericles may turn out to have more life than many a present politician. Not everyone is equally affected by the current deep recession of the temporal economy. An individual opinion is justified by the force of its arguments. A single insuperable flaw can do it in. A movement is validated by the irresistible force of its influence. Hence one principled staunch resister can do *it* in: It isn't the history of my time unless I affirm it. The huge facts of our present that Postmodernism tries to interpret—the fast dispersion of the intellectual center, the rapid supersession of the present, the vast propagation of the electronic image—are undeniable. But I think that their human meaning and our response is to be shaped by our individual understanding and our personal will, not by any inherent dynamic attributed to them. They are, for all their enormity, dead forces until a thinking human being imparts to them their vis viva.

What is Postmodernism? 1. A set of sophisticatedly revealing texts to be gotten to when all that preceded them have been properly studied. 2. The latest "ism" and the last on the long list of recommended inquiries for a young lover of wisdom.

18

Why Study the History of Philosophy?

GISELA STRIKER

Gisela Striker has taught at the University of Göttingen, Columbia University, and the University of Cambridge. She now teaches ancient philosophy at Harvard. Her first published work was an influential study of Plato's Philebus. *She is currently preparing a commentary on Aristotle's* Prior Analytics. *This contribution is adapted from the preface to her collection of* Essays on Hellenistic Epistemology and Ethics.

Students of philosophy, undergraduate as well as graduate, are usually required to take at least a few courses in the history of their chosen field—say, a class on Plato or Aristotle, Rationalism or Empiricism, Kant or German Idealism. These requirements are often seen as a burdensome relic from the old and unenlightened times when philosophy was regarded as a collection of comprehensive doctrines or "systems" from which one could choose a *Weltanschauung*. Analytic philosophy, by contrast, has tended to associate itself as closely as possible with the sciences, seeing itself either as a branch of science or as a kind of second-order discipline that studies the concepts of the sciences or indeed of ordinary language.

During the first half of the twentieth century, analytic philosophers would resolutely set aside what used to be called 'metaphysics' as nonsense, and the history of philosophy as a collection of more or less egregious muddles. Given this kind of attitude, it is not surprising that it became a mystery why an aspiring philosopher should waste her or his time studying earlier and outdated versions of the subject. After all, students of physics or chemistry, biology, or astronomy can do perfectly well without knowing anything about the history of the respective sciences, and the history of science has its own separate department in universities.

Although the revolutionary optimism of the earlier decades has largely disappeared, and many analytic philosophers are now quite inclined to take their predecessors seriously, one can still regularly hear variants of the view that real philosophers are or should be concerned with "the problems themselves," while historians think (only) about what earlier philosophers thought. It seems to me that there are two distinct claims behind this view—first, that what historians of philosophy do is not philosophy, and second, that contemporary philosophers can learn little if anything from the history of their subject.

To begin with the first claim: given that historians of philosophy are engaged in the study and exegesis of the philosophical doctrines of the past, how could they be expected to come up with anything that might advance the discipline?

I would grant, of course, that historians are not likely to come up with novel ideas, at least not in their role as historians. But how many philosophers do? Most of the thousands of philosophy teachers working today would not pretend to be of the rank of a Descartes, a Kant, an Aristotle, or a Wittgenstein. What they do, and what they teach their students to do, is to think about philosophical problems in as clear and disciplined, or as deep and imaginative, a way as they can. It would be a mistake to see the point of their activity only in the books and articles that are its tangible results. Most 'systematic' philosophers, whether by inclination or under the constraints of teaching schedules, have come to concentrate on a particular set of questions in some more or less traditional field—ethics, epistemology, philosophy of language, and so on—but they do not therefore conclude that their colleagues who work in different areas are not really doing philosophy. As far as thinking about philosophical problems is concerned, historians of philosophy are doing much the same as specialists in systematic fields. In trying to make sense of the arguments and theories of older philosophers, we cannot help but think about the problems they were thinking about—problems which are often versions or interesting variants of questions that are discussed in contemporary systematic debates.

One polemical way of describing the difference between historians and systematic philosophers would be to say that it's a matter of taste: historians tend to be those who prefer to read, say, Hume rather than the latest issue of a philosophical journal, or who prefer to do ethics with Aristotle (to borrow a phrase from Sarah Broadie[1] to doing it with the latest school of consequentialists or deontologists. Their prejudice is that there may often be more to be learned from these authors than from our technically more sophisticated contemporaries. It seems highly implausible to suggest that the historian is thinking about Hume or Aristotle *rather than* ethics or epistemology, and if she does, she will not get very far.

One might object that this will not eliminate the difference between the exegetical exercise of figuring out what Aristotle was saying about virtue, for example, and a straightforward discussion of questions of desert or moral responsibility. But the line between exegesis and argument is less clear than these labels suggest. The historian who wants to understand a classical author will have to rely on her own sense of what is philosophically plausible, what counts as a strong or a weak argument, and in this respect she will of course be guided by her training as a philosopher, which can only be that of a contemporary philosopher. This also determines to a large extent which authors or texts she will choose to study: historians of logic or ethics are motivated as much by an interest in logic or ethics as by an interest in intellectual history. Obviously, historical interpretations will be constrained both by the texts they are setting out to explain and by historical background information about the author, if only in order to avoid blatant anachronisms. But whether this should be seen as an intellectual limitation seems to me to be an open question. One could also see it as a challenge to the imagination.

Still, there remains the second question: what historical exegesis can contribute to present-day philosophical debate. The historian's contribution consists in keeping available the thought of past philosophers as a resource that would otherwise be lost or inaccessible. In order to engage in a serious discussion with a classical author, to find out what his views were on a given question, or whether his perspective was different from ours, it is usually not enough to read his relevant works, not even if one can read them in the original language. It is the task of historical exegesis to spell out, in contemporary language, what exactly the questions were, how the arguments were supposed to work, and what answers were being offered. Systematic philosophers tend to find historians' debates tedious and exasperating, but since historical exegesis is a matter of interpretation, the historian's work is open to critical scrutiny by others in the same business. (Historians are apt to find the highly scholastic debates of their systematic contemporaries equally tedious and exasperating.) Such debates are needed to keep the historians honest— assuming, as I would, that there is a point in trying to find the correct interpretation of a classical text, and not just to come up with some fanciful or exciting story about what the author might have thought.

Generally speaking, Aristotle and Hume are likely to have been more interesting than their commentators. Debates about questions of interpretation can also be fascinating for those engaged in them, and indeed most historians are no doubt interested in exegetical questions in their own right. It can also be fascinating to follow the development of a historical debate—such as, for example, the epistemological dispute between the Stoics and the Skeptics—while temporally suspending disbelief in some of the premises involved. But this is not all there is to historical research in philosophy, and it seems important to me to emphasize that the invitation to study historical texts with their accompanying burden of commentary need not be understood as an invitation to join this particular kind of debate. Philosophers who don't read Greek may still take a serious interest in Aristotle, or so we hope, even though they cannot enter into disputes about fine points of translation.

The assumption that there is little to be learned from philosophical authors of the past could be justified only by the implausible claim that philosophy has finally reached the sure path of a science, or that we have come up with the one and only correct way of thinking about philosophical questions. It may well be that many people believe just this today, as some of their predecessors have done in the past, but here the history of philosophy provides a strong counterargument. I do not wish to deny, of course, that there has been a lot of progress over more than two thousand years, but progress in philosophy does not appear to be of the cumulative sort. It seems to consist, rather, in the recognition of some egregious errors, the refinement of concepts and terminology, and the invention of alternative explanations and theories—much of which is due to the development of other disciplines, especially the sciences. Given this kind of situation, there can be no guarantee that all that was valuable has been absorbed into subsequent theories, all that was muddled or mistaken has been discarded.

Hence there seem to be several reasons why it makes sense to keep historical texts and theories accessible. One is, of course, that it may help us to avoid repeating past mistakes. Others are more interesting. Sometimes a philosopher may want to find out why her contemporaries are asking the peculiar questions they do ask, by looking at the developments that led to the present situation. This accounts, I think, for the relatively greater interest taken in the more recent past—the nineteenth and early twentieth centuries—as compared to more distant historical periods. On the other hand, the Greeks, and especially the Presocratics, have sometimes been studied by those who wished to see "how it all began." Finally, and perhaps most importantly, there is the possibility of finding in an older author different and illuminating perspectives on questions of contemporary concern; perspectives that have, for one reason or another, been forgotten or neglected by the more recent tradition. This has happened, for example, with Aristotle and Kant in recent work in ethics. It has also happened in psychology, where philosophers have tried to look back beyond Descartes for theories that are not tied to the dualism of mind and body; and in epistemology, where empiricism, at least in the Anglophone tradition, seemed for a while to have reached the status of an obvious fact rather than a philosophical theory.

I tend to believe, naturally enough, that present-day philosophers should often find it useful to compare notes, as it were, with their distinguished predecessors. In this modest sense, then, I would claim that the historian's work is also a contribution to philosophy itself.

19

The Geology of Norway: Poem on Wittgenstein with Introduction

JAN ZWICKY

Jan Zwicky's books include Wittgenstein Elegies, Lyric Philosophy, Songs for Relinquishing the Earth, *and* Wisdom and Metaphor. *She teaches in the Philosophy Department at the University of Victoria.*

On Wittgenstein, Philosophy, and Poetry

Over the years, Wittgenstein made a number of working visits to Skjolden, a village on the Sognefjorden in Norway. The first, and perhaps most significant, of these occurred in 1913–14, at which time Wittgenstein began to work intensively on ideas that were to receive their final form in the *Tractatus*, the only book published in his lifetime. The last occurred over twenty years later, by which time Wittgenstein was attempting to rework material he had dictated in lectures at Cambridge in the mid-1930s and which we now know as *The Blue and Brown Books*. He left Norway late in 1937 without having wrestled the material into what he felt was publishable form. He did return one more time for a brief holiday in the summer of 1950, a visit cut short by the illness from which he was to die a year later—but his departure in 1937 marked the end of his use of Norway as a working retreat.

He was drawn to Norway by its isolation, convinced he could not focus sufficiently in Cambridge where he was constantly subject to both the irritations of intellectual society and the temptations of concerts. His life in Norway was not entirely that of a hermit (though it was, as it was elsewhere and always, Spartan)—he made a number of friends in the community. But it was, except for his correspondence, non-academic—a circumstance Wittgenstein found especially congenial to philosophical concentration.

The material in *The Blue and Brown Books* is among the earliest in the *Nachlass* to reflect the techniques and preoccupations that were to become the foundation for the posthumously published *Philosophical Investigations*. And there can be little doubt that Wittgenstein's conception of the *mechanics* of linguistic meaning underwent serious revision between the publication of the *Tractatus* in 1921 and the work that we now think of as constituting his later views. But there remains a considerable range of opinion on what, if any, other intellectual dynamic may have been involved in the transition. The relation between the *Tractatus* and later works is complicated not only by the apparent discontinuity in the views, but also by difficulties in interpreting the views themselves—difficulties compounded by the fact that Wittgenstein tended to present his thought in dense, often highly metaphorical fragments, eschewing the standard argumentative style with which professional philosophers are most comfortable.

The poem that follows, like its five older cousins, published in 1986 under the title *Wittgenstein Elegies*, is an attempt to address some of these themes and issues. Like the earlier poems, it incorporates phrases from Wittgenstein's work and incidents from his life, but unlike them, it does not limit its preoccupations to matters that *might* have concerned the living Ludwig Wittgenstein. The voice of this poem, for example, is apparently familiar with both poststructuralist narratology and plate tectonics, neither of which was really on the scene when Wittgenstein died in 1951. Its trajectory nonetheless is, I hope, "Wittgensteinian"—though clearly its take on Wittgenstein's views on meaning must be regarded as controversial.

As for the latter: Wittgenstein once remarked to M. O'C. Drury, "It is impossible for me to say one word in my book about all that music has meant in my life; how then can I possibly make myself understood?"[1] An interesting question on a number of counts, not least for what it reveals about Wittgenstein's sense that his lifelong passion for music was *linked* to his philosophical endeavours. It is also interesting for what it suggests about the nature of musical meaning—that it is real, but somehow resists linguistic expression. This, I believe, is a clue to one of the fundamental links between the early and late views: the conviction that linguistic meaning is merely one *facet* of a larger phenomenon, and not always a paradigmatic facet at that.

The larger project of which this poem is a part is a book-length collection entitled *Songs for Relinquishing the Earth*. Its meditations range in subject matter from Kant, Hegel, and Pythagoras to Beethoven, Bruckner, and Hindemith, unified by questions about the nature of home and our responsibilities to it. I have defended elsewhere[2] the view that lyric poetry and philosophy are not mutually exclusive pursuits, and rest this claim on a demonstration that we (professional philosophers) have not actually provided a *defence* of the claim that clarity of thought (the erotic pull of which I take to be defining of philosophical activity) can be provided only by systematic analysis. In the absence of such a defence, I have suggested, we must take seriously numerous examples of philosophy pursued according to other lights, and, indeed, must take seriously the possibility that there exist compositions which, owing to their form, have never been considered philosophical but which nonetheless *are*. This view, not surprisingly, turns out to point to an understanding of meaning both deeper and broader than that which can be provided by formal semantics. *How* we say, I argue, is integrally bound up with *what* we mean; and, I suggest, there exists a particular subclass of formally anomalous works, conditioned by a (lyric) demand for coherence *as well as* the (philosophical) demand for clarity—which thus might reasonably be called lyric philosophy. In their contexts, it turns out that one of the tests for truth becomes compositional integrity.

Seamus Heaney, in his Nobel lecture, "Crediting Poetry," remarks: "I credit [poetry] ultimately because [it] can make an order . . . where we can at last grow up to that which we stored up as we grew. An order which satisfies all that is appetitive in the intelligence and prehensile in the affections. I credit poetry, in other words . . . for making possible a fluid and restorative relationship between the mind's centre and its circumference . . . for its truth to life, in every sense of that phrase."[3] An integrative understanding of history and perception, mind and emotion, knower and known—how, if there is even a chance that Heaney's assessment is accurate, can we as philosophers not be urgently interested in such a medium?

The Geology of Norway

But when his last night in Norway came, on 10th December, he greeted it with some relief, writing that it was perfectly possible that he would never return.
—Ray Monk, *Ludwig Wittgenstein*

I have wanted there to be
no story. I have wanted
only facts. At any given point in time
there cannot be a story: time,
except as now, does not exist.
A given point in space

is the compression of desire. The difference
between this point and some place else
is a matter of degree.
This is what compression is: a geologic epoch
rendered to a slice of rock you hold between
your finger and your thumb.
That is a fact.
Stories are merely theories. Theories
are dreams.
A dream
is a carving knife
and the scar it opens in the world
is history.
The process of compression gives off thought.
I have wanted
the geology of light.

They tell me despair is a sin.
I believe them.
The hand moving is the hand thinking,
and despair says the body does not exist.
Something to do with bellies and fingers
pressing gut to ebony,
thumbs on keys. Even the hand
writing is the hand thinking. I wanted
speech like diamond because I knew
that music meant too much.

And the fact is, the earth is not a perfect sphere.
And the fact is, it is half-liquid.
And the fact is there are gravitational anomalies. The continents
congeal, and crack, and float like scum on cooling custard.
And the fact is,
the fact is,
and you might think the fact is
we will never get to the bottom of it,
but you would be wrong.
There is a solid inner core.
Fifteen hundred miles across, iron alloy,
the pressure on each square inch of its heart
is nearly thirty thousand tons.

That's what I wanted:
words made of that: language
that could bend light.

Evil is not darkness,
it is noise. It crowds out possibility,
which is to say
it crowds out silence.
History is full of it, it says
that no one listens.
The sound of wind in leaves,
that was what puzzled me, it took me years
to understand that it was music.
Into silence, a gesture.
A sentence: that it speaks.
This is the mystery: meaning.
Not that these folds of rock exist
but that their beauty, here,
now, nails us to the sky.

The afternoon blue light in the fjord.
Did I tell you
I can understand the villagers?
Being, I have come to think,
is music; or perhaps
it's silence. I cannot say.
Love, I'm pretty sure,
is light.
        You know, it isn't
what I came for, this bewilderment
by beauty. I came
to find a word, the perfect
syllable, to make it reach up,
grab meaning by the throat
and squeeze it till it spoke to me.
How else to anchor
memory? I wanted language
to hold me still, to be a rock,
I wanted to become a rock myself. I thought
if I could find, and say,
the perfect word, I'd nail

mind to world, and find
release.
The hand moving is the hand thinking:
what I didn't know: even the continents
have no place but earth.

These mountains: once higher
than the Himalayas. Formed in the pucker
of a supercontinental kiss, when Europe
floated south of the equator
and you could hike from Norway
down through Greenland to the peaks
of Appalachia. Before Iceland existed.
Before the Mediterranean
evaporated. Before it filled again.
Before the Rockies were dreamt of.
And before these mountains,
the rock raised in them
chewed by ice that snowed from water
in which no fish had swum. And before that ice,
the almost speechless stretch of the Precambrian:
two billion years, the planet
swathed in air that had no oxygen, the Baltic Shield
older, they think, than life.

So I was wrong.
This doesn't mean
that meaning is a bluff.
History, that's what
confuses us. Time
is not linear, but it's real.
The rock beneath us drifts,
and will, until the slow cacophony of magma
cools and locks the continents in place.
Then weather, light,
and gravity
will be the only things that move.

And will they understand?
Will they have a name for us? —Those
perfect changeless plains,

those deserts,
the beach that was this mountain,
and the tide that rolls for miles across
its vacant slope.

Notes

1. Rousseau and the Modern Cult of Sincerity

1. Jean-Jacques Rousseau, *Émile or On Education*, Introduction, Translation, and Notes by Allan Bloom (New York: Basic Books, 1979), p. 4.

2. *Ordinary Vices* (Cambridge, Massachusetts: Harvard University Press, 1984), p. 45.

3. Richard Sennett, *The Fall of Public Man: On the Social Psychology of Capitalism* (New York: Vintage, 1974).

4. Lionel Trilling, *Sincerity and Authenticity* (Cambridge, Massachusetts: Harvard University Press, 1971), pp. 23–25.

5. *The Culture of Narcissism: American Life in an Age of Diminishing Expectations* (New York: Norton, 1979). Lasch also points to the fact that practicing psychiatrists have reported "a shift in the pattern of the symptoms displayed by their patients. The classic neuroses treated by Freud, they said, were giving way to narcissistic personality disorders" (p. 238).

6. *Democracy in America*. Edited by J.P. Mayer. Translated by George Lawrence (Garden City: Doubleday, 1969), pp. 530–34.

7. Whereas Tocqueville sees democratic citizens as free of aristocratic formality, and hypocrisy, he emphasizes that they tend to their own unique form of hypocrisy and conformism—stemming, in his view, from the tyranny of the majority.

8. This fact, observed by many interpreters, is the great theme of Starobinski's study, *Jean-Jacques Rousseau: La transparence et l'obstacle* (Paris: Gallimard), 1971.

9. See *Émile*, pp. 358–360, 370–71, 385, 387.

10. See *On the Social Contract*, translated by Judith R. Masters (New York: St. Martin's Press, 1968), p. 69; *Émile*, p. 120; Preface of a Second Letter to Bordes, in *The First and Second Discourses*, translated by Victor Gourevitch (New York: Harper and Row, 1986), pp. 114–15. See also Starobinski, *La Transparence et l'obstacle*, pp. 125–26; and Judith N. Shklar, "Rousseau's Images of Authority," in Maurice Cranston and Richard S. Peters, eds., *Hobbes and Rousseau: A Collection of Critical Essays* (Garden City: Doubleday, 1972, pp. 333–365.

11. *Eloge de la Sincérité*, in *Oeuvres complètes*, Texte présenté et annoté par Roger Caillois (Paris: Gallimard, 1949), Volume I, p. 101. This essay seems to have been written some time between 1716 and 1728. See also the passage from Duclos's *Considérations sur les moeurs de ce siècle*, quoted by Rousseau in *Émile*, p. 338.

12. *Second Discourse* in *The First and Second Discourses*, translated by Roger D. and Judith R. Masters (New York: St. Martin's Press, 1964), p. 180. See also pp. 156, 194; *First Discourse*, pp. 36–39; *Émile*, p. 230.

13. See *First Discourse*, p. 51; *Preface to Narcissus*, in *The First and Second Discourses*, translated by Victor Gourevitch (New York: Harper and Row, 1986), p. 105.

14. *Preface to Narcissus*, p. 105. See also *Second Discourse*, pp. 156, 172–75, 193–95; *Discourse on Political Economy* in *On the Social Contract*, translated by Judith R. Masters (New York: St. Martin's Press, 1978), pp. 216–17; Letter to Beaumont in *Oeuvres complètes*, edited by Bernard Gagnebin and Marcel Raymond (Paris: Bibliothèque de la Pléiade, 1959–69), p. 936.

15. It will seem strange to call the man of Rousseau's aristocratic age a "bourgeois" but that is Rousseau's own usage (see *Émile*, p. 40), adopted in full knowledge of its provocative character (perhaps on the model of Molière's comic title, "Le Bourgeois Gentilhomme"—only reversed). Rousseau does not accept the traditional distinction of classes. The true class division of the human species should follow the division of the truest social good—which, for Rousseau, is neither wealth nor privilege but freedom. Thus, there are three classes of men. The first is the "citizen," who enjoys "civil freedom" because, while needing other human beings, he also loves and lives for them. A second class is the asocial "savage" (and to some extent the free peasant) who, neither needing others nor loving them, enjoys "natural freedom." Virtually all the rest of humanity forms a third, slavish class midway between the other two: the social individual—archetypally, the "town dweller," the urban non-citizen—who, while needing others, loves and lives for himself alone. This is the "bourgeois." It includes the French aristocracy, for "one who believes himself the master of others is nonetheless a greater slave than they." (But see *Émile*, pp. 346, 451, for the conventional use of "bourgeois").

16. *The Theory of Moral Sentiments* (Indianapolis: Liberty Classics, 1969), p. 128.

17. *History of European Morals from Augustus to Charlemagne*. Two volumes (New York: Appleton, 1879), p. 138. Cf. p. 155. See also Schopenhauer's, "The Wisdom of Life," in *The Essays of Arthur Schopenhauer*, translated by T. Bailey Saunders (New York: Willey, 1935), pp. 70–73.

18. Bourgeois honesty will be less hypocritical in the degree to which the "additional moral or religious impulses" mentioned above are dominant. The bourgeois virtues become genuinely and intrinsically attractive through the nobility of "self-reliance," the pleasures of sympathy and approbation, the proto-Kantian dignity of foresighted self-denial and rational self-mastery, and the religious faith that God helps those who honestly help themselves. But Rousseau, who doubted man's natural sociality, had little faith in the power of any morality outside of the total moralizing environment of the militantly patriotic city-state. In general, the more skeptical one is, the more hypocrites one sees.

19. See Mills's account of the "new entrepreneur" in "The Competitive Personality," *Partisan Review* XIII (September 1946), pp. 433–441; and Eric Fromm's description of the "marketing orientation" in *Man for Himself: An Enquiry Into the Psychology of Ethics* (New York: Fawcett, 1947), pp. 75–89. See David Riesman with Nathan Glazer and Reuel Denny, *The Lonely Crowd: A Study of the Changing American Character* (New Haven: Yale University Press, 1950), especially pp. 17–24, 45–48.

20. See, for example, *Dialogues* in *Oeuvres complètes* I, p. 936; *Letter to Beaumont*, p. 965; *Émile*, p. 474; *Letter to Perdriau*, September 28th, 1754.

21. *Émile*, pp. 212–13; *Second Discourse*, pp. 95, 221–22.

22. Consider *Second Discourse*, p. 142; *Émile*, pp. 42, 61; *Oeuvres complètes* II, p. 1124–25; *Dialogues*, pp. 805–06.

23. On the argument of the last several paragraphs, see also Arthur Melzer, *The Natural Goodness of Man*, pp. 35–46 and Pierre Burgelin, *La Philosophie de l'Éxistence de Jean-Jacques Rousseau* (Paris: Presses Universitaires de France, 1952), pp. 115–148.

24. Here again we see a stark contrast with Montesquieu's *Praise of Sincerity*, the first premise of which is that self-knowledge through introspection is impossible. That is precisely why "sincerity" is so crucial: others must frankly tell us the truth about ourselves, for we have no other means of discovering it (see pp. 99–102). In this essay, Montesquieu is really praising "frankness" about others—and precisely on the premise that true Rousseauian sincerity— that is, accurate self-disclosure—is impossible.

25. For Rousseau's own later misgivings about the adequacy of introspection, see *The Reveries of the Solitary Walker*, translated by Charles E. Butterworth (New York: New York University Press, 1979), pp. 43, 75. See also Starobinski, *La Transparence et l'obstacle*, pp. 216–17.

26. Consider *Dialogues*, pp. 668–671, 822–25; *Reveries*, p. 77. From here one sees most clearly the fundamental difference between Rousseau's new concern with hypocrisy and sincerity—his increased "inwardness"—and the apparently similar concern found in the Gospels (and in the late Stoics, like Marcus Aurelius). The latter clearly grows from a heightened longing for moral purity. It calls for inwardness, self-scrutiny and confession in order to increase our moral striving and to intensify our repentance. Rousseauian sincerity, by contrast, intends and produces the opposite effect: it encourages self-acceptance and the release from shame. It would have us acknowledge our inner weaknesses, saying: "This is the way that I am. I cannot change how I feel. I will not lie about it." It makes the acknowledgement of vice into a virtue. The only true sin is insincerity itself.

27. See *Émile*, pp. 91, 94, 97; *La nouvelle Héloïse* in *Oeuvres complètes* II, pp. 563, 568.

28. See *Dialogues*, pp. 805–06, 1324–25; *Émile*, pp. 67, 159, 168; *Reveries*, pp. 92, 95. See also Ronald Grimsley, "Rousseau and the Problem of Happiness," in *Hobbes and Rousseau*, pp. 437–461.

29. See *Reveries*, p. 81; *Émile*, pp. 220–231. One sees from this point the essential inner connection between sincerity and compassion, that other great idol of Rousseau's thought and of our world. This connection, in turn, further grounds or justifies the ideal of sincerity, by reassuring us that "being oneself" will in fact make one, if not actively moral or "virtuous," then at least "good," that is, compassionate and disinclined to harm others.

2. Existential Phenomenology and the Brave New World of *The Matrix*

1. Essays on *The Matrix* mentioned in this chapter can be found in Grau, ed., *Philosophers Explore the Matrix* (New York: Oxford University Press, 2005).

2. Imagine how his heart ached . . . and yet he never blinked;
his eyes might have been made of horn or iron . . .
He had this trick—wept, if he willed to, inwardly.
(Homer, *The Odyssey*, translated by Robert Fitzgerald [New York: Vintage, 1990], p. 360.)
Of course, the Homeric Greeks must have had some sort of private feelings for Odysseus to perform this trick, but they thought the inner was rare and trivial. As far as we know, there is no other reference to *private* feelings in Homer. Rather, there are many *public* displays of emotions, and shared visions of gods, monsters, and future events.

3. Saint Augustine, *Confessions*, translated by R.S. Pine-Coffin (London: Penguin, 1961), p. 114.

4. Letter to Gibieuf of 19th January 1642; *Descartes: Philosophical Letters*, translated by Anthony Kenny (Oxford: Oxford University Press, 1970), p. 123.

5. René Descartes, "Meditations on First Philosophy: Meditation VI", in *Essential Works of Descartes*, translated by Lowell Bair (New York: Bantam, 1961), p. 98.

6. Gottfried Leibniz, *The Monadology and Other Philosophical Writings* (London: Oxford University Press). A monad, according to Leibniz, is an immaterial entity lacking spatial parts, whose basic properties are a function of its inner perceptions and appetites. As Leibniz put it: A monad has no windows.

7. Immanuel Kant, *Critique of Pure Reason*, translated by Norman Kemp Smith (New York: Humanities Press, 1950).

8. Edmund Husserl, *Cartesian Meditations: An Introduction to Phenomenology*, translated by Dorion Cairns (The Hague: Nijhoff, 1960).

9. See Martin Heidegger, *Being and Time*, translated by J. Macquarrie and E. Robinson (New York: Harper Collins, 1962).

10. See Maurice Merleau-Ponty, *Phenomenology of Perception*, translated by C. Smith (London: Routledge, 1962).

11. Charles Taylor, "Overcoming Epistemology," *Philosophical Arguments* (Cambridge, Massachusetts: Harvard University Press, 1995), p. 12. See also, Samuel Todes, *Body and World* (Cambridge, Massachusetts: MIT. Press, 2001).

12. *Phenomenology of Perception*, p. 355.

13. René Descartes, "Dioptric," *Descartes: Philosophical Writings*, edited and translated by Norman Kemp Smith (Modern Library, 1958), p. 150.

14. The point has been made explicitly by John Searle: "[E]ach of us is precisely a brain in a vat; the vat is a skull and the 'messages' coming in are coming in by way of impacts on the nervous system." *Intentionality: An Essay in the Philosophy of Mind* (Cambridge University Press, 1983), p. 230.

15. Names in the movie are generally well chosen. The fact that the word "matrix" refers both to the womb and to an array of numbers works perfectly. Likewise, Neo is both a neophyte and the one who will renew the world. These names are so fitting that one can't help looking for the aptness of the name Morpheus, but it is hard to find. The Greek Morpheus is the god of sleep but the Morpheus in the movie is trying to wake people up. The only way to make some sense of the name is to think of the Greek god, not as the producer of sleep, but as the one who has power over sleep: both to put people to sleep and to wake them up. Thus, Morpheus's first message to Neo, conveyed by Trinity, is "Wake up Neo."

16. This is true for the phenomenologist describing the first person experiences of those inside the Matrix. From a third person perspective of someone outside the Matrix, however, the Matrix world is not connected to the causal powers of the physical universe, and so the experiences of those in the Matrix world do not count as perceptions. In that sense, the Matrix world, while not "in the mind," is merely virtual, although, since it is an intersubjective experience, it is still not like a dream.

17. The Matrix foot, moreover, unlike a phantom foot, can have its "reality" confirmed by coping (kicking a football, walking around in a city). In contrast, a phantom limb does not take part in gaining a maximal grip.

18. There are limits of course. The Matrix programmers can't give a human being a dog's body. It's also unlikely they could make a brain in a female body the causal basis of a man's body in the Matrix world. The hormones of the body in the vat wouldn't match the physical attributes and emotions of that person in the Matrix world.

Indeed, a good way for the AI programmers to prevent bodies being rescued to the hovercraft would be to give each brain the experience of a radically different body (within whatever limits are imposed by biology) in the Matrix world than the body that brain is actually in. If rescued, such people would quite likely go crazy trying to reconcile the body they had experienced all their life with the suddenly alien body on the hovercraft.

19. Likewise, their beliefs about entities such as viruses and black holes would be true if, like empiricists, they held that theoretical entities are just convenient ways to refer to the data produced by experiments. See Bas van Frassen, *The Scientific Image* (Oxford: Clarendon, 1980).

20. Indeed, his coping skills were presumably not based on beliefs at all. See Ludwig Wittgenstein, *On Certainty* (Harper Torchbooks, 1969).

21. John Haugeland suggests that Cypher's choice is, from some ethical points of view immoral, because, in asking that when he returns to the Matrix world all his memories be erased, Cypher is in effect committing a kind of existential suicide, even if the body in the vat, which has been the causal basis of Cypher up to now, will live on as the causal basis for as a powerful actor named Reagan in the Matrix.

22. Granted it's hard to resist believing in the Matrix even where causality is concerned, nonetheless, Neo learns he can stop believing in it. This new understanding of reality is described by Morpheus talking to Neo near the beginning of the movie, and by Neo at the end, as like waking from a dream. But the brains in the vats are not literally dreaming. Their world is much too coherent and intersubjective to be a dream. Or, to put it another way, dreams are the result of some quirk in our internal neural wiring and full of inconsistencies, although when dreaming we don't usually notice them. They are not the result of a systematic correlation between input and output to the brain's perceptual system that is meant to reproduce the consistent co-ordinated experience that we have when awake. That is why we correctly consider them private inner experiences. When someone from the hovercraft returns to the Matrix world, it looks like their hovercraft body goes to sleep, but they do not enter a private dream world but an alternative intersubjective world where they are normally wide awake, but in which they can also seem to dream and wake from a dream, as Neo does after the Agents take away his mouth.

23. There is one unfortunate exception to this claim. At the end of the movie, Neo catches a glimpse of the computer program behind the world of appearances. This is a powerful visual effect meant to show us that Neo can now program the Matrix world from inside it, but, if what we've been saying is right, it makes no sense. If the computer is still feeding systematic sensory-motor impulses into Neo's brain when he is plugged into the Matrix world, then he will see the world the program is producing in his visual system. What the sight of the rows of symbols is meant to do is to remind us that Neo no longer *believes* the Matrix is real but now understands it and can manipulate it, but even so, he should continue to *see* the Matrix world.

24. In *The Matrix*, the Agents, who are computer programs, presumably don't have this freedom. It might seem that Agent Smith shows his freedom and deviates from his program of maintaining order in the Matrix when he tells Morpheus how disgusted he is with the Matrix world. But in *Reloaded* we learn that Agent Smith has a new freedom because he has some of Neo mixed up in him. This is supposed to explain how he can distance himself from the Matrix, so it would seem that his early diatribe against the Matrix is premature and should not be taken at face value. We think the only way to understand this confession consistent with the limitations of the Agents is to understand this as Smith's playing the good cop routine; trying to get Morpheus to believe Smith is on his side, so that Morpheus, in his

weakened state, will give Smith the access codes for Zion, but the movie does not exploit this possibility.

25. Not to be confused with Neo as "the One" who will save people from the Matrix. For Heidegger's account of the power of the one, see his *Being and Time*, and also H. Dreyfus, *Being-in-the-World: A Commentary on Heidegger's Being and Time, Division I* (Cambridge, Massachusetts: MIT. Press, 1991), Chapter 8.

26. Friedrich Nietzsche, *Beyond Good and Evil: Prelude to a Philosophy of the Future*, translated by Walter Kaufman (New York: Vintage, 1966), p. 199.

27. See Colin McGinn's essay, "The Matrix of Dreams."

28. Given the kind of bodies we have—that we move forwards more easily than backwards, that we can only cope with what is in front of us, that we have to balance in a gravitational field—we can question to what extent such body-relative constraints can be violated in *The Matrix* if what is going on is still to make sense.

To test these limits, the filmmakers occasionally blow our minds by using a wrap-around point of view from which action looks so far from normal as to be awesomely unintelligible. At the same time, they have successfully met the challenge of discovering which body-relative invariances can be intelligibly violated and which can't. For example, in the movie, gravity can be overcome—Neo can fly—but he can't see equally in all directions, cope equally in all directions, nor can he be in several places at once. What would it look like for a single person to surround somebody?

Time too has a body-relative structure that can't be violated with impunity. The way we experience time as moving from the past into the future thus leaving the past behind depends on the way our forward directed body enables us to approach objects and then pass them by (see Todes, *Body and World*). Could we make sense of a scene in which someone attacked an enemy not just from behind, but from the past? If, in the movie, the liberated ones were free of all bodily constraints governing their action we couldn't make sense of what they were doing and neither could they. They wouldn't be liberated but would be bewildered, as we often are in our dreams.

29. Although being disruptive is the best one can do in the Matrix world. That's why Neo, a hacker who, as Agent Smith says, has broken every rule in the book, is the natural candidate for savior.

30. In the course of their work the Agents do take over the bodies of innocence bystanders, but such interference is gratuitous and does not show that being used as a battery is intrinsically enslaving. Likewise, if there always is an anomaly in each Matrix world, as we are told in *Reloaded*, unless that can be shown to be necessary, it doesn't show that humans' being used as batteries requires AI intervention to keep order.

31. *Being and Time*, pp. 25–26.

32. W. Caudill and H. Weinstein, "Maternal Care and Infant Behavior in Japan and in America," in C.S. Lavatelli and F. Stendler, eds., *Readings in Child Behavior and Development*, (New York: Harcourt Brace, 1972), p. 78.

33. Among AI researchers, Douglas Hofstadter has seen this most clearly, See his "Metafont, Metamathematics, and Metaphysics," in *Visible Language* 16 (April 1982).

34. "An existent mere physical thing is given beforehand (when we disregard all the . . . 'cultural' characteristics that make it knowable as, for example, a hammer . . .)," *Cartesian Meditations* (Nijhoff, 1960), p. 78.

35. See Martin Heidegger, "The Question Concerning Technology," in *The Question Concerning Technology,* translated by W. Lovitt (New York: Harper, 1977).

36. See Martin Heidegger, "The Origin of the Work of Art," in *Poetry, Language, Thought,* translated by A. Hofstadter (New York: Harper and Row, 1971).

37. Nietzsche, *The Gay Science* (Vintage, 1974), p. 335.

38. See Charles Spinosa, Fernando Flores, and Hubert Dreyfus, *Disclosing New Worlds: Entrepreneurship, Democratic Action, and the Cultivation of Solidarity* (Cambridge, Massachusetts: MIT. Press, 1997).

39. This is not to say that a world generated by computer algorithms couldn't exhibit radical novelty. Perhaps Artificial Life does. But it seems to be taken for granted in the film that the AI intelligences are operating with *symbolic representations* and so consider any deviation from their Matrix world, modeled on the world on the late twentieth century, an anomaly which signals a potential breakdown of their simulation.

40. Hubert Dreyfus would like to thank Rick Canedo for his many helpful suggestions.

3. On (and Beyond) Love Gone Wrong

1. Alain de Botton, *On Love* (New York: Atlantic Monthly Press, 1993). In the title there is already an allusion to classical philosophical discourse, particularly to the stoic essay or declamation.

2. "Liberalism" might best be understood for our purposes as a "letting live" or "letting be" attitude and its appropriate ensuing (and supporting) commitment. This understanding is consonant with the novelist's specific intent as well, though what I write is not by any means to be construed as an exercise in literary criticism. In any case I shall use these helpful phrases, "letting live" and "letting be," in what follows. (Obviously liberalism is a complex historical phenomenon and has many meanings, both political and social. These, however, are not my primary focus in this current undertaking.)

3. Plato's discussion is a considerable one, found mostly in his *Symposium*. It is this work, along with the *Republic*, which bequeath to the West the major parameters for its understanding of love and related species of human affection.

4. The notion of sublimation and, thus, of the alterability of human desire with respect to its "object" is a latecomer on the historical scene. Renunciation and extirpation precede it by some centuries. We find sublimation especially in Freud's notions of compensatory pleasure and substitute satisfaction. But it is also in Schopenhauer and Nietzsche slightly earlier in the nineteenth century. In the "classical" world, however, the concept of sublimation is largely lacking.

5. Consumption is not quite the issue when the "object" of desire is companionship, though at the same time something is definitely "consumed." Suffice it to say for now that to the extent that consumption is involved, the notion has become quite metaphorical. What is consumed, after all, remains in existence to be further consumed. Or is the term "consumption" more misleading than helpful in this regard? This set of complexities cannot help but concern us as our discussion proceeds.

6. If for companionship we substitute openness and informative candor, then we know that such circumstances are not so wildly implausible, especially among interrogators in unsupervised and unmonitored environments in which "intensive questioning" takes place.

7. This is a most tangled situation indeed. Along with quite normal and healthy elements of self-esteem, aspects of narcissism, egoism, and grandiosity tend also to fuse and very unsuccessfully disentangle, within the lives of individuals, as is often confusedly reflected in broadly psychoanalytic literature. If this were not enough, quite obvious and real experiences of shame,

guilt, and inadequacy also come into play, casting doubt on the "positive" dimensions of self-experience, whether these latter are deemed healthy or pathological.

8. As we know, the undertaking of the Enlightenment Project was meant to liberate us from superstition, thereby freeing our energies for an unfettered pursuit of our full potential. That this Project, in the midst of its many successes, would turn out in just over two centuries to undermine the inspiration for accomplishment (and any meaning that accomplishment might have) was an unintended result of the highest magnitude. At the heart of the matter was what would happen to the very notion of human potential—that it would come more and more to converge with the (albeit flexible) concepts of purchasing power and consumer satisfaction.

9. Classically, all actions are doings, all passions undergoings. Thus religious language which speaks of the "passion of Christ" for example, is referring to what was undergone by this historical figure, what he suffered. Similarly, when Kierkegaard speaks of "suffering" as the essential stage of the religious, he means that religion is something undergone, not something "done." This intensely close connection between undergoing, suffering, and passion has been largely lost in the twentieth century.

10. Is it any wonder, one might ask, albeit rhetorically, that standing at the beginning of the modern era of political philosophy, John Locke would make the most critical and crucial right be that of possession? What we see in this maneuver is the aspiration of agency and the consequent, though as yet unsystematically applied logic of consumption emerging well before the advances of large-scale capitalism.

11. In Hegel, we know, possession comes nearly to be action's very meaning, something foreshadowed in Kant and Fichte and pursued in earnest in and through the deteriorating dynamics of late capitalism.

12. An attempt was made in the early phenomenological tradition, particularly in the work of Husserl with his insistence on the centrality of the phenomenon intentionality, that all of our consciousness was always consciousness of something. As Heidegger and others remarked, however, the objectivity this fostered was largely undermined by the Cartesian, Fichtean influences: in Husserl, influences which more or less collapsed classical phenomenology into a sophisticated form of idealism, sophisticated, but idealism nonetheless.

13. I cannot fail to mention a few liberties I have taken in this paragraph now concluding. Heidegger, of course, speaks not of God, but of Being. The pathway to Being, the "object" of all philosophic inquiry, is through an allowing (and an intensification) of *Angst*, that most basic of moods—so basic, in fact, that all other moods are construed as variants of it. It is on this basis that I assimilate Heidegger to the spiritual logic of Paul and Augustine, a logic mediated to the twentieth century through Eckhart, Boehme, and Luther. We know, for example, that Heidegger's own separation from the Catholicism of his youth was in the teens of the twentieth century and that it was accompanied and followed by an intense reading of Kierkegaard and Luther (and other reformers). Only after these events did the outline and content of *Being and Time* begin to take shape. I should add that for all the people just mentioned, following the paradigmatic lead of Plato, true knowledge is not of the world, but of that which lies beyond it. Though Heidegger himself issues a disclaimer with regard to any notion of a "beyond," it is impossible for him to sustain such a denial. This, however, is another story.

14. I wish to thank Pomona College and Earhart Foundation for their generous support, which has made my work possible.

4. The Space of Love and Garbage

1. Ivan Klima, *Love and Garbage*, translated by Ewald Osers (New York: Knopf, 1990), p. 56.

2. Jacques Derrida, "Eating Well, or the Calculation of the Subject," translated by Peter Connor and Avital Ronell in Eduardo Cadava, Peter Connor, and Jean-Luc Nancy, eds., *Who Comes After the Subject?* (New York: Routledge, 1991), pp. 107–08.

5. The Contest of Extremes: An Exploration of the Foundations and the Peak of Nietzsche's Political Philosophy

1. A blindness Nietzsche cannot be said to have shared: "I have cast my book [*Human, All Too Human*] for the 'few,' and even then without impatience; the indescribable strangeness and dangerousness of my thoughts are such that a long time must pass before there are ears to hear them—and certainly not before 1901" (letter to M. von Meysenbug, 12th May 1887, in L, p. 266).

2. Works in English translation are cited by abbreviation and section number. In a few instances I have made minor adjustments in the translations. Where it is necessary to refer to the German original, I cite by volume and page number the standard critical edition edited by Colli and Montinari. Abbreviations are as follow:

A	The Antichrist, in PN
BGE	Beyond Good and Evil, translated by Walter Kaufmann
BKSA	Sämtliche Briefe: Kritische Studienausgabe, edited by Colli and Montinari
BT	The Birth of Tragedy, translated by Walter Kaufmann
EH	Ecce Homo, translated by Walter Kaufmann
GM	On the Genealogy of Morals, translated by Walter Kaufmann and R.J. Hollingdale
GS	The Gay Science, translated by Walter Kaufmann
KSA	Sämtliche Werke: Kritische Studienausgabe, edited by Colli and Montinari
L	Selected Letters of Friedrich Nietzsche, translated by Christopher Middleton
NCW	Nietzsche Contra Wagner, translated by Walter Kaufmann
PCP	The Philosopher as Cultural Physician, in PT
PHT	Philosophy in Hard Times, in PT
PN	The Portable Nietzsche, edited and translated by Walter Kaufmann
TI	Twilight of the Idols, in PN
UD	On the Uses and Disadvantages of History for Life, in UM
UM	Untimely Meditations, translated by R.J. Hollingdale
WP	The Will to Power, translated by Walter Kaufmann and R.J. Hollingdale
WS	The Wanderer and His Shadow, in HH, Volume 2
Z	Thus Spoke Zarathustra, translated by Walter Kaufmann

3. Alexander Nehamas, *Nietzsche: Life as Literature* (Cambridge, Massachusetts: Harvard University Press, 1985), p. 91.

4. Heidegger argues that the metaphysical position that the world is chaos remained "absolutely determinative" for Nietzsche. See Martin Heidegger, *Nietzsche*, Volume 2, translated by David Farrell Krell (San Francisco: Harper and Row, 1982), p. 93. I would qualify Heidegger's remark by omitting the "absolutely" because of the constant battle in Nietzsche's thought between the view that the world is chaos and the view that the world exhibits a rank order of desires, human types, and forms of life.

5. Nehamas denies that perspectivism entails a substantive and partisan moral doctrine. Yet if no view of the world is binding on everyone, then views such as the Platonic, Christian, and Kantian, which make universal claims are wrong views. Hence, perspectivism takes definite sides on questions of morality. Perspectivism is not, as Nehamas characterizes it (p. 72), opposed to, but rather is a contemporary form of dogmatism.

6. Eric Blondel criticizes the tendency to reduce Nietzsche's philosophy to strategies for evacuating texts of meaning, in part because this reductivism obscures Nietzsche's basic practical ambition to evaluate reality and redeem life. See Blondel, *Nietzsche: The Body and Culture*, translated by Seán Hand (Stanford: Stanford University Press, 1991), pp. 9–11, 53, 75. Blondel rightly argues that Nietzsche is a moralist from beginning to end, but overemphasizes the importance of culture to Nietzsche's morality. See Ibid., pp. 64, 65.

7. William Connolly does view the death of God in moral terms. For Connolly, the death of God serves Nietzsche "as an interpretation of the modern condition." See Connolly, *Political Theory and Modernity* (Ithaca: Cornell University Press, 1993), p. 7. Connolly holds that the death of God gives rise to the imperative to abandon the effort to see the world in terms of definitive standards and authoritative convictions, and points toward an ethic or sensibility that aims at questioning, contesting, and problematizing beliefs and practices, particularly one's own. Yet precisely where Nietzsche's ethics needs most to be questioned vigorously, Connolly affirms unequivocally. That is, Connolly treats the death of God as true, the unproblematic basis for a philosophy of the future. He presents as a charitable interpretation of Nietzsche's teaching what looks on closer inspection like an uncritical embrace of an interpretation that he himself finds congenial or useful. This is unfortunate, for it encourages the conclusion that what Connolly favors is not exactly respect for difference and appreciation of ambiguity but rather agreement that dwelling upon difference and celebrating ambiguity are good for human beings. See Connolly, pp. 7–15, and 137–197.

8. In his remarkable study of nineteenth century Germam thought, Karl Löwith emphasized that while one can find in Nietzsche's thought whatever one wishes, the contradictions in which Nietzsce's thought abounds reflect a fundamental unity: "Nietzsche's actual thought is a thought system, at the beginning of which stands the death of God, in its midst the ensuing nihilism, and at its end the self-surmounting of nihilism in eternal recurrence." Löwith, *From Hegel to Nietzsche*, translated by David E. Green (New York: Columbia University Press, 1991), pp. 192, 193.

Similarly, Leo Strauss's reflections on Nietzsche emphasize the fundamental and unresolved tensions that form Nietzsche's thought. Strauss, "Note on the Plan of Nietzsche's Beyond Good and Evil" in *Studies in Platonic Political Philosophy* (Chicago: University of Chicago Press, 1983), especially pp. 183, 185, 190; see also the Preface in *Spinoza's Critique of Religion*, translated by E.M. Sinclair (New York: Schocken, 1965), pp. 12–13, 30–31.

9. Mark Warren wrongly asserts that "Nietzsche's refusal to use metaphysical categories of agency, such as 'will', 'self', 'soul', or 'subject', distinguishes his approach from his precursors in the German tradition from Kant through Schopenhauer." Warren, *Nietzsche and Political Thought* (Cambridge, Massachusetts: MIT Press, 1988), pp. 9–10. But, as I will show, Nietzsche uses "metaphysical categories" freely and often. Of course he also severely criticizes metaphysical language and demands its repudiation. What call for explanation are the more fundamental considerations that drive Nietzsche to both repudiate and to embrace traditional metaphysical notions.

Bernard Yack contributes to such an explanation by providing an enlightening analysis of Nietzsche's dependence on a dichotomy between human freedom and natural necessity that, Yack argues, he inherited from post-Kantian philosophy. See Yack, The *Longing for Total Revolution*

(Berkeley: University of California Press, 1992), pp. 310–365. But Nietzsche's thought is also dependent on opinions about moral and intellectual virtues more typical of ancient philosophy than of Kant. See for instance Karl Löwith, *From Hegel to Nietzsche*, pp. 188–200, 323.

10. See, for example, BT ASC, p. 1; BT, p. 7; UD, p. 6; GS, p. 344; BGE Preface, pp. 44, 48, 62; A, pp. 8, 51; EH IV, p. 3.

11. See, for example, BT, pp. 7, 18; GS, p. 377; WS, p. 86; Z, Prologue; Z II, "The Child with the Mirror."

12. See, for example, UD, pp. 4, 78; GS, p. 382; Z, Preface, p. 4, Z I, "On the New Idol," Z II, "The Dancing Song"; BGE, pp. 22, 30, 32, 45, 265, 287; GM III, pp. 14, 19, 20; A, Preface, p. 37; EH I, p. 8; letter to Carl Fuchs (18th July 1888) in BKSA VIII, pp. 358, 359.

13. See for instance Z I, "On the Three Metamorphoses," "On the Way of the Creator," and Z II, "Upon the Blessed Isles" and "On Redemption"; BGE, pp. 29, 44. See also Z, Preface, p. 4, Z I, "On the New Idol."

14. See for example GS, p. 382; BGE, pp. 11, 261, 265; GM III, p. 14. Also Z I, "On the Three Metamorphoses."

15. See for example BGE, pp. 201, 214, 224, 227, 295.

16. See for example UD, p. 6; BGE, p. 265; GM II, p. 11; TI, "Skirmishes of an Untimely Man", p. 48. Consider also Z I, "On the Adder Bite"; Z II, "On Scholars."

17. See for example BT, pp. 7, 8; BGE, pp. 220, 265; A, p. 57.

18. See for example BGE, pp. 6, 30, 213, 219, 265, 287.

19. See for example GS, Preface, p. 2; p. 344; BGE; GM, Preface, pp. 1, 2; A, p. 7.

20. Although Charles Taylor does not pursue the matter in connection with Nietzsche, this understanding of the contest of extremes in Nietzsche's thought is in harmony with his argument that many of the achievements that modernity most prizes have their roots in and are sustained by premodern categories of thought. Taylor, *Sources of the Self: The Making of the Modern Identity* (Cambridge, Massachusetts: Harvard University Press, 1987). For another account of modernity's fruitful engagement with tradition see Robert Alter, *Necessary Angels: Tradition and Modernity in Kafka, Benjamin, and Scholem* (Cambridge, Massachusetts: Harvard University Press, 1991).

21. Heidegger, *Nietzsche*, Volume 1, translated by David Farrell Krell (San Francisco: Harper and Row, 1972), pp. 3–11; Volume 3, translated by Joan Stambaugh, David Farrell Krell, and Frank A. Capuzzi (San Francisco: Harper and Row, 1987), p. 8; also pp. 187–192.

22. See Heidegger, "The Word of Nietzsche: 'God is Dead'" in *The Question Concerning Technology and Other Essays*, translated by William Lovitt (New York: Harper and Row, 1977), p. 61; Heidegger, *Nietzsche*, Volume 2, p. 205, Volume 3, p. 166.

23. Jacques Derrida argues that deconstruction must work within the tradition of metaphysics to overturn and displace it. Derrida, "Signature Event Context," in Margins of Philosophy, translated by Alan Bass (Chicago: University of Chicago Press, 1982), p. 329. On the implausibility of the attempts by post-Nietzscheans to escape metaphysics see Alasdair MacIntyre, *Three Rival Versions of Moral Enquiry* (Notre Dame: University of Notre Dame Press, 1990), pp. 45–46.

24. Eric Blondel also stresses both the greatness of Heidegger's interpretation and its arbitrary truncating of Nietzsche's thought; see Blondel, in *Nietzsche*, p. 5.

25. Heidegger, *Nietzsche*, Volume 1, pp. 3–6; Volume 2, pp. 5–8.

26. Ibid., *Nietzsche*, Volume 3, pp. 1–9, 173–183, 230–31; Volume 4, translated by Frank A. Capuzzi (San Francisco: Harper and Row, 1982), pp. 8, 116–18. See also "Who is Nietzsche's Zarathustra?" in ibid., Volume 2, pp. 232–33; and Heidegger, "The Question Concerning Technology," in *Basic Writings* (New York: Harper and Row, 1977).

27. Almost twenty years ago Walter Kaufmann criticized the "methodological scandal" involved in Heidegger's interpretations of Nietzsche, which depend on "systematic preference for non-contextual readings—for taking bits out of context and using them willfully and arbitrarily." Kaufmann, *Existentialism, Religion, and Death* (New York: New American Library, 1976), pp. xiii, 29–30. Since Kaufmann wrote, Heidegger's methodology has become the norm.

28. Nehamas uses such a method while claiming to read carefully. But he does not use "carefully" in the ordinary sense of the word, that is, as denoting painstaking attention or precision: "We shall have to read a number of apparently unrelated passages and interpret them carefully (that is to say, creatively) in order to show that they are relevant to our concerns." See Nehamas, *Nietzsche: Life as Literature*, p. 47. One example of such careful reading, crucial to Nehamas's overall argument, must suffice. According to Nehamas, Nietzsche employs a variety of styles as a rhetorical strategy to convey a basic theoretical truth, "that there is no single, neutral language in which his views, or any others, can ever be presented. His constant stylistic presence shows that theories are as various and idiosyncratic as the writing in which they are embodied" (p. 37). But it is very unlikely that Nietzsche understood his use of many styles as an effort to vindicate the theory of perspectivism, for he explicitly offers a quite different explanation. And, interestingly enough, he offers that different explanation in the very paragraph in *Ecce Homo* from which Nehamas quotes to provide the title for his chapter on Nietzsche's style, "The Most Multifarious Art of Style" (p. 19). In the paragraph in question in *Ecce Homo*, Nietzsche makes clear that the problem for him is not, as Nehamas asserts (invoking for support a passage from *The Will to Power*), that there are no facts only interpretations (p. 20), but rather that of communicating accurately the facts about his inward states (EH III, p. 4). For Nietzsche the question is not one of the perspectival character of all knowing, but rather how to make an accurate image of his inner experience available to others. For Nietzsche, at least according to the passage in *Ecce Homo* that Nehamas himself highlights, the aim in deploying a variety of styles is not grand and general, as if to contribute to the construction from his own experience and thoughts of a literary character in his works, but rather quite specific, to reveal the quality and variety of his actual inner life. In sum, by transforming carefulness into creativity Nehamas can claim fidelity to Nietzsche's works while making Nietzsche teach nearly the opposite of what he says. One disadvantage of the creative redefinition of carefulness as creativity is that it obscures Nietzsche's account of the character of genuine creativity.

29. For example, Gilles Deleuze asserts, against those who understand the eternal return as the return of "a particular arrangement of things," that "on two occasions in *Zarathustra* Nietzsche explicitly denies that the eternal return is a circle which makes the same return." Deleuze, *Nietzsche and Philosophy*, translated by Hugh Tomlinson (New York: Columbia University Press, 1983), p. xi. But Nietzsche does not speak in *Zarathustra*. Rather, it is within Zarathustra, characters with their own complicated motives enmeshed in an elaborate narrative, who speak. Moreover, the denials are accompanied by affirmations. For example, Zarathustra calls himself "the advocate of the circle" (Z III, "The Convalescent," p. 1) and proclaims his "lust after eternity and after the nuptial ring of rings, the ring of recurrence" (Z III, "The Seven Seals"). If one may treat any utterance by a character in Zarathustra as a teaching of Nietzsche's, then one can make Nietzsche teach anything one wishes.

30. For an instructive discussion of this problem see Maudmarie Clark, *Nietzsche on Truth and Philosophy* (Cambridge: Cambridge University Press, 1990), pp. 17–21.

31. While one could advance any number of interpretations of Nietzsche's thought, Nehamas believes that a "single view," perspectivism, connects and accounts for the key paradoxes in his thought. Nehamas, pp. 1, 19, 105. Tracy Strong appears to have transcended the

laws of perspectivism to discover that "Perspectivism . . . is at the center of Nietzsche's understanding of our presence in the world and of its availability to us." See Tracy B. Strong, *Friedrich Nietzsche and the Politics of Transfiguration*, expanded edition (Berkeley: University of California Press, 1988), p. 304. Mark Warren's observation that Nietzsche's "most pressing problems" lie in the historically, politically, culturally, and linguistically bound character of subjectivity appears to identify an objective feature of Nietzsche's thought. Warren, *Nietzsche and Political Thought*, p. 2. Jean Granier seems to have moved beyond interpretation to the knowledge that "one of the principal themes in Nietzschean thought" is the primacy of interpretation. See Jean Granier, "Nietzsche's Conception of Chaos," in David Allison, ed., *The New Nietzsche* (Cambridge, Massachusetts: MIT Press, 1985), p. 135. And so on.

32. Nietzsche himself affirms the continuity and unity of his thought in BT, ASC, and GM, Preface, pp. 2, 8. Among the pioneering efforts to examine one of his books as a whole is Leo Strauss's "Notes on the Plan of Nietzsche's *Beyond Good and Evil*," in *Studies in Platonic Political Philosophy* (Chicago: University of Chicago Press, 1983). In the last decade a number of studies have taken Nietzsche's books seriously. Foremost among these is Laurence Lampert's *Nietzsche's Teaching* (New Haven: Yale University Press, 1986). There is also a helpful collection of essay-length studies of individual books: Robert C. Solomon and Kathleen M. Higgins, eds., *Reading Nietzsche* (New York: Oxford University Press, 1988).

33. Derrida argues that "the hypothesis of a rigorous, sure, and subtle form is naturally more fertile." Jacques Derrida, "Plato's *Pharmakon*," in Disseminations, translated by Barbara Johnson (Chicago: University of Chicago Press, 1981), p. 67. And so it is. It remains an open question whether slow and careful reading, on "the hypothesis of a rigorous, sure and subtle form," results in the discovery of a secret, deeper organization other than the one inscribed by the author, as Derrida contemplates, or rather of the organization and arguments the author inscribed.

34. There is no reason to forego study of Nietzsche's unpublished writings. Although I shall refer to passages from his notebooks in the process of interpreting his books, I shall avoid invoking a statement from outside the book at hand as a basic premise or missing step in an argument intended to vindicate a particular interpretation of Nietzsche's meaning in the work under study. For a good discussion of the ambiguous status of the posthumously published collection of writings from Nietzsche's notebooks called *The Will to Power* see Bernd Magnus, "The Use and Abuse of The Will to Power," in *Reading Nietzsche*, pp. 218–236.

35. "Immoralist" is a term Nietzsche uses in a variety of contexts to describe the self and to indicate the morality to which he believes himself subject. Speaking of "we immoralists," he holds, contrary to the "dolts and appearances," that immoralists are bound by exacting duties (BGE, p. 226). In the preface to *Daybreak*, he emphasizes that he and his like are "men of conscience" who "still obey a stern law [strengen Gesetze] set over us—and this is the last morality [die letzte Moral] which can make itself audible even to us." This last morality requires the rejection of unworthy beliefs, of lies, and of compromise, and it says no to Christianity, romanticism, nationalism, and pleasure seeking. On account of this last morality, Nietzsche explains, "we still feel ourselves related to the German integrity [Rechtschaffenheit] and piety [Frömmigheit] of millennia, even if as its most questionable and final descendants, we immoralists, we godless men of today, indeed in a certain sense as its heirs, as the executors of its innermost will . . . In us there is accomplished—supposing you want a formula—the self-sublimation of morality" (D, Preface, p. 4). Moreover, he declares himself "the first immoralist"; identifies Zarathustra with the achievement of immoralism—"the self-overcoming of morality, out of truthfulness"; and claims the word immoralist as "a symbol and badge of honor for myself" (EH IV, pp. 2,3,6; EH III, on UM, p. 2). Nietzsche's immoralism is the ethics of a type that

deserves to be highest, and governs one who not only "conceives reality as it is" but also "is reality itself and exemplifies all that is terrible and questionable in it" and thereby achieves greatness (EH IV, pp. 4,5). In a letter, Nietzsche recommended that he be characterized "as an Immoralist" and defined an immoralist as "the highest form, till now, of 'intellectual integrity' [intellektuellen Rechstchaffenheit]" (letter to Carl Fuchs, 29th July 1888, in L, p. 305).

36. In an early fragment, Nietzsche explains how art depends on philosophy: "The philosopher ought to know what is needed; and the artist ought to make it" (KSA VII, p. 423). Stanley Rosen comments on this fragment: "Nietzsche's relatively early statement (1872–73) on the relation between philosophy and art continues to hold true throughout his mature thought and writings. . . . This [statement] is Nietzsche's Platonism." Rosen, *The Question of Being: A Reversal of Heidegger* (New Haven: Yale University Press, 1993), p. 174. I agree with Rosen's assessment and I would add that in his later writings, Nietzsche envisages a supreme type who unites in his own person the work of the philosopher and that of the artist. In his sympathetic reconstruction of Nietzsche's thought, Leslie Paul Thiele asserts that "Nietzsche's aim was theoretically and practically to incorporate the philosopher, artist, and saint into one person." Thiele, *Friedrich Nietzsche and the Politics of the Soul: A Study of Heroic Individualism* (Princeton: Princeton University Press, 1990), p. 163. No contradiction arises from seeing the saint in the image of a supreme type who unites knowing and making, inasmuch as the saint, as Thiele himself observes (p. 155), is understood by Nietzsche as the highest-ranking kind of artist.

37. Rosen's examination of the tension between knowing and making is very helpful. See "The Quarrel Between Philosophy and Poetry" in *The Quarrel Between Philosophy and Poetry* (New York: Routledge, 1988) and his chapter "Theory and Interpretation" in *Hermeneutics and Politics* (New York: Oxford University Press, 1987).

38. Charles Taylor develops the argument that even the most radical criticisms of morality, particularly the "neo-Nietzschean" criticisms that assume or seek to show that morality is ultimately based on fiat or power, themselves of necessity issue from "moral orientations" that take a stand on what is right and good. Taylor, *Sources of the Self*, pp. 98–103. My account suggests that what Taylor claims is true of the neo-Nietzschean theorizing is true as well for Nietzsche's philosophical explorations.

39. On the back of the original edition of *The Gay Science*, Nietzsche wrote: "This book marks the conclusion of a series of writings by FRIEDRICH NIETZSCHE whose common goal it is to erect a new image and ideal of the free spirit. To this series belong: / Human, All Too Human. With Appendix: Mixed Opinions and Aphorisms. / The Wanderer and his Shadow. / Daybreak: Thought about the Prejudices of Morality. / The Gay Science." (GS, p. 30). Although I do not give these books the attention they deserve, Nietzsche's remark about the common goal that unites them, taken in conjunction with the brief discussion of *The Gay Science* suggests that these books point to the constellation of problems inhering in Nietzsche's efforts to articulate the character of the supreme type. For a thoughtful discussion of the enduring philosophical significance of *The Gay Science* see Richard Schacht, "Nietzsche's Gay Science, Or, How to Naturalize Cheerfully," in *Reading Nietzsche*, pp. 68–86.

40. Nietzsche's account of the intellectual conscience also recalls the opening remark of Aristotle's metaphysics (*Metaphysics* 980a): "All men by nature desire to know."

41. In his final writings Nietzsche describes the philosophical life he lived in characteristically ethical terms that evoke the intellectual conscience: "Philosophy, as I have so far understood and lived it, means living voluntarily among ice and high mountains—seeking out everything strange and questionable in existence, everything so far placed under a ban by

morality. . . . How much truth does a spirit endure, how much truth does it dare? More and more that became for me the real measure of value. Error (faith in the ideal) is not blindness, error is cowardice. . . . Every attainment, every step forward in knowledge, follows from courage, from hardness against oneself, from cleanliness in relation to oneself. . . . Nitimur in vetitum [We strive for the forbidden]: in this sign my philosophy will triumph one day, for what one has forbidden so far as a matter of principle has always been—truth alone (EH, Preface, p. 3).

42. The aspiration to become a god is scarcely an isolated occurrence in German literature. For example, Goethe's Faust yearns to know the innermost secrets of the world (Part I, 382, 383), wonders whether he is a god (Part I, 439), is mockingly called a "superman" by the spirit he summons (Part I, 490), and associates his passion for eternal truth and his sharing in God's creativity with the idea that he was created in God's image (Part I, 614–622).

43. Because of his intense concern with the ultimate structure of the cosmos, Nietzsche's own term "antimetaphysician" is preferable to Richard Rorty's characterization of Nietzsche as one of modernity's "paradigm nonmetaphysicians." Rorty, *Contingency, Irony, Solidarity* (Cambridge: Cambridge University Press, 1989), p. 98. It is hardly, as Rorty argues, that Nietzsche has no opinion about the ultimate structure of the cosmos or that Nietzsche thinks his opinions lack moral and political significance. Rather, Nietzsche is opposed to metaphysicians of the past precisely because they misunderstood the true character of the cosmos.

44. Nietzsche himself suggests such an understanding in a notebook fragment, WP 617. I follow Heidegger in seeing great importance in this fragment. See, for example, Heidegger, Nietzsche, Volume 1, pp. 19–20; Volume 2, pp. 201–04; Volume 3, pp. 156–58, 212–15, 245–46. For difficulties inhering in Heidegger's use of WP 617, see Krell's analysis in Volume 2, p. 257n2. I myself shall lay great stress on the act of falsification to which Nietzsche's note calls attention and which Heidegger sometimes overlooks. I shall suggest that WP 617—which links "the supreme will to power" and the idea that "everything recurs" in the attempt "to impose upon becoming the character of being" and which indicates that the success of this attempt depends upon a "twofold falsification"—articulates the character of Zarathustra's reconciliation with eternity and sheds light on the failure of Zarathustra's quest to make himself a god. But I must emphasize that I do not rely on this notebook fragment as a premise to my study, but ratther ontroduce it as a gloss on results gained by analysis of the text of Zarathustra. Here too I part ways with Heidegger, who insists that we could never understand the doctrine of eternal return but for Nietzsche's unpublished writings. See Heidegger, *Nietzche*, Volume 2, pp. 15, 141.

6. A Psychological View of Moral Intuition

1. "Killing, Letting Die, and Simple Conflicts," *Philosophy and Public Affairs* 18 (1989), pp. 239–258.

2. For a review of this literature, and for discussions of points for which no citations are given, see my book, *Thinking and Deciding* (third edition) (New York: Cambridge University Press, 2000).

3. Matthew H. Schneps, *A Private Universe* (Santa Monica: Pyramid Film and Video).

4. Jonathan Baron, "The Effect of Normative Beliefs on Anticipated Emotions," *Journal of Personality and Social Psychology* 63 (1992), pp. 320–330.

5. See my paper, "Nonconsequentialist Decisions," *Behavioral and Brain Sciences* 17 (1994), pp. 1-42, and my book *Morality and Rational Choice* (Dordrecht: Kluwer, 1993), for additional discussion of the arguments made here.

6. Jonathan Baron and Joan G. Miller, "Limiting the Scope of Moral Obligation to Help: A Cross-Cultural Investigation," *Journal of Cross-Cultural Psychology* 31 (2000), pp. 705–727.

7. See my paper "Norm-Endorsement Utilitarianism and the Nature of Utility," *Economics and Philosophy* 12 (1996), pp. 165–182.

7. The Metaphysics of Ordinary Experience

1. This chapter was taken from a graduate seminar offered at Boston University during the mid-nineties on the problem of ordinary experience. It was originally published in the *Harvard Review of Philosophy* in Spring 1995 and has subsequently appeared as a section in Chapter 7 of *The Elusiveness of the Ordinary*.

8. The Relativity of Fact and the Objectivity of Value

1. Ruth Anna Putnam argues for a similar thesis in "Creating Facts and Values," *Philosophy* 60 (1985), pp. 187–204.

2. Israel Scheffler, *Beyond the Letter* (London: Routledge, 1979), pp. 6–7.

3. Nelson Goodman, *Ways of Worldmaking* (Indianapolis: Hackett, 1978), pp. 109–140.

4. Nelson Goodman, "Sense and Certainty," *Problems and Projects* (Indianapolis: Hackett, 1972), pp. 60–68.

5. But not only then. We may attempt to modify a working system out of curiosity—to see how it works and whether it can be made to work better.

6. Cf. Nelson Goodman, *Fact, Fiction, and Forecast* (Cambridge, Massachusetts: Harvard University Press, 1984), pp. 65–68; John Rawls, *A Theory of Justice* (Cambridge, Massachusetts: Harvard University Press, 1971); Catherine Z. Elgin, *With Reference to Reference* (Indianapolis: Hackett, 1983), pp. 183–193.

7. Jean-Paul Sartre, *Existentialism and Humanism* (London: Methuen, 1968), pp. 35–37.

8. This chapter is copyrighted by the author. It was first published in Michael Krausz, ed., *Relativism: Interpretation and Confrontation* (Notre Dame: University of Notre Dame Press, 1989).

9. Rethinking Progress: A Kantian Perspective

1. References to and citations of Kant's works are given parenthetically in the text, using the abbreviations below, and citing the volume and the page numbers of *Kants gesammte Schriften* ("Academy Edition"; publication started by Preussische Akademie der Wissenschaften, Berlin, 1902). *The Critique of Pure Reason*, however, is cited in its own standard way, by the page numbers of both the first (A) and second (B) editions. I have used and sometimes altered the translations listed below.

C1 *Critique of Pure Reason* (1st edition 1781; 2nd edition 1787), translated by Paul Guyer and Allen W. Wood, Cambridge Edition of the Works of Immanuel Kant (Cambridge: Cambridge University Press, 1998).

C2 *Critique of Practical Reason* (1788), translated by Mary J. Gregor in Practical Philosophy: Cambridge Edition of the Works of Immanuel Kant (Cambridge: Cambridge University Press, 1996).
C3 *Critique of Judgment* (1790)
Contest—*Contest of the Faculties* (1798), translated by H.B. Nisbet, in Hans Reiss, ed., *Kant: Political Writings*, Cambridge Texts in the History of Political Thought, 2nd edition (Cambridge: Cambridge University Press, 1991).
PP Toward Perpetual Peace (1795), translated by Mary J. Gregor, in Practical Philosophy, Cambridge Edition of the Works of Immanuel Kant (Cambridge: Cambridge University Press, 1996)

Religion—*Religion within the Boundaries of Mere Reason* (1793), translated by Allen W. Wood and George Di Giovanni, Cambridge Texts in the History of Philosophy (Cambridge: Cambridge University Press, 1998).
    2. Paul Natorp, *Kant über Krieg und Frieden. Ein geschichtsphilosophischer Essay* [Kant on War and Peace: An Essay in the Philosophy of History] (Erlangen: Verlag der Philosophischen Akademie, 1924), p. 54 (my translation).
    3. Théodore Ruyssen, "La Philosophie de l'Histoire selon Kant" in *La Philosophie Politique de Kant*, Annales de Philosophie Politique 4 (Paris: Presses Universitaires de France, 1962), p. 34 (my translation).
    4. For the purpose of clarity of the following exposition, I changed the order in which Kant gives the three postulates of practical reason.
    5. The claim that progress is to be considered a postulate of practical reason even though Kant himself does not make that point explicitly has been advanced by various Kant scholars over the past decades, most notably by Pierre Hassner, "Immanuel Kant," in Joseph Cropsey and Leo Strauss, eds., *History of Political Philosophy*, third edition (Chicago: University of Chicago Press, 1987), pp. 581–621, at p. 597; Wolfgang Kersting, *Wohlgeordnete Freiheit. Immanuel Kants Rechts- und Staatsphilosophie* (Frankfurt am Main: Suhrkamp, 1993), pp. 86f.; and David Lindstedt, "Kant: Progress in Universal History as a Postulate of Practical Reason," in *Kant-Studien* 90:2 (1999), pp. 129–147. I believe that this claim is entirely justified.
    6. Cf. *Critique of Practical Reason*: "If . . . the highest good would be impossible according to practical rules, then the moral law which commands that it be furthered must be fantastic, directed to empty imaginary ends, and consequently inherently fals." (V:114).
    7. John Rawls, *The Law of Peoples, with The Idea of Public Reason Revisited* (Cambridge, Massachusetts: Harvard University Press, 1999).
    8. In a footnote to this sentence, Kant sets his own project apart from "Plato's *Atlantis*, More's *Utopia*, Harrington's *Oceana*, and Allais's *Severambia*."
    9. Niccolò Machiavelli, *The Prince*, translated by Harvey C. Mansfield (Chicago: University of Chicago Press, 1998), p. 61.
    10. E.H. Carr, *The Twenty Years' Crisis, 1919–1939: An Introduction to the Study of International Relations*, second edition (New York: St. Martin's Press, 1956); Hans J. Morgenthau, *Politics Among Nations: The Struggle for Power and Peace*, brief edition, revised by Kenneth W. Thompson (New York: McGraw-Hill, 1993); Kenneth N. Waltz, *Theory of International Politics* (New York: McGraw-Hill, 1979).
    11. Stanley Hoffmann, "Liberalism and International Affairs" in Janus and Minerva, eds., *Essays in the Theory and Practice of International Politics* (Boulder: Westview, 1987), pp. 394–417, at p. 395. Hoffmann makes explicit reference to Kant's theory: "Freedom as autonomy, or self-mastery, or the triumph of the higher self conceived as the 'civic' part of one's

personality either requires some leap into universality, so that man the citizen of a fragment of mankind becomes a cosmopolitan, a citizen of the world; or else, as long as the political communities confront one another [as long as there is neither a sense of nor a political structure for a community of humankind], it is nothing but a recipe for unhappy consciousness, since the general wills of clashing polities lead men and women not to the realization of the categorical imperative but to rationalized murder" (p. 399).

12. It seems to me highly problematic, if not wrong, to explain the inner workings of modern states solely by referring to them in Realist fashion as hierarchical systems, systems of sovereign orders backed by threats and force. Even for descriptive purposes it seems necessary to assume that many or most citizens follow the laws and rules of society not only because they always fear the power of the state, but often for other reasons: for love of honor (Kant's argument, cf. n.20), or simply because the citizens affirm the rules as reasonably just (what Rawls calls a "sense of justice").

13. This rhetoric must not necessarily be hypocritical (although it often is). As Ronald Dworkin has argued, use of the same concept does not mean that all have the same conception or understanding of what this concept requires. See Ronald Dworkin, *Taking Rights Seriously* (Cambridge, Massachusetts: Harvard University Press, 1978), p. 134. Kant himself pointed out that even a hypocritical appeal to normative standards may reveal something interesting: "The homage which every state pays (in words at least) to the concept of right proves that man possesses a greater moral capacity, still dormant at present, to overcome eventually the evil principle within him (for he cannot deny that it exists) and to hope that others will do likewise. Otherwise the word right would never be used by states which intend to make war on one another, unless in a derisory sense, as when a certain Gallic prince declared: 'Nature has given the strong the prerogative of making the weak obey them'." (PP VIII, p. 355). As one of Andrew Kuper's comments on this paper put it: The discourse in terms of right does to a greater or lesser extent shape policy—some hypocrisies are too great even for tyrants to live with.

14. "The occurrence in our own time which proves the moral tendency of the human race does not involve any of those momentous deeds or misdeeds of men" but is "the attitude of the onlookers as it reveals itself in public while the drama of great political changes is taking place" (*Contest* VII, p. 85).

15. Hope is the form knowledge takes in the practical domain; see the passage of the first *Critique* cited at the beginning of this paper: "with respect to the practical and the moral law [hope] is the very same as what knowledge is with regard to theoretical cognition of things and the natural law." I corrected the syntax slightly to render the parallelism that Kant obviously intended (hope-knowledge, practical-theoretical, moral-natural).

16. *Du Contrat Social*, Book II, Chapter 12, paragraph 2, as quoted in Rawls, *The Law of Peoples*, p. 7.

17. Howard Williams, *Kant's Political Philosophy* (New York: St. Martin's Press, 1983), pp. 3f.

18. Wolfgang Kersting. *Wohlgeordnete Freiheit. Immanuel Kants Rechts- und Staatsphilosophie* (Frankfurt am Main: Suhrkamp, 1993), p. 84 (my translation).

19. I owe this sentence to Andrew Kuper.

20. Kersting, *Wohlgeordnete Freiheit*, p. 84.

21. In §44 of the *Metaphysical Elements of Right*, Kant says that "even if we imagine men to be as benevolent and law-abiding as we please, the a priori rational idea of a non-lawful state will still tell us that before a public and legal state is established, individual men, peoples and states can never be secure against acts of violence from one another" (VI, p. 312; translated by Nisbet).

22. There are two main systematic reasons why Kant does not base his belief in progress on a belief in individual moral progress. One sounds a little bit like the Marxist argument that man's moral dispositions can only prosper under the right circumstances. In *Perpetual Peace*, Kant writes: "we cannot expect their moral attitudes to produce a good political constitution; on the contrary, it is only through the latter that the people can be expected to attain a good level of moral culture" (PP VIII, p. 366). But the second reason shows that Kant definitely avoids the Marxist trap. It is Kant's conviction that individual moral progress has its limits whatever the institutions may be: "[H]ow could the quantity of good of which a person is capable possibly be increased? For it would have to done by his own free agency as a subject, and before he could do it, he would in turn require a greater store of goodness than he already possessed in the first place. . . . [M]an cannot work his way beyond a given limit and go on improving further" (*Contest* VII, pp. 81f). According to Kant, progress will not be produced by an "ever increasing quantity of morality" in men's attitudes, but instead by an increasing number of actions of "legality," i.e. external actions in accordance with the law, "whatever the particular motive behind these actions may be": "Violence will gradually become less on the part of those in power, and obedience to the laws will increase. There will no doubt be more charity, less quarrels in legal actions, more reliability in keeping one's word, and so on in the commonwealth, partly from a love of honor, and partly from a lively awareness of where one's own advantage lies. . . . Such developments do not mean, however, that the basic moral capacity of mankind will increase in the slightest" (*Contest* VII, p. 91).

23. Hassner, *Immanuel Kant*, p. 597. The same point is made by Hilary Putnam: "We are far too ready today to think that we have 'discovered' that progress was an illusion, and that we have to simply give up. But as Kant wrote a long time ago, we must live with an 'antinomy of practical reason'. We cannot prove that progress is possible, but our action is 'fantastic, directed to empty, imaginary ends' if we do not postulate the possibility of progress." ("How Not to Solve Ethical Problems" in *Realism with a Human Face* (Cambridge, Massachusetts: Harvard University Press, 1990), pp. 179–192, at p. 191).

24. This chapter benefited greatly from comments by Paul Dafydd Jones and Andrew Kuper; I am thankful for their thoughtful and constructive criticism. A shorter version of the paper was presented at a Graduate Student Conference on "Rethinking Progress" at Penn State University (hence the title). I thank Michael Blake and John Lachs for important comments on the original abstract.

10. Philosophy as Hubris: Kierkegaard's Critique of Romantic Irony as a Critique of Immanent Thinking

1. Villem Flusser, "Digitaler Schein," in Florian Rötzer, ed., *Ästhetik der elektronischen Medien* (Frankfurt am Main: Suhrkamp, 1991), p. 157. All translations, unless otherwise indicated, are mine.

2. Wolfgang Welsch, "Ästhetik und Anästhetik" in W. Welsch, ed., *Ästhetisches Denken* (Stuttgart: Reclam, 1990), p. 9.

3. Cf. Rüdiger Bubner, *Ästhetische Erfahrungen* (Frankfurt am Main: Suhrkamp, 1989), p. 139.

4. Ernst Behler and Jochen Hörisch, eds., *Die Aktualität der Frühromantik* (Paderborn: Schöningh, 1987), p. 7.

5. Cf. G. Schulte, "Nietzsche und die Postmoderne. Oder: von der vorgeblich heiteren Inexistenz des Menschen," in *Anstöße* 2 (Hofgeismar: Evangelische Akademie, 1986), pp. 54–62.

6. All page numbers refer to Søren Kierkegaard, *The Concept of Irony: With Continual Reference to Socrates*, edited and translated by Howard V. Hong and Edna H. Hong (Princeton: Princeton University Press, 1989).

7. "Thus let us transform our life into a work of art, and we will be able to assert our immortality." (Wilhelm Heinrich Wackenroder and Ludwig Tieck, *Phantasien über die Kunst: für Freunde der Kunst* (Stuttgart: Reclam 1973), p. 57).

8. Kierkegaard claims that the term 'ironic' is equivalent to the term 'Romantic' or 'Romantic aesthetics': "Throughout this whole discussion I use the term 'irony' and 'ironist'; I could just as well say 'romanticism' and 'romanticist'. Both terms say essentially the same thing; the one is more reminiscent of the name with which the faction christened itself; the other, the name with which Hegel christened it" (275 fn).

9. Cf. Klaus M. Kodalle, *Die Eroberung des Nutzlosen. Kritik des Wunschdenkens und der Zweckrationalität im Anschluß an Kierkegaard* (Paderborn: Schöningh 1988), p. 71.

10. With this formulation, Jürgen Habermas characterizes the "paradoxical work" of deconstruction as a "continuation of tradition," in which "the healing energy renews itself solely through spending itself." Jürgen Habermas, *Der philosophische Diskurs der Moderne*, p. 12, Vorlesungen (Frankfurt am Main: Suhrkamp, 1985), p. 216.

11. "Poetry can only be critiqued with poetry. A judgement about art which is not itself a judgement about art, either in the material, as the portrayal of the necessary impression in its development or through a beautiful form and a liberal tone in the spirit of the old Roman satire, does not have a right to exist in the realm of art." Friedrich Schlegel, *Kritische Ausgabe*, edited by Ernst Behler (Paderborn: Schöningh 1967), Volume II, p. 162.)

12. Just at the point where Hegel (for instance in the "Vorlesungen zur Ästhetik") dissolves the contradiction of the early Romanticists (Schlegel's "eternal agility") into a harmony of stillness, Kierkegaard begins to develop it further in its contradictoriness. See especially Kresten Nordentoft, *Kierkegaard's Psychology* (Pittsburgh: Duquesne University Press, 1978).

13. Winfried Menninghaus, *Unendliche Verdopplung. Die frühromantische Grundlegung der Kunsttheorie im Begriff absoluter Selbstreflexion* (Frankfurt am Main: Suhrkamp, 1987), p. 131.

14. Peter Szondi, "Friedrich Schlegel und die romantische Ironie," in Helmut Schanze, *Friedrich Schlegel und die Kunsttheorie seiner Zeit* (Darmstadt: Wissenschaftliche Buchgesellschaft, 1985), pp. 143–161 at p. 155.

15. The "floating" of the imagination is Friedrich Schlegel's central cipher for "irony" (see Schlegel III: 100; IV, No. 1081; XVIII: 287).

16. For an existential analysis of boredom, see Wolfgang Janke, *Existenzphilosophie*. Sammlung Göschen 2220 (Berlin: De Gruyter, 1982), pp. 43–47.

17. Wilfried Grewe, *Kierkegaards maieutische Ethik. Von "Entweder/Oder II" zu den "Stadien"* (Frankfurt am Main: Suhrkamp, 1990), p. 68.

18. For Kierkegaard, the ironist becomes enthusiastic about a sacrificing virtue, "just as a spectator in the theater becomes enthusiastic; he is however a harsh critic who knows very well where this virtue becomes dull and untrue. He even regrets, but he regrets aesthetically and not morally. He is, in the moment of his regret, already over his regret, and examines whether it is poetically coherent, whether it is suitable for a dramatic rendering in the mouth of a poetic figure" (p. 284).

19. See p. 328.

20. After a formulation by Kierkegaard in The *Point of View for my Work as an Author*, translated by Walter Lowrie (New York: Harper, 1962), p. 147.

21. Michael Theunissen, "Der Begriff 'Ernst' bei Søren Kierkegaard," *Symposium* 1 (Freiburg i. Br.: K. Alber, 1958), p. 96.

22. "Bleibt das Ich auf diesem Standpunkt [der Negativität] stehen, so erscheint ihm alles als nichtig und eitel, die eigene Subjektivität ausgenommen, die dadurch hohl und leer und selber eitel wird. Umgekehrt aber kann sich auf der anderen Seite das Ich in diesem Selbstgenuß auch nicht befriedigt finden, sondern [muß] sich selber mangelhaft werden....dadurch aber kommt dann das Unglück und der Widerspruch hervor, daß das Subjekt einerseits wohl in die Wahrheit hinein will und nach Objektivität Verlangen trägt, aber sich andererseits...dieser unbefriedigten abstrakten Innigkeit nicht zu entwinden vermag und nun von der Sehnsüchtigkeit befallen wird, die wir ebenfalls aus der fichteschen Philosophie haben hervorgehen sehen....Dieses Sehnen aber ist nur das Gefühl der Nichtigkeit des leeren eitlen Subjekts, dem es an Kraft gebricht, dieser Eitelkeit entrinnen und mit substantiellen Inhalt sich erfüllen zu können." (G.W.F. Hegel, *Werke*, edited by E. Moldenhauer and Karl Markus Michel (Frankfurt am Main: Suhrkamp, 1980), XIII, p. 96).

23. In the same vein, it has been discussed whether Kierkegaard's criticism of irony in *The Concept of Irony* and his criticism of the aesthetician in *Either/Or* are not themselves communicable solely aesthetically, presentable only in the medium of literature. "What this says is that in Kierkegaard philosophy becomes poetry. Modern philosophers have always thought it possible to be objective; that is, they have claimed to occupy an existentially neutral standpoint, to view reality from the perspective of the angels. Kierkegaard counters: every standpoint is in fact not neutral but biased, not objective but subjective, not angelic but human and finite. Philosophy as understood by modern tradition is impossible." Louise Mackey, *Kierkegaard: A Kind of Poet* [Philadelphia: 1971, p. 266.) Edo Pivcevic, *Ironie als Daseinsform bei Søren Kierkegaard* (Gütersloh: Gütersloher Verlagshaus, 1960), attempts to interpret this process as a "compensatory process" in which the ironic subject consciously transfers its privileges to the Absolute (God)—a "clever act of self-irony, whereby the Romantic fiasco [is to be] thwarted and the possibility of freedom assured" (p. 92).

24. Kierkegaard, *Point of View*, p. 147.

25. Schlegel III, p. 100.

26. Kierkegaard here quotes words spoken by Julius in Schlegel's Lucinde: " 'Only in yearning do we find peace', replied Julius. 'Yes, there is peace only when our spirit remains completely undisturbed in its yearning and seeking after itself, only when it can find nothing higher than its own yearning'" (p. 296 fn).

27. An especially succinct explanation of the manner in which Kierkegaard reveals the Romantic ironist's revolutionary consciousness of its own negativity can be found in *The Two Ages: The Age of Revolution and the Present Age*: "A passionate, tumultuous age wants to overthrow everything, set aside everything. An age that is revolutionary but also reflecting and devoid of passion changes the expression of power into a dialectical tour de force: it lets everything remain but subtly drains the meaning out of it; rather than culminating in an uprising, it exhausts the inner actuality of relations in a tension of reflection that lets everything remain and yet has transformed the whole of existence into an equivocation that in its facticity is—while entirely privately a dialectical fraud interpolates a secret way of reading—that it is not." Søren Kierkegaard, *The Two Ages: The Age of Revolution and the Present Age*, translated by Howard Hong and Edna Hong (Princeton: Princeton University Press, 1978), p. 77.)

28. The well-known 116th Athenaeumsfragment of Friedrich Schlegel reads as follows: "Die romantische Poesie ist eine progressive Universalpoesie. . . . Andere Dichtarten sind fer-

tig, und können nun vollständig zergliedert werden. Die romantische Dichtart ist noch im Werden; ja das ist ihr eigentliches Wesen, daß sie ewig nur werden, nie vollendet sein kann" (Schlegel II, p. 182).

29. Schlegel II, p. 182.

30. Menninghaus, *Unendliche Verdoppelung*, p. 131.

31. Schlegel III, p. 100.

32. Cf. Schlegel II, p. 160 (106th Lyceumsfragment). Using the Romantic fragment as an example, Friedrich Schlegel does not draw attention to the impossibility but rather to the necessity of an "incomplete communication" in the consciousness that the universal whole, or that which the Romantics call life in the emphatic sense, can only be rendered lingually broken. The fragment "contains and stimulates a feeling of the irresolvable conflict of the unconditional and the conditional, of the impossibility and the necessity of a complete communication. It is the freest of all licenses in that through it, one disregards himself; but also the most legitimate, since it is absolutely necessary" (p. 100).

33. Menninghaus, *Unendliche Verdoppelung*, p. 131.

34. Schlegel XVIII, p. 128. Novalis also characterizes this figure of thought as "Assumption—eternal peace is already here—God is among us." Novalis, *Schriften*, edited by Richard Samuel (Stuttgart: Kohlhammer, 1960), III, p. 421.

35. To remind us of this, also with regard to Kierkegaard, is the point of Lore Hühn's work (Lore Hühn, "Das Schweben der Einbildungskraft. Zur frühromantischen Überbietung Fichtes," in *Deutsche Vierteljahrsschrift* 70 [1996], pp. 569–599). The Romantic "reflection renews in its perpetually unsuccessful quest that which without this execution would not be what it is. Precisely in constantly attempting to redeem what is unredeemable, it constitutes, even if negatively, what it strives for. Reflection which by this way always renews its attempt to reach infinity forms a presence which propels and masters the self-renewing process of reflection in the method of revocation" (p. 578).

36. Hühn, *Schweben*, p. 580.

37. Recapitulating the speculative side of the Romantic concept of irony, Kierkegaard explains: "He [Solger] does still have the negation of the negation, but still there is a veil in front of his eyes so that he does not see the affirmation. It is well known that he died at an early age. Whether he would have succeeded in carrying through the speculative ideas he seized with so much energy or whether his energy would instead have been consumed in maintaining the negation, I shall not decide at this point" (p. 323).

38. Strikingly, Kierkegaard does not mention the possibly most interesting theoretician of early Romanticism, since it is Novalis who, in contrast to Solger, thinks in the manner of Kierkegaard in maintaining the reference to an absolute foundation in the perspective of negativity. This absolute foundation can only be represented in a pure feeling (that the Absolute has, but in the status of not-knowing). In the *Fichte-Studien*, Novalis attempted to develop his own approach as a systematic paradox that exists paradigmatically in the fact that philosophy which according to its longings must always be "a striving for the imagining of a foundation [ein Streben nach dem Denken eines Grundes]," "but which can only be relatively satisfied [das doch nur relativ gestillt werden kann]" (Novalis II, p. 269, No. 566). The "highest principle contains the highest paradox in its purpose [das höchste Prinzip enthält das höchste Paradox in seiner Aufgabe]": "Alles Filosofiren muß also bei einem absoluten Grunde endigen. Wenn dieser nun nicht gegeben wäre, wenn dieser Begriff eine Unmöglichkeit enthielte so wäre der Trieb zu Filosofiren eine unendliche Thätigkeit und darum ohne Ende, weil ein ewiges Bedürfniß nach einem absoluten Grunde vorhanden wäre, das doch nur relativ gestillt werden könnte und darum nie aufhören würde. Durch das freywillige Entsagen des Absoluten [sic] entsteht die

unendliche freye Thätigkeit in uns—das Einzig mögliche Absolute, was uns gegeben werden kann und was wir nur durch unsre Unvermögenheit ein Absolutes zu erreichen und zu erkennen, finden. Dies uns gegebne Absolute [sic] läßt sich nur negativ erkennen, indem wir handeln und finden, daß durch kein Handeln das erreicht wird, was wir suchen.... Filosofie, Resultat des Filosofirens, entsteht demnach durch Unterbrechung des Triebes nach Erkenntniß des Grundes" (Novalis II: 269n, No. 566). In his criticism of Solger, Kierkegaard stresses in exactly the same way: "Thus we are not uplifted by the destruction of the great but are reconciled to its destruction by the victory of what is true, and we are uplifted by its victory" (p. 322).

39. Peter Szondi, "Friedrich Schlegel und die Romantische Ironie," in *Satz und Gegensatz* (Frankfurt am Main: Insel, 1964), p. 17n. Paul de Man, *Blindness and Insight: Essays in the Rhetoric of Contemporary Criticism* (University of Minnesota Press, 1983), p. 219n, stresses that this "quotation is right from the point of view of the mystified self, but wrong from the point of view of the ironist. Szondi has to posit the belief in a reconciliation between the ideal and the real as the result of an action or the activity of the mind. But it is precisely this assumption that the ironist denies. . . . Contrary to Szondi's assertion, irony is not temporary (vorläufig) but repetitive, the recurrence of a self-process in exhilarating terms, understandably enough, since he is describing the freedom of a self-engendering invention" (p. 220). But Szondi and Kierkegaard want to emphazise that "freedom as a self-engendering invention" or as, in Schlegel's phrase, an "ever-expanding act of reflection," ("immer wieder potenzierte[r] Reflexion" [Schlegel II, p. 182]), is a temporal invention that only leads to an eternity devoid of content. Therefore it remains temporary with regard to a true eternity (in contrary to a pure rhetoric of temporality). What the Romantics describe as a floating of imagination is a permanent oscillation between two opposites that has no continuity. Therefore it is repetitive in the deeper sense of boredom. The continuity in which the ironist wants to live exists only in the moment. Seen existentially (which the ironist cannot be aware of), this is an empty moment of time (see footnote 44).

This passage continues: "But this ironic endeavor by no means ended with Tieck and Schlegel, on the contrary, in Young Germany it has a crowded nursery. In fact, in the general development of this position, considerable attention is directed to this Young Germany."

40. Revealing for the reflection problematic that Kierkegaard imagines here is his comment: "Like water in relation to what it reflects, the negative has the quality of showing as high above itself that which it supports as it shows beneath itself that which it is battling; but the negative, like the water, does not know this" (p. 262).

41. In his criticism of Solger, Kierkegaard makes clear how the concept of negation is to be speculatively defined in the problematic of an absolute, 'presuppositionless' beginning: "The negative has, namely, a double function—it infinitizes the finite and it finitizes the infinite. But if the reader [Solger] does not know in which current he is or, more correctly, if he is now in one current and than in another, everything is confused" (p. 310).

42. Theunissen, *Ernst*, p. 18.

43. Kierkegaard develops in *The Sickness unto Death* his analysis of desperation, precisely the reflection of the moments "of which the self consists as a synthesis" ("desperately wanting to be itself") and infers from this experience of contradiction an original synthesis of the self posited and created by God.

44. In *Fear and Trembling* and in the *Philosophical Fragments*, Kierkegaard explains that the discontinuous life of the ironist was first severed by Christianity, which in contrast to the specifically heathen philosophy of Platonism is post factum the absolute Other and infers the true, concrete, and as a "fullness of time" defined moment. In Kierkegaard's concept of Romantic irony, irony cannot become history since everything is subjective freedom and every moment

signifies an empty point in the now. Finally Christianity is the qualitative jump that—without being pretended—teaches the experience of actuality as a paradoxical unity of the eternal and the temporal: "In the moment history starts anew." By the fulfilled present of this moment, a differentiation comes into the world that allows time to be developed from the future (next to that which can be called an abstract-steady time) and that divides itself into the three different structures of present, past, and future, making historicity possible in the first place. In contrast to the poetic-aesthetic urge of the ironist "to write himself," the life of the Christian consists of "letting himself be written." Kierkegaard imagines the decisive meaning of this moment both christologically and existentially: christologically he means the absolute paradox of God's becoming man by temporalizing the eternity; existentially he means the absolute paradox that the (preexisting) eternal is only brought through time. But he himself is also the "starting point for the eternal," which formerly was not. This moment of decision that returns into the life of every individual ("for the eternity in time") determines indeed first and foremost the becoming of a Christian but is also interpreted neutrally in the ethical decision, as in *Either/Or*. See Theunissen, "Augenblick" in Joachim Ritter (Darmstadt: Wissenschaftliche Buchgesellschaft, 1971), p. 649n).

45. Kierkegaard's polemic against Schlegel's *Lucinde* goes so far as to accuse it of being inexcusable, even as a noncommittal work of youth, because it is doctrinaire, and indeed he already believes that he recognizes in it a latent anti-Protestantism. Thus he remembers "that Schlegel, as is well known, became a Catholic later in his life and as such discovered that the Reformation was the second Fall of Man, which adequately indicates that he had been in earnest with *Lucinde*" (p. 290).

46. It is Adorno who quotes this sentence from Kierkegaard's novel *Either/Or* in Theodore Adorno, *Kierkegaard: Construction of the Aesthetic*, translated and edited by Robert Hullot-Kentor (Minneapolis: University of Minnesota Press, 1989), p. 136.

47. Theunissen, *Ernst*, p. 23.

48. Adorno, *Kierkegaard*, p. 130n.

49. The original Danish phrase, "at komme gaaende," is just as daring as the English translation. Adorno translates: "gehend kommen."

50. Adorno, *Kulturkritik und Gesellschaft I. Prismen. Ohne Leitbild* (Frankfurt am Main: Suhrkamp, 1977), p. 362.

11. Richard Rorty and the Ethics of Anti-Foundationalism

1. Hilary Putnam, *Realism with a Human Face* (Cambridge, Massachusetts: Harvard University Press, 1990), p. 19.

2. Cambridge: Cambridge University Press, 1989.

3. First published in John Rajchman and Cornel West, eds., *Post-Analytic Philosophy* (New York: Columbia University Press, 1985). Republished in *Objectivity, Relativism, and Truth*, pp. 21–34.

4. First published in John S. Nelson *et al.*, eds. *The Rhetoric of the Human Sciences*, (Madison: University of Wisconsin Press, 1987). Republished in *Objectivity, Relativism, and Truth*, pp. 35–45. References to these essays henceforth will be included in the text.

5. Princeton: Princeton University Press, 1979.

6. I characterize this statement as existential because of Rorty's talk of the need to "give some sense to [our] lives." Why is this a need? Why do we need a "larger context" (with all

the religious implications of that phrase)? One is tempted to answer in terms of existential loneliness, or some such. Rorty, however, makes this existential statement merely as a psychological or sociological observation of human behavior.

7. I accept Rorty's self-designation as a pragmatist, given his uncontroversial similarities to the leading figures of the tradition, and despite his controversial differences. And in any case, to indicate where Rorty misinterprets this or that philosopher would beg all the interesting questions, since, as Hilary Putnam has noted (in a lecture), the philosophical dispute (between Rorty and him) may be interpreted as a struggle over the legacy of pragmatism, a struggle which reflects the complexities present in the tradition from its inception.

8. Does this mean that philosophy has come to end? Yes and no. Rorty would be happy to discard Philosophy, with a capital P, as an academic discipline with pretensions to grandeur. (He sometimes calls this "the end of Philosophy 101.") However, Rorty claims that the end-of-philosophy label is unfair, for he advocates a transformation of philosophy along pragmatist lines. He hopes that people will continue to read Plato and Kant, but he wishes that they would stop trying "to sucker freshman into taking an interest in The Problem of the External World and The Problem of Other Minds" (as he writes in "Putnam and the Relativist Menace," in the *Journal of Philosophy*). To a certain extent, then, the transformation of philosophy involves emphasizing texts over problems. Unfortunately, it is not at all clear why people should continue to read the great dead philosophers, if all they have to offer is bad ideas— ideas which we will find dumber and dumber, as time and our post-Philosophical culture go on. See Rorty's essay "The Historiography of Philosophy: Four Genres," in Richard Rorty, ed., *Philosophy of History* (Cambridge: Cambridge University Press, 1984), p.73, and *Philosophy and the Mirror of Nature*, pp. 389–394.]

9. In response, we may question whether or not this has really been the goal. Rorty, however, certainly believes that it was.

10. The distinction between equating "truth" with "what is good to believe" in the way that this slogan does, on the one hand, and merely associating them or emphasizing their relationship, on the other, cuts to the heart of the struggle over the pragmatist legacy. Investigating this distinction, however, requires further analysis of Rorty's views on truth and relativism—a worthy project, but one which lies outside the scope of this essay. Rorty objects to the caricature of pragmatism which holds that the pragmatists viewed truth as simply made by agreement with one's cultural peers; he insists that truth is not made by anything, and that truth is not the sort of thing about which we shold have a positive explanatory theory.

11. By making this transformation explicit, I also mean to suggest—without any justification, at this point—that it might be optional. That is, an alternative conception might avoid the reduction of either objectivity or solidarity, but rather allow each to rest upon its own "foundation." In this way, Rorty's original formulation of solidarity and objectivity as twin desires is surprisingly well suited to the expression of an alternative position.

12. Obviously, this is something of a caricature. Nevertheless, the difference between this caricature and actual scientific investigation might easily be attributed to the difference between ideal conditions and real ones (by someone who holds to a sharp fact-value dichotomy). Scientific creativity, then, might be conceived of as the ability to imaginatively eliminate such pervasive factors as human error, in order to construct theories which correspond to reality as it is in itself, and which would be confirmed by ideal data.

13. At least, except insofar as some goals (e.g., finding a new drug, or building a new bridge) are considered by us to be more important, while other goals (such as reinterpreting a passage in Milton) might be considered less so. As Rorty points out, the strength of science

is that its institutions—experimentation, public and free debate, and so forth—embody this weaker rationality, at least ideally.

14. While Rorty's account in *Philosophy and the Mirror of Nature* goes into a significant degree of depth and detail, he is no more averse to employing caricatures of the great dead philosophers. In his own defense, he might argue that he is not at all concerned with what Plato or Descartes or Kant actually believed, but rather with the roles that they played in the development of the tradition—which is to say, with the way they were perceived, co-opted, or responded to (see note 16).

15. For example, "Plato's claim that the way to transcend skepticism is to envisage a common goal of humanity" (p. 21) and the post-Enlightenment dream of "an ultimate community which will have transcended the distinction between the natural and the social, which will exhibit a solidarity which is not parochial because it is the expression of an ahistorical human nature" (p. 22) seem to do similar work in the argument.

16. Rorty's brief account (and those elements of *Philosophy and the Mirror of Nature* to which it corresponds) fits his own characterization of "the big sweeping *geistesgeschichtlich* stories," in his article, "The Historiography of Philosophy: Four Genres":

> In contrast [to the genre called 'rational reconstruction'], Geistesgeschichte works at the level of problematics rather than of solutions to problems. It spends more of its time asking 'Why should anyone have made the question of—central to his thought?' or 'Why did anyone take the problem of—seriously? . . . It wants to give plausibility to a certain image of philosophy . . . The question of which problems are 'the problems of philosophy,' which questions are philosophical questions, are the questions to which geistesgeschichtlich histories of philosophy are principally devoted . . . The moral to be drawn [from this sort of history of philosophy] is that we have, or have not, been on the right track in raising the philosophical questions we have recently been raising. (pp. 56–59)

Rorty's own *Geistesgeschichte*, of course, concludes that we have not been on the right track. The particular image of philosophy to which it wishes to give plausibility is one in which all of the important problems are seen as pseudo-problems, and moreover one which refuses to replace those problems with a new set. Instead of coming up with a new answer to the question of "which questions are philosophical questions," it responds by denying that there exists such a class of privileged, fundamental, foundational questions at all. It is, therefore, an anti-*Geistesgeschichte*, or perhaps a *Geistesgeschichte* with no *Geist*.

17. This Nietzschean or skeptical sort of argument also opens the door for another alternative, already mentioned in note 11 above, of not reducing either of these contingent but fundamental desires or intuitions to the other. Once we put both factors on an equally tenuous footing, we can either reject them both, or learn to live with the tenuousness (absence of a secure foundation) of each.

18. Does desiring after objectivity also entail denying one's membership even in the widest possible community, the community of all humans? This question gets to the heart of the issue. Rorty would say that it does, that Plato's instinctive response to the challenge of skepticism and diversity was fruitless because there is no such community, no essence which binds all humans together. This is somewhat paradoxical: the natural, widely-found human impulse to search after objectivity itself constitutes a denial of humanity. Rorty escapes the paradox by denying that objectivity is essential to humanity. An alternative position might argue that the desire for objectivity is as "natural" an intuition as the desire for solidarity, and should be maintained. The escape from the paradox might then be to deny that the desire for objectivity involves a denial of one's humanity—for objectivity is not

inhuman. To desire objectivity is not, as Rorty claims, to attach oneself "to something which can be described without reference to any particular human beings" (p. 21). Rather, objectivity may be considered something less than an unconceptualized inhuman reality, but more than mere intersubjectivity.

As mentioned above (in note 11), a further aspect of this alternative position is one that is suggested by Rorty's conceptual framework—the non-reduction of either objectivity or solidarity, the validation of both. Perhaps each may be considered as relying on its own foundation, as Rorty considers solidarity alone to be. To suggest an alternative picture is not the same thing as to refute the original picture; however, such an alternative would have the merit of not dismissing what had originally seemed to be an authentic human impulse to objectivity.

19. What is remarkable about foundationalist "ethics," especially of the empirical sort, is how non-ethical they sound. On this point, cf. Rorty, Introduction to *Contingency, Irony, and Solidarity*, p. xv. Rorty characterizes the typical consequentialist questions "Is it right to deliver n innocents over to be tortured to save the lives of m x n other innocents? If so, what are the correct values of n and m?" or the question "When may one favor the members of one's family, or one's community, over other, randomly chosen, human beings?" as "hopeless." He continues, "Anybody who thinks that there are well-grounded theoretical answers to this sort of question—algorithms for resolving moral dilemmas of this sort—is still, in his heart, a theologian or a metaphysician."

20. Rorty's mischievous use of the controversial term "ethnocentrism" seems intended to rile his political opponents on the left, for the ethnos he has in mind is (flawed, imperfect, but nevertheless successful) Western liberal democracy: "The liberal culture of recent times has found a strategy for avoiding the disadvantage of ethnocentrism [by making] openness central to its self-image. This culture is an ethnos which prides itself on its suspicion of ethnocentrism—on its ability to increase the freedom and openness of encounters, rather than on its possession of truth" (Introduction to *Objectivity, Relativism, and Truth*, p. 2).

21. Emphasis added. Nietzsche's insight that objectivity lacked metaphysical foundations is taken (by Rorty) to be his "good" side, while his parallel observation about solidarity is considered less charitably.

22. Rorty, in general, impatiently scorns the appeal to philosophical intuitions. In his struggle to eliminate the magical from our conceptions, he cannot suffer (what he interprets as) attempts to retain elements of the metaphysical tradition, hidden underneath talk of intuitions, responsibilities, or obligations. Nevertheless, he privileges the ethical intuition towards solidarity, because he believes that this obligation at least, the obligation towards other individuals, does exist. It should therefore be clear that Rorty has opened himself up to criticism regarding this privileging of one intuition over another, and that his philosophical views are in fact dependent upon a particular picture of what is and what is not fundamental to human nature.

12. Mirror and Oneiric Mirages: Plato, Precursor of Freud

1. Conforming to the general plan of Book Eight, Plato begins by examining the transformation of political regimes before he examines sorts of men, for if it is true that the sort of regime depends on the hierarchy of parts of the soul, then the sort of regime is a paradigm for the corresponding sort of soul, because it permits us to read in capital letters that which, in the soul, is written only in lower-case (cf. Book One).

2. The deduction of different sorts of regimes and souls can be done, in fact, a priori, since it is a function of the different manners in which the soul orders its parts.

3. As for the original change, occurring in the ideal regime where harmony anticipates neither alteration nor decay, Plato explains this by the general law of corruption of all that is born (cf. 546a), the real and occasional principle of decay being a principle of division within the party which governs. As in the *Iliad*, discord is the origin of evil, and discord itself is caused by the ignorance of guardians who do not always reproduce in the right geometric number or at the right generational moment, promoting good mating. These poor unions are responsible for the mixing of "races" and for a division in the guardian class, between the old members, of pure race, and the new ones, more mixed: "This mixing will result in a defect of inequality, of justness and harmony such that, everywhere that the two races meet, there will be war and hatred" (547a). Consequent to this division, the two races of iron and bronze turn to profit, while the other two (those of gold and silver) consider the only riches to be those of the soul—of virtue. The appeal to myth of these four races justifies in nature the differences in the structure of souls and their destiny.

4. Cf. the beginning of Book Eight, 545a.

5. Note the resemblance between the democratic man and the mimic who appears in the city when luxury and superfluity reign, and the soul is guided by no "proper" principle.

6. Cf. also the Phaedra 580e and the Republic 580c, 588d, 589b.

7. The satisfaction of nutritional needs serves as a metaphor for the satisfaction of desires in general. As in dreams, according to Freud (cf. the dream called "The Three Fates"), sexual desire appears in the form of hunger for food.

8. Cf. the Republic Book Ten, 606c and sq. "If you consider that the part of the soul which, moments ago, we endeavored to contain . . . is precisely that which the poet satisfies and celebrates in his representations; and that the part of us which is naturally the best, not being sufficiently fortified by reason and habit, relaxes its supervision on this mournful part, under the pretext that these are the unhappinesses of others that it stages; and that it is not shameful, when another who calls himself a good man pours out his tears at the wrong time, for us to applaud and sympathize—from which expression, on the contrary, we take pleasure, and wouldn't want to deprive ourselves of it by rejecting all poetry . . . are we not likewise ridiculous? And when you listen in a theatrical presentation, or in a private conversation, to a farce that you would be ashamed to put on yourself, and from which you take a vivid pleasure instead of reproving its perversity, do you not achieve the same thing as in poignant emotions? The desire to bring laughter, which you repress by reason, out of fear of looking like a buffoon—you give it free reign in its turn."

9. Plato and his Greek contemporaries could not, before Freud, help but think here (roughly 981–982) of Oedipus Rex: "Numerous are the mortals who dream of sleeping with their mother."

10. Cf. the Republic, 565e, 574a, 615b.

11. Plato does not like madmen. In the *Republic*, in Book Three, it is forbidden to guardians of the city to imitate them (no more so for anyone than for women), and the *Laws* oblige them to be confined (cf. Book Eleven 934d and sq.): "Madmen should not appear in town; rather, each one will be guarded, in his house by his relatives . . . otherwise these relatives will have to pay a fine . . . But there are quite a lot of ways to be mad, and one might say really quite a lot among the Greeks! Among those of whom we are speaking, it is the effect of a sickness . . . there are other individuals for whom it is the simultaneous effect of the perversion of the natural and that of education: men in whom the slightest irritant provoke to shouting and flinging rudely at one another injurious words . . . in feeding his anger with poisonous fuel, in ren-

dering wild again all that his soul had, long ago, tamed by education, this man lapses into a beast from living in irritation."

12. Cf. also *Phaedra*.

13. Plato, here again before Freud, well knew that a total sublimation of desires is impossible, that the base part of the soul, like Schilda's horse—of whom Freud speaks in the fifth of Five Lessons in Psychoanalysis (Payot, p. 65)—needs to be the slightest bit full, if only so as to leave the nobler part in peace.

14. "This part of the soul has a touch of courage and anger, and is hungry to dominate. It has been placed closer to the head, between the diaphragm and the neck such that, amenable to reason, it can, in concert with reason, contain a species of appetite by force, when, from the top of the Acropolis, the commands of reason no longer have the means to obtain obedience by willing agreement" (*Timaeus*, 70a).

15. In the *Phaedra*, divinatory delirium is one of the good forms of delirium.

13. Schleiermacher's Hermeneutics: Some Problems and Solutions

1. For a discussion of this question in Herder's favor, see my *Herder: Philosophical Writings* (Cambridge, 2002), Introduction; also my "Herder's Importance as a Philosopher" (forthcoming).

2. Cf. P. Szondi, *On Textual Understanding and Other Essays* (henceforth OTUaoE; Manchester, 1986), p. 97, for a similar assessment.

3. The chapter will be very selective, omitting a number of other central aspects of Schleiermacher's theory. For example, I shall not discuss his famous conception that hermeneutics should be a *universal* science, or his famous position that the parts of a text/discourse must be interpreted through larger wholes of various sorts and his solution to the problem of hermeneutical circularity that such holism seems to involve.

4. See especially Herder, *Fragments on Recent German Literature* (1767–68).

5. Like Herder before him, Schleiermacher normally in such contexts thinks of language as consisting in speech or writing. However, he does sometimes entertain a broader conception of the "linguistic" which would include quite different linguistic media in addition (see especially Psychology lectures [in *Sämmtliche Werke*, Berlin, 1862], pp. 46, 539–540; cf. *On Religion* of 1799 [Cambridge, 1991], p. 166 on instrumental music). This vacillation leaves a certain indeterminacy in the force of the doctrine.

6. See for example *Hermeneutics: The Handwritten Manuscripts* (henceforth H; Atlanta, 1986), pp. 97–98, 193.

7. See for instance "On the Different Methods of Translation" (henceforth OtDMoT; in A.L. Willson ed., *German Romantic Criticism* [New York, 1982]), p. 20: "the internal and essential identity of thought and expression."

8. See for example *Hermeneutics and Criticism* (henceforth HC; Cambridge, 1998), p. 9: "thinking is an inner speaking."

9. H, p. 34.

10. R.R. Niebuhr, *Schleiermacher on Christ and Religion* (New York, 1964), p. 81; M. Frank, *Das individuelle Allgemeine* (henceforth DiA; Frankfurt am Main, 1977), p. 250.

11. H. Kimmerle's well-known characterization of the later Schleiermacher as breaking with the identity thesis (see H, p. 36) contains an important element of truth, but is a little overstated. Schleiermacher's inclination to distance himself from the identity thesis can be

seen not only by comparing earlier and later versions of his Hermeneutics lectures (as Kimmerle points out) but also by comparing the 1818, 1830, and 1833–34 versions of his Psychology lectures. However, it would probably be an exaggeration to say that he ever unequivocally gave up the identity thesis. For example, to focus on the Psychology lectures, while the sort of emphatic statement of the identity thesis that is found in the lectures of 1818—e.g. "inner speaking[. . .]is completely identical with thinking" (pp. 446-7)—does indeed recede by the time Schleiermacher gives the lectures of 1830 and 1833–34, he can still talk at one point in the 1830 lectures of "the activity of thought in its identity with language" (p. 263).

12. In this context, it should not necessarily be assumed that the rules in question are formulated or even in all cases formulable.

13. H, p. 50. The specific doctrine of "the unity of the word-sphere" which appears here will be discussed below.

14. HC, pp. 234 ff., 271 ff.

15. For example, at Psychology lectures, pp. 147–48 he seems to be thinking of schemata as constituting meanings autonomously of language, language merely being required for the *communication* of meanings.

16. See especially the *Blue Book* and the *Philosophical Investigations.*

17. Somebody might want to object to this that to hypothesize external competence in using the word "red" *is* to hypothesize having sensations of redness or the ability to generate images of redness. However, I would suggest that a little further reflection on the range of possible hypothetical cases shows otherwise.

18. This seems to me a much more satisfactory explanation and justification of doctrine *(1)* on Schleiermacher's behalf than the one suggested by Frank at DiA, pp. 174–75 in terms of Saussure's conception of meaning as arising through a system of oppositions. For, absent some further argument to the contrary, such a system of oppositions, and hence meaning, could occur without language being involved at all.

19. Cf. N. Goodman's recent book title *Languages of Art.*

20. See *On Religion*, p. 166. Cf. lectures on Psychology, pp. 46, 539–540.

21. Aesthetics lectures (*Sämmtliche Werke*, Berlin, 1842), pp. 579–580.

22. Ibid., pp. 584–85. Cf. the similar position that Schleiermacher had earlier adopted concerning instrumental music in *On Religion*, p. 166.

23. Aesthetics lectures, pp. 587–88. Such a rejection of *(a)* and vacillation instead between *(b)* and *(c)* can also be found in Schleiermacher's treatment of music in *Christmas Eve* [*Die Weihnachtsfeier*] (San Francisco, 1990), pp. 46–47.

24. In the *Critical Forests*—a work which clearly forms the foundation for Schleiermacher's lectures on Aesthetics—Herder had been similarly torn between several incompatible positions on the question at issue but had eventually worked his way towards a version of position *(c)*, which he thenceforth retained as his considered view.

25. H, pp. 50, 79; HC, pp. 33–34, 36–37, 247.

26. Pace Frank, the thesis has nothing to do with the *intersubjectivity* of meaning (DiA, pp. 187, 213–14), nor is it even a matter of the identity of meaning in metaphorical uses (ibid., pp. 215–16), though that is much *closer* to what Schleiermacher has in mind.

27. H, p. 79: "Once one has a number of clear and distinct usages by collecting analogies or by referring to dictionaries, the rule for discovering the unity is to put together these contrasting meanings" (cf. H, pp. 62, 121–22).

28. *Institutes* (Edinburgh, 1832), p. 11. Certainly, pace Kimmerle (H, p. 31), Schleiermacher should not be seen as *borrowing* from Ernesti in this thesis. Ernesti does indeed deny

that words have multiple meanings *in particular occurrences* (*Institutes*, pp. 20–21), but that is an entirely different point.

29. He fails to do so. See e.g. HC, p. 247: it is a "necessary . . . principle . . . that two schemata are not the basis of one and the same word."

30. For example at H, p. 76 he contrasts with the "essential meaning" of the connected family of usages of a word the "particular meanings" of the specific usages; cf. HC, pp. 35, 233–34 (he normally distinguishes the two cases terminologically as *Bedeutung* and *Gebrauch* respectively). Accordingly, he is himself by no means shy about detecting ambiguities in words (see for instance *Introductions to the Dialogues of Plato* [henceforth IttDoP; Cambridge, 1836], pp. 69, 113, 120–21).

31. Hence, strictly, "one must be in command of the unity of the linguistic value to arrive at the multiplicity of manners of use" (HC, p. 37).

32. There are also further aspects of meaning-holism in Schleiermacher which make for still further fine-grainedness in his criteria of identity for meaning2. These concern not other usages of the same word but families of cognate words (whether morphologically and conceptually or just conceptually cognate) and the internality of a language's grammar to word-meaning. See for example OtDMoT.

33. HC, pp. 247–48.

34. Psychology lectures, pp. 173–74. Schleiermacher's whole line of thought in this thesis is very similar to one which has motivated more recent linguists to speak of a word's "semantic field"—see for example E. Nida, *Toward a Science of Translating* (Leiden, 1964), pp. 37–40. (Nida also makes an important point which is at least less clear in Schleiermacher, namely that what is essential to specific word meanings is not only what the "unity of the word-sphere"—to use Schleiermacher's terminology—*comprises* but also how it is *structured* [ibid., p. 89 ff.].). I would therefore strongly disagree with Szondi's judgment that Schleiermacher's conception of the unity of the word-sphere stands in sharp *contradiction* with modern linguistics (Szondi, OTUaOE, p. 107).

35. For some relevant discussion, see my *Wittgenstein on the Arbitrariness of Grammar* (Princeton, 2004), Chapter 6.

36. I shall bracket here the interesting question of the extent to which this methodological perspective is Schleiermacher's *own*. However, his stress on conceptual variations across and also within cultures at least coheres well with it (since he would surely have to include the concepts of *meaning* and *conceptual understanding* in such variations).

37. H, pp. 109–110; HC, pp. 21–22.

38. HC, p. 279. Cf. Psychology lectures, p. 20: "All approximation to knowledge must be a reciprocal working of the a priori into the a posteriori and vice versa."

39. "Schleiermacher's Hermeneutical System in Relation to Earlier Protestant Hermeneutics" (henceforth SHS; in W. Dilthey, *Hermeneutics and the Study of History*, Princeton, 1996), pp. 104–110, 134–37, 146.

40. DiA, pp. 152–56.

41. HC, p. 20.

42. H, pp. 164, 195, etc. Cf. Frank, DiA, pp. 310–11.

43. OtDMoT, pp. 4–5, 25. Cf. H, p. 206.

44. OtDMoT, pp. 5–7. Cf. H, pp. 99, 104, 148.

45. OtDMoT, p. 25.

46. Ibid., p. 6.

47. Ibid., pp. 2–3. Cf. HC, p. 230; and, more equivocally, Psychology lectures, p. 509. As Frank mentions, Schleiermacher in this vein concedes that, as he puts it, mere *Wettergespräche*

do occur (Frank, *Das Sagbare und das Unsagbare* [henceforth DSudU; Frankfurt am Main, 1990], p. 209; cf. H, p. 102).

48. Cf. H, p. 57 on "authors in whose works one finds everything one expects and nothing else"; and *Das Leben Jesu* (*Sämmtliche Werke*, Berlin, 1864), p. 11 on the many people who "stand entirely in the power of the collective life."

49. Cf. Aesthetics lectures, p. 636, where Schleiermacher says that understanding is indeed in most cases only approximate but that in some cases "the expression can convey the thought quite identically into the other person."

50. See e.g. HC, pp. 69–70, 275–76; also, though more equivocally, Psychology lectures, p. 509.

51. HC, pp. 276–77.

52. OtDMoT, p. 25 (translation modified): "Every language[. . .]contains within it a system of concepts which, precisely because they touch each other in the same language, because they connect and complement each other, are a *whole* whose isolated parts do not correspond to any in the system of other languages, God and Being, the original noun and the original verb, hardly excepted."

53 Consider, for example, the discrepancy in sense between such co-referring sensory words as the Greek word *Helios* and our word *sun* (for one thing, the former carries an implication of personhood which the latter lacks), or the deep discrepancies between Homeric color conceptualization and our own. (For discussion of the latter case and citation of the most relevant literature, see my "On the Very Idea of Denying the Difference of Radically Different Conceptual Schemes" [*Inquiry*, June 1998].) Interestingly enough, Schleiermacher himself eventually went a long way towards acknowledging that color conceptualization shows striking variability (Psychology lectures, p. 509).

54. C. Kahn, *The Verb 'Be' in Ancient Greek*. Kahn characterizes the late introduction of a purely existential use of the verb *to be* as only a new *use* of the verb rather than a change in its *meaning*. However, if one follows Schleiermacher's equation of meaning with usage and his holism across usages, one will certainly be inclined to draw the more radical conclusion.

55. HC, p. 95.

56. SHS, p. 217; H, p. 29.

57. IttDoP, pp. 2–3; H, p. 104.

58. Hence see for instance IttDoP, pp. 2–3; OtDMoT, pp. 7, 13; H, pp. 92, 104, 171.

59. Psychological and technical interpretation eventually get sharply distinguished by Schleiermacher in their turn, technical interpretation being confined to the pursuit of the necessary development of a text's "seminal decision" over the course of the text (HC, p. 102ff).

60. For instance, in 1829 Schleiermacher still writes that "there is no thinking without words" (H, p. 193), and the 1830 and 1833–34 Psychology lectures continue to assume a dependence of thought on language as well (see e.g. pp. 133–34, 140, 263, 539–540).

61. See HC, pp. 30ff.

62. See the aphorisms from 1805/9–10, especially H, p. 61; and above all, assuming that Virmond's dating is correct, the 1805 lecture on "technical" interpretation at HC, p. 93ff. Also relevant in this connection are the Ethics lectures from the winter semester 1805–06.

63. Herder's key texts for this are *On Thomas Abbt's Writings* and *On the Cognition and Sensation of the Human Soul*, where he adds psychology to Ernesti's purely language-oriented approach to interpretation. For example, in the latter work Herder writes that the wise interpreter "attempts to read more in the spirit of the author than in his book; the deeper he penetrates into the former, the more perspicuous everything becomes."

64. Frank, DiA and DSudU.

65. See for instance HC, pp. 94, 229–230; H, p. 99; OtDMoT, p. 6.

66. See HC, pp. 67–68.

67. See HC, p. 237.

68. H, pp. 70, 99, 149.

69. See e.g. H, pp. 97–98.

70. HC, pp. 254, 229. Skinner often puts his point not simply in terms of a need to fix authorial intentions but, more elaborately, in terms of a need to fix authorial "illocutionary force" and "oblique strategies" (such as irony). I am in the end somewhat skeptical that the notion of "illocutionary force" is helpful here (for example because of intimate connections which Austin gave it with performatives and with social "uptake"). However, I would at least defend a version of the above position framed in such terms against one sort of objection which has been advanced: Frank considers but rejects a rationale for psychological interpretation similar to the one suggested above but articulated in terms of illocutionary force (DSudU, pp. 187–88). His reason for rejecting it (both philosophically and as an interpretation of Schleiermacher) is that illocutionary force is thought of as purely conventional, not subject to originality. This objection does not seem to me a strong one, though. For a theory of illocutionary force could very well accommodate as much originality in illocutionary force as it would be plausible to ascribe to people (even if particular versions of such a theory, such as Searle's, happen not to do so). And if Frank means to object on the ground that authorial intentions are *always* unconventional, then that just seems implausible (even if encouraged by the inferior a priorist strand of Schleiermacher's reflections on authorial individuality discussed earlier).

71. HC, p. 254.

72. See especially F. Schlegel, *Athenäums-Fragmente*.

73. H, p. 202; cf. HC, p. 92.

74. H, pp. 50, 113.

75. See e.g. IttDoP, pp. 1–2; HC, p. 92.

76. See e.g. HC, pp. 28, 102ff; H, p. 192.

77. It seems to be entirely absent from the version of 1805 (assuming this dating of Virmond's to be correct) (HC, p. 94ff), and to be still only ambiguously present in the version of 1809–10 (HC, especially pp. 254–55). By contrast, it is central in the version of 1832 (HC, p. 101ff).

78. SHS, p. 100ff.

79. A minor but interesting illustration of this problem can be seen in the fact that in his *Introductions to the Dialogues of Plato* Schleiermacher gets seduced by his assumption of this model into committing one of his most spectacular errors of chronology concerning the dialogues: assuming this model as a basis for interpreting the Platonic corpus as a whole, he expects Plato's corpus to begin with a dialogue which already contains all of Plato's mature ideas in microcosm, and so he identifies the *Phaedrus* (!) as the earliest Platonic dialogue (see especially pp. 67–68).

80. HC, p. 102ff.

81. Ibid., pp. 117, 132, 136.

82. Ibid., p. 136.

83. Ibid., pp. 102–03.

84. Ibid., p. 140.

85. Ibid., p. 136.

86. Ibid., p. 106.

87. Ibid., p. 140.

88. See e.g. H, pp. 191ff, 205.

89. Ibid., pp. 193–94.

90. Ibid., p. 192.

91. Note that in the 1811 *Dialectics* (translation *Dialectic or The Art of Doing Philosophy*, Atlanta, 1996) Schleiermacher actually calls the closely related process of concept *formation* one of "induction" (ibid., pp. 54–57), and that in the *Dialectics* of 1822 he calls this "induction" a process of "comparative judgments" (ibid., p. 57n).

92. Dilthey, "The Rise of Hermeneutics" (in *Hermeneutics and the Study of History*), pp. 248–49; Gadamer, *Truth and Method* (New York, 1982), p. 164.

93. HC, pp. 92–93.

94. H, pp. 64, 113.

95. HC, p. 23; cf. pp. 134–35.

96. Here I basically agree with Frank, DiA, pp. 314, 331.

97. See especially H, p. 113.

98. Ibid., pp. 42, 150.

99. HC, p. 23. Cf. *Das Leben Jesu*, p. 8: "The maximum of [human-knowing] is a sort of *Prophetie*."

100. See e.g. H, pp. 215–16; HC, pp. 17–18. (To be sure, Schleiermacher is here primarily concerned to combat reliance on a presupposition that a text's *author* is divinely inspired, rather than reliance on a presupposition that its *interpreter* is. However, Ernesti had already forbidden the latter, and the spirit of Schleiermacher's remarks is to *extend* that prohibition to the former *as well*.)

101. See for instance H, p. 207.

102. For the latter point, see especially *Das Leben Jesu*, pp. 6–8.

103. Cf. Frank, *Schleiermacher: Hermeneutik und Kritik* (Frankfurt am Main, 1999), p. 47.

104. H, p. 207. Cf. Schleiermacher's characterization of "divination" in the context of *criticism* as a process of fallible conjecture (HC, pp. 177, 193). Frank similarly understands "divination" as for Schleiermacher a method of hypothesis (DiA, pp. 332–33; DSudU, pp. 66–67, 102). But Frank's claim that its probability cannot be assessed (DSudU, p. 181) is misleading, especially in overlooking the important possibility of *falsification*.

105. See especially *On Thomas Abbt's Writings* and *On the Cognition and Sensation of the Human Soul*.

106. See especially Frank, DiA, pp. 351–364.

107. As the Frank of DiA stresses in this connection, Schleiermacher does imply that meanings are irreducibly individual and hence strictly unattainable by interpreters, that the ("divinatory") method for approaching them is fallible and provisional, and that inquiry in general advances through the sort of communal approximation to truth described in the Dialectics lectures. But, pace the Frank of DiA, these doctrines, so far from conflicting with, *presuppose* an objectivist assumption.

More recently, in his edition of Schleiermacher's Dialectics lectures, Frank has in effect conceded that his original attribution of a consensus theory of truth to those lectures in DiA was a mistake, that they instead assume a realist or correspondence conception of truth (Frank, *Friedrich Schleiermacher: Dialektik* [Baden-Baden, 2001], Volume 1, especially pp. 34, 41, 56). This is an admirable piece of self-correction. However, note that it also pulls the rug out from under Frank's reading in DiA of Schleiermacher's hermeneutics as a position similar to Gadamer's. For the general strategy of that reading was to build on the ascription to Schleiermacher of a consensus-theory of truth in general an ascription to him of a conception of interpretation in particular as, likewise, an ongoing social construction of facts about meaning.

108. This sort of anachronism has indeed recently become something of a cottage industry in Germany. For example, Irmischer has similarly tried to read *Herder* as a sort of proto-Gadamer (in his essay "Grundzüge der Hermeneutik Herders").

109. See especially F. Schlegel, *Philosophie der Philologie*. Therefore, Frank is certainly right to reject Palmer's *equation* of art with science in Schleiermacher's position (DiA, p. 341), but Frank *understates* this point.

110. This is not to deny that there remain important points of contrast. For example, whereas natural scientific hypotheses are always formulated, the hypotheses involved in interpretation are often not, and indeed may not even always be formul*able*. Nor, of course, does mathematics play the sort of role in interpretive hypotheses that it plays in natural scientific ones.

111. This, I take it, is the force of the contrast which he often draws between "divination" and what is merely "mechanical" (see e.g. HC, pp. 10–11, 229, 232). (As I noted earlier, he does think that plain induction plays *a* role in interpretation, namely as the "comparative" method which dominates in linguistic interpretation. But his idea is that in natural science it is the *only* method whereas interpretation also requires "divination," or hypothesis.)

112. The interpretive argument of the last two paragraphs requires some qualification. For Schleiermacher does not consistently sustain the pictures of a sharp art vs. science opposition and of natural science's method as purely plain-inductive, or "mechanical," which I have just ascribed to him. Occasionally, he suggests a contrary picture of natural science as rather like art and as not merely mechanical but also involving imagination (see for example Psychology lectures, pp. 467–68).

113. Examples are Dilthey, Weber, Heidegger, Gadamer, and Frank. A noteworthy exception is Helmholtz.

14. Bentham's Philosophical Politics

1. On this point I am grateful for the observations of Dr David Lieberman of the School of Law, University of California, Berkeley.

2. N. Rosenblum, *Bentham's Theory of the Modern State* (Cambridge, Massachusetts: Harvard University Press, 1978).

3. Dinwiddy has in mind Mary Mack, *Jeremy Bentham: An Odyssey of Ideas 1748–1799* (London: Heinemann, 1962).

4. J.R. Dinwiddy, "Bentham's Transition to Political Radicalism, 1809–10," *Journal of the History of Ideas* 35 (1975), pp. 693, 683. A similar view is enunciated by Michael James, "Work in Progress: Bentham's Political Writings 1788–95," *Bentham Newsletter* 4 (1980), pp. 22–24, and "Bentham's Democratic Theory at the Time of the French Revolution," *Bentham Newsletter* 10 (1986), pp. 5–16.

5. The Bentham manuscripts of 1788–90 and 1993–95 are housed at University College, London: UC 126/1–18, 127/1–19, 170/1–121; and 44/1–5, 170/17–82. Most of this material has been published recently in *The Collected Works of Jeremy Bentham*; see P. Schofield, C. Pease-Watkin, and C. Blamires, eds., *Rights, Representation, and Reform: Nonsense upon Stilts and other Writings on the French Revolution* (Oxford: Claredon, 2002).

6. The argument is made in J.E. Crimmins, "Bentham's 'Radicalism' Re-examined," *Journal of the History of Ideas* 55:2 (1994), pp. 259–281.

7. J.E. Crimmins, "John Brown and the Theological Tradition of Utilitarian Ethics," *History of Political Thought* 4:3 (1983), pp. 523–550, and "Religion, Utility and Politics: Bentham versus Paley," in J.E. Crimmins, ed., *Religion, Secularization, and Political Thought: Thomas Hobbes to J.S. Mill* (London: Routledge, 1990), pp. 130–152.

8. See Bentham mss, esp. UC Boxes 69 and 140.

9. See UC 5/1–32, 96/263–341, and for a detailed discussion J.E. Crimmins, *Secular Utilitarianism: Social Science and the Critique of Religion in the Thought of Jeremy Bentham* (Oxford: Clarendon, 1990), Chapter 3, and for the relationship between science and religion in Bentham's thought generally see Chapter 1.

10. *A Comment on the Commentaries* (begun in 1774, but not published until 1928); *A Fragment on Government* (1776), *An Introduction to the Principles of Morals and Legislation* (printed 1780–81, published 1789); and *Of Laws in General* (substantially completed in 1782, but not published until 1945). Definitive editions of each of these books have been published in *The Collected Works of Jeremy Bentham*.

11. *An Introduction to the Principles of Morals and Legislation*, edited by J.H. Burns and H.L.A. Hart (London: Athlone, 1970), p. 11.

12. E. Halevy, *The Growth of Philosophic Radicalism* [*La Formation du radicalisme philosophique*, 1901–04], translated by M. Morris, 1928 (Clifton: Kelley, 1972).

13. See D.G. Long, *Bentham on Liberty: Jeremy Bentham's Idea of Liberty in Relation to His Utilitarianism* (Toronto: University of Toronto Press, 1977); F.A. Hayek, "The Errors of Constructivism," *New Studies in Philosophy, Politics, Economics, and the History of Ideas* (Chicago: Chicago University Press, 1978), pp. 3–22; C.F. Bahmueller, *The National Charity Company: Jeremy Bentham's Silent Revolution* (Berkeley: University of California Press, 1981); L.J. Hume, *Bentham and Bureaucracy* (Cambridge: Cambridge University Press, 1981); M.H. James, "Public Interest and Majority Rule in Bentham's Democratic Theory, *Political Theory* 9:1 (1981), pp. 49–64; and W.H. Greenleaf, *The British Political Tradition*. Three volumes (London: Methuen, 1983–87), Volume I.

14. F. Rosen, *Jeremy Bentham and Representative Democracy: A Study of 'The Constitutional Code'* (Oxford: Clarendon, 1983); L. Campos Boralevi, *Bentham and the Oppressed* (Berlin: de Gruyter, 1984); G. Postema, *Bentham and the Common Law Tradition* (Oxford: Clarendon, rev. edn. 1989); P.J. Kelly, *Utilitarianism and Distributive Justice: Jeremy Bentham and the Civil Law* (Oxford: Clarendon, 1990); and A. Dube, *The Theme of Acquisitiveness in Bentham's Political Thought* (New York: Garland, 1991).

15. See Long, *Bentham on Liberty*; Hume, *Bentham and Bureaucracy*; and Postema, *Bentham and the Common Law Tradition* (notes 13 and 14 above).

16. Q. Skinner, "Meaning and Understanding in the History of Ideas", *History and Theory* 8 (1969), pp. 3–53.

15. Undocumented Persons and the Liberal State

1. Secretary of the State of California, *California Ballot Pamphlet* (Sacramento, 1994), p. 92.

2. See John Rawls, *A Theory of Justice* (Cambridge, Massachusetts: Harvard University Press, 1971), pp. 11–16, 60–64.

3. Patrick McDonnell and Robert Lopez, "Some See New Activism in Huge March," *Los Angeles Times* (18th October 1994), p. B1.

4. For example, the Family Educational Rights and Privacy Act denies federal funds to "any educational agency or institution" that permits the release of education records of students without parental consent. FERPA, §1232(g).

5. One voter cautioned that the rule would eventually lead to a situation where "everyone carries citizenship papers and anyone who can't prove his or her citizen status is in jeop-

ardy of being reported." See Brad Hayward, "Foes Sharpen Strategies on Immigration Measure," *Sacramento Bee* (4th September 1994), p. A1. When the right to privacy was first proposed, it was a fundamental right thought to belong to all persons; see Samuel Warren and Louis Brandeis, "The Right to Privacy," 4 *Harvard Law Review* 193 (1890), and Dean Prosser, "Privacy," 48 *California Law Review* 383 (1960).

6. Julie Marquis, "Wilson Blames Ills on Illegal Immigrants," *Los Angeles Times* (17th October 1994), p. B1.

7. Plyler v. Doe, 457 US 202 (1982), 221. See also Marianne Constable, "Sovereignty and Governmentality in Modern American Immigration Law," *Law, Politics, and Society* 13 (1993), 249, p. 261. On whether education is or isn't a right for citizens, see Brown v. Board of Education, 347 US 483 (1954), and San Antonio Independent School District v. Rodriguez, 411 US 1 (1973).

8. Plyler, 220.

9. Susan Ferriss, "Immigrant Ballot Issue Imperils Kids," *San Francisco Chronicle* (9th October 1994), p. C1.

10. Ron Unz and Mark Fiore, "Scaling the Heights of Irrationality, *Los Angeles Times* (3rd October 1994), op-ed., p. B7.

11. See Susan Ferris, "Prop. 187," *San Francisco Chronicle* (30th October 1994), p. A1; J. Edward Taylor and Thomas Espenshade, "Seasonality and the Changing Role of Undocumented Immigrants in the California Farm Labor Market," in Francisco Rivera-Batiz, *et al.*, eds., *U.S. Immigration Policy Reform in the 1980s* (New York: Praeger, 1991); and Linda Bozniak, "Exclusion and Membership," *Wisconsin Law Review* 955 (1988).

12. See Taylor and Espenshade; Elizabeth Hull, *Without Justice For All* (Westport, 1985); and Bozniak.

13. See Marquis, and John Mack, "Is Black-Latino Friction a Voting Booth Issue? No," *Los Angeles Times* (24th October 1994), op-ed., p. B7.

14. See R. George Wright, "Federal Immigration Law and the Case for Open Entry," 27 *Loyola Los Angeles Law Review* 1265 (1994), and Plyler.

15. Peter Schuck and Rogers Smith, *Citizenship Without Consent* (New Haven: Yale University Press, 1985), p. 3.

16. See Samuel Scheffler, "The Sources of Special Responsibilities" (unpublished article).

17. Samuel Scheffler, "Families, Nations, and Strangers," The Lindley Lecture (Lawrence: University of Kansas Press, 1995), pp. 6, 11.

18. Bruce Ackerman, *Social Justice in a Liberal State* (New Haven: Yale University Press, 1980), pp. 88–90.

19. Neil MacCormick, "Nation and Nationalism," p. 249.

20. Joseph Raz, "National Self-Determination," *Journal of Philosophy* 87 (1990), p. 448.

21. See Yael Tamir, *Liberal Nationalism* (Princeton: Princeton University Press, 1993), pp. 100–01, 110.

22. See, for instance, Henry Shue, "Mediating Duties," *Ethics* 98 (1988), p. 695.

23. Tamir, p. 121, my emphasis. See also MacCormick, p. 251, and David Miller, "The Ethical Significance of Nationality," *Ethics* 98 (1988), p. 654, both of whom agree with Tamir that "imagined communities" are morally relevant, however "imagined" they may be.

24. Tamir, p. 127. She quotes Michael Walzer, *Spheres of Justice* (Oxford: Oxford University Press, 1983), p. 32.

25. Alicia Doyle and Antonio Olivo, "Proposition 187's Impact on Race Relations," *Los Angeles Times* (4th November 1994), p. B2.

26. Doyle and Olivo, and also McDonnell and Lopez.

27. "A Panoply of Emotions Over Proposition 187," *San Diego Union-Tribune* (22nd October 1994), letters to the editor, p. 7.

28. Tamir, pp. 114, 162.

29. Raz, p. 446.

30. Both senate candidates and both candidates for governor in the November 1994 election had employed undocumented workers at some point.

31. See Hull; and see Bozniak.

32. See Frank Bean *et al.*, eds., *Undocumented Migration in the United States* (Santa Monica, 1990); Milton Morris and Albert Mayio, *Curbing Illegal Immigration* (Washington D.C., 1982); Hull; and Bozniak.

33. Joseph Raz, "Multiculturalism," in *Ethics in the Public Domain* (Oxford: Oxford University Press, 1994), p. 159.

34. See Tamir, pp. 93, 94, 160, 162. Her arguments, however, do seem to be about how nationalism need not be racist or xenophobic, and how nationalism can be compatible with liberalism at its best. Also, while Raz says that numbers do matter sometimes, he suggests that mutual respect for cultures would make this option undesirable. See Raz, p. 159.

35. The quote is from Thomas Pogge, "An Egalitarian Law of Peoples," *Philosophy and Public Affairs* 23 (1994), p. 199. For a depressing history of California, one that chronicles the "conquest, genocide, colonialism, and enslavement" that did occur here, see Tomas Almaguer, *Racial Fault Lines* (1994).

36. See Tamir, pp. 123–24, and Rawls, "The Law of Peoples," in Stephen Shute and Susan Hurley, eds., *On Human Rights* (New York: Basic Books, 1993).

37. This phrase belongs to Kant, "Essay in Theory and Practice," in Carl Friedrich, ed., *The Philosophy of Kant* (New York: Modern Library, 1949), p. 418.

38. See Samuel Scheffler, "Liberalism, Associative Duties, and the Boundaries of Responsibility" (unpublished article), p. 27.

39. The author would like to dedicate this article to his mother as well as to Edward Park, Reiko Furuta, and Gowan Lee.

17. What Is Postmodernism?

1. Ernst Robert Curtius, *Europaeische Literatur und Lateinisches Mittelalter* (Bern: Franke Verlag 1948), p. 259.

2. Richard Kearney, *The Wake of Imagination* (Minneapolis: University of Minnesota Press, 1988), pp. 349–354, 403.

3. Martin Heidegger, "What Is that—Philosophy," translated and annotated by Eva T.H. Brannn, Xerox, St. John's College, Annapolis, Maryland (1991), p. 19.

4. Jean-Franois Lyotard, "Une Note sur le Post," in *Le Postmoderne* (Paris: Galilee, 1986), p. l25.

5. "What Is Postmodernism," in *The Postmodern Condition: A Report on Knowledge* (Minneapolis: University of Minnesota Press, 1984), p. 81.

6. Eva T.H. Brann, *The World of the Imagination: Sum and Substance* (Savage, Maryland: Rowman and Littlefield, 1991), pp. 389–396.

7. Kearny, op. cit., p. 5.

8. Charles Jencks, in Kearney, op. cit., p. 349.

9. Robert Hughes in Kearney, op. cit., p. 24.

18. Why Study the History of Philosophy?

1. Sarah Broadie, *Ethics with Aristotle* (Oxford: Oxford University Press, 1991).

19. The Geology of Norway: Poem on Wittgenstein with Introduction

1. M. O'C. Drury, *The Danger of Words* (New York: Humanities Press, 1973), p. xiv.

2. Jan Zwicky, *Lyric Philosophy* (Toronto: University of Toronto Press, 1992).

3. Seamus Heaney, *Crediting Poetry: The Nobel Lecture* (New York: Farrar Straus Giroux, 1996), pp. 10–11.

About the Editor

PHIN UPHAM has a BA in Philosophy from Harvard University, where he was Editor-in-Chief of the *Harvard Review of Philosophy*. He has a PhD and MBA from the Wharton Business School at the University of Pennsylvania. Phin currently lives in New York City. In 2002 he edited a collection of interviews with great philosophers titled *Philosophers in Conversation*.

Index

spiritual space
  emptying of, 65
  possibility of play in, 61
Spranca, Mark, 91
"status-quo effect," 89
Stoics, 233
"sunk cost effect," 88
surrealistic utopianism, 132
system–building, as dialectical, 118
Szondi, Peter, 153

Tamir, Yael, 214, 225, 227
  Liberal Nationalism, 221–22, 224
Tarski, Alfred
  critique of, 96–97
Taylor, Charles, 21, 22, 25
Thrasymachus, 177, 184
Thucydides, 236
Tieck, Ludwig, 154, 158
Tocqueville, Alexis de, 10
  Democracy in America, 3
Trilling, Lionel, 2
"true,"
  as equivocal, 97–98
  in ordinary language, 97–99
  wholeness of, 102–03
  as wholly visible, 98, 99, 100
truth/falsehood, and seeing/making, 96

undocumented immigrants
  blending in of, 224
  in California, 214, 224
  lack of rights of, 215–16
  problem of, for liberal political theory,
    214–16

utopianism, types of, 132

values and facts, as intertwined, 113–14
Vlastos, Gregory, 232
"the void," spiritual, 62

Waltz, Kenneth
  Theory of International Politics, 133
Warhol, Andy, 243
wasteland, growing of, 65, 66, 67
Wendt, Alexander
  Social Theory of International Politics,
    134
Williams, Howard
  Kant's Political Philosophy, 136
Wilson, Pete, 215, 216
Winfrey, Oprah, 2
Wittgenstein, Ludwig, xiii, 33, 59, 189
  The Blue and Brown Books, 253–54
  on linguistic meaning, 254
  on music, 254
  in Norway, 253
  Philosophical Investigations, 254
  Tractatus, 253, 254
world, as text, 101–03

Xenophon, 230, 234

Zwicky, Jan
  Songs for Relinquishing the Earth,
    254
  Wittgenstein Elegies, 254